THE FIRST FREEDOM

THE FIRST FREEDOM

A HISTORY OF FREE SPEECH

ROBERT HARGREAVES

SUTTON PUBLISHING

First published in 2002 by
Sutton Publishing Limited · Phoenix Mill
Thrupp · Stroud · Gloucestershire · GL5 2 BU

British Library Cataloguing in Publication Data
A catalogue record for this book is available from the British Library

ISBN 0 7509 2923 5

For Martin and Matthew

In whom I am well pleased

Typeset in 10/12pt New Baskerville
Typesetting and origination by
Sutton Publishing Limited.
Printed and bound in England by
J.H. Haynes & Co. Ltd, Sparkford.

Contents

Acknowledgements

When I embarked on my researches for *The First Freedom* some seven years ago, I had no idea what an exhilarating voyage of discovery it would turn out to be. The first and largest debt I owe is therefore to the scores of authors and scholars whose company has made the voyage so enjoyable. Individual attributions will be found in the page notes following the text. I must also express my heartfelt thanks to Jan and Trevor Johnson, whose stimulating writers' seminars in the south of France not only gave me much needed encouragement to persevere, they provided me with a tranquil haven in which to work. Their separate sudden deaths after the manuscript had been completed makes my thanks to them all the more poignant. I am immensely grateful to them both and to the other writers I encountered at Las Cabanes. Their critical contributions were invaluable, their company always stimulating. For detailed scrutiny of the manuscript and their many helpful comments I would like in particular to thank Michael Baldwin, Henrietta Garnett, Martin Hargreaves and Mary Lewis. I would also like to express my gratitude to Christopher Feeney at Sutton Publishing, both for his initial faith in the project and the professional skill and enthusiasm with which he and his staff have seen it through to publication. The London Library provided a civilised environment in which to conduct research; its staff have been unfailingly patient and helpful, as have the librarians at the Reform Club. I must finally add the usual disclaimer that any errors and lacunae are of course my own responsibility.

Robert Hargreaves
Winchelsea, September 2002

Preface

The object of this book is to trace the origins of one of the bulwarks of modern civilisation – our right to free speech. It would be something to show how philosophers have defined that right, but that is not my purpose. Nor, on its own, could a philosophical definition ever be enough. To adapt a phrase often used by Oliver Wendell Holmes, the value of free speech does not lie in logic; it lies in experience. The bravery of individuals in standing against the tide of their times and the felt need to express an unpopular opinion or uncover an inconvenient fact have had as much to do with the development of free speech as the definitions of the philosopher. In order to know what free speech is, we must not only be able to define it, we must know where it came from, what it has been and who its heroes are.

The First Freedom follows this story from its infancy among that awesome generation of ancient Greeks who first threw off the shackles – but also lost the security – of primitive, organic society, in which the tribe was everything, the individual nothing, and free speech had no place. Had the principles established in ancient Greece won universal acceptance, that might have been the end as well as the beginning of the story. But as Karl Popper has shown, western civilisation never fully recovered from the shock of its birth. All too often – and all too recently – attempts have been made to return to the certainties and security of authoritarian rule, where individual rights are suppressed, that of critical discussion prominent among them. Whether they draw their strength from the ideologies of the right or the left, or from the certainties of dogmatic faith, all such movements beguile their followers with the 'magic, mystery and authority' of Dostoevsky's Grand Inquisitor. They offer them the prospect of security, but at the expense of their liberty, leaving those who believe in the value of free speech a beleaguered, and sometimes, a persecuted, minority.

As Lord Acton said, liberty has been beset in every age by its natural enemies, by lust of conquest and love of ease, by the strong man's craving for power and the poor man's craving for food, but above all by everyman's ignorance and superstition. In the Middle Ages, men became obsessed with seeking out the lost secret of the philosopher's stone, believing that an idea was of no value if it was new and that every idea needed the backing of some ancient authority, be it the scholasticism they drew from Aristotle or the revealed word of the Bible. It was Popper again who pointed out that they were right, medieval men *had* lost the key to ancient wisdom. But it was not the teaching of Aristotle they had lost, or the revealed truths of the Bible. The lost key was a faith in reason and liberty. It was the free competition of thought, which cannot exist without freedom of thought.

This can never be a boundless freedom, or the lawless freedom of wild animals; freedom for humans comes essentially within a moral order. And because principles that are morally right are not necessarily compatible with one another, we can strike no precise or entirely rational balance between them. The line will always be drawn where the climate of the age says it should. Only a Robinson Crusoe can have the complete freedom of speech, the right to shout blasphemous obscenities at the top of his voice or utter libels and hurl racist insults about. The rest of us have to live within Holmes's constraint of not being allowed falsely to shout 'Fire!' in a crowded theatre. So the story of the development of free speech is also the story of where different societies at different stages of their development have drawn this invisible line.

In the two and a half thousand years that have elapsed since the age of Pericles, truly tolerant societies have been very rare. The line has more often been drawn on the side of authority and repression, with the heresy of one age often becoming the intolerant orthodoxy of the next. Thus, a man who stood at the top of the Capitol steps in ancient Rome and declared, 'I am a Christian' faced instant arrest and being thrown to the lions. A millennium and a half later, a man who stood on the selfsame spot and declared, 'I am *not* a Christian' faced an equally speedy arrest followed by death at the stake as a heretic. In neither of those societies – nor in any of the intervening centuries – was there anything approaching a belief in free speech or the freedom of conscience. In our own lifetime, dissidents who challenged Marxist dogma were routinely sent to the Gulag, while in libertarian America, where free speech is guaranteed by the constitution, to proclaim oneself a *believer* in the Marxist orthodoxies would until very recently have invited swift and often severe retribution. True free speech must always leave room for the expression of opinions we detest, of arguments we find blasphemous, of viewpoints we regard as seditious. The principle has to be fought out and thought out by each succeeding generation. The battle is never over. Its frontline is never static. But nor is the story of free speech one of steady advance, of positions laboriously captured and made secure, then used as a base for the next push forward. There have been setbacks as well as progress, cataclysmic defeats and long centuries of stagnation along the way.

I have tried so far as possible to tell my story through people. *The First Freedom* is thus an arbitrary series of biographical sketches of the handful of individuals I have chosen to illustrate my theme. I have skipped over the periods of setback and stagnation and written about people who influenced the times when free speech was on the move: the Athens of Pericles, early Christianity, the humanist awakening from the long slumber of the Dark Ages, the Renaissance, the eighteenth-century Enlightenment. If readers feel the latter part of the book concentrates too much on white Anglo-Saxons, I can only reply that for much of the eighteenth and early nineteenth centuries the spread of free speech was very much an Anglo-Saxon phenomenon. It came to maturity in the period which saw the end of press licensing in England, the enactment of the American Bill of Rights and the development of a coherent philosophy by John Stuart Mill and Oliver Wendell Holmes, who painstakingly worked out the boundaries of a principle now enshrined in the Universal Declaration of Human Rights, which states that everyone has the right to freedom of opinion and expression without interference and regardless of frontiers.

Even that has not been the end of the story. Enshrined in constitutions though it may be and seemingly protected by the panoply of international law, free speech faces as many challenges today as it did when John Wilkes was campaigning for the right to criticise government and James Madison drafting his amendments to the American constitution. Though the principle by and large remains the same, its application and relevance to society, and the degree to which it is generally accepted, will always depend on the climate of the age and the resolution of those prepared to challenge it. In a civilisation built on reason and liberty, there can be no final certainties. From Socrates through to Mill and Voltaire, those who truly believe in the value of free speech have never claimed to be the proud possessors of a truth revealed only to them. They are rather the searchers, the enquirers, the sceptical critics, who prefer doubt to certainty, open discussion to blind dogma, an acceptance in argument that 'I may be wrong and you may be right'. They live in the spirit of Marcel Proust when he wrote, 'Cherish those who seek after truth. But beware of those who say they have found it'. It is to that spirit that this book is addressed.

PART ONE

The Classical Legacy

This is true freedom, when free born men
Having to advise the public, may speak free.

Euripides, *The Suppliant Women*

CHAPTER ONE

Why Socrates Died

Five hundred years before the birth of Christ, the Greek city-state of Athens became the first society in recorded history to embrace the notions of freedom and democracy. It was an experiment that went horribly wrong. After a short and spectacular period of success, the democracy collapsed, Athens lost her supremacy and with it, many of her freedoms. Under the strains of a debilitating and seemingly endless war, the city fell into a state of collective hysteria which bears an uncanny resemblance to the ideological neuroses that have blighted our own society's recent past. At the height of the crisis, she forced her most famous philosopher to drink hemlock, solely for the crime of expressing his opinions. It was a miscarriage of justice that still fills us with baffled fascination. How could Athens – the very birthplace of freedom – have so betrayed her most cherished principles? What could Socrates possibly have done – or said – to justify the death sentence? The question is central to the meaning of free speech in a democracy.

SAGE AND GADFLY

Socrates spent the whole of his adult life as a sage. He had no job and never seems to have learned a trade. Apart from two short spells in the army he never left Athens and rarely passed the city gates. His daily habit, which he never much varied, was to stroll down to the sacred groves of the Lyceum or some other gathering place in the open air and talk to his disciples and hangers-on. Everyone was welcome: politicians and poets, aristocrats and artisans. In a city of 100,000 people, he would have been familiar to most of them, an eccentric though harmless figure earnestly engaged in discussions about the meaning of life, the nature of good and evil, or the relationship between virtue and knowledge.

His outward appearance was by most accounts grotesque, with prominent eyes bulging out of a massive bald head, and a broad flat nose that turned up at the end. When he walked, he did so with a comical strut and when he talked, he lowered his head and fixed his interlocutor with a piercing sidelong stare. Even in his younger days he had been given to curious 'rapts' or trances and during his service in the wars is said to have stood spellbound for twenty-four hours in the trenches at Potidaea. Another account has him standing in the dark, gazing up at the sky with his mouth wide open, studying the path of the moon. For all these odd mannerisms and his extraordinary appearance, he has been described as 'all glorious within' and was clearly adored by those close to him. He could always be counted on to be fun at their parties and had a keen sense of the ridiculous.

What he lived on is hard to say. He earned no money and accepted no fees, though he might have been left a small inheritance by his father who had been a stonemason. He lived with his wife and three sons in a tiny house made of sun-dried bricks, his coat was the same summer and winter and he wore neither shoes nor a shirt. Poverty was the badge of Socrates's spiritual independence, though he could be maddeningly self-righteous about it. His friend Alcibiades describes the effect it had:

> There was one time when the frost was harder than ever, and all the rest of us stayed inside, or if we did go out, we wrapped ourselves up to the eyes, and used bits of felt and sheepskin over our shoes, but Socrates went out in the same old coat he'd always worn, and made less fuss about walking on the ice in his bare feet than we did in our shoes. So much so, that men began to look at him with some suspicion and actually took his toughness as a deliberate insult to themselves.

His approach to philosophy was equally provocative. Before him, philosophers had been mainly concerned with cosmology, that is to say the study of the origins and nature of the universe and the movement of the heavenly bodies. Socrates brought philosophy down to earth. He put it into the cities, as Cicero said, and even brought it into the home, compelling people to enquire about life and ethics and good and evil, philosophy's central task to formulate a rule of life to guide men's conduct. His technique was to ask people to put forward a hypothesis about, say, the nature of virtue and then put the hypothesis to the test to see if it worked. If not he would discard it and ask for another, always trying, and invariably failing, to reach an absolute definition of whatever subject was under discussion, whether it was the art of making shoes or the nature of courage and justice.

Although he never wrote a single word himself, examples of his method abound, mostly in the dialogues published after his death by his great friend and disciple Plato. Take, for instance, the *Phaedrus* where, in his search for a definition of knowledge, Socrates discusses horse-trading. He begins with the observation that you obviously cannot take up horse-trading unless you know what a horse is.

How silly it would be, he tells Phaedrus, 'if I should urge you to buy a horse to fight against the invaders, and neither of us knew what a horse was'. So Phaedrus has to provide a definition of a horse, which for Socrates's purposes, must be exact and all-embracing. Of course, Phaedrus fails – his definition could just as well fit an ass – and Socrates has to show him that in order to arrive at an absolute definition of a horse, one must first understand the nature of knowledge. The triumphant conclusion is that he who is ignorant of knowledge does not understand horse-trading or any other trade.

The Socrates depicted by Plato invariably has the last word like this, leaving his victims floundering in their own inadequacy. He had a way of tying them in knots that left them more perplexed at the end of the dialogue than they were at the beginning, and angry both with themselves and with Socrates. In *Meno*, an ambitious young Thessalonian aristocrat ends up unable to speak in public ever again. He had been warned beforehand of the philosopher's negative questioning, but thought it was a case of Socrates being in doubt himself and making others doubt also. 'But now,' he says, 'I find you are utterly bewitching me with your spells and incantations, which have reduced me to utter perplexity.' Socrates was like a stingray or flatfish 'for it benumbs anyone who approaches and touches it . . . and something of the sort is what I find you have done to me now. For in truth I feel my soul and tongue quite benumbed'. In an ominous foretaste of what was to come, Meno goes on to warn Socrates to be careful. 'You are well advised in not voyaging or taking trips away from home,' he says. 'For if you went on like this as a stranger in any other city, you would most probably be arrested as a wizard.'

Socrates's technique was always to affirm nothing positive himself, but to refute others. It is a technique often used in science and is known in philosophy as negative dialectic. Such an approach has its value in the study of philosophy. It helps to remove ambiguities and harden definitions. But it belongs in the realm of thought and is not of much use to practical men wrestling with the day-to-day management of business or government. As US President Harry Truman earthily remarked, the practical man of affairs sees a philosopher as someone with a *phi beta kappa* key at one end of his watch chain – and no watch at the other. In the real world, dialectic can't tell the time of day.

These philosophical complexities went over the heads of most ordinary Athenians, of course. To them, at least in the early days, Socrates was a harmless eccentric, and because of his odd habits even a figure of fun. In 423 BC, when he was about forty-five years old, Aristophanes made him the central character in a comedy called *The Clouds*, a satire on the New Learning which was thought to be putting dangerous and ridiculous notions into the minds of the young. Socrates is cast as the head of a 'Thinkery', or Think Tank, and makes his first appearance on stage suspended from the clouds in a contrivance looking like a gondola in a hot-air balloon, spouting nonsense. The story concerns a well-to-do but ignorant countryman, Strepsiades, who goes to the Thinkery in the belief that Socrates can teach him how to swindle his creditors by proving that wrong equals right. But first he has to learn to lose his belief in Zeus and worship the new gods: chaos, respiration and the clouds, that is to say the forces of nature, the only true divine beings, according to Socrates, the rest the subject of fairy tales. In one passage, which would have offended the religious susceptibilities of the Athenian audience, Socrates is made to say, 'Zeus? Who's Zeus? You really should know better. There is no Zeus.' Strepsiades's education goes badly wrong, of course, and he ends up being beaten by his layabout son, who has also learned a thing or two from Socrates. 'I can dance on the point of a needle,' he tells his father. 'You hit me when I was young for my own good, didn't you? Well, that now entitles me to beat you, for your own good!'

The enraged Strepsiades rounds on Socrates and sets fire to the school, turning out the inmates. The play ends with Socrates trapped in the flames calling out, 'Help, I'm choking to death!' But Strepsiades tells him, 'it's no more than you deserve. For with what aim did you insult the gods, and pry around the backside of the moon?' The mob then descend on the Thinkery crying, 'Stone them! Beat them up! Show no mercy! For many reasons – but most of all because they have blasphemed the gods!'

By the time Socrates was brought to trial more than twenty years later, the satire had been lost. No matter that it was unfair of Aristophanes to show the old philosopher as an atheist – Socrates was in fact devoutly religious, sacrificing regularly to the gods and believing he had his own divine mission to bring wisdom to the city. No matter that it was mere caricature to link him with the itinerant sophists who went from city to city teaching rich young men the art of proving that wrong was right – Socrates in fact regarded the sophists as imposters worthy only of contempt. No matter that Socrates never ventured an opinion on scientific matters – they saw how he lived and concluded he was as bad as the rest of the dissident intelligentsia who had insulted the gods and caused the Athenian world to fall apart. Although it had won only third prize in that year's competition for comedy, the malicious portrayal of Socrates in *The Clouds* permanently damaged his reputation.

But the Athenians did not put Socrates to death just because he had been made fun of in a third-rated comedy. What then was it that turned the mockery of Aristophanes into the hatred that less than a quarter of a century later led the philosopher to be put on trial for his life? Most historians agree that three main factors were at work: Socrates's increasingly outspoken criticism of the democracy, its breakdown in a series of calamitous events that occurred during the war with Sparta, and the nature of Socrates's entourage. All three are closely interwoven.

FREEDOM IN ATHENS

The Athenians' attachment to freedom had been immeasurably strengthened by their victory against the invading Persians a generation earlier. In one desperate year, Attica had been devastated, Athens abandoned by her citizens, the Acropolis captured and its sacred edifices burned. But in the end, after the Battles of Marathon, Thermopylae and Salamis, the Greeks had prevailed against all the odds. 'The decision is now in the balance,' Herodotus had written of the first months of the war. 'Shall we be free men or slaves?' He returned to the theme again and again: the invading Persians were strong, but slaves, the Greeks weak, but free. 'We well know how gigantic is the superior strength of the

Persians,' the Athenians told the supreme Persian commander who called for their surrender. 'We shall nevertheless defend ourselves as best we can, because it is for our freedom that we fight.'

At the end of the war, Herodotus concluded that the Greek victory had proved 'not only by one instance but by many that equality is a good thing; seeing that while they were under despotic rulers, the Athenians were no better in war than any of their neighbours, yet once they got rid of the despots, they were far and away the first of all.' From then on, the Greek city-states, and especially Athens, had become inseparably bound up with the idea of freedom, an overwhelming and mysterious event in the history of the human mind, and one that permeated the whole of Athenian society. It was not yet the idea of individual freedom as it is understood today, but freedom nonetheless for people to choose their own rulers and determine their own destiny. Government by consent had succeeded government by compulsion. All adult male citizens became voting members of the *Ecclesia*, which took the major decisions, while a rotating Council of Five Hundred, the *Boule*, drew up its agenda. A third arm of the democracy was made up of the *dikasteria*, panels of up to 2,000 citizen jurors who met on around 200 days every year to adjudge private disputes, with the added (and more significant) responsibility of calling the city's leaders to account.

Free speech was an inseparable part of the new Athenian order. Never before had ordinary citizens been given the right to debate such vital matters as war and peace, public finance, or crime and punishment. It was a necessary, though ancillary, part of their right to share in government, a right known as *isêgoria*, the equality of speaking rights. Its importance to the Athenians is illustrated in a play by Euripides, *The Suppliant Women*, which tells how the widows of the seven chieftains who went against Thebes returned to the city to claim the unburied bodies of their dead husbands. In a passage aimed at his contemporary audience, Euripides creates an argument between Theseus, the legendary king of Athens, and the Theban herald, which the herald opens by asking: 'Who is king absolute here? To whom must I convey my message?' Theseus replies with a little lecture in democracy. 'You begin on a false note,' he tells the herald. 'This State is not subject to one man's will, but is a free city. The king here is the people.' The herald is unimpressed. 'You concede a point which gives me half the game,' he says. 'The city I come from lives under command of one man, not a rabble.' No one in his city had the power to twist it this way and that by loud-mouthed talk. How can a common man be a guide to sound policy? 'Your poor rustic, even though he be no fool – how can he turn his mind from plough to politics?'

The point was telling enough and has had a long and influential subsequent history. But on this occasion Euripides gives Theseus the last word. Quoting the herald's summons at the opening of debates in the Athenian Assembly, he declares that 'freedom lives in this formula: "Who has good counsel that he would offer to the people?" Where could greater equality be found?' Two thousand years later, these lines were translated by the English poet John Milton into a ringing paeon to free speech:

> This is true liberty, when free born men
> Having to advise the public may speak free.

Profoundly important though this new principle was to become, it was by no means applied universally. The right to take part in debates belonged only to a privileged caste of native-born Athenian citizens, a concept which excluded all women, slaves and the large number of resident aliens (who made up much of Athens' merchant class). It was also exercised in a collective sense. Freedom meant the right to take part in the decisions taken by the *polis* as a whole; it did not bestow the right to individual liberty as it is understood today, nor did it protect a citizen from all interference by the *polis* in the way he conducted his private life. 'We do not say that a man who takes no interest in politics is a man who minds his own business,' Pericles had said. 'We say that he has no business here at all.' He did not contemplate that a man might, without penalty, withdraw from public life altogether. His first duty was always to the *polis*, even when it demanded that he lay down his life or sacrifice his home for it. Even in the freest state in the ancient world, the liberty of expression had its well-recognised limits and, as a philosophical concept in its own right, is now accepted to be the product of a later civilisation.

An episode that shows both the strengths and weaknesses of the Athenians' right to *isêgoria* came in the early part of the long war with Sparta. Athens had laid siege to Mytilene on the Aegean island of Lesbos, and when the Mytileneans eventually surrendered, their fate was, according to custom, referred back for a decision by the Assembly. On the first day of the debate, the people were swayed by a motion put by the demagogue Cleon to raze the city, to kill its entire male population and sell the women and children into slavery. A fast tryreme was at once despatched to carry the fatal message. The next day, however, there was a sudden change of feeling and a petition was put around calling for the Assembly to be recalled. In a speech that vividly illustrates the extent to which liberty of expression was permitted at the Assembly a citizen called Diodotus stood up and made a powerful plea for mercy and moderation. 'It is simply on the basis of the argument which you have heard that I ask you to be guided by me,' he declared. 'For those who make wise decisions are more formidable to their enemies than those who rush madly into strong actions.'

In reply, Cleon scolded the voters for allowing themselves to be swayed by Diodotus's words. 'You are simply victims of your own pleasure in listening, and are more like an audience sitting at the feet of a professional lecturer than a Parliament discussing matters of State,' he told them. If they changed their minds now, they would only be demonstrating that a democracy was not fitted to rule others. Compassion would be taken as a sign of weakness, not of strength.

Cleon spent his eloquence in vain. On a show of hands, the peace party narrowly won the day, and a second tryreme was despatched to Lesbos to countermand the orders carried by the first. Thucydides tells of its dramatic dash across the Aegean Sea after the Mytilenian ambassadors had provided the crew with wine and barley and promised them great rewards if they got there in time. The men rowed non-stop, eating their barley mixture at their oars and taking it in turns to sleep. The commander of the first tryreme had just read out the original decree and was preparing to put it into action, when the second ship put into harbour and prevented the massacre.

It would be hard to find a more dramatic example of how debates in the Assembly could change the course of events. It also provides a neat example of both the fickleness of mass democracy and the restrictive nature of the Athenian idea of liberty. Those who voted to save the Mytilenians saw no incongruity in taking decisions on behalf of another, now subject, people, still less did those who had voted to enslave them. Free speech belonged to the imperial centre, never to the colonial outposts.

Even in Athens itself certain forms of dissent were not tolerated. The old philosopher Anaxagoras, for example, had been exiled for spreading the blasphemous view that the sun was not a god at all, but a huge lump of stone 'larger than the Pelopennese', a view he had formed after observing the fall to earth of a meteorite. In Pericles's day, the politician Thucydides* was ostracised for opposing the building of the Parthenon. He said the city was decorating herself with temples as a harlot decorated herself with jewels, using tribute money stolen from her allies. Pericles disingenuously replied that the allies had contributed the money in order to secure themselves against invasion; Athens had provided that security, consequently she could do what she liked with the money. When their debate in the Assembly failed to resolve the argument, an ostracism† was held, which Thucydides lost. He was banished from Athens for ten years for the sake of the public well-being. The Athenians' attachment to free speech did not extend to ideas which were thought to imperil the State.

Athenian dramatists also faced certain limits to their freedom of expression. They had to observe the laws relating to impiety, or what we would call blasphemy, and could be prosecuted for 'wronging the people', a concept akin to sedition. But within those bounds they were given remarkable latitude to mock or criticise whomsoever they chose. Indeed, the bitter tragedies of Euripides and the biting satires of Aristophanes were, in their very different ways, commentaries on contemporary events. And even while poking fun at their fellow citizens, or pouring scorn on their folly, their underlying purpose was always serious. 'What do you want a poet for?' Aristophanes asked in *The Frogs*. 'To save the city, of course,' comes the reply. His first task was to educate the people. Comedy in particular was used to confront the burning social and political issues of the day, the theatre acting not simply as a place for escapist entertainment, but as a public forum where playwrights could explore the convulsions of a deeply unsettled era.

The two annual *Dionysia* at which the plays were performed went on for several days in front of huge crowds – an audience of 14,000 was not uncommon for the main events in the amphitheatre. As their underlying purpose was religious, impiety would have been inappropriate on these occasions, though the boundaries of religious comment were not hard and fast. Individual gods might

---

* Not the historian.
† So-called because each citizen was called on to write on a potsherd (*ostrakon*) the name of anyone he wished to get rid of. Provided that at least 6,000 votes were cast, the man whose name occurred most often was then exiled for ten years without loss of property.

be freely ridiculed, at least in comedy, but the divine powers they represented had to be treated with reverence, and religious ceremonies mocked only up to a certain point.

The concept of 'wronging the people' was even more imprecise. In a paradoxical reversal of the modern laws of libel, playwrights could abuse individuals in the most outrageous way, but had to watch their step when criticising the community as a whole. Although Aristophanes had freely satirised Pericles as a warmonger and his paramour Aspasia as the keeper of a brothel, he claims to have been hauled up before the Council because of what he said in another play, now lost, called *The Babylonians*. In this play he had not only attacked all the important politicians then in office, but also shown subjects of the newly subdued State of Mytilene as a chorus of Babylonian slaves working on a treadmill – the implication being that imperial Athens behaved no better towards her allies than an oriental despot would have done. The Mytilenean ambassador, who was present, protested to the authorities and they in turn accused Aristophanes of wronging the people. He defended himself on the grounds that he had not been attacking the State, but only its leading statesmen, and appears to have been let off with a small fine. That did not curb his satirical sense of humour and a year or two later he was back with another attack on Cleon, the bullying demagogue who had succeeded Pericles, declaring that it was not his task to make fun of normal men, but to cut down the over-mighty, in this case 'the jag-toothed one' whose reputation 'stank like a camel's arse'. In *The Wasps*, produced in 422 BC, the author himself appears on stage to express his determination to continue poking fun at the new leader he loathed:

> I've heard some people saying that I'm reconciled in amity
> With Cleon, who once tanned my hide* and made me squeal indignantly
> Though they heard me cry for mercy while the dirty deed was happening,
> They only laughed to see the sport and called out very merrily
> To see, if squeezed† and pressed enough, I'd spurt out more buffoonery,
> So I played the fool a little while, but now it's time undoubtedly
> To be unfaithful to the vine – look out! I've pulled away its prop!††

In spite of the legal constraints, dramatists were clearly prepared to use their right to free speech, or *parrhesia*, to the limit, even in wartime. Indeed, the heady new concept of freedom emboldened the entire Athenian intelligentsia, who eagerly used it to explore all fields of knowledge and experience, beholden to nothing but the desire to think things out for themselves, unimpeded by either religious or political dogma. Uniquely for those days, there was no priesthood and no State authority to tell them what to say, to think or to believe, a freedom

---

*   Cleon was a tanner by trade, probably employing many slaves.
†   i.e. 'squeeze' him of a fine.
†† A proverb indicating people who find their trusted support giving way in time of
    need, in this case that Aristophanes was about to break his pledge to mitigate his
    attacks on Cleon.

of the mind which inspired this so-called 'Great Generation' to bring about the first period of enlightenment in human history. Under the leadership of Pericles, Athens not only reached the peak of her imperial influence, she soared to new heights in almost every sphere of intellectual and artistic endeavour. In science and mathematics, in cosmology and medicine, in art and architecture, philosophy and literature, her achievements have never been surpassed by any subsequent civilisation.

But Pericles had died of the plague in 429 BC, while Athens was still at the height of her military and creative power. He was succeeded by demagogues and adventurers who in the next two decades led Athenian democracy down the road to disaster. Most of them were friends and disciples of Socrates.

DANGEROUS FRIENDS

Socrates had always been careless in his choice of friends. He had said that a number of young men with wealthy fathers and plenty of leisure had attached themselves to his entourage to learn the art of negative dialectic. Athens seems to have been swarming with beardless young philosophers who had found an easy way of making laughing stocks of the leading citizens and their most precious beliefs. Some grew ambitious and 'as soon as they thought themselves superior to their fellow-disciples, they sprang away from Socrates and took to politics, for it was for political ends that they wanted him', said the historian Xenophon. Two such disciples were to cause Socrates irreparable harm – the erratic Alcibiades and the anti-democratic Critias. Ambition was the life-blood of both of them, said Xenophon. 'They were eager to get control of everything and outstrip every rival.'

Alcibiades was one of the most dazzling meteors to shoot across the Athenian sky. Handsome and well-born – Pericles had been his guardian – he turned out to be a military commander of genius, a persuasive orator and an accomplished poet. In the bisexual world in which he lived, both men and women found him irresistible; the sort of character who would in every way have been at home in Elizabethan or early Stuart England. At one point, even Socrates seems to have been chastely in love with him. But Alcibiades had a fatal flaw. He was untrustworthy. Perpetually unable to decide which side he was on, he was at various stages in his career an extreme democrat, a military adventurer, a turncoat and an exile. He was later to die in mysterious circumstances at the hand of an assassin, but before then he had played a crucial part in the series of disasters that overtook his native city and brought Socrates to his trial.

The first of these can only be described as a war crime. In 416 BC the long-drawn out war with Sparta was going badly. The little island State of Melos had remained neutral, denying Athens the use of her ports. Athens launched an unprovoked attack on the island and called on its citizens to surrender. After a year-long siege, they finally asked for terms, and following custom, the matter was passed back for a decision by the Assembly.

So far, the story follows that of the surrender of Mytilene ten years earlier. But at Mytilene, *isêgoria* had triumphed. There was to be no such triumph to spare the inhabitants of Melos. Every man on the island was put to death, the women and children enslaved and the island turned over to Athenian settlers. The prime mover in the motion that swayed the Assembly to vote for the massacre was Socrates's great friend and disciple, Alcibiades.

Aged about thirty-five by this time, the ambitious and gifted orator is next seen persuading the Athenian people to embark on one of the most reckless expeditions of the entire Peloponnesian War. In 415 BC, largely at the urging of Alcibiades, a fleet was despatched to invade Sicily, its objective to curb the growing power of Syracuse and gain complete control of the sea. Thucydides relates that at the meeting of the Assembly which took the decision a passionate desire to make the expedition seized everyone present. The general mob and the soldiers were in it for the pay, the younger generation welcomed the prospect of adventure and excitement, the older men thought the very size of the expedition would ensure its safety. 'In such an atmosphere of excessive enthusiasm,' said Thucydides, 'anyone who had misgivings kept quiet, lest he be regarded as a traitor.'

The Assembly voted for Alcibiades to be put in charge, along with two others, but while the expedition was being prepared, Athens was thrown into a superstitious panic by the discovery one morning that the city's *Hermae* had been mutilated. The *Hermae* were quadrangular stone pillars that acted as boundaries and signposts. Each bore an erect phallus – thought to ward off evil spirits – surmounted by a grinning bust of Hermes, the goat-bearded god of procreation. After a boisterous party before the fleet sailed, a gang of drunken young men had gone around the city breaking the phalluses off all of the *Hermae*. Alcibiades was suspected of complicity in the sacrilege and as a result seems to have been demoted to act as second-in-command to the superstitious Nicias, who had been one of the main opponents of the expedition.

The scene was set for disaster. Frightened from attacking Syracuse by an eclipse of the moon, Nicias missed the chance to take the colony by surprise. After a long and bloody campaign, the Athenian forces were annihilated, with Nicias, their unwilling commander, among the fallen. But Alcibiades had characteristically slipped away before the final defeat. Athens had recalled him to answer charges of sacrilege for his part in mutilating the *Hermae*, but he made off instead to join the Spartans. Reeling from a defeat of a magnitude they could still not comprehend, the Assembly sentenced him to death *in absentia* for this gross act of treachery. They would never forget the role that Socrates had played in his education.

His other protégé, Critias, was to bring him still greater grief. Another follower from an aristocratic family (and, as it happens, Plato's uncle), Critias, was all his life a vehement opponent of the democracy. From the account given by Thucydides it seems clear that he and his aristocratic cronies had been preparing for some time to strike against the growingly unpopular rule of the *demos*. Their chance came in the wake of the disaster at Syracuse.

The scale of Athenian losses there had been immense. Thousands of men had been killed in the campaign and at least 7,000 left behind in captivity. Thucydides wrote that all of Athens was weighed down by the thought of the loss of so many *hoplites*, cavalry and men of military age who, they saw, could not be replaced. The entire navy having been lost, they saw too that the numbers of ships in the docks was inadequate, as was the money needed to replace them, and that there were no crews to man the ships. Their allies were falling away or in revolt. Defeat loomed.

In the opinion of the English philosopher, John Stuart Mill, the Athenians' failure at Syracuse decided the fate of the world 'most calamitously'. Looking down on its harbour 2,500 years later, and almost weeping with regret and sympathy, Mill fancied that had the Athenians succeeded at Syracuse they would have added to their maritime supremacy all the Greek cities of Sicily and Italy; Greece would have soon united under their leadership, and might have been too strong for the Romans and Carthaginians. Even if the fleet had sailed and got away safe, Athens would never have been subdued by the Peloponnesians, but it would have been powerful enough to prevent Macedonia from emerging from obscurity, or at all events to be a check on Philip and Alexander. Mill came to the melancholy conclusion that 'perhaps the world would have been now a thousand years more advanced if freedom had thus been kept standing in the only place where it ever was or could then be powerful'. What he does not say is that it was the Athenians' selfish pursuit of a wholly secondary objective that had put their freedoms in jeopardy in the first place. When it came to statecraft, mass democracy had shown itself to be incompetent.

In the panic that followed the defeat at Syracuse, a revolutionary party of oligarchs seized control, but two years later were themselves overthrown and the democracy restored on an unrestricted franchise. Even then, the Athenians' woes were not yet over. Nothing went right for them any more. The war preyed constantly on everyone's minds and, after thirty years, seemed to be as far away from resolution as ever. The new rulers led them into another series of faraway defeats and in 405 BC the Athenian fleet was completely and utterly broken after it had been surprised at anchor by the great Spartan general Lysander not far from Alcibiades' retreat on the Hellespont. The Athenian commanders realised then that they had lost the war. A fast ship, the *Paralus*, was sent home to break the dreadful news. When it reached Athens, Xenophon relates that the sound of wailing extended all the way along the Long Walls from Piraeus to the city. No one slept. They mourned for the lost, but still more for their own fate. 'Besieged by land and sea, they had no ships, no allies and no food; and they did not know what to do.'

In the end, they did what all defeated people do when they have run to the end of their resources. They sued for peace. Harsh terms were imposed, Spartan troops occupied the Acropolis and a puppet regime was installed. This regime, infamous in Athenian history, became known as the rule of the Thirty Tyrants. Their leader was Socrates's protégé, Critias.

The Thirty ruled Athens by terror. Gangs of armed thugs roamed the streets and some 1,500 people were unjustly put to death, some because they were personal enemies of the Thirty, some for their money, others because they spoke up for moderation. In a chilling passage recorded by Xenothon, Critias called for the death penalty to be imposed on Theramenes, the leader of the group of moderate oligarchs who opposed the new alliance with Sparta: 'Gentlemen of the Council, if there is anyone here who has the impression that more people are being put to death than is warranted by the situation, I ask him to reflect that in periods of revolution this is a thing that always happens.'

If people opposed the tyranny, that was only natural, Critias said. They had got used to freedom. But they must be made to realise that Athenian freedom was now at an end. Democracy could never make friends with 'our preservers' from Sparta, though the aristocrats could. They were therefore abolishing the democracy and setting up an aristocratic form of government. Anyone who opposed them would be got rid of, especially if he was one of their own number. The frightful story ends with a gang of thugs dragging Theramenes from an altar in the temple to be escorted through the market place to his death, shouting out at the top of his voice for men and gods to witness how he was being treated. When at last he was forced to drink the hemlock, he threw the dregs out of the cup, as one does when playing *kottabos**, crying with his last bitter words, 'and here's to that delightful fellow, Critias!' Socrates's friend and follower was now the most hated man in Athens.

A drama then occurred that might have come straight from a Shakespearean tragedy. Rumours began to circulate that Critias had paid for the murder of Alcibiades, who had been ambushed by a band of assassins in his lover's bed. The flawed hero died in true dramatic fashion – naked, outnumbered, but with sword in hand. Within the year, civil war had broken out; Critias fell in action in one of its first battles. The remainder of the Thirty fled and in 403 BC the democracy was restored for a second time. On coming home from exile, the democratic leaders immediately declared a general amnesty. One of its terms was that no one still in the city would be prosecuted for events that had taken place in the past. It was a clause to prove important at Socrates's trial.

After two coups and a lost war, Athens had now in effect become a dependant of Sparta, impoverished, and without a fleet, empire or trade. Though restored, the democracy was in decline, the balance of the electorate upset, thousands of people having poured in from the countryside to escape the war. More than half the population had become pensioners of the State. Equality, which had at first liberated the Athenian spirit, now led to an envious levelling down. What the demagogues understood by freedom was that nothing should stand in the way of an all-powerful people, and any speaker in the Assembly who referred to the existing law was shouted down. Decisions were born of the passions of the moment. The law on any given day was what the people said it was. The political freedom they enjoyed came without obligations. Democracy had become the tyranny of the majority, with the *demos* itself ruling as a despot. The very characteristic to which Athens owed its greatness had become its undoing. Not for the last time in history liberty and democracy had parted company.

DANGEROUS ENEMIES

Socrates remained in Athens throughout these turbulent events, living up to his principle that a true philosopher should not stain his soul by taking part in politics.

---

* A game where one threw the last dregs of wine from one's cup while wishing the health of a loved one.

His attitude, as usual, was negative and passive; but while he was known to have despised the democracy, there is no suggestion that he in any way lent his active support to the tyrannical rule of Critias or the excesses of Alcibiades. He just stood aside and continued his life much as before, though on the two occasions when he was called upon to take part in the affairs of the *polis*, he stood up bravely, if passively, for the maintenance of justice and the laws.

The first occurred during the democracy, when Socrates opposed the mass trial of six naval commanders who were put to death after some of their own sailors had drowned in a heavy storm. Ignoring both common justice and the rule of law, an orator called Callixenus had demanded their immediate and collective execution without a hearing. When someone objected, uproar broke out, with many voices heard shouting that it was monstrous to stop the *demos* from doing whatever it wanted. Only Socrates, who had been called up to serve on the jury, insisted on conforming with the law. He too was shouted down and the six commanders were led out to execution forthwith – a further example of the power of the sovereign people at its worst.

Socrates was equally brave on the only other occasion when he was forced to take part in events. During the rule of the Thirty Tyrants he was ordered, along with others, to arrest a *metic*, or resident alien, Leon of Salamis, and take him from his home for execution. The Thirty had decreed the liquidation of rich aliens like Leon in order to expropriate their estates to pay for the Spartan occupation. But their order to Socrates had an additional purpose; it was, he said at his trial, 'one of many instances in which they issued such instructions, their object being to implicate as many people as possible in their wickedness'.

Socrates's response to the order was characteristically negative. He went home. 'I should probably have been put to death for it, if the government had not fallen soon afterwards,' he said at his trial. 'But I made it clear by my actions that death did not matter to me at all . . . but that it mattered all the world to me that I should do nothing wrong or wicked.'

Socrates's detachment from politics did nothing to endear himself to the 5,000 fellow citizens who had suffered the bitterness and hardship of exile. To the newly returned democrats, having stayed in the city during the rule of the Thirty was a badge of dishonour. Though he could show he was not a collaborator, Socrates's disdain for the resistance further poisoned the atmosphere against him.

Socrates viewed the return of the democrats with his usual philosophical detachment. Democracy, he said, did not fulfil man's basic need, which was to look after the well-being of his own soul, or to use the Greek word, his *psyche*. The Assembly was to him no more than an outdoor mass meeting subject to all the irrational emotions and herd instincts that influence any crowd, which can be swayed this way and that by the glib tongue of a skilled orator.

Although he held to it so fully in his own life, Socrates always speaks scathingly of the use of free speech by others. In a dialogue called the *Gorgias*, he dismisses Athens' greatest names – Pericles, Themistocles, Cimon and Miltiades – as little better than pastry cooks, their oratory simply pandering to the appetite of the masses without regard to its results. In Plato's *Republic* he even proposes to censor lines from Homer's *Iliad* lest they should encourage a disposition to evil. He is particularly keen to strike out references to the weeping and wailings of famous men, which could breed disrespect for authority. The verses where Achilles mocks Agamemnon as 'thou ever steeped in wine, dog's face, with heart but of a hart' must also go; kings in this utopian world are never drunk. And so on, cutting a humourless swathe through some of the most memorable lines in Homer.

These of course are the words of Socrates as recorded by Plato. Nevertheless, in all the accounts of his conversations that have survived, Socrates is not once shown to speak up in favour of free speech. Whenever he mentions it, the reference is always disparaging. How ironic then, that he was about to be put on trial for no other crime than practising it himself.

The first clue that some sort of action would be taken to curb his behaviour comes at the end of the *Gorgias* when a materialist friend called Callicles tries to persuade Socrates to drop his philosophy – a 'pretty toy' – and take up some other more down-to-earth occupation. He is worried that Socrates seems unaware that his outspoken views might get him into trouble. 'You seem too confident that nothing can happen to you, as if you were living in another world and not liable to be dragged into court, possibly by some scoundrel of the vilest character.'

Not at all, Socrates replies. 'I would be a fool if I didn't realise that in this State anything can happen to anybody.' He goes on to say that 'if it be alleged against me either that I am the ruin of the younger people by reducing them to a state of helpless doubt or that I insult their elders by bitter criticism in public or in private, no defence will avail me, whether true or not, the truth being simply that in all that I say I am guided by what is right and that my actions are in the interests of those who are sitting in judgement over me. So, presumably, I shall have no alternative but to submit to my fate, whatever it may be.'

TRIAL AND EXECUTION

The final spark that seems to have caused the city fathers to take action against Socrates came in 401 BC, hardly two years after the restoration of the democracy. The prosecution's case against him has not survived; all that remains are the two accounts of his defence by Plato and Xenophon. It is therefore impossible to know with any certainty what was in the minds of his accusers when they finally took action to silence him. It seems probable that their intention was no more than to shut him up and keep him out of harm's way; voluntary exile or ostracism seem to have been the worst punishments they contemplated. But that was to reckon without Socrates's sublime refusal to compromise his views. The scene was set for a tragedy that would blacken the name of Athens for ever.

His principal accusers were all respectable men – not at all the 'scoundrels of the vilest character' that Callicles had warned him of in the *Gorgias*. There were three: Anytus, Meletus and Lycon. Of Lycon, practically nothing is known, other than that he represented the orators. Meletus is described in Plato's account of the trial as an undistinguished young man, with long straight hair, a thinnish beard and a rather beaky nose. He represented the city's poets. By far and away the most important and almost certainly the instigator of the charges was Anytus, a wealthy tanner who probably employed many slaves. Representing the craftsmen and political leaders, Anytus was the archetypal solid citizen – respectable, philistine, upright and principled. In politics, he was a moderate oligarch and had suffered heavy losses when his property was confiscated after he fled the city following the execution of the leader of his faction, the hapless Theramenes. Later, he played a leading part in the armed revolt that overthrew Critias. Now he was back, a hero of the resistance.

Nowhere in Plato's *Apology* is Anytus given the chance to speak for himself, but we can well imagine the cast of mind that caused him to move against the tiresome Socrates. There are even some intriguing clues that Anytus's own son may have fallen under the spell of the philosopher. 'At one time,' Socrates reveals in Xenophon's account, 'I had a brief association with the son of Anytus, and I found him not lacking in firmness of spirit.' Socrates does not reveal the nature of the association, but seems to have tried to persuade the young man 'not to confine his education to hides'. Tanning, after all, was a vulgar trade: the high-minded Socrates might well have tried to entice the young man away from the family business in order to improve his mind and save his soul.

The charges they brought against Socrates were amazingly vague: corrupting the young, and impiety. No specific acts of impiety were alleged. No law was cited which Socrates may have breached. There was no attempt to show he had conspired to incite his young followers to overthrow the city's institutions or commit acts of sacrilege like the louts who had mutilated the sacred *Hermae*. He was on trial solely because his teachings and beliefs were held in some unspecified way to have corrupted the young. In a very real sense the trial would be a test of Socrates's right to free speech – though Socrates himself would never have put it that way. He didn't *believe* in free speech.

His accusers believed in free speech, though. It was an essential – if unwritten – part of their constitution. So why did they couch the accusations in the way they did? One reason, of course, was that it was simply not possible to pin any specific crimes on Socrates. He had broken no law. Another, more important reason, is that Socrates, like everyone else, was protected by the amnesty. Under its terms, charges could not be brought for actions committed before the restoration of democracy three years previously. In the eyes of his accusers, Socrates's real crime was to have educated Critias and Alcibiades, the two men held to have brought about the downfall of the Athenian Empire. Though both were now dead, neither could be mentioned in the charges because of the amnesty – of which Anytus himself had been the chief promoter.

In an Athenian court, even the most serious case lasted only one day and was argued in front of a jury of 501 people, drawn by lot from the population as a whole. Litigants stated their own case, without the help of counsel, first the prosecution, then the defence. After this, the jury voted by a show of hands on conviction or acquittal. If the defendant was found guilty, the two sides spoke again, this time on the punishment they proposed. Finally, the jury voted either for the punishment proposed by the prosecution or for that put forward by the defence. There was no halfway house, no cross-examination, and no judge.

Plato's account of the trial leaves out the prosecution case entirely and jumps straight into Socrates's defence, published after his death as the *Apology*. This consisted of a narration of the facts of his past life, which proved that in the cause of justice and the law, and in insisting on his divine mission from God, he was equally ready to defy democracy as he was the Thirty Tyrants. Unsurprisingly, he ties his young accuser Meletus in dialectical knots and blames his portrayal by Aristophanes in *The Clouds* twenty years earlier for the popular view that he could make the weaker argument defeat the stronger. 'Look around you,' he tells the jury, 'Clear your neighbour's mind on this point. Tell one another whether any one of you has ever heard me discuss such questions, either briefly or at length; and then you will realise that the other popular reports about me are equally unreliable.'

Socrates twice stirred the jury to anger. On the first occasion he claimed the oracle at Delphi had verified his reputation for wisdom. This led to what Xenophon described as a *thorubos*, or uproar, among the jury. 'Please, gentlemen, do not interrupt,' says Socrates. The story had come from one of their own, a friend called Chaerephon, 'a good democrat who played his part with the rest of you in your recent expulsion.' Chaerephon, it seems, had gone one day to Delphi and asked the oracle if there was anyone in Athens wiser than Socrates. The priestess replied there was none.

With typical mock modesty, Socrates claims to have been alarmed and distressed at the oracle's pronouncement. 'I said to myself, "what does the god mean? Why does he not use plain language? I am only too conscious that I have no claim to wisdom, great or small; so what can he mean by asserting that I am the wisest man in the world? He cannot be telling a lie; that wouldn't be right for him."'

Still puzzling over the oracle's pronouncement, Socrates set off on a quest to establish the truth. He went around the men said to be the wisest in Athens and examined them, one by one, to see if any were wiser than he. All were found wanting: politicians, dramatists, craftsmen and poets. Socrates even professes surprise when, after he had shown one politician who thought he was wise but was not really so, 'my efforts were resented both by him and by many of the other people present'. Socrates had discovered that real wisdom belonged only to God. The oracle had said he was the wisest man in Athens only because he realised the extent of his own ignorance.

An even greater *thorubos* arose when he told the jury he didn't care whether he lived or died: he would never change his ways just to save his life. This seems to have been the turning point in his trial. Until that moment, not even the accusers had wanted his blood. They were counting on Socrates agreeing to change his ways, in which case he would have been let off with a light fine or, at worst, banishment. But Socrates would have none of it. He could not compromise.

'Suppose you said to me, "Socrates . . . on this occasion we shall acquit you, but only on one condition, that you give up spending your time on this quest and stop philosophising." I should reply "Gentlemen, I am your very grateful and devoted servant, but I owe greater obedience to God than to you; and so long as I draw breath and have my faculties, I shall never stop practising philosophy and exhorting you to virtue . . . To everyone I meet I shall go on saying in my usual way, "My very good friend, you are an Athenian and belong to a city which is the greatest and most famous in the world for its wisdom and strength. Are you not ashamed that you give your attention to acquiring as much money as possible, or reputation and honour, and give no attention to truth and understanding and the perfection of your soul?"' At this, the jury again began to protest, but Socrates treated them with disdain, saying, 'you can please yourselves whether you listen to Anytus or not, and whether you acquit me or not. You know that I am not going to alter my conduct, not even if I die a hundred deaths.'

The jury was now in uproar. 'Order, please, gentlemen,' Socrates tells them. 'It is to your own advantage to listen. I am going to tell you something else which may arouse a storm of protest, but please restrain yourselves.' If they put him to death they would harm themselves more than they harmed him. Neither Meletus nor Anytus had the power to hurt him 'because I do not believe that the law of God permits a better man to be harmed by a worse'. For this reason, he says, far from pleading on his own behalf, he is really pleading on theirs. If they put him to death, there was no one else to take his place, since it was literally true that 'God has specially appointed me to this city.' He compared himself to a gadfly, appointed by God to sting the city into action as if it were a large but lazy thoroughbred horse. 'All day long, I never cease to settle here there and everywhere, rousing, persuading, reproving every one of you,' he said, 'though in your annoyance I suspect you will finish me off with a single slap; and then you will go on sleeping till the end of your days.' With such a speech, Socrates might as well have put the hemlock to his lips. Sure enough, when it came to the show of hands he was found guilty by a vote of 280 to 221. Even Socrates said he didn't believe it would be such a close thing.

The court now turned to the second stage of the procedure: the punishment it would impose. And once again, the prosecution's case is missing. From Plato's record of the speech made by Socrates, we know only that Meletus had called for the death penalty. He returns us to the trial at the moment Socrates stands up to make his counter-proposal. Any lawyer would think the auguries at this stage of the trial were good; the jury was divided, the death penalty was a disproportionate punishment for so vague an offence, no capital crime had been proved, the prosecution was ready to compromise. A troubled jury could surely have been persuaded to take a lenient view. Ostracism was the punishment they probably had in mind, a procedure used often during that century to deal with citizens held to have endangered the State.

Socrates plainly knew that this was an option the jury would consider. What punishment would they like him to suggest he asked towards the end of his speech. Imprisonment? A fine? Banishment? 'You would very likely accept the suggestion,' he tells them. 'But being convinced that I do no wrong to anybody, I can hardly be expected to wrong myself by asserting that I deserve something bad, or by proposing a corresponding penalty. Why should I? I am not afraid of death.'

At this point, the two accounts of his speech part company. According to Xenophon, when asked to propose a counter-penalty, Socrates 'refused personally and forbade his friends to name one'. Plato, on the other hand, tells a different and far more provocative story. In his version, Socrates teases the jury with a ludicrous suggestion: he had never cared for the things that preoccupy most people – making money, having a comfortable home, high military or civil rank, political appointments, membership of secret societies. Instead, he had tried to persuade each one of them to think of his moral well-being. What did he deserve for behaving in this way? Free maintenance at the State's expense. That then was the punishment he proposed.

Unsurprisingly, the joke fell flat. Socrates tried to retrieve the situation by declaring that he was prepared to accept a fine after all. If he could afford it, it would do him no harm. But of course he had no money. 'I suppose I could afford about a hundred *drachmae*,' he said. 'I therefore suggest a fine of that amount.' The sum was so trifling it amounted to a contempt of court.

His friends had been watching Socrates's performance with mounting alarm – a 'farce' one of them would call it later. Now they intervened. 'One moment, gentleman,' Socrates said in a final dramatic passage. 'Plato here, and Crito and Critobulus and Apollodorus, want me to propose three thousand drachmae on their security. Very well, I agree to this sum, and you can rely on these gentlemen for payment.' But it was too late. Socrates had already goaded the jury beyond bearing. By a bigger majority than before, they voted for his death.

All of Socrates' light-hearted irony now fell away. To those who voted for his condemnation he issued a terrible prophesy. 'Vengeance will fall upon you with a punishment far more painful than your killing of me. You have brought about my death in the belief that through it you will be delivered from submitting your conduct to criticism; but I say the result will be the opposite . . . If you expect to stop denunciation of your wrong way of life by putting people to death, there is something amiss with your reasoning. The best and easiest way of escape is not to stop the mouths of others, but to make yourselves as good men as you can.'

At the gates of death, Socrates had done what he had never done in all of his long life before: issue a clear and ringing defence of the virtues of free speech. It was from the manner in which he faced his trial and death that later generations drew their inspiration for the defence of individual liberty, and not from his teachings during his lifetime. But perhaps it's just another of those Socratic paradoxes that he would have so enjoyed.

The climax was now approaching. Socrates ended his speech with a moving tribute to those members of the jury who had voted for his acquittal. He told them he had just had a remarkable experience: during the whole trial, and even when he left home that morning, the prophetic voice that had been his constant companion since childhood had not once spoken up. The only explanation could be that what had happened to him was a blessing, and it was quite mistaken to think death was an evil thing. He concluded with an elegaic farewell: 'Now it is time that we were going, I to die and you to live; but which of us has the happier prospect is unknown to anyone but God.'

In Athens, a sentence of death was normally carried out on the same day. But the trial of Socrates had coincided with the annual mission to Delos, an important religious festival during the course of which a State galley sailed with thanks-offerings to the island where Theseus is said to have delivered Athens from the yearly tribute of sending young men and maidens as food for the Minotaur. While the sacred galley was at sea, the death penalty could not be inflicted. That year, it was a month before the galley returned. Socrates spent the time in prison turning Aesop's fables into verse and, of course, in conversation with his disciples.

In two dialogues recorded by Plato called *Crito* and *Phaedo*, he prepared his soul for death and reviewed the teachings of his life.

One of the dialogues, the *Crito*, begins with a more practical idea, however. In the darkness before dawn, Crito, one of the wealthy supporters who had offered to stand surety for a fine, visited Socrates in his cell. Socrates was sleeping soundly, Crito waiting anxiously for him to awaken. The ship from Delos was due to dock that day. Before it arrived, Crito had arranged for his friend to escape. Money had been raised, a safe haven provided for him in Thessaly; his wife and young sons would come along too. All that was needed was Socrates's consent.

Crito made a powerful argument that Socrates owed it to his friends, his family and himself to escape. He scolded him for the plight into which he had put himself. 'First, you came into court when it was quite unnecessary,' he said. 'That was the first act; then there was the conduct of the defence – that was the second; and finally, to complete the farce, we get this situation, which makes it appear that we have let you slip out of our hands through some lack of courage and enterprise on our part.'

But Socrates had already chosen to stay and die. He replied to Crito in an imaginary dialogue between himself and the city's laws, in which he for once accepted the arguments of the other side. As a citizen, he had no right to disobey the laws, for the city could not continue to exist and not be turned upside down if its legal judgements had no force, but were open to be nullified by private persons. The only course a citizen should follow if he disagreed with its actions was to use his liberty of speech to persuade them to change. If the state leads him out to war, to be wounded and killed, he must comply, for both in war and in the law courts and everywhere else 'you must do what your city and country commands, or else persuade it in accordance with universal justice'.

Socrates never explicitly referred to the citizen's right of free speech, but his conclusion made it plain that if he is not to be forced to disobey his country's laws the citizen must be free to persuade it to change them 'in accordance with universal justice'. Socrates saw that in a free state such as Athens, the right to disagree went hand in hand with the duty to obey the law. In refusing to flee, he was doing posterity a final service by establishing for all time that in putting him to death, his fellow citizens had not betrayed Socrates, they had betrayed themselves and the principles they stood for.

The sacred ship from Delos did not, in fact, arrive for another day. Another day meant time for another dialogue, the *Phaedo*, with Socrates in mystical mood as he examines the nature of the human soul and the prospects of immortality. Then, at last, it was time for him to die.

On the last day, his followers found him in his cell just being released from his chains, his long-suffering wife Xanthippe sitting next to him with their infant son on her knee. 'Oh, Socrates,' she exclaimed when his friends walked in, 'this is the last time that you and your friends will be able to talk together!' Socrates looked at Crito and said, 'Crito, someone had better take her home.' It was an icy rebuke to a wife he had forced into a life of poverty as she struggled to keep house and bring up their three sons. But even on their last day together, philosophy came before family life or conjugal affection. If he took Xanthippe into his arms, or kissed his infant son, Plato does not record it.

After his wife had gone, the disciples talked all day. Socrates was to drink the hemlock at sunset. Phaedo relates how during the afternoon, the warder came in to tell him not to talk so much: it was making him heated and might affect the working of the poison. Never mind, said Socrates, he can give me a second dose, if necessary – or even a third. Just before dusk, the women and children returned to say goodbye and Socrates retired to take a bath. When he got back, his warder was in the room to tell him what would follow. 'Farewell,' he said, 'and try to bear what must be as easily as you can.' As he spoke, the warder burst into tears.

A little later the hemlock was brought in, which Socrates accepted 'quite cheerfully'. He said a prayer to the gods and with no sign of distaste drained the cup in one breath. Phaedo describes the effect on his disciples:

> Up till this time most of us had been fairly successful in keeping back our tears. But when we saw that he was drinking, that he had actually drunk it, we could do so no longer. In spite of myself, the tears came pouring out, so that I covered my face and wept broken-heartedly – not for him, but for my own calamity in losing such a friend. Crito had given up even before me, and had gone out when he could not restrain his tears. But Apollodorus, who had never stopped crying even before, now broke out in such a storm of passionate weeping that he made everyone in the room break down, except for Socrates himself, who said 'Really, my friends, what a way to behave! Why, that was my main reason for sending away the women, to prevent this sort of disturbance. One should make one's death in a tranquil frame of mind. Now, calm yourselves and try to be brave'.

Socrates began to walk about while the hemlock did its work; his limbs grew heavy and he lay down on his back. The numbness spread through his body, and when it had about reached his waist, Socrates drew back the cover he had placed across his face and made one last ironic jest. 'Crito,' he said. 'We must offer a cock to Asclepius. See to it, and don't forget.' Asclepius was the god of healing and Socrates was implying that death was the cure for life. They were his last words.

THE FINAL PARADOX

The trial and death of Socrates is rich in paradox. It marks the arrival of free speech as a concept for which men were ready to die; and yet the man who drank the hemlock had never defended the concept himself; indeed, there are many indications that he believed in it less than those who sentenced him. The idea of liberty was never seriously discussed in any of his many dialogues or ever subjected to the same rigorous search for a definition as other abstract concepts that concerned him like, say, justice or courage. Perhaps it is easier to resolve the paradox by putting the statement the other way around: the trial of Socrates marked the moment at which a democratic State showed it was capable of putting one of its citizens to death for no more than giving expression to his ideas.

This leads us to a further paradox, with important implications for the arguments about free speech in later civilisations. The trial of Socrates shows as plainly as could be that liberty and democracy are not the same things. They are not even necessarily dependent upon one another. Under the pressure of external events, or the influence of irresponsible demagogues, democracies can behave quite as despotically towards individual citizens as countries governed by a single ruler. The death of Socrates is the first and perhaps plainest example of that. A democracy may be diminished when it dispenses with the freedom of expression, as Athens was diminished, but it remains a democracy nevertheless, governed by the collective and sovereign will of the *demos*. A truly free spirit is just as likely to fall victim to the tyranny of the majority as he is of a single dictator.

The death of Socrates did not mark the end of democracy in Athens, nor of free speech. Both were to survive for about another eighty years. The dialogues of Plato alone – especially, perhaps, his bitterly critical account of Socrates's trial – stand as testimony to the freedom with which the philosophers were able to express their views. So, too, do the great works of Aristotle, Isocrates and Xenophon and the speeches of Lysias and Demosthenes, whose 'philippics' against the kings of Macedon are still remembered as classics of the orator's art. It was not until two lost wars against Philip and his son, Alexander, that Athenian democracy was finally extinguished.

Even then, Athens never lost her reputation for intellectual pre-eminence. During the rule of the Romans, it became as fashionable for their well-born citizens to go to one of the famous schools of philosophy in Athens as to a university. Cicero, Atticus and Horace were all educated there and the author Lucian appreciated its peaceful calm and beauty after the turmoil of Rome.

The Athenians also went on talking, of course. In the days before reading, they talked all the time, in public and in private, and in their literature they elevated it into an art form. From Homer to Thucydides and Plato, Greek literature consists mostly of talk. It was their way of life. They loved debate and argument and were always eager to discuss new ideas. It was a reputation they maintained throughout antiquity as we see from an episode 400 years after the death of Socrates, when the apostle Paul paid a visit to Athens to make converts to the new religion of Christianity. The Acts of the Apostles tells us how the Athenians took him to the Areopagus, the hill to the west of the Acropolis which gave its name to their meeting place, and asked him: 'May we know what this new doctrine is of which you speak? For you bring strange things to our ears; we would know therefore what they mean.' In a charming aside, the Bible adds, 'for all the Athenians and strangers which were there spent their time in nothing else but either to tell, or to hear, new things'. That is perhaps the final paradox of Socrates. The city which loved to talk and was always eager to hear and receive new ideas is remembered by history as the city that stopped the mouth of its greatest talker and idealist.

CHAPTER TWO

The Paradox of Paul

FREEDOM IN ROME

When St Paul spoke on the Areopagus 400 years after the death of Socrates, Athens was still the intellectual centre of the civilised world. But politically she had become a backwater, just one of the many distant provinces of the Roman Empire, ruled by a foreign governor, no longer independent, no longer a democracy.

At the time of Socrates's death, Rome had been a small and backward city-state with a population of no more than 20 or 30,000. Now she ruled most of the known world, from the coast of the Black Sea to the northern outposts of Britain, from the Nile to the Pillars of Hercules. When the city-states of Greece were formally absorbed by Augustus at around the same time as the birth of Christ, the population of the empire was estimated at more than 200 million people, its capital a vast overcrowded city of 2 million, by far the largest in the world.

It was the Greek historian Polybius who first recorded the phenomenon that had brought 'almost all the inhabited world under the single rule of the Romans in less than fifty-three years.'* A native of Arcadia who had been carried off to Rome as a prisoner, Polybius observed with what he called his pragmatic eye that this swift ascendancy was due to more than the acknowledged military superiority of Rome. It was made possible, he concluded, by the nature of her constitution, a particularly happy blend of monarchy, democracy and aristocracy.

The democratic element brought a necessary though limited degree of freedom. The level-headed Romans had no time for the open mass democracy of Athens, or for the unbridled freedom of the individual citizen to 'live as he likes' which had been such a feature of the Athenian *demos* in its later, decadent days. The Romans' *libertas* was an altogether sterner concept, reflecting their pronounced sense of law, order, strict organisation and social discipline. Within those bounds there was nonetheless freedom for the ordinary citizen to play a part in the government of his community according to his individual worth. It was generally accepted that this *libertas* had its natural limits not only in the obligation to conform with fixed laws, but also with *auctoritas*, that is to say the authority of persons and bodies of acknowledged superiority. For centuries, a strong and more or less permanent executive was thus enabled to pursue consistent and purposeful policies for the benefit of Rome as a whole.

The people's *libertas* did not include the right to vote on individual policies, or give them access to *isêgoria* in the way the Athenians would have understood it. Ordinary citizens might have the right to vote; only the well-born had the right

* That is from 220 to 168 BC.

to stand for office. Free speech was confined to members of the Senate, whose rhetoric, it is true, was often magnificently insulting and abusive. But woe betide anyone outside the governing class who ventured to offer political criticism or satire. The output of the theatre, for instance, was always closely policed, and even in prose, where the later Republic remains famous for its rich supply of great literature, its writers as well as its readers were restricted to members of the upper class. Elites could speak to élites; the rest were rigorously excluded.

When the Republican form of government so admired by Polybius eventually gave way to rule by a single emperor, the old balance between *libertas* and authority was destroyed. Political life became a struggle for power between individual men; a change so deplored by the implacable champion of liberty, Cato, that when he heard of the triumph of Julius Caesar, he committed suicide, having spent the previous night reading Plato's *Phaedo*. 'By divine law they were indissolubly united,' wrote Seneca. 'Neither did Cato survive freedom, nor freedom survive Cato.'

Seneca was speaking for the aristocratic group in the Senate, who could not accept that with the civil wars that ended the republic, their own political role had ended, too – as had their previous freedom of speech. This was dramatically brought home to them by the fate of the orator Marcus Tullius Cicero. After Caesar's assassination, Cicero published a series of fourteen philippics against Mark Antony, accusing him of trying to seize despotic power. In response, Antony had the greatest republican politician of his generation condemned to execution. Cicero's head was struck off, so, too, was his right hand, cursed for having written the attacks on Antony, who ordered the severed head and hand to be placed on the rostrum where Cicero had delivered his all too eloquent orations.

Cicero's *Philippics* – modelled on Demosthenes's speeches against Philip of Macedon – turned out to be the last example of truly outspoken republican oratory. Never again would anyone dare to rise in the senate to speak so publicly, so freely and so critically on matters of State importance. In future, political issues would be settled in the emperor's private council. Tacitus had to acknowledge that debate in the senate had become a sham – so meanly obsequious that even the emperor thought his grovelling advisers fit only for slavery.

When Augustus took the imperial purple, disrespect towards the emperor became a treasonable activity. Troublesome philosophers were banished, the poet Ovid exiled for immorality and subversive writings burned. The ordinary people – those the Greeks would have called the *demos* and the Romans called *plebeians* – were kept quiet with bread and circuses. By and large they remained content. They relished the benefits of law and order and above all what Pliny called 'the stupendous majesty of the *Pax Romana*'. This meant much more to them than the mere absence of war. It meant the belief that all the people of the empire could live together in harmony, with justice and order for all. Citizenship was widely available without distinction of race or nationality and even in Athens an orator was able to proclaim that under Rome 'we have one common democracy covering the whole earth under the most excellent man in it as its law-giver and administrator'.

But alongside this agreeable sense of security there grew up a pervasive sense of intellectual servility. Tacitus complained bitterly that the spirit essential to great literature had been killed. 'Genius died by the same blow that ended public liberty,' he wrote. Longinus observed that 'we never drink from the fairest and most fertile source of literature, which is freedom, and therefore we show a genius for nothing but flattery'. And of the book burnings that had by now become commonplace, Seneca wrote, 'How great is the savagery that puts a match to literature! Thank god these punishments of genius began in an age when genius had come to an end!'

In religion, too, it was an age without faith. Though the old gods survived, their worship was performed more by force of prosaic habit than through any feeling of spirituality. Polybius concluded that the endless religious ritual he observed in Rome was just a useful means of keeping the multitude from getting unruly; it instilled in them a deep sense of community and order. In his incomparable way, Edward Gibbon concluded, 'the various modes of worship were all considered by the people as equally true; by the philosophers as equally false; and by the magistrate as equally useful.' Tolerance of the thousands of gods that were worshipped across the empire produced not only mutual indulgence, but even mutual concord. Rome gradually became the common temple of her subjects, and 'the freedom of the city was bestowed on all the gods of mankind'.

This easy and mutual tolerance was about to undergo a profound change, however. A new religion had imperceptibly taken root in the distant provinces of the east and was now ready to burst upon Rome itself. The apostle who brought it to them was a genius at propaganda, his persistence and courage in putting over the revolutionary new message of Christianity was one of the most remarkable stories in the annals of human communication. The apostle's name, of course, was Paul.

It is almost impossible to exaggerate Paul's contribution to the spiritual development of mankind. He was the first to bring them a new kind of freedom, the freedom brought by an inward faith in a God who would redeem them from sin and give them the promise of everlasting life. Belief, he taught, would make them 'more than conquerors'. He told them that if they believed, then neither death, nor life, nor angels, nor principalities, nor powers, nor things present, nor things to come could separate them from the love of God. It was a powerful message, and what is more it was available to all mankind, Jew and Gentile, freeman and slave, men and women: 'for whosoever shall call upon the name of the Lord shall be saved.'

His message carried such force it conquered the whole Roman Empire, survived its fall, preserved the remnants of its culture through the Dark Ages that followed and provided the foundation for the modern civilisation in which we still live. Its effect on the development of free speech was more dubious. Paul had brought his message to Rome against tremendous odds; his successors then clung on to their faith through years of persecution until Christianity had prevailed as the established religion of the empire. But finally, in the aftermath of their triumph, the Christians repudiated the idea of free speech and liberty of conscience for anyone but themselves. As soon as their religion was established as the one true faith of the empire, they turned with ruthless energy not only on the pagans who had harboured them, but also on the heretics in their own ranks, the easy religious tolerance of the Romans giving way to the rigid suppression of all views but their own.

PAUL'S MISSION

What sort of man was the frail and sombre pharisee who made this possible? First of all, he was a humble man, by trade a tentmaker. The biblical accounts of Paul's travels mention how he set up his workframes in one new town after another and began sewing together the goats' hides that he sold to earn his living. And while his hands were busy with the needles and the twine, he preached to his followers, comforting and charging every one of them, he would say, just 'as a father doth his children'. All through his life, while he preached, he also worked, 'labouring night and day, because I would not be a charge unto you'. A driven man, evidently, and judging by the repeated references to his labour and travail, the founder, or at least the forerunner, of the Christian work ethic. 'If any man will not work, neither let him eat,' he once said: a maxim he certainly followed to the full in his own life. And like any good workman, he took care of those few possessions he did own. The Bible's very last reference to Paul, in prison and facing death, comes in a letter to his friend Timothy, where he begs for a visit before winter, telling him, 'bring with you my cloak which I left with Carpus at Troas, and the books, especially the parchments'.

A driven man indeed, who was ready to endure unimaginable hardships in order to bring the gospel to the notice of the world. Take, for instance, this one sentence out of a letter to his followers: 'Of the Jews five times received I the forty stripes save one, thrice I was beaten with rods, once I was stoned, thrice I suffered shipwreck, a night and a day I have been adrift in the deep; in journeyings often in perils of waters, in perils of robbers, in perils of my own countrymen, in perils of heathen, in perils of the city, in perils of the wilderness . . . in weariness and painfulness, in hunger and thirst, in cold and nakedness.' And besides all those things, he adds with an almost audible sigh, there is also 'that which comes upon me daily: the care of all the churches'.

To add to his hardships, Paul was often unwell, suffering from what he called his 'thorn in the flesh', which seems to have been one of the painful eye infections common in that part of the world. During the course of his travels he also picked up another chronic disease, probably akin to malaria, causing splitting headaches and spasmodic attacks of ague which left him prostrate for days on end.

A humble man, a driven man, an introspective man. It is a curious aspect of Paul's writings that, though full of the most intense feeling and personal drama, they rarely lift their head to make an observation about the physical world with which his travels had made him so familiar. Nowhere does he consider the lilies of the field, as Jesus did, or make parables about the mustard seed. Only once does he mention the wonders he must have seen on his travels: that was the temple of the great goddess Diana at Ephesus – and then only because he precipitated a riot there by preaching against idolatry. Paul's heart was not touched nor his vocabulary enriched by the imagery of the external world. Psychology was his domain, his writings addressed always to the inner man and the spiritual needs of his flock.

Tantalisingly, the beginning and end of his story have been lost. There remains only the record of his manhood, from the moment he met St Luke, who began putting him into his diary, to the day thirty years later, when the diaries abruptly stop. They are magnificently amplified by Paul's own epistles, but even so, no record remains of his youth, nor of his old age and death. He comes to us without genealogy, without father or mother, 'without beginning of days or end of life'.

His childhood was spent under the influence of three nations. He was a Jew from a family of pharisees, born with the name of Saul, he was a native of a Greek-speaking colony in Asia Minor, and he was a Roman citizen. All three played their part in the psychological make-up of this most complex of men, though his early upbringing was as Jewish as the blood that ran in his veins.

His native town was Tarsus, situated at the topmost corner of the Mediterranean Sea, where the coastline above Syria turns sharply westward into Asia Minor. It was 'no mean city,' he said with pride; a market town with a thriving trade in the timber which came floating through the middle of Tarsus on the navigable river Cydus on its way down to the sea. Behind the town were the Cilician Gates, the traders' mountain pass to the interior, through which Paul himself was to pass many times in his missionary travels. It was the lair, too, of the robbers who once waylaid him.

Tarsus was also a university town, though Saul, as he was still known, spent no time there. He attended the orthodox Jewish school, where instead of pagan writers like Homer and Thucydides he read only the sacred scriptures of the Hebrews, boasting that in his studies he advanced beyond many of his age. Later, he went to Jerusalem and immersed himself in the narrow complexities of Talmudic law. He returned home a scribe, a theologian and a stiff-necked pharisee. 'I was zealous for the law,' he wrote. 'I led a blameless life.'

Years then passed in silence: the years which saw the crucifixion of Jesus. Afterwards, Saul once again found himself in Jerusalem. He had gone there as leader of a pack of fanatics, 'exceeding mad' against the followers of the heretical new religion and determined to make 'havoc' of it. The Bible's very first mention of Saul has him present at the trial of St Stephen, where a howling mob at first 'gnashed their teeth' at Stephen and then rushed him out of the city gates where they stoned him to death. The Bible reports that those who cast the stones had 'laid down their clothes at a young man's feet whose name was Saul. And Saul was consenting unto his death'. He was at this time about twenty-five years old.

All his life, Stephen's murder preyed on Paul's mind, even into old age. Psychologists would probably agree it was one of the most potent factors in his sudden conversion on the road to Damascus, where he had gone 'breathing out threatenings and slaughter' against the Christians who had fled there. The story of how a blinding light struck him down at the end of his six-day journey is one of the most vivid and familiar in the Bible. He was utterly convinced that the voice of God had called to him from heaven as, trembling and astonished, he fell to the ground in absolute surrender: 'Lord, what wilt thou have me do?'

Explain it how we will, Saul's conversion marked a turning point in human history. The synogogue lost one of its most zealous defenders, the Church acquired its most heroic advocate, who spent the next thirty years in ceaseless toil on its behalf. Without that effort, the Church would in all probability not have spread beyond the scattered Jewish communities of the Middle East. The Christian faith would not have grown to become the powerful historical force it was. Western man would have lived in a different, and in many ways a lesser, civilisation.

The experience on the road to Damascus was certainly real enough to Saul. It left him blind for three days and traumatised for months afterwards, when he retired 'into Arabia' to think through what had happened to him. He came back with an unshakeable conviction that he had seen the risen Lord, and that it had fallen to him to sacrifice his whole life to his service.

After his sojourn in Arabia, he sought out Peter and James, doubtless to hear the whole story of Christ's life and teachings. And then, when he felt he was ready, he changed his name to Paul and began to preach. At first, he was a dismal failure. The Jews would not listen to him. Every speech was the signal for a riot. Every sentence was punctuated with curses and stones. He was hated as a renegade and so stirred up the people against him that his followers once had to lower him over the city walls in a wicker basket in order to save his life. Believing himself a failure, he went home to Tarsus.

More years passed by in silence. The New Testament leaves no record of how Paul spent the time; the next we hear of him is when the apostle Barnabus is sent to Tarsus to seek him out and bring him to Antioch, the multinational seaport 350 miles north of Jerusalem. Antioch was to play a crucial part in the early history of the Church; it was Paul's base for the next twenty years and, of equal significance, it was the centre of the gentile converts who first coined the name of Christian for themselves.

After spending a year with the converts there, Barnabus and Paul set out on their travels, visiting an astonishing number of communities around the eastern Mediterranean where the new religion was taking root: Athens, Corinth, Ephesus, Macedonia, Jerusalem, Caesaria and many more. Two features stand out. The first is the extent of the hostility shown to them by the Jews, the second the extent to which the Romans protected their freedom to speak.

In city after city, Paul and Barnabus were reported to the authorities for making speeches contrary to the law. Each time, the Romans were ready to let them go. Christianity was not yet a seditious religion, and but for this Roman neutrality it might never have survived. One example makes the point: in Achaeia, the Jews there 'made insurrection' and brought Paul before the Roman deputy, a man called Gallio, the brother of the author Seneca. As Paul was about to open his mouth in his defence, Gallio interrupted, telling his accusers, 'If it were a matter of wrong or wicked lewdness, I should bear with you. But if it be a question of words and names, and of your law, look to it yourselves. I will be no judge to such matters.' With those words, Gallio drove the Jews from the judgement seat. The Acts of the Apostles are full of such stories. Over and again, the Romans allow Paul to preach and speak without hindrance. It was only the Jews who stopped their ears.

The reason for this is not too hard to find. The gentiles came to the faith as converts from the pagan gods and saw the Hebrew prophets merely as forerunners of the risen Christ. To the Jews, the Hebrew prophets were *their* prophets and Jehovah was *their* God and no one else's. They had a covenant with him, sealed by Moses. Paul's teachings that Jesus was divine, or the Son of God, or the Second Person of the Trinity were therefore, quite literally, heretical, while to admit Gentiles to the temple defiled and polluted that most holy place. It is easy to understand their anger. Paul was challenging their deepest and most strongly held beliefs.

Indeed, the argument was dividing the Church itself. Many of its founders thought Christianity was just a purer, holier form of Judaism. Some even believed it was necessary to be an actual descendant of Abraham in order to gain entry to the kingdom of God that had been promised by Christ. If he was the Messiah, he was the Messiah of the Jews, foretold by their prophets, who had nowhere spoken of a Messiah for all mankind.

The issue came to a crisis over the practice of circumcision, the painful rite that sealed every male Israelite's covenant with God. It was the essential mark of his faith. There were several among the apostles, led by James, the brother of Jesus, who were telling converts that 'unless you be circumcised after the manner of Moses, you cannot be saved'. So important was the issue that Paul and Barnabus hurried to Jerusalem to join in the debate. Paul's victory in the argument was another decisive moment in the history of early Christianity. It marked what was, in effect, a break with what had been its exclusively Jewish nature. Thereafter, it became a separate faith. It was no longer necessary to pass through the synagogue in order to enter the Church.

For Paul, a break with the religion of his ancestors had seemed likely ever since he lived in Antioch and found he was no longer able to speak in the synagogues there. The moment he mentioned the name of Christ a storm of insults and blasphemies would break out, drowning out his words and obliging him to stop preaching. Paul's always short temper finally snapped at a particularly unruly meeting in Corinth when he shook his cloak at the demonstrators and shouted at them: 'Your blood be on your own heads! I am clean. Henceforth, I will go to the gentiles.'

Around this time, too, Paul began writing to the congregations he had visited on his earlier travels, beginning with one to the Church in Thessaly. The letters survive today not only as great works of literature but also as the origins of the New Testament. No gospels had yet been written – and none would be for another twenty years or so; at that point and for a considerable time afterwards, the Christian message was passed by word of mouth. Until Paul started to send his epistles, nothing whatever had been written down. The converts, after all, were mostly humble folk with an oral rather than a written tradition. In terms of chronology, the first book of the New Testament was Paul's Epistle to the Thessalonians.

Paul turned out to be a writer of genius. He wrote as he taught, while at work on his loom, dictating to Silas or Timothy, who took down his words on sheets of papyrus they had bought from an artist's shop around the corner. At the close of each letter, he would take up the stylus and add a note in his own hand:

'The salutation by the hand of me, Paul, which is the token of every epistle. All the saints salute you.' His style is spontaneous, full of verve and tenderness of thought and as varied as the peoples he was addressing. As works of theology, they are rated as the most profound ever written and every now and again express his thoughts with a splendidly austere beauty. 'Though I speak with the tongues of men and of angels, and have not charity, I am become as sounding brass or a tinkling cymbal,' he wrote to the Corinthians. Paul's dictated thoughts have influenced the hearts of men for nearly 2,000 years.

The climax of his life was now approaching. One day, he suddenly declared, 'I must see Rome.' He had preached to Greek and barbarian, he said, he was ready next to preach in the capital of the empire.

Paul's wish was to be fulfilled in a way he did not expect. He had gone again to Jerusalem to celebrate the Pentecost. On the seventh day, he was suddenly seized in the street by a mob who accused him of bringing an uncircumcised Gentile into the temple. 'Men of Israel, help!' they cried. 'This is the wretch that teaches everywhere against Moses and the Laws and has brought Greeks into the Temple of Jehovah and defiled the holy place.'

The story was not true, but it brought all Jerusalem into an uproar. Paul was rescued by a band of Roman soldiers who bound him in chains and carried him off to the castle. He impressed the captain of the guard by speaking Greek and was given leave to address the people. At first, the crowd fell silent as he told them in their own language of his conversion on the road to Damascus and his presence at the stoning of Stephen. But the moment he mentioned his mission to the Gentiles, pandemonium broke loose. Instead of quietening the crowd, as the captain of the guard had hoped, Paul had roused them into even greater fury so that they 'cried out, and cast off their clothes and threw dust into the air'.

Paul was bound with thongs and ordered to be scourged before being cross-examined by the magistrate. But as the soldiers bound his wrists, Paul suddenly asked their captain: 'Is it lawful for you to scourge a Roman, and uncondemned?'

'What! You are a Roman citizen?'

'Yea,' answered Paul drily.

'My citizenship cost me a great sum,' said the captain.

'But I was free born,' replied Paul with pride.

Now thoroughly alarmed, the tribune in charge dismissed the guard. It was a serious crime to scourge a Roman citizen without trial. He ordered Paul to appear for examination the following day before the Council of the Elders. Paul used the occasion to set the Pharisees against the Sadducees and caused another great uproar. Once again he was passed on to a higher authority, eventually appearing before the provincial governor himself. In an echo of Jesus's appearance before Pontius Pilate, the Jewish elders demanded his execution. But Paul again called on his privileges as a Roman citizen and appealed 'unto Caesar'. So the governor ruled 'then unto Caesar thou shalt go'.

Paul was on his way to Rome. On the way there under escort he was caught in a great storm and shipwrecked off the island of Malta. Luke tells the story in the Acts of the Apostles: 27 with such an authentic eye for seamanship it became known as the 'sailor's chapter' and is said to have inspired Nelson, who read it on his flagship on the morning of Trafalgar.

As the storm raged, Paul had kept his head. Through his efforts and exhortations, all 276 people on board were saved, though the ship was lost. After more adventures, he finally arrived in Rome, a prisoner awaiting trial. It was the year AD 60 and the Emperor Nero occupied the imperial throne. Luke tells us that Paul then dwelt in Rome for two years in his own hired house. Although chained to a guard, he was free to receive everyone who came to him and to preach the gospel with all confidence, 'no man forbidding him'.

Paul's confinement does not appear to have been a great hardship, and he very soon began to make converts among his visitors, and even among the soldiers posted to guard him. The commander of the castle was an educated man who treated him with sympathy, while his presence in Rome seems to have sent a wave of fervour running through the Church. 'Many of the brethren have gained courage by my chains and are much bolder to speak the word without fear,' he wrote.

Now nearly seventy years old, he kept up the ceaseless flow of letters, driven still, and rising to ever greater heights of eloquence as he laid down the enduring rules of Christian theology. As old men do, he was looking too towards his own death, sometimes with longing 'to depart to be with Christ, a lot by far the better', yet knowing that 'to stay on in the flesh is necessary for your sake'. His friends were meanwhile free to come and go, carrying his epistles to the farthest corners of the empire without the least hindrance from the Romans.

Then one day in the spring of AD 63, he was called at last to appear before Caesar's Court of Appeal. The verdict was favourable. He was set free. The Romans' tolerance of religious views they did not share was at this time still intact.

Almost at once, Paul set off to visit his far-flung congregations, encouraging, admonishing, even railing against them when they showed signs of heresy or backsliding. These later travels stamped the Church with an authoritarianism that has marked it to this day. Freedom, as Paul understood it, meant the freedom to embrace the Christian faith. It did not include the freedom to dissent or deviate from it. To worship was to obey.

Paul had offered the world a stupendous new idea: that God himself had appeared on earth and suffered in order to save mankind. Unlike other religions, it worked not by sacrament or magic, but by belief. Here was a religion that for the first time in human history recognised the worth of the individual. However meek and lowly they might be, the gospel was free and open to all. And here came the ambiguity. If you believed, all things were possible; but for disbelievers, all things were denied. To his followers, Paul's religion brought the spiritual freedom or peace of mind that comes from the hope of a saviour. It also raised the question of freedom of conscience, with the Christians' refusal to make obeisance to the pagan gods. But at the same time, it denied that freedom to others. There was only one true faith. Paul's blinding, mystical experience on the road to Damascus allowed for no doubts. If it gave his followers the strength to endure the most horrible persecutions, it also endowed them with an intolerance that in years to come would lead to even more rigorous persecutions than those they had endured themselves. Works they disapproved of would be burned by the thousand, dissenting voices ruthlessly suppressed. Paul himself was present at the first recorded burning of books in the name of Christianity. At Ephesus, we are told, he once urged new converts to pile up their 'superstitious' works and put them to the torch. The resulting bonfire destroyed books worth 50,000 pieces of silver. The easy tolerance of the pagans, now inextricably linked with liberty of conscience, was about to enter a long and melancholy interruption.

Paul's final years, like his first, are cloaked in mystery. There are hints that he planned a last mission to Spain, although no records survive to show that he actually went there. All that is known is that while he was away, Rome was engulfed in a major catastrophe. In AD 64 fire broke out and blazed for six days and nights, leaving two thirds of the city in ashes. The trophies of the Punic and Gallic wars, the holiest temples and the most splendid palaces of the Imperial capital were all consumed by the flames, including Nero's own magnificent apartments on the Capitoline Hill. Rumour put the blame on the dissolute emperor himself. Nero in turn shifted the responsibility to the Christians. On the basis of their teachings they were said to 'hate the whole human race', on the evidence of their liturgy they were depicted as atheists, sorcerers, cannibals and conspirators. Their religion anticipated the end of the world in a widespread conflagration. What could be more natural than the belief that they had started the fire that destroyed Rome, a city they openly despised as a new and even more dissolute Babylon?

Acting under the influence of a palace coterie of Jewish women and actors, Nero issued a decree prohibiting the profession of Christianity: *Christiani non sint*. From that moment on, it became a crime to be a Christian. Mass arrests soon followed and the victims were put to death in the most gruesome manner that the emperor's diseased imagination could devise. Some were clothed in the skins of wild animals in order to enrage the packs of hunting dogs that were set on them in the amphitheatre, living men and women were covered with tar and burned as torches to illuminate the palace gardens at the foot of the Vatican Hill. A 'great multitude' of Christians went to their deaths, according to the historian Tacitus.

Paul had got away only just in time, working on for three more years, mostly among the congregations of Asia Minor. Then in AD 67 he was arrested at Troas, the site of Troy, and sent to Rome in chains. One last epistle is the sole surviving evidence of his sorrow-laden final days, a letter written from prison to his great friend Timothy. Hold fast, he tells him. Be prepared to endure as a good soldier of Christ. Preach the word, in season and out, reprove, rebuke, exhort, 'for I am now ready to be offered and the time of my departure is at hand. I have fought the good fight, I have finished my course, I have kept the faith.' He asks for his cloak and books, left behind in Troas when he was arrested, he salutes his friends and begs Timothy to visit him 'before winter.'

And that is the end. We do not know whether he ever got his winter cloak and the books he so valued. It is unlikely that he ever saw Timothy again. Tradition has it that before summer had gone he was taken out of the city through the Ostian Gate and executed by one blow of the sword as was his due as a Roman citizen. He had given his life for the cause in which he so fervently believed.

CHRISTIANI NON SINT

Historians often refer to Nero's treatment of the Christians as the 'accidental' persecution. Gibbon even believed that Nero confused the Christians with another less passive sect of Galileans. At any rate, the effects, as well as the cause, of Nero's edict were confined to the walls of Rome. It was many years before the religious tenets of the Christians were again made the subject of punishment, or even of inquiry. Later emperors were still inclined to spare a sect that had been subjected to the cruel and unjust rage of a tyrant. The systematic persecution of Christians that began 200 years later had a different and more complex cause.

An impenetrable veil has been drawn across the early history of the Christian Church. From the time of Nero's persecution almost nothing more is heard of its slow but inexorable growth for the rest of the century. The contemporary Roman historians, Tacitus and Suetonius, both mention Christianity only once, each time disparagingly. Tacitus, the only pagan author to refer to Pontius Pilate's role in the crucifixion of Christ, calls their religion 'a pernicious superstition' of Jewish origin. Suetonius refers to it only in the context of the expulsion of the Jews following the abolition of their State by Claudius in AD 44, that is to say a good twenty years before Paul had completed his mission.

During the first century of its existence most educated pagans thus regarded Christianity as just another troublesome sect of Jews – and had it not been for Paul, that is how it would almost certainly have remained. The pagan world disliked the Jews, but tolerated them as a distinct and exclusive race who venerated a different God to theirs. So why did the Jews escape when the persecution of the Christians began? Their God was just as exclusive as the Christians' God; indeed, to the Romans it would seem to be the same God. What was it about Christianity that was so pernicious in the eyes of the otherwise tolerant Romans that alone among the religions of the world, they had to root it out? What separated it from the worship of all the other gods, whose divinity was so easily accepted? One reason, no doubt, was because, in contrast to the Jews, who kept to themselves and did not proselytise, the Christians were always active in seeking converts.

Evidence, however, is tantalisingly scarce. Indeed, we have to wait until AD 111 before we get an authentic glimpse of how an educated Roman regarded the humble new religion that was springing up around him. In that year, Gais Plinius Caecilius Secundus, known to us as Pliny the Younger, took up a post as governor of Bithynia and Pontus, a province on the southern shores of the Black Sea. In the course of his duties there, he came across what was, for him, a new phenomenon – a group of Christians openly practising their faith, and, what was worse, refusing to take part in the public worship of the Roman gods. Puzzled as to how he should respond, Pliny wrote for advice to Emperor Trajan. 'I have never been present at an examination of Christians,' he said. 'I do not know the extent of the punishments usually meted out to them, nor the grounds for starting an investigation or how far it should be pressed.' Should a pardon be granted to anyone retracting his beliefs, he asked the emperor. Or if he had once professed Christianity, should he gain nothing by renouncing it? Is it the mere name of Christian which is punishable, or must another crime go with it, like a refusal to sacrifice to the gods of Rome?

Trajan's reply was, by his own lights, a model of humane concern. Punish such persons who are legally convicted, he told Pliny, but go no further than that. These people must not be hunted out. Pamphlets circulated anonymously must play no part in any accusation, for 'they create the worst sort of precedent and are quite out of keeping with the spirit of our age'.

Here was no implacable zeal to root out heresy. Accusations had to be made openly. The offence had to be proved by due process of law. There would be no witch hunt. They should not be sentenced before they had been given a chance to recant. But the question is still unanswered: why was the Christians' religion of such concern to the Romans? The answer is to be found partly in the respect for law and social discipline observed so many centuries before by Polybius: citizens may not have had the faintest idea of why they made obeisance to any particular god; their endless rituals were more a civic than a religious duty, designed to instil in them their sense of community and order. It was incomprehensible to them that anyone should refuse to participate in such duties. It was not the Christian faith that Trajan wished to punish. It was their defiance of the State. They threatened the stability of the social order.

And in the background, the wildest rumours went around. Cannibalism, incest and human sacrifice were commonly thought to be part of Christian worship – practices which were not only disgusting and illegal, but they also brought bad luck. 'No rain, because of the Christians,' was a familiar Roman proverb. It became a common practice for pagan priests to blame the presence of Christians whenever they were unable to obtain omens at their official sacrifices. By making the sign of the cross, they were said to offend the gods.

We must not forget that this was an age steeped in superstition. Even the most educated Roman believed in divine signs and omens and that the ritual reading of the intestines of slaughtered animals could be used to foretell the future. Anyone who wilfully abhorred the gods was an atheist who could bring catastrophe to the whole community. The Church historian Tertullian summed up the mood in a brilliant and sonorous passage: 'If the empire had been affected by any recent calamity, by a plague, a famine or an unsuccessful war; if the Tiber had, or the Nile had not, risen beyond its banks; if the earth had shaken, or if the temperate order of the seasons had been interrupted, the superstitious pagans supposed that it was due to the crimes and the impiety of the Christians and the cry would go up "Throw them to the lions!"'

SAINTS AND MARTYRS

Revered by the Church as martyrs, the story of the obstinate men and women who defied the emperor's edict is difficult to unravel. The only accounts that survive are of the Christians themselves; and for the purposes of religious propaganda those accounts have been wildly exaggerated. Gibbon found himself unable to decide what to transcribe, 'until I am satisfied how much I ought to believe'. And many of the stories from the early Church are very difficult to believe indeed.

Its early historians – men like Eusebius, bishop of Caesarea – laid down an ideal of martyrdom which the Church has never lost. Their accounts dwell in lurid detail on the horrible tortures believers had to face – though, if Eusebius is to be believed, they always faced their degrading public deaths with a tranquil smile on their lips and a 'steadfast gaze' in their eyes. He tells of how their faces 'glowed', their skin regained 'the bloom of youth' and their bodies enjoyed 'anaesthesia' as they concentrated on the vision of paradise opening up before them. When Polycarp, bishop of Smyrna, went to the stake, we are told the flames encircled his body like the sail of a ship billowing out in the wind, while the middle of it was like baking bread, or gold and silver being smelted in a furnace, giving off a fragrance 'as if from gales of incense or some other costly perfume'.

Eusebius and other Christian apologists counted the numbers of such martyrs in their thousands, even tens of thousands. In later ages the catacombs of Rome would be ransacked for their bones, as though everyone who had ever been buried there was a Christian saint and martyr. It is even thought probable that it was through its contacts with Christianity that early Islam picked up its analogous language and theology for those who died in the faith. In both religions, martyrs take the short cut to paradise, going straight to heaven on the day they die, with pure and spotless souls.

The stories that were handed down can hardly fail to have stirred the emotions of the early Christian congregations. The fate of the noble Vibia Perpetua, martyred in Carthage with all her household in AD 206, is a vivid and typical example. According to Perpetua's own account, she was first put under house arrest and then transferred to prison, where her family was able to bribe the guard to allow her to take fresh air and nurse her infant son. In prison, Perpetua dreamed of a bronze ladder leading to heaven, with a huge and frightening serpent at its base. She at once invoked the name of Jesus and trod on the serpent's head. Having climbed the ladder, she entered a vast garden, with an elderly shepherd milking sheep and surrounded by many thousands clad in white. Perpetua awoke, realising she was destined for martyrdom.

Before long she was led out with other Christians for trial in the forum where a large crowd had gathered. When Perpetua's turn came to offer a libation to the pagan gods and pray to them for the safety of the emperor, her father sprang forward and begged her to pity her baby son. But Perpetua refused to take part in a pagan ceremony and confessed herself a Christian. Sentence inevitably followed and she was condemned with all the other Christians to fight the beasts. They returned joyfully to their cells and Perpetua was separated from her child for the last time.

She had more dreams, all recorded in vivid detail, and was finally led out into the arena to face the beasts, naked and covered in nets, but singing and radiant as befitted a bride of Christ. The crowd was shocked to see her breasts still dripping with mother's milk and called for her to be clothed. She was dressed in a modest tunic and set before a ferocious wild heifer, was tossed, but fell gracefully, and re-arranged her hair.

Meanwhile a leopard had been set on one of the members of her household, Saturus, who bled so profusely the crowd began to yell *bene lava! bene lava* – 'well washed! well washed!' – a hideous parody of the salutation used in the public baths. The wounded martyrs were finally lined up for despatch by a troop of gladiators, all save Perpetua receiving their *coup de grace* in silence.

She, however, screamed out, and when the young gladiator wavered, she guided his sword to her own throat. The narrator concludes his account with the exultant cry, 'O brave and blessed martyrs!' Later, a Church was built in Carthage in memory of Pertpetua, a cult built up around her memory, *The Passion of Perpetua* was regularly read out at Christian services and the anniversary of her martyrdom entered into to the official calendar of the Church of Rome. The blood of the martyrs was indeed the seed of the Church.

But not in the eyes of the Romans. To them, Perpetua had died because she chose to die. The more thoughtful of them found it disconcerting that someone could go to their death voluntarily, as she had done, simply by refusing to utter a few simple words of prayer. A pinch of incense might have been enough to save her life. All that was needed was a gesture of honour to the gods and conformity to tradition. If they only would agree to do that, the Christians could go on worshipping their own gods for as long as they liked. The Romans could not understand that to the Christians, liberty of conscience meant the liberty *not* to utter words they believed were blasphemous or to recognise the existence of gods they abhorred as idols.

That the Christians could be exasperating is not in doubt, particularly when they deliberately courted martyrdom, as many now did. What else could the magistrate do when Christians began shouting outside the courthouse, 'I wish to die, for I am a Christian!' The magistrate said, 'Come in, whoever shouted.' The man entered, carrying the gospels under his arm – and so achieved the end he sought.

On other occasions the would-be martyrs were denied the death they so ardently desired. Tertullian tells that when Arrius Antoninus, the proconsul of Asia, was holding one of his periodic assizes, all the Christians of the town presented themselves in a body before him and demanded the privilege of martyrdom. The astonished proconsul sent a few off to execution, but told the rest, 'If you wish to die, O miserable men, you can make use of ropes or jump off a precipice!' Others who found themselves in a similar predicament bade the Christians, 'Go, all of you and kill yourselves and worship your God and leave us in peace!'

Up until this time, the persecutions came about as the result of what were in effect private prosecutions. Christians had to be brought to court by a named accuser, usually an individual harbouring a grievance against them. Almost always, the initiative came from below, while the emperors looked down from Rome with benign indifference. One of them, Alexander Severus, even had the idea that he could absorb the Christian and Hebrew God into the official pantheon. In his private chapel, he put up statues of Orpheus, Christ, Abraham and Apollo and had his household pay them equal reverence. The experiment was not a success and his reign marked the end of a long period of official toleration.

The barbarians were now pressing on the frontiers and in AD 250, the new emperor, Decius, fearing Christianity as a dissident force, issued a general edict ordering everyone in the empire to swear an oath to the gods of Rome. Dionysius, bishop of Egypt, reported that when Decius's edict arrived there everyone cowered in terror. All the more conspicuous Christians were affected, he said, 'some came forward immediately in fear; others were brought along by their public business, and others were dragged in by the people around them. They were called by name and approached the unholy sacrifices, many of them

pale and trembling with terror.' A large crowd had gathered to watch and heap
mockery upon them, for it was evident, said Dionysius, that they were by nature
cowards – 'cowards in everything, cowards to die, cowards to sacrifice'. Dionysius
describes how many of them ran eagerly to the pagan altars, 'affirming by their
forwardness that they had not been Christians, even formerly'. Of the rest, some
followed to the pagan altar later, others fled, some were captured and foreswore
their faith after a few days in prison, and the rest gave in after being tortured.

Had the Decian persecutions persisted, Christianity would, in all likelihood,
have been eliminated. But the persecutions lasted barely sixteen months. Then
the emperor died, and the ancient pagan laws, though never repealed, sank
slowly into disuse. The disciples of Christ passed the next forty years in a state of
prosperity that was, in Gibbon's phrase, far more dangerous to their virtue than
the severest trials of persecution.

There was, however, one more testing time to come. In AD 303, the Emperor
Diocletian launched the so-called 'great' persecution. Having first consulted the
oracle, he decreed that Christian churches in all the provinces of the empire be
demolished to their foundations, all sacred books handed over to the magistrates
and burnt in public and Christian worship forbidden. Later edicts banned the
Christian name, restored the worship of the pagan gods and ordered all the
inhabitants of the empire to sacrifice.

As before, many Christians fled, many apostatised and many lapsed. Again, there
were the noble exceptions who defied the emperor's edict. But contrary to the
subsequent Christian myths, Diocletian's so-called great persecution was in fact
feebly pursued and had come far too late. In all, just 9 bishops resisted the edict
and were punished with death; in Palestine, no more than 92 Christians earned the
title of martyr. In the whole empire, perhaps 2,000 died for their faith in the ten
years the persecution lasted. By then they had won the argument. The Roman
authorities had shown they simply did not know how to deal with the gentle new
religion that had sprung up so inconveniently in their midst. They understood that
Christianity demanded the exclusive loyalty of its followers, and they were
instinctively aware that there was not room in the empire for both the Christian
and pagan views of religion, yet they were not clear-headed enough to know how to
counter it. Instead of offering an intelligent rebuttal of the points on which they
thought Christianity was wrong, they lashed out in fear and hatred at something
they did not comprehend, persecuting the Christians just enough to arouse their
sense of moral outrage, but not enough to crush them. The odium they incurred
was incurred for nothing. Their half-hearted and clumsy brutality defeated itself.

To Christians, it seemed as though God had allowed the persecution in order
to bring the pagans within the community of the Church. The native cults were
in decline, the signs of collapse to be seen everywhere: abandoned temples,
neglected shrines, stilted ceremonies. Even in Egypt, the old gods were dying
out, mummies embalmed in the most perfunctory fashion and hieroglyphic
inscriptions were going out of use. Country people in particular were now
leaving the gods of their ancestors and converting to the Church. The empire
itself was now in decay, living standards were falling and there was a widespread
belief that the old gods had let them down. Christianity was there in their place
to offer comforts so conspicuously absent from the worship of Jupiter and his

fellows. Christ was proving to be stronger than Caesar. It has been estimated that a fifth of the population of the empire in the west were now Christians and more than a half in large sections of the east. It would be just a matter of time before the Church conquered the empire.

CONSTANTINE'S CONVERSION

And this is exactly what happened. Barely twelve years after Diocletian's great persecution had begun, his successor was himself converted to Christianity. The story of how Constantine came to embrace the Christian faith marks another turning point in the history of the human mind, though the facts surrounding it are shrouded in myth. Even in his lifetime, at least three separate versions were in circulation. The legend that has survived the longest attributes it to a dream while Constantine was in camp with his army, an event immortalised in Piero's great frescoes in the Church of Arezzo. Others put it down to a more worldly cause: Constantine was using the altar of the Church merely as a footstool to the imperial throne.

All we can safely say is that Constantine was proclaimed as Augustus in York when his father died there in AD 306, and six years later marched with his army into Italy to claim his throne. The vision that converted him is said to have occurred after a battle with his greatest rival Maxentius near the Milvian Bridge across the Tiber, in which Maxentius drowned as he tried to make his escape.

Whatever the reason for Constantine's conversion, it came as one of history's great surprises, 'an erratic block which has diverted the course of human history'. The year after it happened, Constantine issued the historic Edict of Milan which granted complete freedom of worship to 'Christians and all others' – the first explicit declaration of religious freedom in the ancient world. It did not endure for very long. Almost as soon as he had issued it, Constantine learned that the last thing Christians wanted was to make religious freedom available 'to all'. They wished to reserve it for those who professed the one true faith, as they made plain at the Council of Nicea in AD 325, when Christianity was in effect established as the official religion of the Empire, even though Constantine himself was still half pagan at the time. He was baptised only on his deathbed in 337.

The Church lost no time in consolidating its unexpected gains. At Nicea, the council had already condemned the works of Arius to be delivered up and burned; concealment of them was forbidden under pain of death. By the 340s the Christians were demanding the total extirpation of pagan worship. Temples were smashed, statues defaced, the ancient gods banned, sacrifices prohibited, heretical writings burned, the first index of prohibited works drawn up. The Jews were anathematised as a deadly sect of parricides who had murdered God's own son. It became a crime for Christians to marry them. Dissent in Christians ranks was ruthlessly stamped on, and any attempt at compromise by the pagans rudely rebuffed. When the Christian Emperor Gratian had the statue of Victory removed from the Senate House in Rome, the pagans protested that the statue was a harmless reminder of the city's great past. Their spokesman, Symmachus, wrote to the emperor to plead for the old indigenous gods: 'We cultivate the same soil, we are one in thought, we behold the same stars, the same heaven and the same world. Why should not each, according to his own purpose, seek the truth? The Great Mystery cannot be approached by only one road. The divine mind distributed various thoughts and spirits among us, just as the *genii* are divided among nations.'

Symmachus's civilised plea for the freedom of each man to seek his own truth fell on closed minds. To the successors of Paul, there was only one road which approached the Great Mystery – and that was *their* road. Since the pagans were not infused with the same zeal to defend their beliefs, the Church's triumph was assured. The pagans gave up with what Gibbon called no more than a 'plaintive murmur'. So rapid, yet so gentle, was their fall that only twenty-eight years after the edict which forbade the worship of their gods the faint and minute vestiges of their faith were no longer visible to the eye.

The early Christians' horror of diversity eventually brought an end, too, to the classical world's last vestiges of free enquiry. In AD 529, they persuaded the Emperor Justinian to close down the Platonic Academy in Athens. Philosophers had speculated there in freedom since the fourth century before the birth of Christ – a span of almost a thousand years, or about twice as long as the period of free thought that has existed from the Italian Renaissance until our own day.

The closure of the school moved Gibbon to pen one of his most eloquent passages as he mourned the passing of an institution that encouraged the freedom of enquiry and submitted only to the forces of persuasion, those who ran it convinced by the experience of the ages that the moral character of philosophers was not affected by the diversity of their theological speculations:

Our sense of the dignity of human nature is exalted by the simple recollection that in these groves Isocrates was the companion of Plato and Xenophon; that he assisted perhaps with the historian Thucydides, at the first representation of the *Oedipus* of Sophocles and the *Iphigenia* of Euripides; and that his pupils Aeschinus and Demosthenes contended for the crown of patriotism in the presence of Aristotle. Here had the Latin conquerors respectfully listened to the instructions of their subjects and captives; the natives of Italy, of Africa, and of Britain had conversed with their fellow students of the East. The systems which professed to unfold the nature of God, of man and of the universe entertained the curiosity of the philosophic student; and, according to the temper of his mind, he might doubt with the Sceptics, or decide with the Stoics, sublimely speculate with Plato or severely argue with Aristotle.

Now it was gone, the victim of a belief whose ministers over-ruled the exercise of reason, resolved every question by an article of faith, and condemned the heretic and the sceptic to eternal flames.

Gibbon provides an eloquent and melancholy epitaph to the spirit of free enquiry that Athens had preserved to the very brink of the Dark Ages. Before long, wave after wave of barbarian and infidel invasions put an end to the world of classic antiquity for ever. Believing he was obeying the will of Allah, one caliph burned the library at Alexandria. By then, the spirit of free enquiry and the liberty of conscience had already been extinguished. Neither was to see the light again for more than a thousand years.

PART TWO

Liberty's Precursors

Here I stand – I can do no other.

Martin Luther

CHAPTER THREE

Renaissance and Reform

THE ROLE OF HUMANISM

When the Roman Empire collapsed, waves of Teutonic migrations reduced Europe to a state of deplorable, though vigorous, barbarism. For several centuries mankind struggled just to stay alive. The people were half-starved, half-naked and superstitious, their rulers illiterate, uneducated and savage. Even the ablest of their kings was unable to write his own name. There were no cities to live in, no paved roads, no formal schools, no money, no banks, and precious little trade. The knowledge of Latin was all but forgotten. And, it goes without saying, there was no freedom. First things came first. As a later Russian writer put it, there are times in human history when boots are of more value than books. The European Dark Ages were decidedly such a time. Liberty is a luxury that comes only after man's more basic needs have been satisfied. It is, in Lord Acton's phrase, the delicate fruit of a mature civilisation.

That western civilisation survived at all was due largely to the Christian Church, particularly its monastic movement. It kept alive literature and learning. It affirmed the dignity of manual labour and preserved the basic agricultural skills. When it was driven from the mainland, it clung on in the remote islands off the northern coast of Britain and in Ireland, where monks took up again the broken traditions, sang the same liturgy, read the same books and, however fitfully, passed down the works of Latin antiquity from generation to generation.*

---

* Though much Greek learning was lost, having gone east to Byzantium, where it was absorbed by the Arabic speaking world.

Even the unlettered barbarians made their contribution. Though uncivilised, they were a virile and adventurous people who invented tools such as the heavy plough and the horseshoe, introduced trousers and soap, and learned how to make hay, an art the Greeks and Romans had never mastered. And due to the work of great evangelists like Gregory and Augustine they eventually became Christians too.

When the turmoil of the Dark Ages subsided, it was found that a new civilisation had taken root in the soil of the old. It was a profoundly Christian civilisation, in which practically everyone, from the king to the peasants, devoutly followed the ritual of the Catholic Church. Physically as well as spiritually, the Church was at the centre of every community, however remote and however small.

But freedom still had no role to play. So long as it had the power to do so, the medieval Church withheld the freedom of conscience, freedom of speech and, later on, the freedom of the newly invented press. Its concern was with what it saw as the higher necessity of Christian salvation in a life to come. The way to the divine was to be found through prayer and plainsong, and certainly not through the exercise of reason. What intellectual activity there was, the Church confined to a study of the ancient authorities, as synthesised by St Thomas Aquinas.

That is not to say there was no culture. Throughout the later, more prosperous, Middle Ages the arts had flourished, not only in Europe but also in Islam and the Orient, whose civilisations were, at that time, in many ways more advanced. The philosophy and porcelain of China, the palaces of Byzantium, the wondrous temples of Rangoon and Angor Wat, the work of the great Arab scholars and mathematicians – and in Europe, the paintings of Giotto, the writings of Chaucer and Dante, the music of Monteverdi and the magnificent cathedrals of Chartres and Rouen – owed more to patronage than they did to liberty. The artists relied on their own genius, as always, but their freedom to express it depended on the wealth and protection of powerful patrons, the Church prominent among them. Raphael worked for the most corrupt of all medieval popes and Leonardo was to declare, 'I serve the one who pays me'. Michelangelo, too, could boast that he worked only for noble patrons and was 'never the kind of painter who set up shop for that purpose'. He was a gentleman in service, who had to sit at table with the tailors, musicians and engineers employed by his noble master. It is a romantic fallacy to assert that art can only exist in conditions of intellectual *laissez faire*. The virtues of liberty lie elsewhere.

However, one development did play a crucial part in emancipating men's minds. By the fifteenth century, the arid scholasticism of the Church and universities was being subtly undermined by a new generation of Christian humanists. These scholars of the liberal arts, or *studia humanitatis*, promoted the ideal of a peaceful and prosperous pan-European culture fostered by a ruling class educated according to the principles of ancient Greece and Rome. In Jacob Burckhardt's phrase, they based their philosophy on that which lay on the other side of the Middle Ages. They were influential because they knew what the ancients knew, they tried to write as the ancients wrote, they began to think, and soon to feel, as the ancients thought and felt. They had the patronage of powerful and enlightened lay patrons, and, just as momentous, they made use of printing.

In their insistence on returning to the original sources, the humanists also exposed the contradictions inherent in medieval theology. They showed that hope, not the fear of purgatory or the fatalism and quiet serenity of the oriental religions, was Christianity's main characteristic, the core of its message intensely individualistic. Man's relationship with his God was a personal one, his redemption in his own hands.

Such sentiments were a world away from the beliefs of the high Middle Ages, encapsulating what has been called the fundamental value-shift in modern European history. They set man on the road to liberty and prepared the ground for the arrival of free speech and the spirit of free enquiry, concepts which spring from and depend on discord. They were, however, concepts in direct contradiction to the doctrines of the medieval Church. Free speech implies that the search for truth is not yet over – the Church preached certainty. The liberty of conscience depends on the right to disagree peaceably about the eternal verities – the Church sent those who argued with its dogma to the stake. The scientist arrives at the truth through free enquiry – the Church taught that its own authority over such matters was absolute. Liberty implies diversity – the Church demanded unity.

Something had to give. Either the Church would reimpose its authority, in which case the whole western world would in all likelihood have sunk into the state of intellectual servility that subsequently overtook Catholic Spain; or the humanist principles would prevail, and lead in due course to the establishment of the modern concepts of tolerance, intellectual curiosity and individual human rights.

In the west, the road to free speech therefore necessarily began as a struggle against the authority of the Church itself. The men who first led that struggle would have been horrified if they had realised where their rebellion would lead. Those who laid the foundations of our modern civil liberties had not the least idea that this would be their lasting and most cherished memorial. But philosophers now accept that 'something like the modern understanding of liberty of conscience and freedom of thought began then'. The vision of equal liberty, which Christianity had engendered, was now to be turned against the Church itself.

'PRAISE OF FOLLY'

The chief exemplar of the humanist spirit was a timid, unmarried former monk who wrote only in Latin and yet became the best-selling author in Europe and the friend of four kings and two popes. They knew him simply as Erasmus of Rotterdam. Though his works were later to spend 300 years on the Church's *Index Expurgatorius*, Erasmus freed European scholarship from its intellectual servitude to the past and prepared the way for the reformation of the Church. It became almost a cliché to say that Erasmus laid the eggs that Luther hatched. That western thought is today supported on the twin pillars of tolerance and reason is due in no small part to this gentle, though waspish, humanist.

All we know of his early years is that he was born in Rotterdam sometime in the late 1460s, the bastard son of a copyist of manuscripts and his widowed mistress,

Margaret. The boy was christened Desiderius, a name he later dropped in favour of the single Latinised surname Erasmus, who saw himself as a citizen of the world.

We learn from his own works that he was raised 'amidst the sound of hymns and canticles', but when he was thirteen, both his parents died of the plague and he was put into the care of monks in a religious house at s'Herogenbosch – 'a sick and solitary child, ignorant of things of the world, passing from school to school', and, incidentally, haunted for the rest of his life by schoolboy memories of Lenten fasts and rotten eggs. In 1486 he was enrolled in a monastery at Steyn, near Gauda, where in his spare time he recopied some classical texts he had discovered and recited them by candlelight to his fellow noviates. He was ordained in 1492 – the year that Christopher Columbus discovered America – but quit the priesthood the following year to follow his true vocation as a scholar and writer, settling for a while into a tutorship, 'that humble anteroom of a literary career'. He next moved to Paris to pursue his studies at the Sorbonne, and later spent several happy years in England – which enchanted him – before visiting Florence and Rome to refresh his mind at the sources of classical learning.

Although Erasmus had from an early age acquired the precious gift of making friends, women were to play no part in his life, even after he left the monastery. 'If this happened to me by chance, then I have been very lucky,' he said. 'If it was by my own choice, I have been very wise.' He lived for his studies and sometime during his travels had come across a precept from an unknown philosopher, which influenced him profoundly: 'Live as if you are to die tomorrow; study as if you are to live forever.'

From then on, and for the rest of his life, words poured from his pen – adages, letters to his friends and patrons, pioneering translations of the New Testament and the pagan classics, grammatical text books, works on theology and philosophy, all written in elegant Renaissance Latin and achieved without any of the tools of modern scholarship such as dictionaries, encyclopaedias or reference books. Thanks to the newly invented art of printing, his books circulated throughout Europe and, because he wrote them in Latin, were as well understood by the intelligentsia of London as they were of Geneva, Paris and Rome. His technique was 'not to write in such a way that everyone understands everything, but so that they are forced to investigate things and learn'. So influential did he become that over the next two generations, his works, especially the book known as *De copia*, became the inspiration for the widespread innovations that transformed the structure of western education, to the extent that one critic could say of the link between humanist education and artistic achievement, 'Without Erasmus, no Shakespeare'. The link is the more remarkable when we consider that Erasmus spoke not a word of English.

He wrote wherever he found himself, even on horseback, the paper pressed against the pommel of his saddle, writing out a fair copy at the inn where he was spending the night. 'I give my pen daily practice in writing letters,' he wrote, 'throwing off any kind of nonsense and rattling on in the way one man talks to another in the intimacy of a glass of wine between friends and cronies.' The books of others he devoured with the appetite of a true bibliophile. They were, he said, friends who never thrust themselves upon you uninvited yet were at once at your disposal, who never flattered or feigned or dissembled, who were frank in telling you of your faults but never complained of them, who went with you into every perilous situation and stayed by you till the very end of your life.

Erasmus's religion was based on a mild and liberal blend of classical culture and the Christian scriptures (as opposed to Church dogma). He preferred Socrates to Duns Scotus, and found the myth of Prometheus just as compelling as the Garden of Eden. Although devoutly religious, he was offended by the sterile theology of the Church, its pretentious verbiage and its authoritarian logic. The pomp of Rome disgusted him, the worship of relics outraged him and the sale of indulgences he found superstitious and corrupt. He was equally disillusioned with the mercenary ambitions of Pope Julius II and the pagan atmosphere he found in the Vatican, where, he tartly observed, studies lay dormant whereas wars were hotly pursued.

On his way home on horseback over the Alps he began to write down his thoughts in what became one of the classics of Renaissance literature. He finished it in a few days when he got to London and dedicated it to his best friend, Sir Thomas More, its Graeco-Latin title, *Moriae Encomium*, meaning both in praise of folly, and in praise of More.

In writing *Praise of Folly*, Erasmus had resolved that what was wrong with the Church could be put right by laughter. Published in 1511, it became one of the first bestsellers in the history of print, running to forty-two separate editions in Latin and many more in its French, German and English translations. It was read in Rome by the Pope, in London by Henry VIII, in Paris by François I and by Martin Luther in Thuringia. At once a savagely satirical attack on a venal Church and lyrical praise of the wise foolishness of authentic Christianity, this strange book has only one character – Folly. She is, says Erasmus, everywhere, and present throughout human life. She accompanies us from morning to night and from night to morning. Her bells sound in every head, and when they are no longer heard, death cannot be far away. 'I've no use for cosmetics,' says Folly, 'my face doesn't conceal my innermost feelings. I am myself, and no one can pretend I'm not.'

After thus introducing herself, Folly steps forward to claim that she is mankind's greatest benefactor. Folly bestows happiness, and the happiest people to be found are the young, the foolish and those who undermine dignity, hierarchy and authority. She makes a withering attack on the futility of war – whose only glory goes to the 'scum of the earth' – and she cites Socrates as an example of 'just how useless these philosophers are'. What society ever took its laws from Socrates, she asks? Who would invite a wise man to dinner? He'd only upset everyone by his gloomy silence or tiresome questions. Invite him to dance and you'll have a camel prancing about.

The satire bites ever more deeply as it moves from the young and hot-blooded to the pitiful drybones and grotesque old women with sagging withered breasts whose folly is to live with their illusions, going around saying 'life is good', still on heat, longing for a mate, and seducing some young Phaon they've hired for large sums of money.

When she begins to describe the follies of the Church, parody drops away and the lighted-hearted tone of the earlier chapters turns to bitter invective as she derides the pious superstitions of the faithful, the supercilious arguments of theologians and the noxious way of life of the impious pontiff himself. The list of superstitions alone fills an entire chapter as she picks off the cult of the saints, one said to cure the toothache, another to stand by women in childbirth, a third to retrieve stolen objects, a fourth as a saviour at shipwrecks and another to protect the flocks – sillinesses, says Folly, which are readily permitted and encouraged by priests who are 'not unaware of the profit to be made thereby.'

As for the mendicant religious, the whole tribe was so universally loathed that even a chance meeting was thought to be ill omened. Yet they were gloriously self-satisfied. 'In the first place,' says Folly, 'they believe it's the highest form of piety to be so uneducated they can't even read.' Then, when they bray like donkeys in Church, repeating by rote the psalms they haven't understood, they believe they are charming the ears of their heavenly audience with infinite delight. Many of them make a good living out of their squalor and beggary, bellowing for bread from door to door, and making a nuisance of themselves in every inn, carriage and boat. 'This, then, is the way these smooth individuals, in all their filth and ignorance, their boorish and shameless behaviour, claim to bring back the apostles into our midst.'

The attack on theologians has them ready to send any doubter to the stake as a heretic rather than refute him by argument. Meanwhile, these same theologians wasted their own time discussing mysteries of concern to no one but themselves. In what might be taken as pure parody, but is not, Folly runs through some of the absurder issues that were gravely discussed by the scholastic theologians of the day: in what measure and how long was Christ formed in the virgin's womb? What was the exact moment of divine generation? Could God have taken on the form of a woman, a devil, a donkey, a gourd or a flintstone? If so, how could a gourd have preached sermons, performed miracles, and been nailed to the cross? And what would Peter have consecrated if he had performed the sacrament at a time when the body of Christ still hung on the cross?

Moving on to the pope himself, Folly asks who would want to spend his resources on the purchase of the position, which once bought has to be protected by the sword, by poison and by violence of every kind? Any work the popes have to do they leave to Peter and Paul, who have plenty of time on their hands, while claiming all the pomp and pleasure for themselves. For them, it is outdated and outmoded to perform miracles; teaching the people is too much like hard work, interpreting the scriptures is for schoolmen, and praying is a waste of time; to shed tears is weak and womanish, to be needy is degrading; to suffer defeat is a disgrace and hardly fitting for one who scarcely permits the greatest of kings to kiss the toe of his sacred feet; death, finally, is an unattractive prospect, and dying on a cross ignominious. The only weapons the popes have left are fine-sounding benedictions, which they scatter around with a lavish hand, along with interdicts, superstitions, excommunications and anathemas, painted scenes of judgement, and that dreaded thunderbolt whereby at a mere nod they can despatch the souls of men to dreaded Tartarus.

Towards the end of the book, Folly abandons satire for a form of divine wisdom, which is itself the highest form of foolishness, the supreme reward for man no other than a kind of madness. Plato had written that the madness of lovers is the highest form of happiness, 'for anyone who loves intensely lives not in himself but in the object of his love'. Likewise, the folly of the Cross is the purest and highest of all follies; it recognises neither prayers nor merits, neither sacrifices nor texts; it is enough to love.

Erasmus was not the first Renaissance writer to criticise the Church. Boccaccio and Machiavelli had both blamed her for the faithless and wicked nature of the age, though neither went as far as Erasmus, whose savage attack was not only directed against the pope himself but printed and published for the whole world to read. He got away with it partly because of his international reputation for scholarship and partly because he wrote to amuse. If Folly sometimes laughs in order not to cry and pours ridicule on the Church, she never ridicules God. Her avowed purpose was to help, not to hurt, to correct abuse and not to destroy what was good.

Like all the humanists, Erasmus also wrote under the protection of enlightened and powerful patrons. He had no wish to share his thoughts with *hoi polloi* – that 'mighty, powerful monster' easily swayed by trumped up tales and absurdities. His books were for the educated élite, among whom his books engendered a mounting conviction that a golden age of enlightenment was at last on the way. The mood of confidence did not last long, but while it did last, it accomplished wonders.

All the same, Erasmus was lucky to escape a charge of heresy. At one point, the conservative theologians at the Sorbonne moved to have him condemned and were only prevented from doing so by the direct intervention of King François, an enlightened Renaissance prince who seems to have enjoyed Folly's joke, even though the Sorbonne had declared that 'it is part of the Catholic faith not only that one can, but that one must, punish heretical opinions by execution.'

Erasmus's triumph was to be short lived, the remainder of his life spent under the shadow of schism and war, his dreams of a peaceful Age of Gold lost to view in the thunderstorm which now broke over the whole of western Christendom. Only seven years after the publication of *Praise of Folly*, Martin Luther posted his celebrated ninety-five theses attacking the scandalous sale of papal indulgences on the door of his Church in Wittenberg. The Protestant Reformation was under way. Between them, the two movements – humanist and protestant – would set mankind on the path to the liberty of conscience and, ultimately, to the secular freedom of speech.

'HERE I STAND'

The abuse of indulgences had been going on for centuries. Chaucer's Pardoner peddled them to the gullible in his *Canterbury Tales* and in Martin Luther's own town of Wittenberg, when the local Elector needed cash to build a new bridge over the River Elbe, he had the Church sell indulgences which excused people from fasting during Lent. It was known as the butter tax. Pardon for more serious offences had to be bought direct from the Vatican, and in 1477 Pope Sixtus IV began openly selling relief, for money, to souls in purgatory. People were able to buy a papal indulgence, inscribed on parchment, which they believed would help commute the amount of time their souls would spend in torment because of the sins they had committed here on earth. For an extra fee, indulgences could also be bought to help relieve the suffering of relatives already dead. The Church never actually claimed that forgiveness could be simply bought and sold – an indulgence was only a part of the sacrament of penance and had to be accompanied by true repentance and confession – but it allowed people to believe that it was an essential step towards salvation. Overcome by fear and superstition, most ordinary folk complied. They believed that the moment their coin dropped in the money chest, the soul they had absolved would jump straight from purgatory into heaven.

Indulgences were big business and the Church had become heavily dependent on the money they brought in: so much so that the Vatican had farmed out their management to the banking house of Fugger, whose high fees had become another source of scandal. Corruption was rife, and the Church's demands were growing ever more extravagant. In Rome, the new pope, Leo X, was building the vast Basilica of St Peter. To pay for it, Leo issued a special Jubilee Indulgence, offering plenary pardons in exchange for a contribution towards the building works. He was helped by the newly licensed printing trade, which found that printing indulgences was a lucrative business, especially if they ran off rather more copies than had been ordered and sold the extras on the black market. Orders of 20 or 30,000 printed indulgences were not uncommon.

To preach the indulgences, specially trained friars were engaged to carry them from town to town with great pomp. The ceremony at which they were handed out was regarded as an 'occasion of grace', usually coupled with the sacrament of confession, without which a remission of sins could not be had. One April day in 1517, the most famous indulgence vendor of his day, the Dominican Friar John Tetzel, arrived in the little Saxon town of Jüterborg to set up his banners and preach the Jubilee Indulgence. People came from miles around to watch the procession, confess their sins, and hand over their coppers for one of the precious indulgences that hung from Tetzel's banners.

Tetzel's sermons were skilfully constructed: frightening to start with, then consoling. 'How many mortal sins have you committed today?' he would demand. 'One? Two? Then just think how many mortal sins are committed in a week, how many in a year, how many in a lifetime? They are all but infinite, and for each one there is need to do penance for seven years, either in this life or in the flaming punishment of purgatory.' At this point, he would produce one of his indulgences and declare, 'and yet, in virtue of these confessional letters, you shall be able to gain, once in a life, full pardon of the penalties due . . .' He would then take a theatrical step forward and place a coin in the chest to gain an indulgence for his own father. The watching sinners would drop to their knees to confess, coins would ring in the friar's coffers and the people would believe they had been granted a miraculous reprieve from the torments of purgatory.

Eighteen miles away at his seminary of Wittenberg, the young Doctor Martin Luther learned of Tetzel's display in Jüterborg with a feeling of disgust. His objections were not that gullible people were being cheated of their money, but that the use of indulgences was doctrinally unsound. From his own experience as a confessor, he knew that genuine penitence was only marginally present; many of his flock believed they had to be granted absolution simply because they came to him carrying an indulgence and its accompanying letter of confession.

As the lecturer in theology at the new University of Wittenberg, Luther had recently completed a *Treatise on Indulgences*. On All Saints' Eve 1517, he suddenly swept his previous work aside, and settled down at his cluttered desk to write a series of ninety-five theses, intended for debate. He wrote them quickly, in short sharp dialectical sentences, some of them practical, some theological, all stressing the spiritual inward character of the Christian religion and the need for a life of repentance, many of them attacking the worthlessness of purchased indulgences. When he had done, he nailed his theses to the door of the parish Church* and sent copies to his archbishop with a covering letter. They invited anyone interested to discuss the matter, either at a meeting, or by correspondence. To his archbishop he wrote: 'What a horror, what a danger for a bishop to permit the loud noise of Indulgences among his people while the gospel is silenced. I beg you . . . to command them to preach in another way.'

Father Martin, as he was known, had been born of affluent peasant stock in Eisleben, on the edge of the Thuringian Forest, his father having prospered as part-owner of a smelting furnace at the local copper mine. Martin had gone into the Church against his father's wishes soon after graduating from the University of Erfurt and had risen to become a Doctor of Theology at the age of twenty-nine. He was now one of the principal Deans at Wittenberg and always incredibly busy. 'All day long I write letters,' he confided to one of his friends. 'I am a preacher at the monastery, I am a reader during mealtimes, I preach daily in the city Church, I have to supervise the studies of the novices, I am a vicar (and that means I am eleven times prior), I am caretaker of the fishpond at Leitzkau, I lecture on Paul and am assembling a commentary on the psalms . . . I hardly have time to say the "Hours" and celebrate the Mass. Besides all this are my own struggles with the flesh, the world and the devil. See what a lazy man I am!' And now, in his spare time, so to speak, he was about to begin the Protestant Reformation.

Martin Luther was a mass of contradictions. The hearty cheerfulness that comes through in the letter to his friend often gave way to lengthy bouts of despair and self-doubt. Profound thoughts on scripture were mingled with coarse jokes about his bowels. Relations with his overbearing father were complex and ambivalent and are seen by some as the psychological key to a character torn between subservience on the one hand and rebellion on the other. Later in life, Cranach the Elder painted a portrait of Luther's father, Hans, in which his shrewd, earthy, determined character clearly shows through. Hans Luther was ambitious for his gifted son and had sent him to the university; but he went mad with rage when Martin dropped his studies in the law and entered the Church.

There was another crisis on the day Martin conducted his first Mass, an experience that had stricken him with a kind of holy terror. During a noisy party

---

* Not in itself an act of defiance, as legend would have it. Church doors were the customary place for medieval publicity.

afterwards Hans exclaimed that he hoped Martin hadn't been lured into his vocation by the devil. When Martin answered back, Hans crudely put him down with a quotation from the Ten Commandments, 'have you not read, "honour thy father and mother"?' The remark haunted Martin for the rest of his life. Many years later, when he was perhaps the best-known man in Europe, he told his father the rebuke had penetrated to the depths of his soul.

Luther clearly had a psychosis about authority which instilled in him the feelings of guilt that hounded him all his life, in spite of constant scourgings and fastings. It infused his works with a kind of vehemence, which often came close to rage. 'You are a fool,' his old confessor once told him. 'God is not angry with you. It is you who are angry with God.'

Early in his career at the university, despair had engulfed him. He found he hated God. And the more he hated, the more guilt he felt. He was on the way to a major nervous breakdown. Then all at once his feelings of despair yielded to a great, overwhelming certainty. He was probably straining to relieve his chronic constipation, when he was struck by a stupendous insight: salvation came through faith alone. Not good works, not Church ceremony, not liturgy, just a strong and simple faith was the necessary foundation of a religious life. The Church was to be found wherever the gospel was preached and believed.

Luther had come across his text in the writings of St Paul: 'I am not ashamed of the gospel of Christ, for therein is revealed the righteousness of God, from faith to faith. As it is written: the just shall live by faith.' Luther's hatred dissolved. He felt born again. He had found the precepts on which he built an entire theology: the authority of the scriptures alone, justification by faith alone, man's individual responsibility to God alone. They later became the three pillars of the Protestant Reformation.

While scripture was to be the only source of religious truth, its interpretation was entirely Luther's. The translation was his also, for he added the word 'alone' to the phrase 'the just shall live by faith,' insisting that the meaning in German demanded it. 'It is true these four letters *sola* do not stand in the Greek and Latin texts,' he wrote. 'So the blockheads stare at them like cows in front of a new gate.'

With the immediate crisis behind him, Luther applied his tremendous energies to deepening and developing his theology, rising to become one of the most distinguished luminaries of Wittenberg University, which Frederick had founded only six years before Luther joined it. Set in flat country on a sluggish stretch of the Elbe 200 miles before it reaches the sea, Wittenberg was remote, provincial and dull. Frederick had ruled there for thirty years, and next to amassing his collection of holy relics, the university was his favourite project. He got it a charter from the Emperor Maximilian and agreed to provide the buildings if the Augustinian Order would provide the professors. Stone and brick structures soon replaced the thatched wooden houses along the main street, the town council bought desks and benches, and, as well as the mandatory theology, the university had chairs in Greek, Medicine and Law. It enrolled about 150 new students a year and quickly attracted some brilliant people. Albrecht Dürer and Lucas Cranach were both there for a while and another great theologian, Philip Melanchthon, became its Professor of Greek. Frederick had good reason to be proud of his new university.

He kept himself away from any direct involvement and ruled it, as he ruled all his lands, through an efficient network of civil servants, who kept him well informed about developments in both Saxony and the rest of the Holy Roman Empire. He was aware, too, of the sense of unease that was spreading across Europe, both inside the Church and outside it. There had been riots not far away in Erfurt and in the countryside the peasants were on the edge of open revolt against economic exploitation by the Church. There were similar stirrings in England, France and Holland, religious as well as social.

Europe was beginning to emerge from its Middle Ages, but the people's beliefs were still based on frightening and only partly understood myths. It was a morbid and neurotic age, its mood reflected in the art of Hieronymous Bosch, with his ever-more terrible pictures of sinners roasting in the fires of hell and the sufferings of Christ on the Cross. Even at Wittenberg, sixty-four priests were attached to the castle Church to celebrate the daily requiem masses funded by the relatives of the dead. Frederick's own spare time was spent amassing a collection of holy relics that might fairly be described as incredible. In his thirty years as Elector, he had acquired over 5,000 such items, including a phial of milk from the breast of the Virgin Mary, a thorn from the Crown of Thorns worn by Jesus before his crucifixion, the entire skeleton of one of the holy innocents slaughtered by King Herod, eleven pieces of the original crib, a wisp of straw from the manger and gold pieces specially minted for the three wise men. Collecting them was not only Frederick's hobby: they were a useful source of income from the credulous who paid to view them. Based more on superstition than they were on faith, the ceremonies in Frederick's own castle Church offered no access to the words of the New Testament even to those who could read. Luther himself had only handled a Bible for the first time when he entered his religious order.

But by then printing was beginning to make the Bible accessible to the people, not just in Latin, but also carefully selected parts in German. Travelling merchants were a common sight on market day, selling printed copies of the seven penitential psalms, St John's gospel or the Book of Revelation, which had provided Hieronymous Bosch with his inspiration. Many of these pamphlets were illustrated with woodcuts and printed anonymously for fear of reprisals: at this time the press was so new the printers were unsure whether it was permitted or forbidden. However, it was now about to play its part in spreading Luther's revolutionary message far beyond the borders of provincial Saxony.

When his time of crisis arrived, Martin Luther had by his side two powerful allies to shield him from the fate of earlier heretics: the Elector Frederick, now a potential successor to the Emperor himself, and the printing press, invented seventy years before by Johannes Gutenberg on the other side of Germany in Mainz. They proved to be an unbeatable combination. Luther was the first person in history to use print to pursue a major public controversy. That alone earns him an important place in the history of free speech. His incomparable translation of the Bible into the simple, pure German used by the people would later confirm the importance of the printing press as the most powerful medium of communication the world had yet known.

THE POWER OF PRINT

Once Gutenberg had marshalled the essential components into a coherent whole, print caught on with astonishing rapidity. After years of experimentation, he had discovered how to combine moveable type with the manufacture of an oil-based ink, reliable supplies of paper and the printing press itself, which he adapted from the vast wooden wine presses that were common throughout Europe. His invention transformed the transmission of ideas. From then on, the history of free speech would be indissolubly coupled with the freedom of the press.

Born into a wealthy family of Rhenish goldsmiths, Gutenberg had been in a race with several other entrepreneurs who had seen the commercial possibilities of mechanising the process of transferring ink to paper. After prolonged and expensive experiments, Gutenberg finally found the means to make his new technology work. One breakthrough came after his realisation that paper rather than the old-fashioned vellum or parchment was the most efficient medium for the mass production of books. After that came the invention of a new type of ink made from a mixture of varnish and lampblack,* which paper absorbed more readily than the old water-soluble inks based on such substances as gallnuts or cuttlefish emissions. Then came the crucial invention of moveable type – that is, pre-cast letters that can be used again and again – which Gutenberg made from an alloy of tin, lead and antimony, which together ensured that it was both durable and easy to cast. He also had to overcome problems with the wooden screw press he used for printing, which at first had a tendency to cause the ink to smudge. This was caused by the fact that tightening the screw used to press the platen – the flat plate that spreads the pressure over the page being printed – also caused it to rotate slightly, and thus blur the printed impression. Gutenberg overcame this difficulty by inserting a vertical wooden box, known as a 'hose', between the screw and the platen. The presses he finally assembled were so successful they would remain in use virtually unaltered for the next 300 years.

Like many inventors since, Gutenberg's single-minded pursuit of perfection had put him heavily into debt, having borrowed from a neighbour, who eventually foreclosed. Before then, Gutenberg had produced the first printed edition of the Bible (still, of course in Latin). He began cutting the type for the project in about 1450 and began composition two years later. Employing six compositors, working simultaneously, he completed the hugely expensive project in 1456, running off 185 copies, 40 of which still survive. Although Gutenberg himself went bankrupt and later died in poverty, his invention enriched his partners and quickly spread along the principal trade routes of the Rhine. By the time Luther arrived at Wittenberg, printing presses had been set up in at least sixty German towns and were being installed by itinerant printers in just about every country in western Christendom.

In those early days, printed books were valued as art objects as much as sources of knowledge (though at a much more affordable price than a personally commissioned version copied out by a scribe). Indeed, it was at first hard to tell

---

* Made from the soot deposited by candle flames on a cold surface.

the difference between an elaborately illustrated printed manuscript and one produced by hand. It was the humanists, more than anyone, who saw the opportunity of using printed books in order to spread ideas. Erasmus was particularly adept at ensuring that his books were made available through the most prominent and successful publishing houses in Europe.

Thanks to print, the humanists were also able to circulate both Greek and Latin copies of the Bible and works of antiquity that had been hidden from sight during the Middle Ages in private and monastic libraries. At the same time, Greek mathematical and scientific works, lost to the west for centuries, began to seep in from Byzantium, including books by Euclid, Archimedes and Ptolemy, the impact of which was arguably greater than the rediscovered works of Homer, Euripides and Plato. Printed mathematical tables made possible significant advances in astronomy and navigation, while humbler readers were provided with a steady stream of poems, chronicles, Bible stories and booklets about the saints. By the beginning of the sixteenth century over 25,000 separate titles had been published in Germany alone, excluding broadsheets and pamphlets. In Europe as a whole it has been been estimated that up to 20 million items had been set in print, more perhaps than all the scribes of Europe had produced since the beginning of the Christian era more than a thousand years before. By Luther's lifetime, books were being bought and sold as freely as loaves of bread.

As with most new inventions, printing's potential for creating controversy dawned only slowly. Luther himself had not at first thought of using the press to spread his ideas. Only when he received no reply from the Archbishop in Mainz did he seek further publicity for his theses. Thinking they had fallen flat, he went round to the Wittenberg printer, Johan Grünenberg, and got him to print off forty copies of them, which he sent around to his academic friends for further comment.

The moment it was in print, the controversy took off. By the end of November, new editions were on sale in Leipzig and Magdeburg. By December, it had been published in Nüremberg and Basle under the title in German: *A Disputation of Master Martin Luther, Theologian, for the Purpose of Making Known the Efficacy of Indulgences*. Dürer sent him a set of printed woodcuts in thanks for expressing what everyone wanted said. 'Ho! ho!' exclaimed the old Prior of Muldenstein when he saw the printed theses posted up in his own friary. 'Here is a man who is going to do something.' Copies were by now flying around Europe in their thousands. Erasmus sent one to his friend Sir Thomas More in England and Cardinal Wolsey's agents found one being smuggled into the country inside a bale of wool. But once in print, the debate was unstoppable. Luther had not only said the unsayable, he had spread his message right across Europe. Printed copies of his theses were being used as a manifesto for revolution.

In other circumstances, Luther's death at the stake would have quickly followed. But a quirk of fate now brought the proceedings to a halt. The Holy Roman Emperor, Maximilian, had fallen ill and was not expected to live. His successor would be chosen by the seven Prince Electors of the Empire, one of whom was Frederick, Luther's protector and himself a candidate for the imperial crown. Indeed, he was favoured by the Medici pope in order to block the election the Hapsburg king of Spain, Charles V, who was growing too powerful for the comfort of the Vatican. In the circumstances which had unexpectedly arisen, Leo could not afford to antagonise Frederick over the incidental matter of Father Martin Luther. With more important issues now at stake, he ordered Luther to be handled with tact. So rather than being carried off to Rome as a heretic, he was summoned to a personal interview with the papal legate in Germany, Cardinal Thomas Cajetan, a fatherly Italian diplomat with orders to smooth things over. Luther was given an imperial safe conduct, arriving at the cardinal's palace in Augsburg on 7 October 1518, just short of a year after he had posted the theses on the door of the castle Church in Wittenberg. As naive as he was stubborn, he still believed that he could win over the cardinal by the force of his arguments. Reform was his aim, not schism.

The meeting was a disaster. Cardinal Cajetan had been put in an awkward position, caught between the different demands of a degenerate papal court, his own Dominican Order, and a local ruler who was a potential emperor. The Order wanted Luther condemned to death as a heretic, the elector was determined to protect him, the pope kept changing his mind. First he had wanted Luther interrogated, then arrested, but now His Holiness wanted compromise. Get Luther to recant, Cajetan was told, use your charm, and if that fails, impose your authority.

Cajetan did his diplomatic best. An emissary called Serralonga was sent round to Luther's quarters to remind him that all he needed was the simple little word 'revoco', 'I recant', and all would be well. There would be no further reprisals. But there would be no academic disputation either. The cardinal was not inviting Luther round for a debate on theology. He was sincerely trying to help him resolve the unfortunate misunderstanding that had arisen. The only way to do that was for Luther to recant. At this point, Luther seems to have hinted that he had the protection of the Saxon elector. Serralonga asked him where he would go if the elector disowned him. '*Sub coelis*' was Luther's famous reply: under the sky, under heaven, he had the protection of God. It was the answer of a mystic.

The series of interviews with Cajetan began next morning. Luther opened with his customary obsequies in the presence of authority, prostrating himself full length before the cardinal, his face on the ground. He then offered to submit to the authority of the Church if they could show him 'wherein he had erred'. Cajetan selected two of the theses and declared them contrary to the Church's teaching. Luther needed to know where this could be proved in scripture. Cajetan refused: the authority of the Church rested as much on tradition as it did on a literal reading of the scriptures. Luther must recant. That was the wish of the pope. As the interviews progressed, the cardinal was in stages patronising, charming, avuncular, irritable and finally threatening, as Luther grew more and more obstinate. The discussions became technical: they went through such issues as the doctrine of the treasury of merits and the sacrament of penance, and at one point Luther tripped up Cajetan on a recondite point of philology. 'You should not believe, most reverend father, that we Germans are ignorant even in philology,' he proclaimed, his eyes flashing triumphantly.

At the end, the cardinal disdainfully threw back Luther's 'little piece of paper' and shouted at him to recant. 'Almost ten times I started to say something,' Luther wrote to the head of his university at Wittenberg, 'but each time the legate thundered back and took over the conversation. Finally, I started to shout too.' Luther ends his account with Cajetan still shouting for revocation, 'Go, and do not return to me unless you want to recant!' The interview was over. The cardinal had misjudged his man.

Frederick was now faced with an awkward choice. Cajetan was demanding that he hand Luther over to Rome on charges of open heresy; the alternative he offered was exile, in either Holland or Bohemia. After much to-ing and fro-ing, the elector came to the momentous decision to stand by Luther and let him stay in Saxony. He wrote personally to Cajetan, enclosing Luther's printed rebuttal and saying he awaited scriptural proof of the doctor's heresy. Until then, Martin Luther would remain under his protection in Wittenberg. It was another crucial moment in the progress of the Reformation.

Luther was now a celebrity. People swarmed into Wittenberg to hear him preach and Grünenberg's presses could barely keep up with the torrent of words that gushed from his pen. There were comforting religious works on such themes as *The Lord's Prayer* and *Preparing to Die*, serious works of theology as he deepened his studies of the scriptures, and immensely popular secular works in which he gave voice to the rising sense of German nationalism.

For three and a half years, the printing presses were kept busy day and night in their efforts to keep up with the output of Luther's pen. Each spring, wagonloads of his works were sent off to the annual Frankfurt book fair. So much work was coming his way that Grünenberg had to farm some of it out to another printer 40 miles away in Leipzig, Melchior Lotther. Both of them made a fortune, although little of it seems to have come back to Luther. Erasmus, the only other best-selling author of the day, was occasionally given a fur coat, or some other gift, by his Basle publisher, Fröben, but Luther, it would seem, got nothing. Then as now, books were a more profitable business for printers and publishers than they were for their authors. But Luther made no complaint: he was, after all, bound by his monk's vow of poverty.

As the months went by, he became more convinced than ever that the Church's problems were rooted in Rome. Everyone there, he wrote, had become 'mad, foolish, raging, insane, fools, sticks, stones, hell and evil'. Antichrist was enthroned in God's very temple. 'Farewell, you unhappy, lost and blasphemous Rome; the anger of God has come upon you at last.' The schism that had so long been dreaded could no longer be avoided.

EXCOMMUNICATION

In May of 1520 Leo was finally persuaded he needed to act. He had been outmanoeuvred over the election of the new emperor and, for all the papal intrigues to prevent it, Charles V of Spain had been appointed to the imperial throne. The curia's appeasement of Frederick had been in vain. It was time to cast around for revenge.

Leo was at his hunting lodge in the Italian hills when the formal papal bull of excommunication was presented for his signature. Made a cardinal at thirteen and appointed pope at thirty-eight, this Medici son of Lorenzo the Magnificent was essentially a man of pleasure. Business, we are told, was a matter for his morning *levée*, leaving the rest of the day free 'for the chase, the banquet, family affairs, and all the glorious social life.' Although short-sighted, His Holiness was often to be seen, sword in one hand, gold monocle in the other, giving the *coup de grâce* to some unfortunate wild beast held by his gamekeeper. When he came to sign the formal document, *Exsurge Domine*, it was natural that he should look to the hunt for a metaphor with which to preface it. 'Arise, O Lord,' he wrote in his own hand. 'There is a wild boar loose in the vineyard.' His edict gave Luther sixty days in which to recant or face excommunication and, following that, death at the stake as a heretic. Meanwhile, all his books were to be burnt in public.

Leo's bull was the signal for outright schism. Luther was a German hero. So strong was his support that Church officials found it impossible to publish the edict outside the episcopal towns of Merseburg, Meissen and Brandenburg. In Erfurt, it was thrown into the river and at Leipzig students gathered in the street to sing rude songs about it. In Cologne, the archbishop and his entire cathedral chapter boycotted the bonfire of Luther's works. Elsewhere, wastepaper or the Church's own publications were thrown onto the bonfire instead of Luther's. Luther himself wrote to the new emperor asking him to 'protect the truth' and not allow him to be condemned without the pope's charges being heard and defeated.

There could be no turning back. On the day he was due to recant, Luther's friend Melanchthon organised a huge bonfire at Wittenberg, where a copy of the Church's own canon law was symbolically consigned to the flames. At the last moment, Luther threw the papal bull into the fire for good measure. No one knew it yet, but the issue was about to divide the Church into two distinct and hostile camps. In these few weeks in 1520, the seeds were sown of the appalling wars of religion that soon rent Europe apart.

'Something serious is at hand,' Luther wrote. 'There is such tremendous turmoil, I think it cannot be quieted except by the arrival of the Last Day.' The whole Empire was dividing against itself. At least half of the electors supported Luther, though the new emperor had come down on the side of tradition – 'a single friar who goes against all Christianity for a thousand years must be wrong,' he said. 'I will proceed against him as a notorious heretic.' Compromise was impossible, civil war a real risk. The Imperial Diet, or high council, was due to meet shortly in the Rhineland city of Worms, where the new emperor would be staying on his way to be crowned by the pope in Rome. All sorts of sub-plots and intrigues were in play, but after much debate, it was resolved that Martin Luther should be summoned to appear before the Diet in Worms to explain himself in person.

For Luther, here was a chance to put his case before the emperor himself. Armed with a safe conduct and a sizeable escort, he set off across Germany in a horse and cart in the spring of 1521, attracting thousands to gawp and cheer as he made his two-week trek to his lodgings in Worms. The day after he arrived, he was to make his first appearance before the emperor, an encounter that would determine the course of European history for years to come. It was also an important milestone in the history of free speech. In effect, Luther was being put on trial for the books he had written.

He appeared at the imperial court in mid-afternoon, a provincial country friar with a freshly shaven tonsure, tense and apprehensive as he prostrated himself before the throne of the emperor in the presence of princes, dukes, ambassadors, bishops, archbishops, counts and knights. His accusers came straight to the point. The chief prosecutor, Johann von Eck, Chancellor to the Archbishop of Trier, swept his arm towards a great pile of books and bluntly asked Luther whether they were his and if he wished to retract any of them. Through his lawyer, Luther asked for their titles to be read out. Then, realising they thought he was here solely to recant, he asked for time to prepare his reply. He was given twenty-four hours.

The hearing was resumed next day in an overcrowded room, which grew too hot. Feeling faint and perspiring heavily, Luther began in his usual obsequious way, asking forgiveness if, through ignorance, he had not given anyone his proper title or in any other way offended against court etiquette. Then, as his confidence grew, he delivered a measured and carefully prepared defence of his right to publish.

We have agreed that these books are all mine, he said, and they have all been issued rightly in my name. But not all of them were of the same kind. The first group were simple gospel works; to renounce them would 'condemn the very truth upon which my friends and enemies readily agree'. A second group attacked what he called the power of the keys, that is to say the papacy. But everyone knew the papacy had ravaged Christendom and especially 'this illustrious nation of Germany'. How could he withdraw what everyone accepted was true? A third kind of book had attacked certain individuals, all of them defenders of Rome and enemies of religion. He admitted he had been rougher with them than perhaps befitted a monk. But he was not a saint and was not defending his own life but the teachings of Christ. He was therefore not free to retract them.

The only way for him to defend what he had written was to use the same method as his saviour. When he was being questioned about his teachings by Annias, the High Priest, a servant struck him in the face, and Jesus replied, 'If I have spoken lies, tell me what the lie is.' Therefore, said Luther, tell me what the lie is: if someone can expose my errors, I shall be the first to pick up my books and throw them on the fire.

Eck replied to him in measured terms. Certainly the emperor was ready to make a distinction between the harmful and the harmless, he said, but Luther was putting himself above other, perhaps wiser, theologians. 'Do not, I entreat you Martin, do not claim for yourself that you are the one and only man who has true understanding.' Do not throw doubt on the holy, orthodox faith, the faith defined by sacred councils and confirmed by the Church: it is your heritage and we are forbidden to dispute it. 'I must therefore ask again,' he said, 'I must demand that you answer sincerely, frankly and without horns, yes or no, will you or will you not retract your books and the errors contained therein?'

'Since your serene majesty and your lordships demand a simple answer, you shall have it,' said Luther, 'without horns and without teeth. Unless I am shown by the testimony of the scriptures and my own conscience is captured – for I don't trust popes or councils not to err – I cannot and will not recant. To act against one's conscience is neither safe nor honest. Here I stand; God help me; I can do no other.'

His final plea – in German, *'Hier stehe ich; ich kann nicht anderst'* – are probably Luther's most famous words and are still used as the defiant rallying cry of a free conscience. They sent a thrill round Europe and mark a notable moment in the progress towards the liberty of thought.

Fearing for his safety after making his defiant stand before the emperor, Luther hurried back again to Wittenberg. As they passed through the forest near his boyhood home at Eisenach, his party was ambushed by a group of bandits, who bound and gagged Luther before carrying him away. 'God help us,' Dürer exclaimed when he heard the news, 'if Luther is dead, who is going to explain the gospel to us?' But Luther was not dead. The ambush was a ruse intended to get him out of harm's way. The 'bandits' were a group of friends who had spirited him away to the Wartburg, a deserted hilltop castle, where Luther grew a beard and disguised himself as the local landowner and called himself Junker Georg.

He spent his time working on his classic translation of the Bible into German (from a text which had been sent to him by Erasmus). In the words of a Catholic theologian, its verbal felicity and its accuracy stand as permanent witnesses to the calibre of Luther's religion, the thoroughness of his studies and the power of his intellect. Using many printers in many cities, the text illustrated by lovingly carved woodcuts, it was a publishing feat without previous parallel. Over the next ten years Luther would sell more than 200,000 copies of the New Testament alone. Historians believe that perhaps more than anything else, it was the strong pure language of Luther's German Bible which enabled the Protestant Reformation to spread so fast and solidly. Until it was published, said a contemporary writer, 'none of us knew in what darkness we were living'.

When he had finished, it was safe to return to Wittenberg, where Luther was to live and work for the remaining twenty years of his life. In outlawing him, the Church had in effect outlawed itself. In those lands being swept by the Reformation, the old order quickly gave way to the new. Belief was based on the word and the word was to be found in the Bible, now available in the believer's own language. Church services were conducted in the vernacular, indulgences were no more, mendicant monks returned to the community and priests and nuns were allowed to marry. In 1525, Luther himself married one of the former nuns in the local convent, Katherine von Bora, then twenty-six. Children followed within the year, and Luther settled down to become head of a large and happy family. And at long last, he made peace with his father.

He was now widely regarded as a prophet in his own time, his influence probably greater than any other man's then alive. His energy was undiminished, his output still prodigious, his reputation immense, though clouded by two unhappy episodes that showed up the harsh and intolerant side of his nature. The first was his attitude of crude hostility towards the Peasants' Rebellion that broke out in the year he was married. The second was his quarrel with Erasmus, which left them on opposite sides of the now permanent religious divide.

The dispute with Erasmus brought out the weaknesses in both men – Luther's boorishness, Erasmus's timidity. On the face of it, they were in manifest agreement: heaven was not for sale, both of them opposed scholastic theology and loathed monastic piety, both saw the way to reform was through a return to the scriptures. Realising this, Luther at first tried to flatter Erasmus – 'my glory and my hope' – into supporting him. Although in sympathy with Luther's aims, Erasmus disliked his methods and had no wish to involve himself in civil strife. Torn, as always, between the reformers and the orthodox, and 'lacking the strength' for the martyrdom which overtook his friend, Sir Thomas More, he sent Luther a non-committal reply and at the same time wrote to the new pope, his friend Adrian VI, denying that he had any connection with the Protestant Reformation.

Adrian replied with a plea for Erasmus to come to Rome to launch an attack on the new heresies, a task he said God had reserved especially for a man possessing 'such intellectual powers, extensive learning and a readiness in writing such as in living memory has fallen to the lot of few or none'. Doubtless gratified to be flattered in such terms, Erasmus nevertheless declined the offer to go to Rome, which he said was like telling a crab to fly. 'The crab answered, "Give me wings," and I shall reply, "Give me back my youth."' He coupled these evasions with a half-hearted defence of religious liberty 'at the sweet name of which all men will breathe afresh.' But he found the courage to declare that 'the burning of his books will perhaps banish Luther from our libraries; whether he can be plucked out of men's hearts I am not so sure'. While he disliked schism and faction, he was repelled by the idea of repression and complained of being himself accused of heresy by preachers who were more hot-headed than enlightened. 'Nowadays, if anyone disagrees with some newfangled reasoning thought up yesterday by some sophister in the schools, he is called a heretic,' he wrote in another letter. 'Anything they do not like, anything they do not understand, is heresy. To know Greek is heresy, to speak like an educated man is heresy.' But that was as far as he was prepared to go. 'I neither wish to, nor can, serve any faction,' he wrote to an ally of Luther's.

Having lost all hope of enlisting his support, Luther reacted with an exasperated attack on Erasmus's pamphlet, *The Freedom of the Will*. 'I confess you are far superior to me in powers of eloquence and native genius,' he began in his usual over-hearty way, 'all the more as I am an uncultivated fellow who has always moved in uncultivated circles.' However, Erasmus's book was 'so cheap and paltry that I felt sorry for you, defiling as you did your very elegant and ingenious style with such trash'. Such unworthy matter conveyed in such rich eloquence was like dung being carried in gold vases.

The dispute brought out all the contradictions in Luther's character, his mighty eloquence marred by coarse passions, his disagreements over theology lost in vulgar abuse. Though he was essentially a rebel, a radical and a non-conformist himself, in matters like this Luther could be as dogmatic and authoritarian as any pope. Erasmus sincerely believed that it was enough to put the words of the gospel into the language of the ordinary people and not worry about the theology. His dream was to hear the farmer singing the words of the New Testament in his own language as he followed the plough or 'the weaver warble them at his shuttle'. His approach to their interpretation was that of the detached humanist scholar: questioning, enquiring, sceptical, and even agnostic on some issues. He was quite able to accept that the meaning of scripture was not always clear, and was sometimes downright ambiguous. His theology always left room for doubt.

But Luther demanded certainty. While he shared Erasmus's belief that all members of the Church should have access to the Bible in their own plain language, they needed doctrine and theology, too. Since his God was unfathomable, his faith must be unquestioning. There was no room for the rational arguments of the humanists. Religion was a matter of faith, not of reason. The cool scepticism of Erasmus was absolutely inadmissible. Take away the dogma, Luther once said, and you deprive us of Christianity.

The attitude of both men was now irreconcilably hostile, perhaps fuelled on Erasmus's side by a feeling of pique. The foremost intellectual of Europe was being displaced by a bigger personality with a more powerful mind. He grew increasingly out of sympathy with Luther's dogmatic certainties. He was offended by his coarseness and strongly disapproved when he called the pope 'Antichrist'.

On the issue of individual freedom, the two men also ended up on opposite sides, Erasmus as a forerunner of the modern concept of individual and religious liberty, Luther, with his absolute dependence on faith alone, the progenitor of intolerant fundamentalism. Nevertheless, they both stand as giants on the road that leads to the emancipation of the human spirit. Their simultaneous but very different contributions to the development of western civilisation were immense, their legacy to free speech pivotal. Luther's ringing cry, '*Ich kann nicht anderst*', broke the hold of the medieval Church over man's individual conscience and paved the way for the liberty of dissent, which the modern world accepts as an essential human right. His translation of the Bible and his use of the printing press opened the minds of ordinary men and women to a truth that had previously been available only to an élite priesthood. It gave them the ability to think for themselves, to argue and to speculate, first about the eternal verities contained in the Bible, then about the secular issues raised by the society in which they lived. In the next century, the two themes would come together, as the vernacular Bible became one of the principle engines of social revolution. While in Luther's day, the secular concept of free speech did not yet exist, it could never have happened had he not made his stand against the authority of the medieval Church.

Erasmus died in Basle in 1536 reciting the words of the twenty-third psalm. Luther lived on for ten more years, growing increasingly ill and fat, but working ceaselessly to the very end, dying at the local inn on a visit to his home town of Eisleben at the age of sixty-two. When they carried the news back to Wittenberg, his great friend and protégé, Philip Melanchthon, who was to carry forward his reformation, called all the students of the university together and announced, in an echo of the death of the prophet Elijah, 'The charioteer of Israel is fallen'.

TYNDALE'S ENGLISH BIBLE

Even before Luther's excommunication, printed vernacular translations of the Bible had energised practically every country in northern Europe, producing a totally different view of everyday Christianity from that taught by the Church.

A German Bible had been published in Strasbourg as early as 1466, followed by another in 1470 and seven more by 1483. The first printed Bible in French dates from the 1470s, as do translations into Czech, Dutch and even Danish. Two generations later, when Luther settled down in the Wartburg to translate the New Testament from the original Greek, he had fourteen earlier versions of German vernacular Bibles to draw from. Only pre-reformation England remained without its own printed Bible. Translating it was a criminal offence, punishable by death.

Fear of heresy seems to have been the main cause. A distaste for the vulgar native tongue may have been another. In any event, the ban on translating the Bible into English went all the way back to a decree of 1408 known as the 'Constitutions of Oxford', imposed long before the invention of printing in an attempt to stamp out John Wycliffe's heretical Lollards. The ban was reinforced when Henry VIII's chief minister, Cardinal Wolsey, realised the damage a vernacular Bible could do to the wealth and authority of the Church. If ordinary people were allowed to read the word of God in their own language, they would discover that there was no mention of purgatory in the Bible, no mention of five of the seven sacraments and nothing at all about priests and bishops, aural confession or the need to do penance, pay tithes and purchase indulgences. Instead, it would reveal a stress on individual faith and personal responsibility. That, and only that, could redeem the sinner, whose fate was in the hands of God, not of the bishops and the pope.

Such shocking disclosures would surely undermine the whole edifice of clerical domination over people's lives and beliefs. The Church, therefore, stuck to its century-old ban on translating any text of Holy Scripture into the English, or any other language, and that 'any such book, pamphlet or tract, whether composed recently or in the time of John Wycliffe, or in the future, shall not be read in part or in whole, in public or in private'. The result was to cause English to become the language of the religious underground. Even the Dean of St Paul's, John Colet, was suspended from his living for translating the Lord's Prayer into English.*

Apart from a few copies of Wycliffe's illegal manuscript translations made at the time of Chaucer, the only Bible available in England was the Latin version compiled by St Jerome a thousand years earlier. It was full of omissions and inaccuracies, and in any case few but the more learned clergy could understand it. By the time the news of Luther's reformation started to seep into England in the 1520s, lay men and women were so hungry for a Bible in English that some of them were prepared to die for it. That, at least, was the fate that overtook the greatest of all English translators, William Tyndale, who devoted his life to producing an English Bible from the original Greek and Hebrew.

Born in Gloucestershire in about 1495, Tyndale was educated at Magdalen Hall, Oxford, where in his day the entire university possessed only sixty books in the English language. All the rest were in Latin, then the only acceptable tongue for learning, theology and the law. Oxford dons might speak to their college servants in English; to each other and their students they spoke and taught in

---

* Reported by Erasmus, Foxe and Tyndale himself, though sometimes disputed.

Latin. It was Tyndale and his immediate successors who established modern English as a language capable of expressing the most subtle and complex thoughts with an eloquence that has scarcely ever been surpassed. In the words of a modern biographer, at a time when English was struggling to find a form that was neither Latin nor French, he gave the nation a language that was English in words, word-order and lilt. He did so by using the language that people spoke, not as the scholars wrote. He invented new words such as 'scapegoat' and 'Passover' and created phrases which have gone deep into the English-speaking consciousness such as 'the powers that be' or 'let there be light' or 'the salt of the earth.' He wrote mostly in powerful monosyllables, as in the start of his description of the fall of man: 'And they heard the word of the Lord God as he walked in the garden in the cool of the day. And Adam hid himself and his wife from the face of the Lord God. And the Lord God called Adam and said unto him: Where art thou?' Or again, from the New Testament, 'There were shepherds abiding in the field, keeping watch over their flocks by night. And lo, the angel of the Lord came upon them, and the glory of the Lord shone round about them, and they were sore afraid. . . .'

In writing like this, Tyndale made a language for England. Without knowledge of his translated Bible it would be impossible to understand the literature, philosophy, art, politics and society of the following four centuries. There would have been no *Paradise Lost*, no *Pilgrim's Progress*, no Handel's *Messiah*, and no Gettysburg address. It remains arguably the greatest work of English literature and the foundation of the hugely influential King James's or Authorised Version of the Bible that followed a century later, nine-tenths of which is based on Tyndale.

Mentally as well as physically an austere man, Tyndale had resolved soon after graduating from university that he wished to devote his life to the translation of the New Testament from the original Greek. In his own words, he did so 'because I had perceived by experience how that it was impossible to establish the lay people in any truth except the scripture were plainly laid before their eyes in their mother tongue, that they might see the process, order and meaning of the text.'

His initial intention was to translate the New Testament while staying in London, where he arrived in 1523, just as Luther's German tracts were beginning to reveal the possibilities of a new form of Christianity built on personal faith discovered through reading the scriptures. In search of a patron who might provide financial support for his project, Tyndale approached the new Bishop of London, Cuthbert Tunstall, a deeply learned man with a reputation for moderation and a close friend of Erasmus. But Tunstall was also a wily politician, all too aware of the dangers of such a radical proposal, and Tyndale was rebuffed. With the secret backing of a group of English merchants, he made his way instead to Germany, where he may well have gone to visit Luther at Wittenberg before settling down to work in Cologne. There, he found a printer, who by 1525 had reached about three-quarters of the way through Tyndale's translation of the book of Matthew when the authorities closed him down. Tyndale and his assistant fled up the Rhine to the Protestant city of Worms, taking their work with them. It was there that the first printed edition of the full New Testament in English was published in 1526, beautifully printed by Peter Schoeffer in an exceptionally clear local typeface. Copies were successfully smuggled into

England, where they caused an immense sensation. Further editions followed in 1534 and 1535, providing a text that brought its English readers 'a blissful sense of release and new awakening'.

At first, no one knew where the forbidden Bibles had come from. Their title page carried the name and place of neither a printer nor a translator. The text went straight into St Matthew's gospel, without preface or acknowledgement. But so popular did it become that by October 1526, some 6,000 copies were in circulation, about half of them from Tyndale's printer at Worms, the other half in a less well-produced pirated edition printed in Antwerp. Many copies came hidden inside cargoes of hides or bales of cloth – often in the form of unbound printed sheets which could be assembled later. Others were distributed by the half-dozen or so London booksellers who were still able to import more or less what they liked. All were eagerly devoured by their readers, the new Bible, we are told, often read and shared 'till it was all in pieces'. At one point, the Church itself sent an emissary to buy up as many copies as he could find in order to destroy them. The result was that Tyndale's printer simply ran off more copies and ploughed the proceeds back into the business.

A more serious attempt to stem the flow quickly followed. Motivated by his horror of heresy, Wolsey ordered that all 'untrue translations' should be burned. Having worked out that the translation was the work of Tyndale, Cuthbert Tunstall delivered a fierce missive (in Latin) to the city authorities and ordered that as many copies as could be found were to be ceremoniously piled up outside the cathedral and burned by the public hangman.

Tyndale was deeply shocked. To have your own works condemned as heresy was one thing. To burn the word of God himself was barbarous, not to say sacrilegious – doubly so when it was done on the orders of a friend of Erasmus known to be deeply versed in the original Greek, and who would therefore know better than anyone how philologically faithful Tyndale's translation had been. In Tyndale's eyes, Cuthbert Tunstall had betrayed his own humanist principles in order to curry favour with Wolsey and the king.

A particular problem for the bishops was caused by Tyndale's provocative, though perfectly accurate, translation of words in the original Greek that did not tally with the Latin of the Vulgate. Tyndale was right to translate the Greek *metanoeo* as 'repent' instead of the Church's 'do penance' (*penitentiam agite*) even though he knew it contradicted one of their dogmas. He was right, too, to give 'congregation' rather than 'Church' for the Greek *ekklesia* and 'elder' (or 'senior') for *presbeteros* in preference to the vulgate's 'priest' – words which he inserted in full knowledge that they would undermine the authority of the established Church. The problem was made worse by the fact that to many lay people – and perhaps many members of the clergy – it came as a terrible shock to learn that the original New Testament had been written in Greek. Jerome's Latin vulgate was the Bible they had been brought up on, and it was upon this version that the Church had based its doctrinal teachings for more than a thousand years. But now, 'ignorant and illiterate monks, alarmed at the progress of the new learning, thundered from the pulpit that a new language had been discovered called Greek, of which people should beware, since it was that which produced all the heresies' and filled the Bible with 'thorns and briers'.

During the controversy which now erupted, Tyndale's fiercest and most intemperate opponent was no ignorant and illiterate monk. It was none other than the foremost intellectual in England, Erasmus's friend, the subsequently sainted Sir Thomas More. His polemics against Tyndale border on the hysterical and still embarrass his modern admirers by their foul tone and filthy language. Even in the more moderate passages, Tyndale is dismissed as 'an idolator and devil worshipper . . . discharging a filthy foam of blasphemies out of his beastly, brutish mouth'. In his calmer passages, More stressed that faith meant belief in the dogma of the Church as formulated, discussed and defended by its fathers over the past 1,500 years, starting with the apostles before any of the scriptures had been written down. To assert otherwise was damnable heresy. At bottom, More's venom was motivated by a scholar's conviction that if the common people were allowed to read the Bible in English they would get it wrong – especially the passages that expounded the doctrine of justification by faith, which contained 'such high difficulties as very few learned men can attain'.

While controversy over his New Testament raged at home, Tyndale moved from Worms, first to Hamburg, then to Antwerp, the thriving commercial city at the mouth of the River Scheldt, which was at that time a far more important centre of printing than London. It was also the home of an English company of Merchant Adventurers, who gave him shelter and a place to work. Here, he revised the next edition of his New Testament before moving on to an ambitious project to translate the whole of the Old Testament from the original Hebrew, a language then virtually unknown in England, but which Tyndale had mastered while living in Germany. For the rest of his life, Antwerp became his home, a city that became in a very real sense the cradle of a free press and new ideas. By the 1500s, Antwerp had some sixty well-equipped printing houses employing skilled technical staffs, learned readers and editors who were producing over 2,000 books a year, in a variety of European tongues. London, by contrast, was hard-pressed to produce 300.

Early in 1530, copies were smuggled into England of a well-made little book entitled *The first book of Moses called Genesis*, the first fruits of Tyndale's translation of the entire Pentateuch. Again, his work came to his readers as an immense revelation, written in strikingly simple Anglo-Saxon phrases – 'And God said, Let there be light: and there was light', or his almost comic description of Pharoah's 'jolly captains' being drowned in the Red Sea, and his description of Joseph as 'a lucky fellow'. No one before had ever attempted to translate direct from Hebrew, which Tyndale discovered goes even better into English than it does into Latin. In many ways, readers of his *Genesis* felt they were meeting the God of the Old Testament for the first time. Here, in wonderfully readable prose was the story of the Creation, of Adam and Eve, Noah's Ark, Jacob's dream and Joseph's coat of many colours – stories still as fresh and readable as they were when Tyndale wrote them 500 years ago. It remains one of the great glories of English literature.

Yet when it first arrived in England, people were forbidden to read it on pain of death. By the 1530s, the burnings there had started in earnest – not only of books, but of the people who sold and read them. A priest named Thomas Hitton became the first such martyr, burned alive at Maidstone after confessing that he had smuggled a New Testament and a primer from abroad. Others quickly followed: Thomas Bilney, a 'godly man of little stature', who, when he read Tyndale's translation of St Paul, 'seemed unto myself inwardly to feel a marvellous comfort and quietness, inasmuch as my bruised bones leapt for joy' and who had laughed when carrying his faggot to the stake in the Lollard's pit at Norwich; James Bainham, caught in possession of all five of Tyndale's books, was burnt at Smithfield after being tortured in Sir Thomas More's house in Chelsea; John Bent and Thomas Harding, were burnt in 1532; Richard Bayfield and Thomas Benet, burnt in Devon; Andrew Hewet, John Frith, and Elizabeth Barton, burned on the same day in 1533, and many others. Several hundred more were arrested for having an English Bible and forced to abjure, all commemorated in John Foxe's *Book of Martyrs*, which often listed their usually humble occupations – skinner, glazier, serving man, tailor, harper, bookbinder, weaver, priest. More himself was sometimes present when they were tortured and rejoiced when they went to the stake. Bainham, he wrote, was a mere chatterer who, with other heretics, deserved the stake – 'and after the fire of Smithfield, hell doth receive them where the wretches burn for ever'. Although More himself became a martyr, one wonders at his frenzied loathing of the English Bible, a trait which, in the words of one leading historian of the period, 'does perhaps make the reader think a little about the qualities normally expected in a saint of the Catholic Church'.

Meanwhile, Tyndale laboured away in Antwerp, producing his revised edition of the New Testament in 1534 while beginning work on the remaining chapters of the Old. This time, he added a prologue to each of the chapters, most merely explanatory, but some of the later ones highly inflammatory. That preceding Paul's epistle to the Romans, for instance, was, at thirty-six pages, taken almost verbatim from Luther: anathema, of course, to the Catholic Church. It was in this edition that he also settled on 'elder' for *presbeteros*, a translation he knew was bound to arouse the hostility of the Church. It could be these marginal comments and individual words that eventually sealed Tyndale's fate.

There can be no doubt, though, that the 1534 New Testament was Tyndale's masterpiece. The language was sharper and clearer and even more strongly English in rhythm and syntax. To give but one example, 'Blessed are the maintainers of peace' in Christ's Sermon on the Mount had become 'Blessed are the peacemakers,' and he amended the end of the chapter to bring it to an even more eloquent conclusion: 'Take therefore no thought for the morrow: for the morrow shall take thought for the things of itself. Sufficient unto the day is the evil thereof.' Tyndale's translations made the words sing with a wholly English rhythm that reflected the poetic quality of the original Greek in a way the Vulgate did not.

But the net was now closing in, and Tyndale was not as secure at the English House in Antwerp as he might have thought he was. In May 1535, his presence there was betrayed by an impoverished ne'er-do-well called Henry Philips, who was then bribed to entice Tyndale away from the house by inviting him to supper. The invitation was a trap, since as Foxe relates it, as soon as he came through the door 'Philips pointed with his finger over Master Tyndale's head down to him, so that the officers who sat at the door might see that it was he whom they should take'.

He was spirited away to a secure castle between Brussels and Louvain in the Catholic area of the Low Countries, and a year and a half later he was formally condemned as a heretic. Early in October 1536 he was handed over to the secular authorities for execution and, with the Procurator-General of the Holy Roman Emperor looking on, led out to the stake, which had been piled high with brushwood, straw and a sprinkling of gunpowder. But at least he was not burned alive. As Foxe relates it, though he deserved no death, he was 'brought forth to the place of execution, was there tied to the stake, and then strangled first by the hangman, and afterwards with fire consumed'. As the procurator-general gave the signal for him to be hanged, Tyndale cried out with fervent zeal and a loud voice, 'Lord, open the King of England's eyes!'

By a strange irony, a similar fate had overtaken his old enemy, Sir Thomas More, who was executed on Tower Hill in 1535 on a charge of high treason. He had incurred the wrath of Henry VIII by refusing to attend the king's wedding to Anne Boleyn and subsequently by defending the papal authority over England. The scene was now set for Henry's own reformation, starting with the dissolution of the monastries and at last authorising publication of the Bible in the English language. This was 'set forth with the king's most gracious licence' in 1539 and was, though unacknowledged, based on the work of William Tyndale, with the uncompleted books of the Old Testament added by his younger protégé, Miles Coverdale. With minor variations, this became the Bible used throughout the long reign of Queen Elizabeth and was superseded only by the definitive Authorised Version, published by order of King James in 1611. This again drew largely on the magnificent translation of William Tyndale, who has rightly been credited not only with one of the most influential works in the English language ever written, but with creating the rhythm and lilt of the language itself – an achievement which cost him his life and which places him in the highest ranks of those who died and suffered for the freedom of speech and a free press.

Less than a decade after his execution, the Catholic Church launched its counter-Reformation at the Council of Trent, starting a crusade to purify the faith by the extirpation of heresy and the suppression of free thought. At Trent, the Church reaffirmed the sole authority of the Vulgate version of the Bible, revived the work of the Inquisition and created the Index of Forbidden Books, authority's first systematic attempt to censor the press, and yet another important milestone on the tortuous road that ultimately led to the freedom of speech.

CHAPTER FOUR

Galileo Dares to Know

'ALL COHERENCE GONE'

Throughout the age of faith, Christians of all denominations accepted the words of the Bible as literally true. God created the world in seven days, mankind was descended from Adam and Eve, the earth was the centre of the universe and the sun moved around it, rising and setting, and then 'hastening again to the place where he arose'.

In the century following Luther's Reformation, these seemingly eternal verities became subject first to doubt and then to outright challenge. The engine of that doubt was men's growing awareness of the world around them. In Luther's own lifetime, they had gone off on voyages of discovery and exploration that proved conclusively that the world was round. The voyages were made possible by the newly developed art of navigation, which depended in turn on an understanding of geography and astronomy. By the middle of the sixteenth century, Verspucci and Mercator had produced maps of the world that enabled the explorers to plot their course with an accuracy previously denied to them. Henry the Navigator had set up a school of mathematicians and astronomers that helped them to harness the stars of the sky to fix their position on the open ocean, which with the aid of the magnetic compass made it possible for them to sail out of sight of land for weeks and sometimes months on end.

Out of these practical needs grew a system of independent and disinterested curiosity about the world that depended not on dogma, nor on faith, but on meticulously observed fact. The medieval pseudo-sciences of alchemy and astrology gradually gave way to true scientific enquiry, which over the following three centuries gave man the power to transform the environment, and in doing so, to alter fundamentally the way he thought about himself and his place in the celestial order. No longer would he be the centre of creation around which the rest of the universe revolved, but an insignificant and transient speck of life hurtling through space on a minor planet – 'this earth a spot, a grain, an atom, with the firmament compared and all her numbered stars', in John Milton's celebrated phrase. At the time he wrote those lines in *Paradise Lost*, man had embarked on one of the most profound changes in his history on earth. The primacy of faith was giving way to the primacy of science.

The old beliefs did not give up without a struggle, of course. As with all great upheavals, the vast majority of people found the new ideas deeply unsettling; none more so than the guardians of Christian orthodoxy. With the hindsight of almost four centuries, it is easy to condemn the blinkered prejudice with which they refused to believe the evidence of their own senses, refused even to look through the telescope which could prove beyond any doubt that their orthodox view of man's place in the world was no longer valid. But before they are condemned, it should be considered what it was they were being asked to abandon. This was not merely one hypothesis replacing another in the modern scientific manner; this was a hypothesis that overturned the whole static system of beliefs on which western civilisation had rested since the end of the Dark Ages. To the layman, the new proposition seemed simply absurd. If the earth moved through the heavens, 'the lark would not be able to hover over her nest and the crow over the snail on the rock'. If it turned on its axis, it would be impossible to stand up. Such people preferred to believe what they thought they saw: the sun and the moon arising and going down in their appointed paths, just as the Bible told them they did.

To the theologian, the consequences of the proposition were even more alarming. It suggested that there was no difference between heaven and earth, that motion in the heavens obeyed the self-same laws as they did on earth, that we are therefore in heaven, and heaven is here on earth. On countless other points, the proposition contradicted holy scripture, and since holy scripture was the revealed word of God, the proposition was not only erroneous, it was heretical.

The Church fathers responded in the only way the logic of their literal reading of the Bible would allow. If the new ideas were heretical, they must be suppressed. For most people, there was no enormity in this. Saving their own souls was a more pressing need than the right to free enquiry. The Church's dogma offered them certainties; the new philosophy called all in doubt. In John Donne's mournful words, ''tis all in pieces, all coherence gone'. From this, they went on to link the new ideas with political subversion and anarchy – 'prince, subject, father, son, are things forgot' – and every man, like every planet and every atom, was on his own. The tragi-comedy that resulted from this bewildered incomprehension was to create one of the most disastrous episodes in the history of free speech. In 1633, the leading mathematician and astronomer of the age, Galileo Galilei, a child of the Florentine Renaissance and a devout and faithful member of the Catholic Church, was hauled before the Inquisition and forced to recant.

'THE STARRY MESSENGER'

Born in 1564, the same year as Shakespeare and in the very month that Michelangelo died, Galileo was destined to become the last great figure of the Italian Renaissance. He was educated by the Jesuits at the monastery of Vallombrosa, not far from Florence, and it was from them that he acquired his lifelong interest in astronomy. He left at seventeen, steeped in the scholastic science of Aristotle, and an accomplished musician and painter. Intended for a career in medicine, he went to the University of Padua, where he developed a precocious aptitude for mathematics and science, after attending by chance a lecture in geometry. At eighteen, he made his first independent discovery, demonstrating that a swinging pendulum marks time in a way that is unconnected with the size of the arc it describes. Four years later, he gave up his studies in medicine and devoted the rest of his life to mathematics and physics. There is an old, though probably apocryphal, tale that he once climbed to the top of the Leaning Tower of Pisa to drop a cannonball and a bullet over the edge in order to prove that all falling objects accelerate at the same speed. Eventually, his gifts won him an appointment to the chair of mathematics at the University of Padua, where he spent eighteen fertile and creative years laying the foundations of the modern science of dynamics, the study of the properties of moving bodies.

A tall and bellicose extrovert with unruly ginger hair, a bristly square beard and a massive intellectual's brow, Galileo had a magnetic charm that made it impossible not to love him. He was a master stylist and raconteur, with a bewitching style of conversation, 'full of wit and conceits', according to his contemporary Italian biographer, 'rich in grave wisdom and penetrating sentences'. Deeply read in music, letters and poetry, he was able to quote by heart from Virgil, Ovid, Horace and Petrarch and he could recite the entire oeuvre of Ariosto, his favourite poet. When provoked, he had the tongue of a Tuscan peasant and would dismiss the ideas of his opponents with cries of 'elefantissimo', 'buffalocaccia', 'villan poltrone' or 'ridiculoso'. His private life was just as tempestuous. At thirty, he took a young Venetian girl, Marina Gamba, as his mistress, fathered three children, but never married her, probably because his university post did not permit it. When he left Padua in 1610, he broke off the union and, since they had been born out of wedlock and were, therefore, unmarriageable, put his two teenage daughters into a convent, innocent little victims of his devotion to science. They were cold and half-starved, and the youngest of them sank into a lifelong depression, but the eldest, who had taken the name of Maria Celeste, adored and comforted her negligent father into his old age. Even his abandoned mistress kept up a friendly correspondence with him, and eventually married someone else.

Though loved by his friends and family, he was unpopular with his fellow academics, largely because he treated them with such sarcastic contempt. In these years, much of his venom was spent on the followers of Aristotle, whose brilliant but incorrect speculations on the laws of physics, astronomy and motion had become enshrined in the so-called 'scholastic' philosophy approved and taught by the Church. Aristotle, who had studied under Plato in about 360 BC, was, in effect, the inventor of the natural sciences. A philosopher of great genius, he had constructed a comprehensive view of the entire physical universe which was a masterpiece of Greek logic, though unsurprisingly by Galileo's day – almost two thousand years later – it was in places outdated and often erroneous. His ideas had come down to western civilisation via the Arabs, from whose language it had been translated as late as 1200. The Christian world, then avid for knowledge, had harmonised his works with the words of the holy scriptures under the supervision of Thomas Aquinas. So closely had Aristotle's view of science been interwoven with Christian doctrine, it had become heretical to challenge it.

Ultimately, it was this that caused Galileo's downfall. He had already disproved Aristotle's theory of motion; now another conflict was brewing over Aristotle's teachings on astronomy. The Greeks had deduced that the world was round, both from the spherical shadow it threw on the moon during an eclipse and by the fact that different stars are visible in different latitudes. But Aristotle supposed that the earth was at rest and the heavens revolved around it. Because the constellations did not alter shape, they must rotate around the earth, just like the sun and the moon. Under Aristotle's later disciple, the Egyptian astronomer Ptolemy, an elaborate universe was constructed around a stationary earth surrounded by a series of fifty-five invisible rotating spheres, which carried with them the sun, the moon, the various planets and the stars.

It is one of the oddities of astronomy that this false version of the universe is the one that survived, while the truer versions also formulated by the ancient Greeks did not. Democritus and Aristarchus of Samos had both put forward theories that were closer to the truth than Aristotle's, but somehow their work was lost and only rediscovered after the argument had been settled.

One reason for this is that for most purposes the system devised by Aristotle, and later refined by Ptolemy, seemed to work. The risings, the settings and the eclipses of the heavenly bodies could be predicted with a high degree of accuracy. The four seasons were duly accounted for. And when the world was circumnavigated, the same sun rose and set over the antipodes, just as Aristotle and Ptolemy predicted it would. Equally important in those days, theologians had shown that it was compatible with every line in holy scripture, and thus as central to Catholic dogma as the resurrection of Christ or the immaculate conception.

In 1543, twenty years before Galileo was born, the brilliant Polish astronomer, Nicholas Copernicus, had postulated a simpler explanation for the movement of the heavenly bodies. He placed the sun at the centre of the universe and had the earth orbit around it. Copernicus's great thesis, *Revolution of the Celestial Orbs*, which he had dedicated to Pope Paul III, had been scoffed at for fifty years. Most scholars dismissed his mathematics as something for the *virtuosi*, while the Church fathers refused to take seriously his adventurous speculations into the 'divine secrets'. It was enough to follow the teaching of St Ambrose that 'to discuss the nature and position of the earth does not help us in our hope of the life to come'. It was necessary only to know that scripture stated, 'He hung up the earth upon nothing.' Why then raise a controversy as to how the thin air could support the earth, or why the earth did not go crashing to the bottom of the sea? The majesty of God's will had caused it to endure 'stable upon the unstable and the void'. Besides that, the respected official astronomer, Ticho Brahe, had declared against the new theory. As far as the Church was concerned, that settled the matter.

But to Galileo, Copernicus's theory came as a marvellous revelation. His powerful mind saw at once that it must be true. As early as 1597, he wrote to his friend in Prague, Johannes Kepler, that it meant that one would 'have to mould anew the minds of men'. But while he knew intuitively that the theory was true, he could not prove it. And for so long as he could not observe and quantify it, he refused to come forward to pronounce its truth, held back not by any fear of persecution by the Church, but by his pathological fear of professional ridicule. Although he had told his young friend that he had adopted Copernican opinions 'many years ago', and used them to arrive at explanations of many natural phenomena which were otherwise inexplicable, he had not dared bring them to light for fear of following the fate of Copernicus, who in laying up immortal fame for himself had been ridiculed during his lifetime by the 'multitude of fools' in the Church and universities. If there were more folk in the world like his friend

Kepler, Galileo would not hesitate to put forward his own views. But since there were not, he would refrain from busying himself with such matters.

In spite of young Kepler's idealistic pleadings – 'have faith, Galileo, trust in the power of truth' – Galileo kept his views to himself for twelve more years. Indeed, there is evidence that during this period he went on teaching the theories of Aristotle, although knowing them to be untrue.

One of the happy accidents of history then intervened. The means became available to prove that the Church's view of the universe was incorrect. In June or July 1609, Galileo conducted an experiment with an optical instrument invented by a Dutchman which had the 'marvellous effect' of making distant objects appear near at hand. Galileo set to work with single-minded enthusiasm and, in his own words, 'I applied myself entirely to seeking out the theory and discovering the means by which I might arrive at the invention of a similar instrument'. A little later, he had developed a theory of refraction which led him to fit two glass lenses at either end of a tube of lead, each lens being flat on one side, but one concave on the other side and the other convex. The trumpet-shaped instrument thus prepared was then mounted on a stand. Galileo had built the world's first working telescope.

He spent the next twelve months in a frenzy of activity, grinding his own lenses for a succession of increasingly effective instruments, which he simply called an *occhiale*, or spyglass. 'Sparing neither time nor labour,' he wrote, 'I finally succeeded in producing so excellent an instrument that objects seen by it appeared over thirty times closer than when regarded with our actual vision.' In August 1609 he took his finest instrument to the top of the campanile of St Mark's Cathedral in Venice and showed the astonished Doge and Senate how they could discover their enemies' ships approaching more than two hours before they could see the Venetians. The demonstration was so effective, Galileo was promptly confirmed in his post for life at what might fairly be termed the astronomical salary of 1,000 florins a year.

Towards the end of that same year, he turned his *occhiale* on the night skies above Padua, first at the crescent moon, which he found was covered in mountains, thus at once discrediting the age-old belief that the heavenly bodies were smooth, uniform, precisely spherical and composed of an incorruptible celestial substance known as aether. Over the next few enthralling months, Galileo discovered the 'almost inconceivable' number of stars in the Milky Way, charted the constellations of Orion and the Pleiades, discovered stars 'never seen by anyone before me', and came to the firm conclusion that 'the earth is a wandering body surpassing the moon', and not the sink of all the dull refuse of the universe that Aristotle supposed it to be.

He went on to record with mounting excitement how 'on the seventh day of January in this year 1610 at the first hour of night' he turned his finest telescope towards the planet Jupiter. That first night, his curiosity was aroused by three small, very bright stars lying in an exact straight line, two to the east of Jupiter, one to the west. Next night, he noticed them again, but was certain they had changed their position, all three now being in a straight line to the west of Jupiter. Here were stars moving in relation to one another, something the old astronomy did not allow for. Could this be the proof he was seeking that Copernicus was right all along?

The following night, he waited with growing impatience to view the phenomenon again, but to his fury and disappointment the sky was completely overcast. He spent the next twenty-four hours in an agony of frustrated expectation, but to his great relief the next night's sky was clear as he swung his telescope once more towards Jupiter. The little stars had moved again. Now there were only two of them, both west of the planet. Knowing that there was no way in which this could be attributed to the movement of Jupiter, his perplexity was transformed into amazement. Night after night he watched the three little stars dance around the planet, always precisely in line with the zodiac, and later he discovered a fourth star, following precisely the same pattern. The only possible explanation could be that they were moving around it in orbit. Jupiter had four moons. He kept up his observations for five weeks until not the slightest shadow of doubt remained in his mind. Copernicus was right.

Galileo ended his observations at the end of March and began to write. By the end of the month, he had completed a pamphlet announcing his discoveries to the world, *Nuncius Siderius*, the Starry Messenger. Publication presented no problems. He had dedicated the pamphlet to his patron, Cosimo II, the Grand Duke of Tuscany, after whom he had shrewdly named the moons of Jupiter. He also took care to confine himself to a factual account of his observations without referring to their doctrinal implications. He was still unconcerned with the effect his pamphlet might have on the Church; his worry was the old one, the reaction of his fellow professors. And sure enough, while the rest of the world received his Starry Messenger with wonder and delight, his academic colleagues treated it with disdain. When he invited them to look through his telescope and see his discoveries with their own eyes, some looked and professed to see nothing, others said the *occhiale* was only a toy that could show them nothing of philosophical value, others that he must have taken the invention from Aristotle, since the ancients had been the pioneers of everything. Two old pedants, Giulio Libri and Cesare Cremonini, the chief professor of philosophy, refused to look through the telescope at all. 'To look through that spyglass of his would make me dizzy,' Cremonini said. '*Basta*! I don't want to hear any more about it.'

Galileo reacted with amused exasperation. 'My dear Kepler,' he wrote to his friend, 'what would you say of the learned here, who with all the pertinacity of the asp, have steadfastly refused to cast a glance through the telescope? Shall we laugh, or shall we cry?' Shortly afterwards, when one of the old pedants died, Galileo wrote sardonically, 'Libri did not choose to see my celestial trifles while he was here on earth. Perhaps he will do so now he has gone to heaven.'

While Galileo poured scorn on his academic colleagues, the Church stayed aloof: the doctrinal and theological implications of his discoveries had not yet sunk in. Galileo was also working under the protection of the Venetian Republic, who were constantly threatening to follow the example of England and break away from the Church altogether. Galileo was himself in Venice when the republic threw out three of the most militant papist orders, including the Jesuits, who were led away, as Galileo himself recorded it, each with a crucifix hanging around his neck and a lighted candle in his hand – 'to the great regret and sorrow of many women who are devoted to them'.

With the Jesuits away, the most prized sage in the republic was safely beyond the reach of the Inquisition. But his larger ambitions now got the better of him. In 1610, only a few months after his triumph with the telescope, he accepted an offer to return to his native Tuscany to become chief mathematician and philosopher to the Grand Duke Cosimo. The Doge and Senate in Venice never forgave him for this act of base ingratitude. His supporters were equally concerned. 'Your departure produces an inconsolable unhappiness,' wrote his best friend, Giovanfrancesco Sagredo. 'Here is a place so beautiful and so different from all others, with a freedom and way of life perhaps unique in the world.' There were great dangers in serving the court of an absolute monarch where the Jesuits were so influential.

But Galileo was adamant. His new post gave him the leisure to draw his work to a conclusion without any tiresome teaching or having to take in scholars as boarders. 'I should like my books to become my source of income,' he wrote to Cosimo – 'to say nothing of such inventions as no other prince can match.' He had a wider ambition, too, and once settled in his new post, he conceived a bold and imaginative plan to fulfil it. He would go to Rome. There, he would persuade the pope himself of the truth. He would free the Church forever from its bondage to Aristotle and Ptolemy. It was a madcap idea that was to obsess Galileo for the rest of his life. His belief in his own genius had persuaded him that 'since it has pleased God in our age to vouchsafe to human ingenuity the admirable invention of perfecting our sight by multiplying it as much as forty times', any good mind could now grasp the new truth. If he could give the theologians in the Vatican the facts, they would surely draw the correct conclusions. It would take time, but he was sure his invention would bring the universal acceptance of the Copernican theory.

In order to bypass the die-hard academics who had become such an obstacle to the spread of new ideas, Galileo began writing in the vernacular. His readers were no longer confined to scholars who wrote only in Latin, but were drawn from educated independent-minded men of affairs, who had proved over the past few generations how powerfully free discussion and independent thought could influence the progress of civilisation. He believed that intelligent men with a proper respect for the facts could arrive at the truth through free and open discussion – men with whom he liked to say 'it is a great sweetness to go wandering and discussing together among truths'. It was the easy and open intercourse of powerful minds that led to progress and the clarification of ideas, a belief that was a world away from both the old scholasticism and the new-fangled insistence on blind obedience demanded by the Jesuits. Who had ever heard that a man's mind, created free, must submit itself passively to the decrees of a single Church order? Outside his faith, a man's intellect was free, especially to explore the new sciences – of which there was not the smallest mention in scripture, which took so little notice of astronomy that it mentioned none of the planets by name.

Although he wrote in an earthy vernacular prose, Galileo's appeal was not to the vulgar uneducated masses. Along with Machiavelli and the other members of the intelligentsia of who produced the Florentine Renaissance, Galileo believed ordinary people were incapable of rational thought and were all too easily stirred up by rabble-rousers and demagogues to become 'a club wherewith to crush the endeavours of science'. In all his printed works, Galileo was speaking to his equals, educated men of open mind and 'wise ignorance'.

He was going to Rome to add to the Christian truth, not to oppose it. Believing himself a shrewd man of the world, he had prepared the ground with care, opening a correspondence with a friend he had made on an earlier trip to Rome, the eminent German mathematician, Father Christopher Clavius. By then an old man, best known for his work in reforming the calendar under Pope Gregory XIII, Clavius had an enquiring mind and a host of valuable contacts. Though he never embraced the views of Copernicus, he wrote to Galileo to tell him that he and his colleagues had built themselves a telescope and verified all his observations. 'In very truth, you deserve great praise for them,' he said.

It was an encouraging start, and Galileo set off to Rome with high hopes and a collection of his finest telescopes. He had a long conversation with Clavius and his colleagues on the first day and was told that the fathers, being finally convinced that the moons of Jupiter were real, had devoted the past two months to continuous observation of them. 'We have compared notes and found that our experiences tally in every respect,' Galileo reported to the Tuscan Secretary of State.

There was not the slightest sign that the Church had found anything objectionable in the new discoveries. Indeed, Galileo was now lionised wherever he went, one enthusiastic cardinal writing to the grand duke that 'were we living in the ancient republic of Rome, I verily believe that a column would have been erected on the Capitol in his honour'.

Galileo, now forty-seven and at the height of his powers, returned to Florence thinking his mission had accomplished all he had hoped for. He had convinced Father Clavius and the Vatican astronomers that Aristotle's views on the nature and movement of the heavenly bodies were no longer tenable. They were not ready to go the whole way with Copernicus, but they at least accepted that the heavens contained more mysteries than they had supposed. They realised, for instance, that the phases of Venus provided incontrovertible proof that the planets revolved around the sun. It was now surely only a matter of time before the Church itself accepted that the earth, too, was in orbit around the sun. Yet within eight months of his triumphant return from Rome, Galileo was in trouble with the Inquisition and doomed to spend the remaining thirty years of his life under the shadow of heresy.

What had gone so dramatically and tragically wrong? There was nothing inevitable about the collision that was about to take place between the opposing philosophies of faith and science. In the tragi-comedy that now unravelled, jealousy, intrigue, stupidity, arrogance and fear all played their part. Due to this deadly combination of human failings, Galileo was on his way to become an unwitting martyr to the principle of free and unfettered enquiry.

THE TRIDENTINE INDEX

In the forty or so years since the Council of Trent, the Catholic Church had hardened and purified itself. The counter-reformation launched under the inspiration of Ignatius Loyola, the founder of the Jesuit order, had led the papacy out of the moral and spiritual morass into which it had sunk, and in doing so had checked the once inexorable spread of the Protestants. Italy, France and Spain stood firm for the faith; Bavaria, Bohemia and Poland were recovered; after Trent, only England and Republican Holland were lost. Under Loyola's brilliant and single-minded leadership, the Jesuits rose through their prodigious energy to become the cutting edge of the counter-reformation, the Church's intellectual and religious élite. The Church's best moralists were all Jesuits, its leading humanists, its best scientists, and, as it happens, far and away its best and most up-to-date astronomers. But they were no friends of freedom. Together with their rivals, the Dominicans, they provided the Church's censors, ruthlessly controlling the flow of new ideas. They condemned all 'inquisitive curiosity' about Church dogma and policed the chilling decree that 'faith excludes not only doubt, but even the desire to subject its truth to demonstration.' They coined a new and subsequently sinister phrase in the history of ideas, the College of Propaganda, a body charged with spreading the faith to the farthest corners of the newly discovered world. '*Libertas credendi perniciosa est,*' was one of their mottoes – freedom of belief is pernicious; '*namnihil aliud est quam libertas errands*' – it is nothing but the freedom to be wrong.

The Church's main instruments of control were the Inquisition and the Index of Forbidden Books, both revived and reformed after the Council of Trent. By the use of the Inquisition – which in Spain maintained a record of almost no acquittals – it terrified the people into submission, put thousands on the rack, and sent as many as 100,000 to the stake as heretics. In Rome, the so-called Holy Office was a relatively milder body, but a formidable instrument of suppression nonetheless. With criminal jurisdiction over all accusations of heresy, the Holy Office – presided over by the pope himself – differed in two important respects from every other court of law. In contrast to any other tribunal, there were no limits to its jurisdiction, either in terms of territory, of persons or of subject matter. Its remit ran throughout the world. Only the cardinals and the pope himself were immune from its scrutiny. The second characteristic was its secrecy: a person accused of heresy knew neither the name of his accuser nor the nature of his supposed crime. The Inquisition's first question was always: 'Do you know, or can you guess, why you are here?' So effective was the technique, it has been copied by totalitarian regimes ever since, culminating in the ideological show trials of the Soviet Union, which were modelled closely on the methods of the Catholic Inquisition.

Working hand in hand with the Inquisition was the so-called Congregation of the Index, responsible for censorship. Books had been burned for years by local tribunals, but after the Council of Trent the Church compiled a centralised list of forbidden works, the so-called Tridentine Index, which was to continue in existence for the next 400 years. Under it, all the works of Erasmus, Machiavelli and Boccaccio were banned and even the writings of Dante were thoroughly expurgated before they could be published and read by the faithful. Luther was on the Index from the start, of course, as was the Church of England's Book of Common Prayer. To these would be added, among many others, the works of Descartes and Montaigne (whose *Essays* were placed on the Index in 1676 after freely circulating for close on a century), all the works of Balzac, Rousseau,

Locke, Voltaire, John Stuart Mill and, in our own day, Sartre and Simone de Beauvoir. The Church justified this on the grounds that it sought only to keep faith and morals unpolluted from the ravages of a pernicious press.

All new works in countries controlled by the Church became subject to prior restraint: in other words they had to obtain an official licence, or *imprimatur*, before they could be published. In charge of this complex operation was the Master of the Sacred Palace, or *Padre Maestro*, who employed a large staff of theological experts who spent their time, in John Milton's scornful phrase 'raking through the entrails of many an old good author with a violation worse than any could be offered to his tomb'. Nor did they stay in matters heretical, but meddled in any subject that was not to their palate, ordaining that no book should be published unless it were approved and licensed 'under the hand of two or three glutton friars'.

Of course, Milton wrote as a critical Puritan. But there was the sharp edge of truth in his criticism of the Church's censorship. In rescuing the papacy from its moral decline, the Council of Trent had set it against the new spirit of intellectual enlightenment that was beginning to sweep across Europe. By withholding authorisation for new editions of the Bible, by stressing the need for lay obedience, by attempting to channel the flow of literature along narrowly prescribed lines, the Church had already set its face against most of the new forces Gutenberg's invention had unleashed. It now prepared to launch itself into a battle that threatened to obliterate the independent-minded enquiry and critical speculation that were so vital to the development of the scientific method.

AT ODDS WITH THE VATICAN

The first hint that Galileo might be in trouble with the Inquisition came in the form of a court intrigue, the very peril his Venetian friend Sagredo had warned him of when he took up his post in Tuscany two years previously. The plot was hatched by the poisonous old professor of philosophy at the University of Pisa, Cosimo Boscaglia, who was seen whispering over the dinner table into the ear of the grand duke's mother, the Dowager Grand Duchess Christina, a domineering old lady who had fallen under the spell of the Jesuits. After dinner, Galileo's friend Benedetto Castelli was summoned to the dower duchess's private apartments and informed that she had heard Galileo taught that the earth moved through space, something she said could not take place since it was contrary to scripture.

Warned of this danger by Castelli, Galileo sent him a long letter about the relationship between theology and the sciences – a letter which was to lead him into his first conflict with the Church. A layman had dared to enter the rarified world of theology. Without realising it, Galileo had handed his enemies the weapon they had been waiting for.

As a work of literature, the missive to Castelli, later expanded into a letter to the grand duchess herself, was a model of dialectical skill. But as an instrument intended to quell the theological objections to Copernicus, it had just the opposite effect. The pamphlet declared that while the Bible cannot err, it had always been understood to speak figuratively in many of its passages. Otherwise, it would be necessary to give God hands and feet and ears and human and bodily emotions such as anger, repentance, hatred and sometimes forgetfulness of things past and ignorance of the future. Scripture had therefore to be accommodated to the common understanding. But nature cared not one jot whether her secrets were above man's understanding. Natural effects could in no way be revoked because of certain passages in the Bible, which may be turned and twisted into a thousand different meanings. As we cannot be certain that the interpreters are all divinely inspired, it would be prudent if men were forbidden to employ passages of scripture to sustain what demonstrable proof denied.

Galileo then penned a rhetorical plea to let man's intelligence roam where it will: 'Who can set bounds to the mind of man? Who dare assert that he knows all that in this universe is knowable?' It would be well not to burden the scriptures with official interpretations beyond need; the more so when the demand came from people who claimed to be divinely inspired, yet were destitute of the intelligence necessary not merely to disprove, but to understand the demonstrations of science. The intention of holy writ was to persuade us of the truths necessary to salvation; it did not demand us to believe that the God who gave us our senses, our speech and our intellect would have us put them aside when they could help us find out things for ourselves, particularly in the sciences.

Galileo's expression of his faith in reason and his hopes for intellectual freedom won the admiration and support of writers, thinkers and practical men of affairs everywhere. But the academics hated it. As Arthur Koestler perceptively observed, the inertia of the human mind and its resistance to new ideas are most clearly demonstrated not, as one might expect, by the ignorant mass – which is easily swayed once its imagination is caught – but by professionals with a vested interest in tradition and in the monopoly of learning. Innovation is a twofold threat to academic mediocrities, he said, it endangers their ocular authority, and it evokes the deeper fear that their whole, laboriously constructed intellectual edifice might collapse. He argued that academic backwoodsmen have been the curse of genius from Aristarchus to Darwin and Freud: 'they stretch, a solid and hostile phalanx of pedantic mediocrities, across the centuries.' It was this threat that had silenced Copernicus and the earlier Galileo. Now, the silence broken, Galileo's enemies were still firmly entrenched in academic chairs and preachers' pulpits, waiting to strike back.

For a year, not much more happened. The letter circulated among the educated élite, as Galileo had intended. Inevitably, it also fell into the hands of his enemies, who muttered among themselves without daring to be the first to strike at such a famous and well-connected figure. Then, in 1614, just as the storm seemed to have blown itself out, a public attack was made on Galileo by name. Its author was an obscure Dominican monk called Tomasso Caccini, who had been put up to preach a sermon in Florence by a gang of Galileo's enemies who called themselves The League. Caccini's text from the gospels – 'Ye men of Galilee, why stand you gazing up into heaven?' – was a pun, of course, on Galileo's name. But while the text was witty enough, the sermon itself was pure vitriol. Mathematics was of the devil, Caccini said. Mathematicians should be banished from all Christian states. Their ideas about a moving earth were akin to heresy.

When he heard of it, the preacher-general of the Dominicans quickly apologised for the friar's intemperate outburst. But the damage was already done. A scandal blew up. Another friar who had not heard before of the strangely-named 'Ipernicus' acquired a copy of Galileo's letter to the grand duchess and was so profoundly shocked by its contents that he sent a garbled copy of it to a cardinal on the board of the Inquisition, underlining Galileo's claim that scripture does not always mean what it seems to mean and urging the cardinal to provide 'such remedies as will seem advisable'.

The machinery of the Inquisition rolled inexorably into motion. Caccini was called to Rome, where he testified that the city of Florence was a nest of Galileists publicly holding discourses inspired by their master. The attention of the Inquisition was drawn to Galileo's recent work on sunspots, which claimed that the sun revolved on its axis. As the process ground on, the Church authorities spent much time pondering texts from the Bible that did not square with Galileo's hypothesis. Two in particular caused them much perplexity. The first was from Joshua:

> Sun, stand thou still upon Gibeon
> And thou Moon in the valley of Ajalon;
> And the sun stood still, and the moon stayed
> Until the nation took vengeance on their enemies.

How could the sun stand still, the Church fathers wondered, when the Copernicans asserted that it never moved in the first place? The second passage, from the nineteenth psalm, provided even firmer proof that the sun was in motion. It told them:

> He is as a bridegroom coming out of his chamber,
> And rejoiceth as a strong man to run a race.
> His going forth is from the end of heaven
> And his circuit unto the end of it.

With such earnest quibbles about what most people would regard as poetic similes, Galileo's enemies set the snare that would entrap him. And being the proud tempestuous man he was, Galileo walked straight into it.

His friends in the Vatican advised him to lie low, but fearing all his gains of the past two years might be lost, he asked for his letter to be sent to Rome for the attention of Father Clavius and, if possible, the pope himself. Messages flew back and forth between Florence and Rome through 1614 and 1615, most of those from Rome advising prudence. Galileo's theories were being exaggerated. People were starting to believe he taught that there were men on the moon and were wanting to know how these lunar people could have descended from Adam and Eve or to have issued from Noah's Ark. Cardinal Bellarmine, the chief theologian, reminded everyone that the man who wrote that the sun rises and sets and returns to its place was Solomon, who not only spoke from divine inspiration but was wise and learned above all others.

With the arguments taking on a surrealist air, Galileo decided to go back to Rome to argue for his beliefs in person, obsessed with the idea that 'all his future life and being' depended on persuading the world of the truth about Copernicus's universe. He now sincerely believed he could persuade the Vatican that his system was in accord with the Catholic faith. His Italian biographer tells us he set out for Rome in the winter of 1615 'with the heroic blindness of an apostle and the enthusiastic faith of a boy.'

Galileo arrived in Rome 'purring with optimism'. He was boisterous, confident and back to vigorous good health after a painful bout of arthritis brought on by the severe winter weather in Florence. The debate was now out in the open and Galileo relished the controversy. 'He turns the laugh against all his opponents and answers their objections in such a way as to make them look perfectly ridiculous,' one admirer wrote. The Tuscan ambassador was more anxious about the fate of his unwanted house guest. 'Galileo gets hotly excited about these views of his,' he reported. 'This irritability makes the skies of Rome very dangerous for him.' Galileo himself remained blithely certain he had done the right thing. 'From day to day I am discovering what a good inspiration it was for me to come here,' he said, 'for such snares have been laid against me that I could not have hoped to save myself later.' He lobbied assiduously, always amid fifteen or twenty guests, now in one house, now in another, pestering and wearying several cardinals, we are told, before he found one who would speak to the pope on his behalf, the 22-year-old Alessendro Orsini.

The result was a cold rebuff. The pope cut Orsini short and told him the matter had already been referred to the Holy Office. In a matter of days, the eleven learned theologians who had been charged with investigating the Copernican theories came to a conclusion that has made them a laughing stock ever since. They censured the proposition that the earth rotates around the static sun as 'foolish and absurd in philosophy and formally heretical'. The proposition that the earth moves as a whole, with a diurnal motion, earned the milder censure that it was 'erroneous in faith'.

The finest minds of the Church had fallen into the self-same trap that had been set for Galileo. He had been accused of entering the sacristy; they had pronounced on a matter of science, in which they were unqualified. It represents the moment at which faith and science parted company, to the advantage of neither. Catholic apologists point out that the findings of the Inquisition's theologians never became part of the official doctrine of the Church, which requires ratification by Ecumenical Council. Nevertheless, the damage was done. The Church had publicly condemned the Copernican system as 'formally heretical'. In doing so, they had set the face of the Church against the principle of free and dispassionate enquiry.

The leaders in the Vatican seem at least to have sensed the enormity of the dilemma they now faced. The last thing they wanted was a martyr on their hands, especially one as famous and well connected as Galileo. After a few days of intense diplomatic activity, Cardinal Bellarmine was directed to instruct Galileo to desist. There are two versions of what happened at that fateful meeting, still hotly debated. The first has Galileo agreeing that he would no longer defend the Copernican doctrine. The second has it that Galileo agreed to relinquish the forbidden opinion altogether, and not to hold, defend or teach it in any way.

The troubles that fell upon Galileo sixteen years later, when he was formally denounced to the Inquisition, were due to his alleged breach of the injunction to abandon Copernicus's theories, his trial turning on the presence of that little word 'teach' – a word many historians believe was inserted later and that the injunction itself was either a forgery or had at least been tampered with.

But for now, Galileo had won a victory, of sorts. He had escaped any form of punishment or censure, he was received in audience by the pope, who assured him of his continuing esteem, and the decree which was read out from the pulpit of every Catholic Church in Christendom simply forbade the presentation of Copernicus's theories as philosophical truth. They could still be discussed as a mathematical hypothesis, since Copernicus's work was not to be banned outright but only withdrawn for 'correction'. Nevertheless, by this action, the censor had entered the world of free scientific enquiry. The year 1616, which saw the gagging of Galileo and the deaths of Shakespeare and Cervantes, is sometimes said to mark the end of the European Renaissance.

After this initial brush with the higher authorities of the Church, Galileo was ordered back to Florence, where he did some work on the causes of tides, which before Newton's discovery of gravity, he supposed to be caused by the rotation of the earth interacting with its orbit of the sun. He was now in continual poor health, a painful rheumatic condition often confining him to bed. He had the consolation of an excellent salary, a comfortable villa overlooking the Arno, the pleasant company of his friends, a keen interest in his garden, where he became an expert on the grafting of vines, and above all the devoted attention of his daughter, Maria Celeste, then just turned seventeen. From her rural convent at Arcetri, she sent him little delicacies, mended his linen, picked the last December rose for him from the nunnery garden, and, during the plague years, sent him home-made pots of electuary as a preservative. 'A piece the size of a walnut is to be taken each morning, fasting, with a little Greek wine,' she wrote, though she was sorry the pot was baked too much: 'we did not take into account the tendency of the figs to get into lumps.' She undertakes to try to make it better next time and has only one regret about her life in the convent: 'It prevents me from attending on you personally, though my thoughts are always with you and I long to see you daily.' Galileo eventually bought the house next door to the convent in order to be nearer to her and to help him pick up what remained of his broken family life. And though officially silenced, he never lost hope that he would eventually triumph over what he called those three most powerful operators – ignorance, malice and impiety.

For seven years he published nothing. Then in 1623 came *Il Saggiatore*, a witty polemic written in the form of a dialogue defending the experimental method, though not yet entering the forbidden world of astronomy. Having successfully tested the waters, as he supposed, he returned to astronomy in the book that was to bring him before the Inquisition, a dialogue between proponents of the two world systems: Ptolemaic and Copernican. He worked on it for seven more years, during which a number of events occurred that were to have an important bearing on his future. First, the Grand Duke Cosimo died unexpectedly, depriving him of his patron, and, even worse, putting in his place as regent the pious old dowager duchess who had started all his troubles in the first place. In Rome, Pope Paul V had also died, to be followed by Gregory XV, a man so aged and infirm his reign lasted less than two years. He was succeeded by one of Galileo's oldest friends and supporters, Cardinal Maffeo Barberini, who took the name of Urban VIII. A wit, a poet, an accomplished horseman and immensely ambitious, the new pope was a man of monumental vanity who claimed to know 'more than all of the cardinals put together'. He commissioned Bernini's vast black baldachin with twisted columns which still adorns St Peter's, and he tore down the bronze ceilings in the Pantheon to make cannons for his castle, leading to the Roman pun '*quod non fecerunt Barbari, fecerunt Barberini*' – what is not the work of the barbarians is the work of Barberini. With an almost insatiable lust for worldly power himself, he was a noted cynic when it came to the power of others. On learning of the death of Cardinal Richelieu, he remarked: 'If there is a God, Richelieu will have much to answer for; if not, he has done very well.' After the two former popes, he was welcomed on his accession as a man of the Renaissance, skilled and knowledgeable in the arts, politics and diplomacy. 'I am fully confident that this is going to be a papacy of the *virtuosi*,' wrote the Tuscan ambassador. Some of Galileo's friends had been appointed to influential posts, and the pope himself had eagerly asked when he could expect a visit from Galileo – at that time perhaps the only man in Italy whose ego matched the size of his own.

'I swear to you that nothing pleases his Holiness so much as the mention of your name,' one flattering admirer wrote to Galileo from Rome. 'After I had been speaking of you for some time, I told him that you, esteemed sir, had an ardent desire to come and kiss his toe, if his Holiness would permit it, to which the Pope replied that it would give him great pleasure, if it were not inconvenient to you.'

Galileo arrived as soon as his health would allow and was given six long audiences, where he was eulogised as 'this great man, whose fame shines in the heavens, and goes on earth far and wide'. During their private discussions, Galileo tried to persuade the new pope of the truth of the Copernican system. But though clearly infatuated with Galileo, Barberini would neither admit the truth of the theory himself nor allow the decree of 1616 to be in any way relaxed. However, 'the Holy Church has not condemned the opinion of Copernicus,' the new pope said. 'Nor was it condemned as heretical, but only as rash. If anyone could demonstrate it to be necessarily true, it would no longer be rash.' The eversanguine Galileo assumed this to mean he could write more or less what he wanted about Copernicus so long as he kept away from theology and spoke always *ex hypothosi*.

Back home, he laboured away at his dialogue in a house now overcrowded by the arrival of his layabout younger brother, together with his wife and nine children. But at last, in 1630, the *Dialogue* was ready, a book still revered as a lucid and witty masterpiece of Italian literature, again cast in the form of a conversation almost Socratic in its form. It takes place in a palace on the Canale Grande between three friends, two of them named after Galileo's own old friends from Venice, Salviati and Sagredo, both now dead. Sagredo is cast as the man of the world, endowed with the statesmanship and open-minded curiosity of a

Venetian nobleman, Salviati as the idealist proponent of the Copernican system. The third character, Simplicio, a genial defender of the status quo, becomes the butt of the other two and a harmless figure of fun.

The three friends spend the whole of one day discussing the arguments about the earth's diurnal motion. Sagredo puts forward the view that, if the earth did rotate eastward on its axis at high speed, the birds would lose their bearings in mid-air, autumn leaves would always scatter to the west of the trees, and cannonballs fired to the west would travel farther than those to the east. Salviati responds by comparing the motion of the earth to that of a ship at sea. Passengers on board could freely wander up and down the decks even as their ship made its way at great speed from, say, Venice to Alepppo. Just so with the whirling of the earth, which takes along the air itself, and everything else that is suspended in it, just as it carries the clouds. So there was no need to worry about the birds in the sky; so far as that is concerned. they could forever be asleep.

On the third day of their dialogue – actually written by Galileo after an interval of several years – the three friends speculate about the enormity of the heavens. Salviati begins with a spirited argument showing how the errant wanderings of the planets could be explained by earth plying a yearly orbit around the sun, between those of Venus and Mars. He goes on to muse about the vastness of the entire universe, pushing the stars away to unimaginable distances in order to explain the constancy of their positions and the apparent lack of any stellar parallax. Simplicio responds by saying he could not believe that God would have wasted so much space on something of no possible use to man. The medically-minded Sagredo squashes him by showing how arrogant it was to say 'since I do not know how Jupiter or Saturn is of service to me, they are superfluous, and even do not exist . . . because, O deluded man, neither do I know how my arteries are of service to me, nor my cartilages, spleen or gall; indeed, I would not even know I had a gall, or a spleen, or kidneys, if they had not been shown to me in many dissected corpses.' He ends with the exasperated remark, 'What does it mean to say that the space between Saturn and the fixed stars, which these men call vast and useless, is empty of worldly bodies? That we did not see them perhaps? That the four satellites of Jupiter . . . came into the heavens when we began seeing them, and not before? That the nebulae, which were once only little white patches, became clusters of bright and beautiful stars only after we looked at them with our telescopes? O, the presumptuous, rash, ignorance of mankind!' To imagine an infinite universe was merely to grant Almighty God his proper due.

After 500 pages of such argument, touching on every point of difference between the Aristotlean, Ptolemaic and Copernican systems of science, the three men amiably end their three days of discourse, come to no conclusions of their own, but agree that while they are making up their minds 'we may, according to our custom, spend an hour in taking the air in the gondola that awaits us'. Readers, like the characters, were left to make up their own minds. Galileo had taken great care not to assert in words the truth of the Copernican system, but the arguments led irresistibly to the conclusion that no sensible person could hold any other opinion but the Copernican.

Galileo's *Dialogue* was always more a work of propaganda than a contribution to science. Indeed, Arthur Koestler argued that after his sensational discoveries of 1610, Galileo neglected both observational research and astronomic theory in favour of his propaganda crusade, with which he had become obsessed. By the time he wrote the *Dialogue* he had lost touch with new developments in that field, particularly those made by his friend Kepler. The arguments put forward in the *Dialogue* were thus flawed and out of date.

None of this affected the enormous impact of the *Dialogue*, which was written not for the specialist but for educated lay opinion, to whom it came as an immense revelation. By his masterly skill as a dialectician, Galileo had run rings round the terms of the censorship imposed by the injunction of 1616 and put before the whole world a theory that was to change their view of the universe. But before publication, there still remained the task of getting an official *imprimatur* – and the problem that his characterisation of Simplicio would be seen as a joke at the expense of the pope, to whom Simplicio was seen to carry an uncanny resemblance. It does not seem to have occurred to Galileo that this might cause offence and he set off for Rome with his manuscript in May 1630 optimistic as ever that he would soon have the *imprimatur* he sought.

There then began one of those intricate dances familiar to anyone who has submitted a contentious work for approval by the censors. Galileo presented his manuscript to the chief licenser, the master of the sacred palace, Father Niccolo Riccardi, who had looked so favourably on his earlier work, *Il Saggiatore*. A genial and loveable old friar whose official title was *Padre Maestro*, he was known to everyone as *il Padre Mostro*, or Father Monster, because of his immense girth – the origin, presumably, of Milton's 'glutton friar'. As a Florentine, he was proud of his famous compatriot and quite neutral on the arguments between the Ptolemaic and Copernican systems of astronomy, since the good friar had a childlike belief that the planets were directed in their course by angels. But he was well versed in the requirements of his office and immensely conscientious.

At first the censorship went well, but then Riccardi began to have doubts, and the longer he thought about it, the more profound were the doubts. The manuscript was revised, re-revised, and then revised once more. At last, Riccardi gave permission for Galileo to publish in Rome, provided he agreed to alter the beginning and end of the book in whatever way the censor required. Galileo agreed and returned to Florence to escape the heat of Rome, with a promise that he would be back in the autumn.

Once again, chance intervened. Galileo's prospective publisher and his strongest supporter in the Vatican, Prince Cesi, suddenly died; then a severe epidemic of plague broke out all across Italy, disrupting communications.* With the censors in Rome and the precious manuscript in Florence, Galileo organised a cabal of his friends to persuade Riccardi to allow printing to take place in Florence. Reluctantly, and under intense pressure, the harassed old friar agreed, on condition that he himself saw and approved the preface and conclusion, and that some responsible person in Florence revised the rest. More manoeuvring took place, as a result of which Galileo more or less nominated his own censor and joyously accepted Riccardi's revised preface and an insertion insisted on by

---

* The outbreak of plague that features in Manzoni's *I Promessi Sposi*.

the pope. Then he took care to ensure that these were printed on different paper and in a different typeface, so making quite clear which part of the work was Galileo's and which was the censors'.

In explaining the storm that subsequently broke over Galileo, in spite of having obtained an official *imprimatur*, Catholic historians put the blame on his own underhand manoeuvres and the way he browbeat poor conscientious Riccardi into letting his *imprimatur* appear on the book. But while Galileo may well have been unscrupulous, he was up against a dilemma known to writers down the centuries who face prior restraints on their work. Which represents the greater good: obeying the rules or outwitting the censor in order to publish what they conceive to be the truth? For there is no doubt that had he played strictly by the rules and not resorted to subterfuge, the *Dialogue* would have been suppressed, Galileo would never have been brought to trial and the issues it raised about man's place in the universe would have been set back, perhaps for generations.

As it was, the book was in print in the spring of 1632, to the jubilation of his friends and the praise of most of his early readers. The Vatican's response came more slowly, possibly because the book took some time to reach Rome owing to the plague. By May, only two copies had arrived, to be followed by eighty others in June. As soon as they got round to reading it, the Vatican authorities realised they had been outwitted. 'The Jesuits will persecute him most bitterly,' lamented Riccardi when he saw the form the book had taken. But before the Jesuits had time to make a move, the pope himself intervened. Galileo's old friend was beside himself with fury, believing Riccardi had been hoodwinked into permitting publication and persuaded that he had been personally caricatured in the person of Simplicio.

Publication of the *Dialogue* had come at an awkward time for Barberini. The religious wars then devastating Europe were going badly for the Vatican, the pope's diplomatic manoeuvres foundering in disaster. Cardinal Richelieu, the effective ruler of France, had succeeded in prizing apart the Austro-Spanish coalition under the Hapsburgs, but only with the help of King Gustavus Adolfus of Sweden, a Protestant. When they learned that Barberini had not only sided with Richelieu, but was also in alliance with a Protestant, Austria and Spain were predictably furious. Cardinal Gaspare Borgia, the Spanish Ambassador, denounced the pope for supporting the heretics, throwing in his face not only his own secret alliance with Richelieu and the Swedes, but the diabolical publications of Galileo Galilei.

The consistory meeting at which he spoke ended in tumult. Blows were exchanged. Attendants intervened. Borgia meanwhile distributed copies of a leaflet denouncing the pope for his easygoing attitude towards the enemies of religion at a time when it behoved them all to stand guard. From now on, he insisted on intransigence towards heretics and innovators and strict surveillance of orthodoxy in Rome itself. Threats were made to depose Barberini as a protector of heresy.

At this critical moment, Barberini lost his head. 'The pope lives in terror of poison,' wrote a diplomatic correspondent. 'He has gone up to Castel Gandolfo and shut himself in. No one is admitted without being searched. The ten miles of road are heavily patrolled. The garrisons and lookouts on the coast have been reinforced.' The Jesuits were meanwhile whispering in his ears that Galileo was in breach of a solemn undertaking given sixteen years earlier that he would neither hold nor teach the proposition that the earth moved around the sun: and for the first time they now produced the document that seemed to prove it.

Suffering from a deep sense of personal failure, the pope had to show the world he could impose his authority on the man who had betrayed him. 'Your Galileo has dared to meddle in things he should not,' he shouted at a meeting with the Tuscan ambassador. 'And with the most perilous questions which can be stirred up at this time.' The acrimonious meeting ended with the pope complaining, 'I have used him better than he has used me, for he deceived me'.

BEFORE THE INQUISITION

In Florence, Galileo was aware that trouble was brewing, but had no idea how serious it might be. He was, after all, a friend of the pope. His book had the sanction of authority, with no fewer than five separate *imprimatura* on his '*piazza*' of a title page. He had Cardinal Bellarmine's personal account of the promises he had made all those years ago during the reign of the previous pope. His book was everywhere acclaimed, even eulogised. Any trouble could surely be shrugged off, as it had been so many times before.

Galileo was therefore aghast when the Inquisition's representative in Florence turned up on his doorstep with an order to present himself in Rome within thirty days. The charges he was to face were, as always, unspecified, the sentence that might follow unspecified, too. As far as he knew, he might be tortured, put to the rack, imprisoned, burned at the stake, his life's work obliterated. Stricken with terror, the old man took to his bed.

The Tuscan ambassador at the Vatican tried to intercede, but the pope was adamant. Ill or not, Galileo must come to Rome. Galileo sent a medical certificate signed by three doctors: he was suffering from intermittent pulse, frequent attacks of giddiness, hypochondriacal melancholy, weakness of the stomach, a hernia and 'flying pains about the body'. The pope was unmoved. Evasions would not be tolerated. If there were any further delay, Galileo would be brought to Rome as a prisoner in irons. The case would go the full Inquisition.

When they broke the news to Galileo, he saw at last the truly desperate situation he was in. 'He fell into the deepest dejection and since yesterday has sunk so low that I am greatly concerned for his life,' his host reported. 'We are all trying to ease and comfort him, and to work for him through our connections, because truly he deserves everything good; and all this house of ours, which loves him extremely, is stricken with great sorrow.'

On the night of 11 April 1633, Galileo was removed to the custody of the Inquisition, and next morning summoned for his first examination by its commissary-general, Father Vicenzoi da Firenzuola. He was put on oath and asked if he had any idea why he had been summoned. He supposed it was because of the book he had written. This established, the interrogators moved immediately to the events of 1616, seventeen years previously. Why had he come to Rome that year? Of his own accord, he replied, in order to learn what opinion it was proper to hold in the matter of the Copernican hypothesis. And what instructions had he been given? Galileo carefully spelled out the terms of the contract he had signed all those years ago agreeing that he would neither hold nor defend the Copernican system, but was free to discuss it as a hypothesis. That was all he had ever done, from that day to this. On and on they went, but Galileo held his ground. Then suddenly the questions changed.

Did he get any permission to write the book? No, because he did not consider writing it was in any way contrary to the command not to hold or defend that opinion. When seeking permission to print the book, did he tell the *Padre Maestro* about its prohibition? No, because he had no doubts about it. The book neither maintained nor defended the opinion that the earth moves and the sun is stationary.

With that the first day's proceedings came to an end. Galileo signed the record with a shaking hand and returned to his place of custody to await his fate. Meanwhile, a record of the day's proceedings, together with a copy of the *Dialogue*, was sent for detailed examination by professional theological lawyers. Their report, when it came, utterly rejected Galileo's defence. By use of copious quotations the counsellors proved beyond doubt that the accused did, in fact, hold, defend and teach the mobility of the earth and the fixity of the sun and had sought to prove it by holding up to ridicule those who did not share it, for instance by calling them dumb mooncalves who hardly deserved the name of human beings. What is more, the defendant had written his book in Italian, 'not to extend the hand to foreigners or other learned men, but rather to entice to that view common people in whom errors very easily take root'.

By their own lights, the theologians had a cast-iron case. Galileo had clearly violated even the loosest interpretation of the injunction placed on him in 1616. Yet it is worth noting that they spent not a moment in discussing whether Galileo's ideas might be correct, and were not in the least concerned with the pursuit of truth, or the freedom to put forward an argument, even if it might turn out to be wrong; they were concerned solely with asserting the Church's authority. Galileo had broken a solemn and binding oath not to hold or defend a forbidden opinion. His right to hold that opinion was not an issue they spent any time over. In matters that touched on faith, it was for the Church to decide what was true and acceptable, not some troublesome individual unversed in the finer points of theology.

The more tolerant minds on the board of the Inquisition now reached out for compromise. The commissary-general met Galileo privately and asked him to admit his disobedience and plead for mercy, when in all probability he would be let off lightly; a binding vow of silence was the worst punishment the board had in mind, provided that he promised in future to conform. If, on the other hand, he continued his obstinate denial of his guilt – well, the commissary-general hinted, in that case, you will compel us to proceed further. In other words, he threatened Galileo with cross-examination under torture, the standard procedure for unrepentant heretics.

'After many arguments and rejoinders had passed between us, by God's grace I obtained my objective,' Firenzuola wrote to one of the inquisitors. 'He clearly recognised that he had erred and gone too far in the book, and to this he gave expression in words of much feeling, like one who had received great consolation in recognition of his error, and is willing to confess it judicially.' Firenzuola trusted the pope and the Inquisition would be satisfied that the matter could now be swiftly and amicably settled. In that way, 'the court will maintain its reputation; it will be possible to deal leniently with the culprit; and whatever the decision arrived at, he will recognise the favour shown to him'.

Two days later, Galileo was called before the Inquisition to make a personal statement of submission. He had spent some days in continuous and attentive reflection on his interrogation, he said, and as a result he had re-read his book with the utmost diligence. As he had not seen it for so long, it presented itself to him like a new writing by another author, and he could see that in several places it might contravene the injunction of the authorities: 'My error then has been – and I confess it – one of vainglorious ambition, and out of pure ignorance and inadvertence.'

Galileo was dismissed into the care of the Tuscan ambassador, and the stage set for one of the most shameful episodes in the entire history of free speech. A frightened old man was to return under threat of torture to renounce what he sincerely believed to be true and, in doing so, to disown a lifetime's work. He returned to the Tuscan embassy that night 'more dead than alive'. But here was no Socrates refusing to renounce his beliefs and prepared to lay down his life for them. Here was an intelligent man who had gambled and lost in an attempt to persuade others of a scientific truth that would remain true whether he renounced it or not. The idea that he was about to become a martyr to the principle of free speech did not occur to him.

On 10 May he appeared before the Inquisition for the third time. Once again he produced Cardinal Bellarmine's signed certificate, once again he declared his belief that it merely decreed that the doctrine of the motion of the earth and the stability of the sun must not be held or defended, but that it contained no mention of the requirement that he may not teach it in any way whatsoever. Such words struck him as quite novel, as if he had not heard them before; nor had he the need to give any particular thought to them, having in his possession so authentic a reminder in writing. He had come as close as he dare to accusing the Inquisition of basing the case against him on a forgery – in other words, the mysterious injunction suddenly produced by the Jesuits which had come as much as a surprise to the pope as it had to Galileo.

Still sure that he would be let off with a light reprimand, Galileo concluded with a humble plea for mercy. 'It remains for me to beg you to take into consideration my pitiable state of bodily indisposition, to which at the age of seventy years, I have been reduced by ten months of constant mental anxiety and the fatigue of a long and toilsome journey at the most inclement season.' He bowed to his judges and left the court believing the worst was now over. He had fulfilled the terms of his deal with Commissary Firenzuola.

In Tuscany, his friends and family confidently expected his early return home. Maria Celeste, who had earlier had all his papers removed from the house for fear of a raid by the Inquisition, was now certain he would soon be with her again. 'My beloved lord and father,' she wrote. 'Your letters have come like *zoccolanti* [the wooden clogs worn by friars] not only in a pair, but like them with much noise, giving me more than ordinary pleasure. As to your return, God knows how much I desire it.' But she pleaded with him to stay a while with the Archbishop of Siena and recover his health before returning to 'this your dear hovel, which truly laments your long absence'. She tells him of the barrel of wine that has been spoilt and of the potted oranges that had been damaged in a storm, so they had transplanted them in the earth until he was there to tell them what should be done. His little mule had become so haughty it would not be ridden by anyone else and had bucked their poor servant Geppo, while she had brought six bushels of wheat ready to bake bread for him when he came home.

In Rome, the Tuscan ambassador had been told the matter would be over within ten days and that Galileo would then be allowed to go. But weeks passed by in silence and nothing happened. In the higher reaches of the Vatican, another crisis had arisen. The papers had gone to the pope for a final decision, and when he read them, Barberini concluded leniency was out of the question. Galileo had disobeyed direct orders. The understanding with Commissary Firenzuola was consequently over-ruled. The prisoner was to be interrogated as to his intention, threatened with torture and then forced to recant. After that there would be a formal sentence in full penitential dress for his heresy *de vehementi* accompanied by rigorous examination, public abjuration and imprisonment.

The following week, Galileo appeared before the Inquisition for the fourth and last time. 'I held, and still hold, as most true and indisputable, Ptolemy's opinion, namely, the stability of the earth and the motion of the sun,' Galileo pronounced. The board rejected this desperate act of perjury. The very fact that he wrote his book was evidence of his real opinions. Would he therefore freely tell the truth? If not, he would be tortured. 'I do not hold this opinion of Copernicus, and I have not held it after being ordered by injunction to abandon it,' Galileo replied dully. 'For the rest, I am here in your hands. Do with me what you will. I am here to obey and I have not held this opinion since the decision was pronounced, as I have stated.'

The well-known final act of the tragedy took place next morning in the Temple of Minerva, the goddess of wisdom, now converted into a Dominican convent. Barefoot, bareheaded and clad in the white shirt of penitence, the broken old man was forced to kneel in the shadow of a gigantic crucifix as the sentence was read out in the presence of the cardinals and other high officials. He was to abjure the Copernican system, the *Dialogue* was to be prohibited by public edict, its author was committed to formal prison and was to repeat the seven penitential psalms daily for the next three years. The sentence was held by the Church to be remarkably lenient.

The hearing then ended with Galileo's personal denial of all he believed in, a statement written for him by someone else:

I, Galileo Galilei, son of the late Vicenzo Galileo, Florentine, aged seventy years, arraigned personally before this tribunal and kneeling before you, swear that I have always believed, do now believe, and by God's help will always believe all that is held, preached and taught by the Holy Catholic and

Apostolic Church . . . Therefore, desiring to remove from the minds of your Eminences and of all faithful Christians, this strong suspicion reasonably conceived against me, with sincere heart and unfeigned faith, I abjure, curse and detest the aforesaid errors and heresies, and I swear that in future I will never again say or assert anything that might furnish occasion for a similar suspicion regarding me. So help me God, and these his holy gospels, which I hold in my hands.

His humiliation complete, the old man stumbled to his feet. As he did so, there is a story that he muttered *'Eppur si muove'* – it does so move – but the words are almost certainly apocryphal; the earliest mention of them coming only in the eighteenth century. Like so many of the stories surrounding Galileo, it is based on subsequent myth, representing what opponents of the Church think he ought to have said.

The whole miserable business was now drawing to an end. He spent twelve days at the house of the Tuscan ambassador, very downcast at his public degradation, and was then released for a further six months into the custody of the Archbishop of Siena, where Maria Celeste wrote to him offering to take upon herself the daily recitation of the seven penitential psalms in order to spare him the trouble. 'Had I been able to substitute myself in the rest of your punishment,' she said, 'most willingly would I elect a prison even straiter than this one in which I dwell if by so doing I could set you at liberty.' But that could never be. Her convent's rules of enclosure meant that she was forbidden to leave its grounds, and could speak to her visitors only through a grille. Galileo returned to his 'dear hovel' in December, condemned to spend the remaining eight years of his life under perpetual house arrest next door to his equally confined daughter.

Even there, misfortunes continued to fall upon him. Less than six months after he had moved back to Acretri the steadfast Maria Celeste, worn out by anxiety for him, contracted dysentery and died, a few days past her thirty-third birthday. Galileo was enveloped by 'an immense sadness and melancholy, complete lack of appetite and disgust with my existence.' His dearest daughter was dead; his sister-in-law and her three children had died of the plague, he himself, forlorn and alone, was going blind, and forbidden to teach or even receive casual visitors. To one old friend he wrote, 'Woe is me, *signor mio*, your dear friend and servant Galileo has become totally and irreparably blind; so that this heaven, this earth, this universe, which I by marvellous discoveries and clear demonstrations have enlarged a hundred thousand times beyond the belief of the wise men of bygone ages, henceforward for me is shrunk in such small space as is filled by my own bodily sensations.'

In spite of his manifold sorrows, the amazing old man kept on working. Forbidden any longer to discuss astronomy, he had turned his attention to the science of dynamics, producing before he went blind what is sometimes regarded as his finest work, which laid the foundations of modern physics and which his friends had to smuggle out of Italy to get it published in Leyden.

In 1638, the poet, John Milton – himself destined to go blind – wrote after a visit to Florence:

There it was that I found and visited the famous Galileo, grown old, a prisoner of the Inquisition for thinking in astronomy otherwise than the Franciscan and Dominican licensers thought. I could recount what I have seen and heard in other countries, where this kind of inquisition tyrannises, when I have sat among their learned men (for that honour I had) and been counted happy to be born in such a place of philosophic freedom as they supposed England was, while they themselves did nothing but bemoan the servile condition into which learning among them was brought – that this was it which damped the glory of Italian wits, that nothing had been there written now these many years but flattery and fustian.

Three years later, his course now run, Galileo took to his bed and died in the early hours of 8 January 1642, having received the last sacraments of the Church to which he remained ever faithful. He had asked to be buried with Maria Celeste in the family vault in the Church of Santa Croce in Florence, where the city fathers planned to honour his memory with a public funeral and a marble mausoleum. But the pope's unabating vendetta pursued him even to his grave. Barberini himself vetoed the marble mausoleum and the Inquisition forbade a public funeral. Not until 1737 were the great man's bones laid to rest in the cathedral alongside his compatriots Michelangelo and Machiavelli. And a further 100 years had to go by before the Church could bring itself to remove his works from the Index of Forbidden Books.

By then, the glittering Italian Renaissance which had flourished through the tolerance of the free expression of ideas was long since over, the intellectual freedom on which it depended lost at the hands of the Holy Office. But Galileo's contribution to the emancipation of the human mind has lived on, though it would be other lands and other cultures that built on his stubborn and sometimes belligerent insistence that material facts and the laws of science were to be established by independent enquiry, unfettered by the power of any outside authority to overrule them. Like Socrates before him, he showed that mere authority cannot suppress the search for truth. The lead he gave set scientific enquiry on a course it has followed for three and a half centuries, and engendered a passion for truth that gave the eighteenth-century Enlightenment its motto, *Sapere aude* – 'Dare to know.'

PART THREE

Areopagitica *and After*

The liberty of the press is the birthright of a
Briton, and is justly esteemed the firmest
bulwark of the liberties of this country.

John Wilkes, 1762

CHAPTER FIVE

Towards a Free Press

One hot day in the spring of 1638, the same year that Milton paid his visit to the
aged prisoner of the Inquisition in Florence, a young man in London was tied to
the tail of a cart and 'smartly whipp't' all the way from the Fleet Prison to New
Palace Yard, where he was to be put in the pillory. The young man's name was
John Lilburne. His crime was to have distributed copies of an unlicensed
pamphlet criticising the unpopular government of Charles I. The struggle for
free speech was beginning to engage the common people.

John Lilburne, by his own account a 'rough hewn' north-countryman who had
come to London at fourteen to seek his fortune, had some months earlier been
seized in the street by five or six ruffians hired by the Stationers' Company to
stamp out illicit printing and brought before the court on suspicion of importing
'factious and scandalous' books from Holland. Repeatedly asked by the
examining magistrate why he had gone to Holland and who he had met there,
Lilburne replied: 'Why do you ask me all these questions? I am not imprisoned
for knowing and talking with such and such men. I think by the law of the land
that I may not answer your interrogatory.'

The young man destined to become the seventeenth century's most famous
champion of individual liberty was asserting two important principles, one new
and one old. The new one was the liberty of free expression, an idea which was
just beginning to find its voice; the older principle was the right of an
Englishman brought before the courts to know of what he is accused, and by
whom. In Lilburne's view, the means used to control access to the printing press
met neither of those criteria.

The examining clerk read out the anonymous accusation: Lilburne had printed 10 or 12,000 unauthorised books in Holland, he had rented a room in Delft where they were stored, he had made £80 out of the enterprise.

All lies, said Lilburne.

'You received money of Mr Wharton since you came to town, did you not?'

'What if I did?'

'It was for books?'

'I do not say so.'

'For what sort of books was it?'

'I do not say it was for any.'

'We have power to send you back to the place from whence you came,' threatened the exasperated clerk.

'You may do your pleasure,' replied Lilburne. He did not refuse to answer out of any contempt; he was just ignorant of what properly belonged to an examination on such a charge. 'I have answered punctually to the thing for which I am imprisoned, and more I am not bound to answer,' he said. 'As for my liberty, I must wait God's time.'

Realising he had a more recalcitrant prisoner on his hands than he could manage, the magistrate sent Lilburne up for examination by the attorney general, as the spread of scandalous pamphlets was becoming a matter of concern to the State. But the attorney general made no better headway than the magistrate had done. Rather than answer questions, the prisoner offered to write and sign his own statement, though he had got no further than 'the answer of me, John Lilburne, is . . .' when the pen was snatched from his hand and he was dismissed, his case referred to the Star Chamber, the prerogative court which dealt with all serious infringements of the printing laws.

An institution almost as much feared in England as the Inquisition was in the Catholic countries on the Continent, the Star Chamber no longer had the power to impose a death sentence, but it could and often did sentence offenders to mutilation. Only a few weeks earlier it had sentenced the Puritan divine who wrote Lilburne's pamphlets to have his ears cropped off at the pillory. Lilburne was now to appear before them for unlawfully publishing seditious books and knew he faced a similar sentence.

But their new prisoner was no more afraid of the Star Chamber than he had been of the attorney general, even though it was presided over by the archbishop of Canterbury in person. With the whole company of clerks beginning to 'look and gaze', Lilburne was called forward to take the oath, told to take off his glove and put his hand on the proffered Bible.

'What to do, sir?'

'You must swear.'

'To what?'

'That you shall make true answer to all things that is asked you.'

'Must I so, sir? But before I swear, I must know to what I must swear.'

'As soon as you have sworn, you shall.'

'Sir, I am but a young man and do not well know what belongs to the nature of an oath, and therefore before I swear, I must be better advised.'

With his usual exasperating mixture of innocence and guile, Lilburne was getting round to the point that the oath he was being asked to swear would give the court the power to question him about any matter they chose, whether he was accused of it or not. It was therefore illegal.

'I dare not take this oath,' he said. It was not in accordance with the Common Law of England, which allowed no man to accuse himself. If he did take an oath, it should be before a magistrate. If he was to be tried, he must be told of what he was accused and his accusers brought to face him in court. If asked to accuse himself, he would give them the reply of Jesus Christ to his accusers, 'Why ask ye me? Go to them that heard me.' If more recent history were needed to support his case, the Parliament's Petition of Right laid down that none should be tried or imprisoned except by the laws and statutes of the realm. He was a free-born Englishman, entitled to claim the protection of the laws of the land. 'Upon these grounds,' he declared breathlessly, 'I did, and do, refuse the oath.'

At this point, Archbishop Laud lost patience with his obstinate prisoner. 'Pull off his glove,' he told one of the clerks, 'and lay his hand upon the book.'

'Most honourable and noble lords,' Lilburne replied. 'With all reverence and submission unto your honours . . . yet must I refuse the oath.'

'My lords, do you hear him?' Laud exclaimed. 'With all reverence and submission he refuseth the oath! This fellow has been one of the notoriousest dispensers of libellous books in the kingdom.'

'Submit yourself unto the court,' the lord keeper demanded.

The prisoner responded with his usual mock humility: 'Most noble lords, with all willingness I submit my body unto your honours' pleasure.'

With that, the insolent youth was sentenced to be 'smartly whipp't from the Fleet to Westminster', a distance of more than 2 miles.

But they were not done with Lilburne yet. When the day of his sentence dawned, the streets of London were crowded with onlookers, some come to hoot and jeer at a common criminal being whipped to the pillory, but most to offer support and sympathy to a man they had already nicknamed 'Free Born John' for his courage in standing up for himself before the Star Chamber. The people of England were growing increasingly restless under the arbitrary rule of the king, who for the past nine years had governed them without a Parliament. The country was on the brink of a momentous divide, and John Lilburne's punishment played its part in focussing their discontent. In the words of a leading historian of the age, the government's attempts to silence its critics merely added 'fresh zest to the banquet of libel and invective'. The people's appetite for unlicensed literature had grown too strong to be baulked.

Hence the sympathetic crowds that lined the streets as Lilburne was led behind the cart towards the pillory, stripped to the waist, his hands bound to the cart's tailgate, the warder striking him with a three-thonged knotted whip every three or four paces as John cried out, 'Hallelujah, Hallelujah, Glory, Honour and Praise be given to thee O Lord, for ever!'

His progress became more of a triumphal procession than a punishment as people ran alongside him offering words of comfort and exhortation. At the pillory, they locked him in, his painful weals undressed, his beaten shoulders swelled 'almost as big as penny loaves', left to stand hatless in the hot sun with his head through the hole in the pillory, his back stooped because it was too low for him, the very figure, one would suppose, of ignominy and shame.

But John Lilburne was a genius at propaganda. Bowing sardonically in the direction of the Star Chamber he told the crowd the whole story of his arrest and his reasons for refusing to take the *ex officio* oath. It is true, he said, that he was a young man and no scholar, yet a divine providence had brought him thither that day. 'I speak not words that are rash and unconsidered,' he said, 'but words of soberness and mature deliberation.' He stood before them as a soldier fighting under the banner of a great and mighty captain. Therefore, 'I dare not hold my peace, but speak unto you with boldness in the might and strength of my God, come life, come death'.

When he was hereabouts in his speech, he relates, 'there came a fat lawyer and commanded me to hold my peace and leave off preaching.'

'Sir,' John replied, 'I will not hold my peace, but speak my mind freely though I be hanged at Tyburn for my pains.'

His words achieved the effect he probably sought. He was gagged so tightly that the blood spurted from his mouth. As the crowd gaped and cheered, he somehow conjured copies of the forbidden pamphlets from his pockets and scattered them around the Yard. And when he could speak no more, he stamped his feet until the punishment was ended. His cheerful courage and resourcefulness at the pillory had made him an instant hero. Great crowds escorted him back to prison, where his wounds were dressed by a surgeon, who reported that the weals on his back were 'the miserablest that ever I did see'.

Though still feverish and exhausted, he was the next day removed to the common jail and put in irons as a punishment for his behaviour on the pillory. Lying in this 'tormenting condition, full of extremity and bodily pain', hungry, ill and in fear of being murdered, he nevertheless managed to write or dictate a full account of his sufferings, which was smuggled out of jail and printed on one of the secret presses now springing up all over London and sold openly on the streets under the title *A Work of the Beast*. England's printing laws were collapsing around the government's ears. An intense struggle to establish the freedom of the press was now inevitable.

A number of factors had combined to bring the issue to a head. The first and most obvious was that the press in recent years had grown so cheap and prolific it was no longer possible to control it. Dissenting minorities distributed their own books and pamphlets, and in doing so spawned new ideas, new images and new slogans with which others might also contend for the freedom of thought, of expression and of the press itself. Historians believe that out of this ferment the modern doctrine of liberty emerged – not yet accepted by all, or even by the majority, and still to be bitterly fought over, but a coherent intellectual concept nonetheless, and one with immense significance for the future.

To add to this ferment of ideas, the government of Charles I was losing its grip on events. At the time Lilburne was brought before the Star Chamber, John Hampden was arguing with the judges in the Exchequer in the notorious dispute over ship-money, an arbitrary tax imposed without the consent of Parliament, which did as much as anything to alienate the king's English subjects. At odds with his people in all three of his kingdoms, Charles and his ministers were set on a course that would bring a civil war in which the printing press and its effect on public opinion would find a new and important role and the liberty of expression would become one of the issues most hotly fought over.

THE COMING OF THE CORANTO

The laws under which the English press was at that time controlled went back to the reign of Queen Elizabeth. A Star Chamber decree of 1586 had restricted the number of master printers authorised to operate in London to twenty-four, with strict limits on the number of presses they could own and the journeymen and apprentices they could employ. All books were required to be licensed either by the archbishop of Canterbury or the bishop of London (though in practice this task was delegated to professional deputies). The Star Chamber was the body ultimately responsible for punishing any breaches of censorship by outsiders, but in a masterstroke of Tudor policy-making the printers were given the day-to-day task of policing themselves. The Company of Stationers, to which every master printer belonged, was empowered to deface the type and smash the presses of any illicit printers they found and to search them out 'whenever it shall please them in any place, shop, house, chamber or building'. As they also maintained strict control over entry to their own craft, London's master printers had become a self-perpetuating, conformist monopoly, willing accomplices to censorship, the government's main instrument of control.

However, without the spur of competition, the stationers grew greedy and began to employ only half-trained staff. Workmanship became shoddy, mistakes more frequent. A 1631 edition of the Bible became an instant collector's piece when it erroneously printed the seventh commandment to read, 'Thou shalt commit adultery'. Archbishop Laud was so incensed that he lodged a formal complaint. 'I knew the time when great care was had about printing,' he said. 'Good compositors and the best correctors were gotten . . . the paper and letter rare and fair, every way of the best. But now the paper is naught, the compositors boys, and the correctors unlearned.' The Stationers simply farmed out their work to others. 'Heretofore, they spent their whole time in printing, but these look to gain, gain, gain.'

Naturally enough, those excluded from this cosy monopoly also began to protest. As early as 1614, the journeymen printers had presented a petition complaining that the master printers were growing rich and fat while the journeymen were without means to make a living. The Stationers were high handed in the use of their right to break and enter journeymen's homes looking for illegal presses; the Star Chamber decrees were 'contrary to the laws of God and nature.'

The Stationers held down the lid on this seething cauldron for as long as they were able. Illegal presses were constantly being defaced and made unserviceable in the presence of the Stationers' warders and their assistants. Searches and seizures became regular occurrences. Yet for every press that was smashed, another would spring up elsewhere, while control of imports from abroad was never more than a pious hope.

At first it was the religious pamphlets and polemics that caused the greatest concern, but as Charles I's reign progressed a new type of publication began to seep into England alongside the dissenting tracts and sermons. These were the newsbooks, then known as corantos, the forerunner of the modern newspaper. While the corantos found a large and eager readership among a people avid for news of the wars of religion then raging on the Continent of Europe, they carried not one word of English news. This was partly due to prudence, partly to the fact that they were usually printed in Holland and translated verbatim from the Dutch.

Nonetheless, they met a demand, and it was not long before presses in London were printing their own corantos, though still 'honestly translated from the Dutch'. They came out about twice a week, but still without English news, and being ephemeral, did not need to be licensed. They were the work of two entrepreneurs, Nathaniel Butter and Nicholas Bourne, who thus became England's first newspapermen, a calling that then as now their countrymen held in low regard. Ben Jonson dubbed them 'newsmongers' and Donald Lupton, a character-writer of the day, scoffed that they had used the trade so long everyone could now say it's as true as a coranto – meaning it's all false. He went on to express sentiments newspapermen have had to contend with ever since:

> Ordinarily they have as many lies as lines. They are new and old in five days. They are busy fellows, for they meddle with other men's affairs. No pope, emperor, or king but must be touched by their pen . . . If they write good news of our side, it is seldom true; but if it's bad, it is almost too true. I wish them to write either not at all, or less, or more true; the best news is when we hear no news.

In spite of the disdain, news had become a marketable, though soon to be forbidden, commodity, and with the arrival of the corantos that were smuggled ashore in the 1620s and 1630s the beginnings of a free press can be dimly discerned, the rudimentary outline of the craft of journalism and the first skirmishes in the struggle to establish the right to publish news.

The government was unable to stop the demand for news, of course. But it did what it could to stem the supply. As early as 1629, the warden of the Stationers Company was informed of the king's express wish that 'hereafter none do presume to print or publish any matter of news, relations, histories, or any other thing in prose or in verse that hath reference to matters and affairs of State' without a specific licence. When that decree didn't work, he issued another one prohibiting all 'seditious, schismatical or offensive books', plugging the loopholes in the censorship. The number of licensed printers was reduced to twenty, each of them placed under a bond of £300, which would be forfeit if they printed anything unlicensed. The pillory and the whip were prescribed for those who printed without authority, and carpenters were required to report any press they were asked to build. Licences were required for ephemeral material such as ballads and newsbooks. The name and *imprimatur* of the licenser had to be carried on all publications and reprints had to be separately licensed. The import of books in English was prohibited, with instructions to the port inspectors to take particular care to search all 'dry vats, bales, maunds, or other fardels'. Finally, an attempt was made to control the flow of news by granting the exclusive right to print corantos to Butter and Bourne. For the privilege of printing and publishing 'all matters of history of news of any foreign place or kingdom' they contracted to pay £10 a year towards the repair of St Paul's and were subject to the strictest censorship. But English news was still off limits.

The king's decree was draconian only on paper. In practice, it failed like all its predecessors. That is not to say there was no control. The threat of punishment was always present, as John Lilburne's trip to the pillory testified. Awareness of the decree led more cautious souls than Lilburne to abandon their projects and others to submit them to official scrutiny. Lord Herbert, for instance, was told that his account of the recent war with France 'cannot but reflect upon the honour of King and State and ought not to be published'. Private papers, too, were regularly subject to search and scrutiny, and sometimes impounded. But those determined and courageous enough could always make themselves heard. The most recent historian of Charles's personal rule concluded that England was not a country in which all criticism and dissent were stifled. But nor was it a realm in which men were free to publish or read what they saw fit. Royal control only collapsed altogether when Charles was forced to recall Parliament at the end of 1640, at which point the crown itself was foundering.

Charles had convened Parliament in order to raise an English army to fend off an invasion from Scotland, but from the moment of its recall, Parliament seized the initiative. Before it would vote a penny to the king, it demanded redress of grievances stored up over twelve years of personal rule. With England on the brink of a civil war and power about to pass from king to Parliament, a number of consequences would flow of great importance to free speech and the liberty of the press.

The first and perhaps most significant of these is that the principle of free speech was secured in Parliament itself. Ever since the beginning of the century, the Commons had been trying to assert that every member 'hath and of right ought to have the freedom of speech', but when they presented their demands in a Petition of Right, James I ordered the offending resolution to be ripped from the pages of the Commons Journal. Any privileges the House enjoyed, he said, were 'derived from the grace and permission of our ancestors and us'.

The concession finally won from his successor was still a strictly limited freedom, confined to the few hundred members of the Commons, who were to remain liable to prosecution for seditious words spoken in Parliament for another fifty years. During the later Commonwealth and Protectorate, Parliament also became little more than a cipher, rent by schism and notoriously intolerant of views they did not share. Nevertheless, the liberty established in 1641 for an elected assembly to speak and vote without royal restraint ensured that when Parliament re-asserted its authority after the restoration, England would be able to boast with the ancient Greeks that theirs was a forum where 'free born men, having to advise the public, may speak free'.

There was general rejoicing, too, when Parliament abolished the hated Star Chamber. In its earlier days, the Star Chamber had been a respected and valued prerogative court frequently used by private plaintiffs to obtain rights denied them elsewhere. But the Stuarts had also used it to punish political crimes, such as a too free expression of opinion. Great offence had been given by the corporal punishment meted out to John Lilburne, and to the three leading Puritans who a few months earlier had had their ears hacked off at the pillory. Respectable folk were scandalised that a punishment usually reserved for riff-raff and vagrants should be meted out to learned professional men – a doctor, a lawyer and a clergyman. The result was that the Star Chamber was widely perceived to be an instrument of royal tyranny. In 1639, Sir Henry Wotton closed a letter to his nephew with the words, 'my lodging is so near to the Star Chamber that my pen shakes in my hand'. And the Venetian ambassador remarked that the spectacle of the three Puritan martyrs standing in the pillory was 'a pest which may be the one which will ultimately disturb the repose of this kingdom'. Only three years later, his prophetic words came true.

Once the prop of the Star Chamber had gone, the whole edifice of Stuart censorship collapsed. With war imminent and Parliament's attention diverted to issues elsewhere, there was a period in which the press, though often harassed, was comparatively free. The immediate result was a burgeoning of corantos devoted to news of the impending civil war.

Butter and Bourne were driven out of business as a succession of competing mercuries poured from the London presses – *The Diurnal, The True Diurnal, The Perfect Diurnal* – confusing titles at first, largely devoted to Parliamentary proceedings, but later augmented by news-sheets which carried weekly reports of the war – *The Kingdom's Weekly Intelligencer, Mercurius Civicus, Mercurius Britannicus* and a score of others. Parliament passed an ordinance to regulate the press in 1643, but its attempts were half-hearted, and effective control was not re-imposed until the end of the decade, after the war. As a result, by 1645, the year of the decisive Battle of Naseby, London saw the publication of 722 editions of the various newsbooks, an average of fourteen separate weekly titles. Most supported the Parliament, but among them were a scattering of royalist pamphlets, often smuggled in from the king's headquarters in Oxford by travelling pedlars, notable among them *Mercurius Aulicus*, a witty and well written compendium which was to be a thorn in Parliament's side throughout the war. From this brief taste of freedom a coherent theory of liberty was to emerge.

MILTON'S *AREOPAGITICA*

Through all the hubbub of civil war and revolution, more contemplative minds than Lilburne's had applied themselves to the question of liberty. The best known to posterity is the poet and Puritan revolutionary, John Milton, who became the seventeenth century's most eloquent advocate of the right to the liberty of unlicensed printing as well as the author of its most sublime heroic poem, *Paradise Lost.*

From his earliest manhood, Milton had trained himself to become a great writer. After the usual seven years spent at Cambridge – where he was known as 'the Lady of Christ's' – he rejected the idea of becoming a preacher, having conceived a vocation as a poet, then regarded as the highest and noblest of the literary arts. If he was to leave something 'so written to aftertimes that they would not willingly let it die', he must embark on a life of 'labour and intense study'. On coming down from Cambridge in 1632, he settled in his father's house in the country where he spent the next six years preparing himself for his great task with single-minded devotion. He mastered the laws of poetry and read industriously in the classics, scripture and history. His lofty aim was to compose heroic poetry in the English language worthy to compare with Homer and Virgil.

With this ambition always in his mind, he undertook his pilgrimage to Italy in 1638, staying there for fifteen months, a time of 'bliss without alloy'. He took part in discussions at the literary academies, wrote verses in Italian, inspected the literary treasures of the Vatican, visited the ruins of Rome, was shown around Naples by Tasso's friend and patron, the Marquis de Villa, and paid a visit to the aged Galileo in Florence, where he was shocked by the intellectual ravages of the counter-Reformation.

He was about to embark for Greece, whose history, literature and philosophy had been by far the most potent influence in shaping his thought, when news arrived that England's pent-up grievances against the king were about to burst out in civil commotion. He returned home at once and by the time the Long Parliament was called in 1640, he had settled in a house in London 'feeling more English and more Protestant than ever'. He rarely left London again.

The question of Church government was then at the forefront of debate, and Milton found himself inexorably drawn into the pamphlet war that was raging. It was a task he hated. He had spent years in seclusion preparing himself to be a poet, but now 'sad conscience clear' had left him with no alternative but to put aside his life's vocation and enter into the dust and turmoil of controversy. It was not that he felt the task he had set himself was petty or ignoble, it was that he despised his antagonists. Accustomed to arguments that led to better understanding and greater enlightenment, he found himself up against bigots like William Prynne, who based all his arguments on the citation of authorities and custom and clubbing quotations with men whose learning and belief lay in 'marginal stuffings'.

He endured because 'as I had from my youth studied the distinction between religious and civil rights, I perceived that if I ever wished to be of use, I ought at least not to be wanting to my country, to the Church, and to so many of my fellow Christians, in a crisis of so much danger'. He joined the fray convinced that the issues were not less than those for which men had contended in the previous great crises of human history.

He came to his theme of free speech almost by accident, the result of his troubled domestic life. In 1642, at the age of thirty-four, Milton was feeling the need for a wife, and seemingly under pressure from his family, married the daughter of an Oxfordshire squire. The marriage lasted but a few weeks, the young wife leaving her husband to return to her own people, who soon afterwards declared for the king. Reconciliation was out of the question, the marriage barely consummated, and Milton left lonely and abandoned in London. The outcome was his series of tracts in favour of divorce, an argument based on deep rational thought – and doubtless even deeper feelings – but one that his contemporaries found profoundly shocking. In an age when marriage at all levels of society was universal and lifelong, a tract that advocated divorce was regarded as the work of the most profligate libertine. The first of the divorce tracts was published in the summer of 1643 without a licence, and was followed in the next six months by two more, one of them carrying Milton's initials, J.M. It was as though he was courting prosecution. Prynne thundered from the pulpit, angry speeches were made in a Parliamentary committee, and the Stationers Company moved in to exculpate themselves. They cited the author before the Committee on Printing, but in the middle of the war they had more pressing business to pursue and Milton was never prosecuted. His tracts were, however, condemned, and Parliament issued an ordinance that laid down that in future no book, pamphlet or paper should be published without the prior approval of an official licenser.

It was this order which led Milton to write his great tract on the liberty of unlicensed printing, the *Areopagitica*, printed in November 1644, again without a licence. Constructed according to the rules of classical rhetoric, the *Areopagitica* stands today as the most perfect literary expression of the ideal of freedom produced during the Puritan revolution. As his model, Milton turned to Isocrates, in whose rhetoric he had been steeped since his early manhood. In his own work he cast aside the style of 'ragged notions and babblements' that he so hated – they were like being compelled to write with his left hand, he said. The appeal of the *Areopagitica* was to be timeless.

It is built around a vision of England which would be extraordinary at any time for its optimism, its self-confidence and its boundless faith in the destiny of his country and his countrymen, and which is doubly extraordinary for springing from the chaos and turmoil of a people at war. The struggle had clearly set Milton's imagination afire as he drew the picture of 'a nation not slow and dull, but of a quick, ingenious and piercing spirit, acute to invent, subtle and sinewy to discourse, not beneath the reach of any point the highest that human capacity can soar to' – 'a knowing people, a nation of prophets, of sages, of worthies' – a people taken up even in the midst of war 'with the study of the highest and most important matters to be reformed'. Here was London, 'this vast city, a city of refuge, the mansion house of liberty', full of anvils and hammers beating out the instruments of war, with battle oft rumoured to be marching up to her walls and suburb trenches, but not less full of pens and heads 'sitting by their studious lamps, musing, searching, revolving new notions and ideas wherewith to present, as with their homage and their fealty, the approaching Reformation'.

What could a man require more from a nation so prone to seek after knowledge? Why else was this nation chosen above all others to sound forth the first tidings and trumpet of Reformation to all Europe? Now the opportunity for her to lead the way was occurring again. 'God is decreeing to bring some new and great period in his Church, even to reforming Reformation itself; what does he then but reveal himself to his servants, and as his manner is, first to his English-men.'

This belief in the moral superiority of his own countryman makes it sound as though Milton believed the abolition of the English licensing laws was a central part of God's plan for the redemption of mankind. But Milton was giving voice to a sentiment widespread among English Protestants of his day. Having led the way into the Reformation they believed they had a divine mission to set an example to the rest of the world – an attitude of lofty condescension which bears an interesting resemblance to the claim of modern Americans that they are the 'last, best hope of mankind', and the guardians of its democratic ideals. Perhaps the resemblance is not so surprising when we consider that the Americans who hold such views are the direct spiritual descendants of the English Puritans of Milton's day. A sense of moral superiority seems to go with the race.

Milton found his title in the Areopagus, the hill to the west of the Acropolis where the Athenian council used to gather to give their advice to the *polis* and where St Paul preached his famous sermon. Milton uses it as the citadel of free speech, and after quoting the lines of Euripides that 'this is true liberty where free born men, having to advise the people, may speak free' starts the *Areopagitica* with a homily on the virtues of reading. Books, he says, are as active as the soul whose progeny they are. True, they may be as dangerous as the fabled dragon's teeth, which being sown up and down, may spring up armed men. Yet on the other hand it is almost as good to kill a man as kill a good book, since 'who kills a man kills a reasonable creature, God's image; but he who kills a good book, kills reason itself, kills the image of God, as it were in the eye'. While no age can restore a life, the revolutions of ages do not often recover the loss of a rejected truth, for the want of which whole nations fare the worse.

How much better, he says, to imitate the old and elegant humanities of Greece, to whom we owe that we are not still Goths and Jutlanders like our barbaric ancestors, and where the only writings the magistrate took notice of were libels and blasphemies. He surveyed the censorship in Rome, where books met with no interdict until the conversion to Christianity in the fourth century. Until then the issue of the brain was no more stifled than the issue of the womb; 'but if it proves a monster, who denies but that it was justly burnt or sunk in the sea'. The erudite review goes on for five or six more close-set pages dealing with the Bible and the classical authorities. It was the papist Roman Church, he says, who first started raking through the entrails of good old authors and who had created a new department in purgatory reserved for books. They behaved as if St Peter had bequeathed them the keys of the press out of paradise, ordaining that no book, paper or pamphlet should be published unless it were approved and licensed under the hand of two or three glutton friars. The government of Charles I had tried to copy their repressive ways, but Laud's efforts to control the flow of ideas through the licensing laws had been as futile as trying to pound up the crows by shutting the park gates. No nation or well-instituted state, if they ever valued books at all, had used a system of licensing. If their orders to control them were not to be 'vain and frustrate' the English Parliament would be bound to go down the same road as Trent and Seville – 'which I know you abhor to do'. Even if they did consent to this, the order would still be fruitless and defective. The truth would spread, just as the Christian faith had spread before any gospels or epistles had been written down.

And what quality of man would they recruit as licenser? 'If he be of such worth as behoves him, there cannot be a more tedious and unpleasing journeywork, a greater loss of time levied upon his head, than to be made the perpetual reader of unchosen books and pamphlets, oft-times huge volumes.' Such a task would be an imposition 'which I cannot believe but that he who values time and his own studies, or is but of a sensible nostril, should be able to endure'.

Those who now did the job wished themselves well rid of it, and 'no man of worth, none that is not a plain unthrift of his own hours is ever likely to succeed them. We may easily foresee what kind of licensers we are likely to expect hereafter, either ignorant, imperious, and remiss, or basely pecuniary'.

From that, he soars towards his majestic climax.

Methinks I see in my mind, a noble and puissant nation, rousing herself like a strong man after sleep, and shaking her invincible locks; methinks I see her as an eagle, mewing her mighty youth, and kindling her undazzled eyes at the full mid-day beam; purging and unscaling her long abused sight at the fountain itself of heavenly radiance; while the whole noise of timorous and flocking birds that love the twilight, flutter about, amazed at what she means, and in whose envious gabble would prognosticate a year of sects and schisms.

What should you do then, should you suppress all this flowery crop of knowledge and new light? Should ye set an oligarchy of twenty engrossers over it to bring a famine upon our minds again, when we shall know nothing but what is measured to us by their bushel? Believe it, Lords and Commons, they who counsel you to such a suppressing, do as good bid ye suppress yourselves . . .

He ends with his famous paeon to the strength of truth.

And though all the winds of doctrine were let loose to play upon the earth, so truth be in the field, we do injuriously by licensing and prohibiting to misdoubt her strength. Let her and falsehood grapple; who ever knew truth put to the worse in a free and open encounter? . . . Truth is strong next to the Almighty; she needs no policies, no stratagems nor licensings to make her victorious; those are the shifts and defences that error uses against her power. Give her but room, and do not bind her when she sleeps. If it comes to prohibiting, there is not aught more likely to be prohibited than truth itself; whose first appearance to our eyes bleared and dimmed with prejudice and custom is more unsightly and unplausible than many errors. [Above all liberties] give me the liberty to know, to utter and to argue freely according to conscience.

The *Areopagitica* stands today as probably the most eloquent plea for a free press ever penned. Its intellectual power, its lofty ideals, its erudition, its ordered demolition of the notion of licensing are concepts which have appealed with peculiar force to literary and radical minds through the ages. It was the voice of Milton that inspired the men who led the struggle for a free press on the eve of the American Revolution, which anticipated much of Rousseau and Voltaire, and which spoke to Wordsworth and the English romantics, and a little later to John Stuart Mill as he composed his own great work on liberty. Milton's unqualified faith in reason and scholarship presented a case so forceful it could never again be ignored.

But his appeal was to the future. To his own contemporaries, Milton's great tract went almost completely unnoticed. Where Lilburne and the other Levellers sold their pamphlets by the thousand, Milton ran to only one edition and perhaps no more than a 100 or 200 copies. Where Lilburne published to noisy controversy, Milton roused no echo of either condemnation or applause. William Haller, the historian of the Puritan pamphlets, has searched through everything printed in the entire decade and has not found a single reference to the *Areopagitica*. The truth seems to be that Milton was unknown to the general public and not regarded as a person of importance until he allied himself with the revolutionary leaders after the execution of the king in 1649. Five years earlier, he was known only as someone who argued for a man's liberty 'to put away his wife, whenever he pleaseth' – an example of the sort of licentious view that would run rife if toleration were allowed.

Thus, Milton's *Areopagitica* had no discernible effect on the controversy to which it was addressed. Agitation for free speech and the liberty of unlicensed printing was a battle fought in the political arena, not in the poet's study. Milton – poet, thinker, scholar, prophet – stood above the current hurly-burly and addressed instead the fundamental issue between the squabbling factions, namely how the great body of ideas that had been brought into the world by the invention of the printed book should be absorbed by the modern State that was emerging from the upheaval of war. His dazzling, idealistic answer was to give unrestricted access to the truth, which would always vanquish error without the aid or intervention of authority. It was a vision that captured the imagination of the future. But in the tooth and nail struggle for supremacy then going on between Presbyterian, Independent, Separatist and Leveller, such lofty notions were as so much hot air. Milton had written not a polemic, but a poem.

Perhaps for that reason, Milton was never persecuted, as others were, for his violation of the printing laws. Lilburne spent years in prison, rebellious preachers were deprived of their livings, the Levellers constantly had their presses raided and destroyed. Milton was simply reported to the Committee on Printing, who then let the matter lapse. The Presbyterian faction that harried the others so relentlessly regarded Milton as a harmless dreamer. His freedom of speech was for serious-minded writers who held deeply reasoned, though differing views on important matters of religion or philosophy. It neither covered all forms of literature, nor contemplated the freedom of speech for any but high-minded Protestant scholars of Milton's own class. He would have been horrified to think that he had expounded a principle that would one day be extended to give the liberty of the press to Catholics, Deists, and atheists, whose opinions he thought 'should be extirpat'. As a later Dean of St Paul's concluded, it was clear that, far from being a libertarian, Milton would have excluded 'not only the overwhelming majority of Christians but the greater part of the human race from the benefit of his tolerance'. *Areopagitica* may be a literary classic and an unparalleled argument in favour of intellectual liberty; it is not a comprehensive plea for the freedom of the press, nor one for religious toleration. And in spite of its influence on posterity, it played no part whatever in prising open the shackles placed on the printing press during the decade in which it was written. At the Restoration of the monarchy in 1660, it was forgotten entirely.

CHAPTER SIX

Towards Toleration

The Restoratian held back the freedom of the English press for another generation. True, the political balance of the constitution had been changed forever – the Convention Parliament was not summoned by Charles II; it summoned him – but after twenty years of civil strife, the country yearned, above all things, for peace and stability. There was a widespread feeling among the new rulers that the free circulation of pamphlets and news-sheets had contributed to what they called 'the late rebellion' and that next to settling the Church and the armed forces, control of the printing press was the most necessary step towards securing a permanent peace.

Within a week of his recall Charles II had given back to the Stationers Company its previous authority to search and seize printed material critical of the government. Under the Licensing Act of 1662, which provided the framework for censorship and control for the next thirty years, the newsbooks were suppressed, a rigid censorship imposed and the number of licensed London printers reduced again to twenty. Only four foundries were licensed to cast type in the entire country, while all master printers and founders had to post a £300 surety against transgressions. The act forbade the publication of any book or pamphlet unless it was first 'lawfully authorised' according to its category. History books, for instance, were to be licensed by the Secretary of State, works of philosophy or science by the Church. Booksellers and even street hawkers were forced to post bonds, while pamphlets and other ephemeral works were placed under an official surveyor of the press, Roger l'Estrange, who was given a monopoly of printing news and empowered to destroy and deface the equipment of his unlicensed rivals.

In an unsavoury career that lasted more than twenty years, l'Estrange became the government's enthusiastic instrument of censorship and suppression. Only the homes of peers of the realm were immune from his right of search and entry, though he was not above winking at unlicensed books 'if the printer's wife would but smile upon him'. When l'Estrange wasn't seducing their wives and raiding their workshops, he sought to limit output to a few carefully chosen favourites whose publications he could control himself, as an officer of the crown. This approach was based on a deep distrust of the Stationers' Company, whose members he regarded as both parties and judges in their own cause. He also helped to introduce a more fearsome threat to the freedom of expression than Laud's Star Chamber had ever been. In 1663, he raided the house of a bookseller called John Twyn and had him brought to trial on a charge of treason.

Derived from a 1352 statute of Edward III, the treason laws had been formulated long before the invention of printing. They rested on such concepts as levying war against the king, encompassing his death, or adhering to his enemies. Never before had mere scandalous words been held to be treasonable, but after the Restoration such words when written or printed were held to amount to overt acts of *constructive* treason. Twyn was arrested after proofs were found in his shop of a pamphlet entitled *A Treatise on the Execution of Justice.* Written by a former officer in Cromwell's army, it argued that the supreme magistrate was accountable to the people and that the people were entitled, in some circumstances, to take matters into their own hands – sentiments later to be shared by the Whigs, but which on this occasion were held by the judge to be an overt threat to the king's life. After refusing to reveal the name of the author or to implicate others, Twyn was taken from his cell at Newgate in February 1664 to be hanged, drawn and quartered as a traitor, more as an example to the rest of the printing trade than as a punishment for his crime.

On the face of it, the English press was now more tightly controlled than it had ever been, subject to the regulatory scrutiny not only of Roger l'Estrange and the law courts, but also of the king and his council, the secretaries of State, the bishops and the Stationers Company (whose interest was largely concerned with preserving its own monopoly). In reality, the regulators faced an impossible task. Printing was now so cheap and prolific it was no more possible to secure a compliant press than it had been in Charles I's day. Between 700 and 1,000 different items were being printed each year and new outlets for the exchange and discussion of ideas were springing up everywhere. Handwritten tracts were widely available in the coffee-houses, often found pasted to the walls. Later to be dubbed 'penny universities', the coffee houses had become the focus of the political parties that were then emerging: the Tories favouring Gray's Inn Coffee House, the Whigs Kid's Coffee House. In 1666, Clarendon, the lord chancellor, had recommended their suppression, but others, fearful of losing their licence fees, pointed out that 'it had been permitted in Cromwell's time, and that the king's friends had used more liberty of speech in those places than they durst do in any other'. It would therefore be better to leave things as they were.

Five years later, Roger l'Estrange was still referring to the coffee houses as 'nurseries of sedition' and complaining that men sat there half the day 'talking of news', a still forbidden activity. He urged the government to close them down, but the resulting edict caused such an outcry it was rescinded within ten days, though only on condition that the coffee-house keepers entered into a recognisance to prevent scandalous papers from being brought to their premises or read there. As it turned out, this was but a foretaste of the upheavals that were to shake the country during the course of the next turbulent decade, when even the Church resorted to the underground press to express its opposition to the king.

JOHN LOCKE'S INFLUENCE

As Charles II's reign drew to a close, the country was rocked by one constitutional crisis after another. Most were precipitated by attempts to bar the king's openly Roman Catholic brother from succeeding to the throne. Widespread apprehension that James would inaugurate another Stuart despotism was aroused by repeated allegations of a Popish plot backed by the French under

Louis XIV. But each time the Commons attempted to introduce exclusion measures, the king used his prerogative to close their proceedings. The dispute went to the heart of the relationship between the monarch and his Parliament and eventually led to a fundamental and irreversible realignment of political forces that would endure for the next 250 years.

With the most profound and puzzling constitutional issues at stake, a hitherto obscure Oxford don emerged to articulate the views of those opposed to the absolutist rule of the Stuarts. In 1667, John Locke left Oxford to join the household of Anthony Ashley Cooper, soon to become the Earl of Shaftesbury, and one of the country's most aggressive and ambitious statesmen, as well as the most able. Shaftesbury was at various stages of his career lord chancellor, a prisoner in the Tower, leader of the opposition and an exile in Holland, where he died before his ambitions could be realised. As his fortunes ebbed and flowed so did those of his protégé, who spent his own years in exile composing classic works of philosophy that were to inspire both the creators of the European Enlightenment and the framers of the American constitution. He also wrote his *Letter Concerning Toleration* which, after Milton, provided the seventeenth century's most intellectually persuasive justification for the right to free speech.

The two men had met casually enough when Shaftesbury went up to drink the spa water at Oxford to relieve a chronic liver complaint. They struck up an immediate friendship and within a year Locke had been taken on as Shafesbury's household physician, where he supervised the surgical removal of a suppurating renal cyst.* Surprisingly for those days, the operation was a success and from there Locke went on to become the statesman's intellectual *alter ego*.

They made a strange pair: the audacious, sometimes reckless aristocrat and the asthmatic, deeply Puritan Oxford don, a man with an ascetic face, a long thin nose and a cold expression. He had been born in Somerset in 1632, his father becoming an officer in the Parliamentary army during the civil war and later a moderately successful country attorney. He had used his army contacts to find a place for his son at Westminster School under the legendary Doctor Busby, who groomed him for a place at Christ Church, Oxford – an institution as yet untouched by Puritan reforms. To remedy the narrowness of its scholastic syllabus, Locke read contemporary philosophy; he became the equivalent of a Fellow, declined holy orders and, had he not encountered Shaftesbury, would in all probability have spent the rest of his days in academic obscurity.

While still at Oxford, he had been occupied in constructing a philosophical theory of knowledge and had worked on an essay, unpublished in his own lifetime, arguing *against* religious toleration – in the climate of the times he thought it was impracticable. He discarded these views only after taking up with Shaftesbury, who had throughout the vagaries of his public life stuck firmly to the principle of toleration. In the face of an Anglican conformity that fined, imprisoned or, if necessary, deported Dissenters, denied them public office and

---

* Although not a doctor himself, Locke had systematically studied medicine with his friends Robert Boyle and Thomas Sydenham, a pioneer in the treatment of infectious diseases.

took away their right to teach or preach, this was both brave and dangerous. It was an era in which the gentle Quakers endured their martyrdom or fled to America and John Bunyan comforted thousands of poor non-conformists with his *Pilgrim's Progress*, which he wrote while incarcerated in Bedford jail. Baptists, Independents and Presbyterians all nursed their own grievances against the Tory squires and landowners who enforced the vindictive and often brutal provisions of the Clarendon Code.*

Shaftesbury himself was in the process of putting together the nascent Whig Party whose objectives were to establish the supremacy of Parliament, strengthen the restraints on the Crown and secure the succession of a Protestant monarch who could be trusted to exercise his functions in a constitutional manner. Locke was in sympathy with all of these aims, and for the rest of their time together the statesman and his aide worked in perfect harmony. As Locke thought through his own highly original ideas about the philosophical basis of political authority and ethics, he also undertook various practical tasks in his patron's 'library and closet'. He was for a time secretary to a group set up to foster trade with America, became an expert on the currency and helped to draft a constitution for the new colony of Carolina (the first such document to permit the freedom of worship). Meanwhile, he persevered with his studies and went to France for the sake of his asthma, where he immersed himself in French philosophy and the works of Descartes.

By the time he came back to England in 1679 he found the country swept by wild rumours of plots and counter plots. Riots had broken out over allegations that the Catholics intended to murder Charles and put James on the throne. A score of innocent people were hanged for a conspiracy that never was; the streets were taken over by the mob – a word recently distilled from the more cumbersome *mobile vulgus*. Shaftesbury himself had just been released from the Tower, where he had been confined for his part in precipitating the Exclusion crisis, which had used the anti-Catholic rumours to try and bar James from the succession. When the repeated attempts to exclude James failed, Shaftesbury was again arrested, tried and finally acquitted by a London jury. Fearing for his life and wracked by pain and ill health, he fled to Holland, where in 1683 he died.

None of Shaftesbury's friends were now safe in England. Locke himself was put under close surveillance, and on one occasion had his house ransacked by l'Estrange's men on the lookout for seditious libels. He was lucky that they failed to find his unpublished manuscript of *Two Treatises on Government*, an extremely seditious work which roundly endorsed the people's right to rebel against a monarch who had grossly abused his powers – the exact sentiments that only a few years earlier had led John Twyn to be hanged, drawn and quartered as a traitor. Realising that his own life was now in danger, Locke also slipped away to Holland, where his name was posted on a list of eighty-four traitors wanted for extradition

---

* Statutes passed after the Restoration compelling the nation to conform to the Church of England. In 1662, the Uniformity Act drove dissenters from the church, while the Conventicle Act of 1664 penalised all religious meetings outside the church. The Five Mile Act of 1665 then banned dissenting ministers from entering corporate towns.

by the English government. He went into hiding for a while, but eventually the danger passed and he spent the next five and a half years in fruitful and not unhappy exile, though his experiences had left him with an obsessively secretive nature, a characteristic he was to retain for the rest of his life.

After he had fled, the failure of the Rye House Plot to kidnap Charles and James on their return from the races at Newmarket led to the arrest of the other leading members of the Whig opposition, Algernon Sidney, Lord William Russell and the Earl of Essex. Sidney and Russell were executed; Essex cut his own throat while a prisoner in the Tower. Due to a constitutional anomaly the printing laws had fallen into temporary abeyance at the time – the king had prorogued Parliament in order to prevent passage of the Exclusion Bill; a vote needed to renew the Licensing Act could therefore not take place. The press was unexpectedly off its leash. The result was one of the most ferocious propaganda wars England had ever witnessed. On the Whig side, sympathetic printers were on hand when Russell went to the scaffold, putting copies of his final speech on sale within the hour. By the end of the year, it is estimated that at least 25,000 copies were in circulation. On the other side, the government spared no expense to discredit their reviled opponents. More than 50 officially sponsored tracts spread the word that 'forty-one had come again' – the realm was in danger. Illustrations had come into vogue and the now knighted Sir Roger l'Estrange published pamphlets featuring a picture of 'a frog and a mouse at variance which shall be king', while a kite hovered overhead ready to swoop down on them both.

The undignified squabble came to an end only when the king re-imposed censorship by royal proclamation the following May. From then on, according to the historian, G.M. Trevelyan, 'no Whig could raise his voice in speech and writing without imminent danger of being brought up for sedition or libel, and ruined by packed juries and new judges who had been put in the place of predecessors not sufficiently servile'. There was no more freedom of the press than there had been under Laud and the Star Chamber. With the accession of James II in 1685, the second Stuart despotism came into being, backed by a standing army financed by Louis XIV. That same year, Louis stirred further Protestant outrage when he revoked the Edict of Nantes and so unleashed one of the most barbarous and unprovoked religious persecutions of the age. Though forbidden to emigrate and forced on pain of torture to convert to Catholicism, nearly half a million Huguenot refugees fled to settle in England, Brandenberg and Holland – bringing with them tales of menfolk sent to the galleys and women entombed in nunneries or prisons, their children torn from their homes to be 're-educated' by priests and nuns. 'Heresy is no more!' proclaimed Bishop Jacques-Bénigne Bossuet. 'God alone could have done so marvellous a thing.'

A LETTER ON TOLERATION

This then was the climate that prevailed as John Locke settled down in exile to write two of the abiding works of English philosophy, *An Essay Concerning Human Understanding* and the *Letter on Toleration*. Already passed the age of fifty, he had previously published nothing of the least consequence. The two works he wrote in his late middle age were to bring him enduring fame and would influence the development of liberal values for the next three centuries. Though in that sense they were timeless, both documents were written in response to contemporary events with which Locke was intimately concerned. At first during the Exclusion crisis and later in the congenial company of Dutch theologians and Huguenot refugees he had come to see that the interests of the religious dissenters and those of political freedom were closely intertwined. The issue of toleration was less a matter of State policy than it was one of individual human rights.

In the *Essay*, he argued that because the human mind is free, people must think and judge things for themselves. Reason should be their guide, for without reason their opinions were 'but the effects of chance and hazard, of a mind floating at all adventures without choice, and without direction'. He accepted that 'all reason is search, and casting about', which is why there was more falsehood and error in the world than truth and knowledge. He spent much of the *Essay* discussing what the human mind can know and what it cannot, why it so often works badly in practice and how matters could be improved. In the main, his conclusions are optimistic and were later to be seized on by the leaders of the Enlightenment to show how, by the application of reason, the human condition could proceed to improvement.

In a separate letter, Locke said that if the discourse towards understanding was simply a taste, like that for different foods, then he would put aside books and think his time 'better employed at push-pin than in reading or writing.' But he was convinced of the contrary. 'I know there is truth opposite to falsehood, that it may be found if people will, and is worth the seeking, and is not only the most valuable, but the pleasantest thing in the world.' In this, Locke was at one with Milton: the search for truth is the philosopher's highest duty and one that demands the unfettered freedom to speculate, to argue and, if needs be, to be wrong. So frail is the human mind, so limited its understanding and so involuntary its beliefs, men ought, above all things, to be sceptical of the validity of their own opinions – for in this fleeting state of blindness 'where is the man who has uncontestable evidence of all that he holds, or of the falsehood of all that he condemns; or can say he has examined to the bottom all his own or other men's opinions?' We should be more busy and careful to inform ourselves than to treat others as obstinate and perverse because they will not renounce their own and receive our opinions, or at least those we would force upon them.

In the *Letter on Toleration*, Locke's argument was made even more plainly explicit: it is wrong for governments to impose their authority on their citizens' beliefs. For its day, this represented a daring break with the orthodox. In an age when belief in God was all but universal, it was taken as a *sine qua non* that the various forms of Christian worship could not co-habit one with the other within the same State. How could there be toleration of dissent when Anglicans, Catholics and Puritans were each profoundly convinced that theirs was the only true way to heaven? Under such a system, people were forced to conform, not only for the sake of their own salvation but also to ensure the peace and stability of the nation. In a country where the monarch determined the form of his people's worship, heresy and non-conformity were therefore identified with treason and sedition. Freedom of expression was synonymous with conspiracy, religious dissent with disorder and revolution. Whether the government was Catholic, as it had become under James, Anglican, as it was under Charles, Puritan as it had been under Cromwell or Presbyterian as it was (and long remained) in Scotland, the compulsory uniformity of belief necessarily imposes restraints on the freedom of expression.

Locke demolished these illusions in the discourse he wrote while living under an assumed name in Amsterdam during the winter months of 1685. Originally written in Latin as the *Epistola de Tolerantia*, it was superbly translated into English by his friend William Popple, but only published after his return home with William of Orange during the Glorious Revolution of 1688 – and then anonymously. Popple's introduction stated its purpose with admirable brevity: no nation under heaven stood more in need of religious toleration than England. Narrowness of spirit on all sides had undoubtedly been the principal occasion of the recent miseries and confusion. It was high time to seek a thorough cure. What the country needed was 'Absolute Liberty, Just Liberty, Equal and Impartial Liberty'. Locke's discourse was intended to inspire that spirit in all men who had souls large enough to put the interest of the public before that of their party.

Locke stated his premise with an equally simple clarity: toleration was the chief characteristical mark of the true Church. Religion was instituted solely to regulate men's lives according to the rules of virtue and piety; it had no business forcing them to profess things they did not believe. As the gospels said, no man could be a Christian without a faith which works, not by force, but by love. Those who maintained that people should be compelled by fire and sword to profess certain doctrines could hardly be motivated by love.

Without any of the soaring phrases that marked Milton's *Areopagitica*, Locke esteemed it necessary above all things to settle the just bounds between the business of civil government and that of religion. The commonwealth seemed to him to be a society of men constituted for protecting civil interests – by which he meant life, liberty, health and property. It was the duty of the civil magistrate, by the impartial execution of equal laws, to secure the just possession of such things. His power was confined solely to the care of interests belonging to this life; it neither could nor ought in any manner to be extended to the salvation of souls.

Locke then put forward the proposition that no man can so far abandon the care of his own salvation as blindly to leave it to the choice of any other. 'All the life and power of true religion consist in the inward and full persuasion of the mind,' he said. 'Faith is not faith without believing.' But the power of the civil magistrate consisted only in outward force, which could not compel the inward persuasion of the mind. 'Confiscation of estate, imprisonment, torments, nothing of that nature can have such efficacy as to make men change the inward judgement that they have framed of things,' he wrote. The rigour of laws and the force of penalties would not help at all in the salvation of their souls. And though the princes of the world determined the faith of their subjects, they were themselves much divided in their opinions on religion. But since there was but one truth and one way to heaven, only one country could be in the right, and all the rest obliged to follow their princes in the ways that lead to destruction. What heightened this absurdity and ill suited the notion of a deity was that men would owe their eternal happiness or misery to the places of their nativity. In vain therefore do princes compel their subjects to come to their Church under pretence of saving their souls. If they believe, they will come of their own accord; if they believe not, their coming will nothing avail them. For all these reasons it was sufficient to conclude that the power of civil government was confined to the care of things of this world, and had nothing to do with the world to come. When all is done, religion must be left to people's own consciences.

> No peace and security, no, not so much as common friendship, can ever be established or preserved among men so long as this opinion prevails, that dominion is founded in grace and that religion is to be propagated by force of arms.

Locke wrote with an intensity of moral outrage unparalleled in any other important work of political philosophy. Although his tract confined itself to religious issues, it soon became plain that it applied equally to secular matters: at that time they were, in any case, inextricably mingled. The freedom of worship, and with it the freedom of speech, would at last become a *right*, soon to be embedded in the Anglo-Saxon tradition. If any one man can be said to have created the principle of toleration on which that right rests, that man was John Locke. His writings while in political exile inspired one of the two main strands of western political discourse, the liberal and radical strand that played such an important part in the constitution-building of America and France and the long slow march towards political and religious liberty in eighteenth- and nineteenth-century England, and from there to much of the rest of the world.

At first, though, Locke's argument seemed to have been lost in the political turmoil that erupted during James II's quarrel with his bishops in the summer of 1688, when the established Church itself felt compelled to resort to the underground press. After James had ordered his second Declaration of Indulgence to be read out in every parish Church in the country, seven of his bishops delivered a petition declining to promulgate it. They were immediately arrested and charged with seditious libel. That same evening, the document they had put into the hands of the king appeared word for word in print and was laid on the tables of all the coffeehouses and hawked around the streets. It was said that the printers cleared £1,000 in a few hours from a penny broadside that played a significant part in the downfall of the king, whose actions had by now alienated even a loyal priesthood and the landed gentry. He was overthrown that same autumn after the disputed news that he had been presented with a male heir (and thus a Roman Catholic successor).

At Parliament's invitation, James's nephew and son-in-law, William of Orange, set sail in November on a providential 'Protestant wind', landing at Torbay with 11,000 men and a portable printing press. The men barely saw action; the press was used to flood the country with copies of a pamphlet giving the prince's reasons for appearing in arms in the kingdom of England. A password was devised to prevent leaks, and bundles of free copies were distributed for booksellers to sell at their own profit. It was cleverly timed propaganda, which reportedly had 'a wonderful effect' in persuading the people that William came as a selfless deliverer to overthrow a tyrant who had planned to hand over his country to Louis XIV and the Jesuits. By the following February William was on the throne at the invitation of a free Parliament, sharing the crown with his wife Mary, James's eldest daughter, a device invented to preserve the dynastic proprieties.

Locke, too, was back in England, having crossed with the party that accompanied the Princess of Orange, soon to be crowned Mary II. In the course of the same year, his three great works of political philosophy at last appeared in print. Two appeared anonymously, *A Letter Concerning Toleration*, first in the Latin version printed in Holland and then Popple's English translation licensed to be printed in London in October, followed by *Two Treatises on Government* at the end of the year. In the same month a fine folio volume of the *Essay Concerning Human Understanding* was published with his own name prominently displayed on the title page.

Locke's triumph was complete; he was accepted by all as the intellectual leader of the Whigs and the trusted adviser to the country's leading statesmen. Though his asthma had returned and he was forced to leave London for a house in the country, his commitments remained as diverse as ever. Oddly though, he remained obsessively secretive about his authorship of both the *Letter Concerning Toleration* and the *Two Treatises on Government*, and became more than a little hysterical when friends disclosed it for him. As late as 1698, he was still denying he wrote them, though by then it was common knowledge.

In any event, they and the *Essay* had firmly secured his reputation for posterity, and they are as relevant today as they were when he first wrote them more than 300 years ago. It should always be remembered, though, that Locke wrote as a seventeenth-century Protestant dissenter. His writings were a product of their own time, and however apposite they may seem today, they were directed by their author at the narrower issues of his own day. He did not intend his argument to be applied to secular politics, nor even to be applied universally to all religions. Catholics in particular were outside the scope of his plea for toleration since – rather like Communists in post-war America – they were regarded as the enemy within, beholden to a foreign power and an inflexible dogma, biding their time until they were strong enough to re-impose their own form of tyranny, just as they had done under Louis XIV in France. More than 100 years had to pass before Catholics were accepted on equal terms with their fellow Christians, and even now are barred from sitting on the English throne.

For Locke and his fellow Englishmen these were academic questions to be settled at some distant date in the future. For now, there was work to be done in settling the form of their own constitution. After a hard-fought compromise with the Tories, the Glorious Revolution came to a climax in 1689 when Parliament passed a Bill of Rights securing the liberties of the subject and the privileges of Parliament. The bill removed the king's prerogative to suspend the laws and impose taxes without Parliament's consent. There was to be no standing army during peacetime and there would be free elections and freedom of speech for Members of Parliament. There was, however, one notable omission. The Bill of Rights made no mention of the freedom of the press.

THE END OF LICENSING

In a sense, England's Glorious Revolution had come too early. Freedom of the press was not among the ancient rights and liberties the new government sought to restore. It could not be traced back to Magna Carta. The political leaders of the revolution had no interest in the question. They may have suffered under the Stuarts, but they came to power with no useable intellectual tradition in support of free speech, having distanced themselves as far as they could from the earlier revolutionary radicals who had first formulated the idea – men such as Milton, Lilburne and William Walwyn, none of whose tracts were republished in 1689. Though the new leaders had frequently violated the printing laws in their own struggles to regain power, once they had achieved it, they were content to see the same restrictions imposed on the press as those employed by the Stuarts. Consequently, there was no mention of the liberty of the press in the Heads of Grievances, which formed the first draft of the Declaration of Rights presented to William and Mary in February 1689, nor in the Bill of Rights itself, which received the royal assent in December. From that day to this, whatever freedom of the press exists in England has come about by a removal of restrictions rather than as the result of a separate and independent legal right enshrined in the country's constitution. It was an omission, which ensured that the English struggle for free speech continued for at least another century and would never wholly be resolved.

The revolutionary government – that most conservative of bodies – at once assumed responsibility for the regulation of the press. In the six years after it took office there were seventeen trials for unlicensed printing. And in June 1693 a Jacobite printer, William Anderton, suffered the same gruesome fate as poor John Twyn; he was hanged, drawn and quartered as a traitor after a press was found hidden in a secret room at his home on which he had printed seditious material against the new Protestant monarchs.

But then in 1695, again under the influence of John Locke, there came a true watershed in the history of the English press. The Licensing Act was allowed to lapse, never to be renewed. This came about through no suddenly awakened belief in public liberty. The impetus for change was Parliament's desire to eliminate the more blatant abuses of the old act, particularly the lucrative monopoly given to the Stationers Company over patents and copyright. Locke and others had bitterly complained that the printers' monopoly was preventing publication of the classics without their prior permission. He cited, in particular, a recent edition of *Aesop's Fables* whose author, he reasonably pointed out, had died some years before the invention of printing. Locke himself was still burning with indignation that fourteen years earlier l'Estrange's men had ransacked his own home while on the lookout for seditious libels during the Exclusion crisis. 'I know not why a man should not have liberty to print whatever he would speak and to be answerable for the one just as he is for the other if he transgresses the law in either,' Locke wrote in memorandum to the House of Commons. Gagging a man for fear he should talk heresy and sedition was no better than binding his hands for fear of what he might do with them if they were free. The censors' power to search people's homes and seize what they suspected may be forbidden was 'a mark of slavery'.

At Locke's urging, the Commons resolved on reform. When the Licensing Act came up for renewal in February, they rejected it without a division and instead appointed a committee 'to prepare and bring in a Bill for the better regulation of Printing and Printing presses'. No one foresaw that this was the moment that would mark the end of licensing for ever.

Indeed, with the old act now dead, the Commons prepared to put forward their new and in some ways more stringent regulations. Instead of pre-publication censorship, printers would have to deliver contentious works to the authorities sheet by sheet as they came off the press. Unregistered printers would be liable to a fine and disablement from the trade, as would anyone publishing material contrary to the established religion. But the number of presses and apprentices would be no longer restricted, no controls were to be imposed on the import of books and there was to be no protection for copyright.

The proposals were met by a storm of opposition. Vested interests in the Stationers Company lobbied to preserve their monopoly. The court faction worried that they would lose the profitable power of granting patents. The bishops argued for the continuation of licensing on the grounds that the prevention of mischief was preferable to its punishment, pointing out that a public trial would only draw attention to the views it sought to silence. Between them, these factions persuaded the House of Lords to call for the restoration of the old act rather than the enactment of the new.

With the two Houses of Parliament at loggerheads, the Commons sent the Lords an eighteen-point document stating why they no longer favoured licensing. Echoing Locke, they cited the unnatural and damaging monopoly of the Stationers Company, the lack of a definition in the old act of what constituted 'offensive' literature, the invasion of privacy involved in raiding people's homes in search of unlicensed books, and the subjection of learning to 'the arbitrary will and pleasure of a mercenary, and perhaps ignorant, licenser'.

But they said nothing whatever about the liberty of the press. 'On the great question of principle, on the question of whether the liberty of unlicensed printing be, on the whole, a blessing or a curse to society, not a word is said,' observed the Whig historian, Lord Macaulay. The Licensing Act was condemned not as a thing essentially evil, but on account of the petty grievances, the exactions, the jobs, the commercial restrictions, the domiciliary visits which were incidental to it. It was pronounced mischievous because it enabled the Company of Stationers to extort money from publishers. The Commons complained that the measures made it penal to open a box of books from abroad except in the presence of one of the censors of the press. How, it was very sensibly asked, was the officer to know that there were books in the box until he had opened it? Such, said Macaulay, were the arguments which did what Milton's *Areopagitica* had failed to do.

One last attempt to introduce a new bill was made when Parliament re-assembled in November, but a hundred 'petty objections' were made to it and it was referred again to a committee, and there it eventually petered out, never to re-emerge. Its expiry caused no excitement and in the country at large went virtually unnoticed. Freedom of the press had crept into England all but incidentally to the elimination of a commercial monopoly. The Commons knew not what they did, said Macaulay, or what a power they were bringing into existence. Yet, in his view, the lapse of the licensing laws did more for English liberty than Magna Carta or the Bill of Rights itself. That too can be counted among John Locke's abiding achievements. He may not have met Macaulay's exacting *post facto* moral requirements, but he had personally drafted the practical arguments that won the day in the House of Commons, although he was by then an ill and exhausted man.* As a result of his labours, the prerogative powers of the crown to control the press had gone forever, as had censorship and prior restraints on publication. The Stationers' monopoly had at last been broken and the press was both cheap and open to all.

SEDITION AND THE STAMP ACTS

In the decade after the end of licensing, scores of new publications came into existence, including *The Daily Courant*, the first regular daily newspaper in the English language. Journalism became a recognised social force under writers such as Addison, Steele and Defoe. Emancipated from censorship, literature was on the eve of its Augustan age, whose eminent adornments would include Pope, Swift, Gibbon and Samuel Johnson. Politically, the Glorious Revolution had brought stability – some thought the English constitution 'the most perfect form of government that ever was devised by human wisdom' – though with stability came an arrogant complacency that led them to resist all further efforts at constitutional reform for another century and a half. Not the slightest effort was made to enfranchise the common people or to alleviate their economic lot. The press was free, but not free enough. Parliament still guarded news of its debates with a jealous ferocity, the law of treason was an ever-present threat, while the establishment of the day never gave up its search for new devices to curb its independence.

In the twenty years after the lapse of the Licensing Act, eight bills were initiated for the general regulation of the press, though none completed all of its stages, usually because of disagreement between the two houses of Parliament or between the rival parties that had now become a permanent feature of English political life. Both parties had by now enjoyed their periods of ascendancy, and both were aware of the part that the press had played in bringing them to power. Each was afraid to entrust the other with the administration of a licensing act and each had learned that the official censors were unreliable. As one historian of the English press has observed, 'the work was too arduous for a leader in the party, too dangerous for an underling'. So the government reached out for other means to regulate a medium that all were agreed was not fit to regulate itself. Uppermost in their minds was not the glory of a free press, but the need to control it. Not

---

* Locke died in the country house of his friends the Mashams, at Oates, Essex, in October 1704.

until much later in the century was the liberty of the press seen as an essential bulwark of the constitution. And by then it had fallen under new and in some ways more subtle and indirect forms of control, in that they achieved one goal – that of suppression – while purporting to aim at another, more principled goal, whether it be crushing sedition, raising revenue, or subsidising virtue.

The first and perhaps most insidious of the new devices to curb the freedom of the press was the introduction, in 1712, of the hated Stamp Act. This imposed a tax on all printed papers, pamphlets and advertisements, an imposition which later in the century was to play its part in precipitating the American War of Independence. Queen Anne was now on the throne and her governments had been constantly searching for a way to control the flood of pamphlets and newspapers that meddled with the affairs of the State and the Church. The queen's own proclamations had gone unheeded – 'the publication of false news or of books of this kind is to stop', she had once ordered, peremptorily but fruitlessly. After almost ten years of unavailing effort, one of her ministers hit upon the discovery that a tax on publication would serve the double purpose of providing revenue and curbing the press, the revenue being needed at the time to fund the prizes in a national lottery that had been created to pay for the Duke of Marlborough's wars in Europe.

The author of the act, Viscount Bolingbroke, had made a timely discovery. When only a few copies of their writings were wanted, the early pamphleteers could afford to have them printed at their own expense. But now that great numbers were in circulation, the cost had, to a great extent, to be met by the readers. Taxation would make their distribution more difficult, and as Dobson Collet, the historian of the Stamp Acts, has observed, when anyone attempted to evade the tax, he could be punished, not as a libeller, but as a smuggler, with the added advantage that the character of what was printed would not come under discussion by the courts, as it would in a trial for libel. Accordingly, the act required a stamp to be placed on every piece of printed material it chose to call a newspaper. The costs varied, but were based on a tax of $1d$ for every printed sheet, with an additional tax of $1s$ on advertisements.

The outcry was immediate. 'This is the day on which many eminent authors will publish their last words,' wrote Richard Steele in the *Spectator*. 'All Grub Street is dead and gone,' said Dean Swift. 'No more ghosts or murderers now for love or money!' Addison, who could never resist a pun, called the mortality among the weekly magazines the Fall of the Leaf. Five of the existing newspapers did indeed go under, but four survived, including the influential *Daily Courant*. Among the casualties were Addison's own *Spectator*, Steele's *Tatler*, and Defoe's *Review*.

However, within a year wily newspaper publishers had found ways of evading or avoiding payment of the hated tax. A loophole was discovered in the clauses that imposed a tax of $1d$ 'for every printed copy' smaller than a whole sheet (equivalent when folded to four pages) and a $3s$ tax 'on *one* printed copy' of newspapers larger than a whole sheet. The publishers concluded that they were liable to pay only $3s$ *in all* for their larger works and $1d$ *per copy* for the smaller ones. The effect was an overnight growth in the size of the English weekly newspaper as editors employed larger type, wider margins, heavier leadings and, more significantly, critical essays and editorials to fill the extra space. As a result, the daily newspapers, who found it impossible to expand to six pages, continued to pay the tax and went into decline, while the tax-free six-page weeklies flourished as the main organs of party passion and controversy.

In another irony displeasing to the government, the editors who found a way around the new tax all supported the opposition Whigs while those who supported the ruling Tories felt more or less compelled to pay the tax and were being driven out of business. Instead of removing the inequitable levy, the politicians introduced the even more insidious remedy of paying secret subsidies to pro-government newspapers with money drawn from public funds, another device which contributed to the corruption of both press and politics. Statesmen as prominent as Sir Robert Walpole dug deep into the coffers of the Secret Service to make payments to the publishers and editors of daily and weekly newspapers favourable to their cause, while the opposition was either bought off or prosecuted in the courts.

It was Walpole, too, who closed the loophole in the Stamp Act when it was pointed out to him that the London press included four supporters of the rebel Jacobites, and thirty-four 'High Fliers', or supporters of the main opposition. The hand of the law fell even upon the unfortunate street sellers, who were liable to be committed to a House of Correction for three months for hawking illicit goods. And when another war with France broke out in 1757, the tax was put up from 1*d* to 1½*d* on the cynical principle that in time of war a patriotic public ought to pay more for news of England's victories at land and sea. Meanwhile, the tax on advertising was doubled to 2*s*, driving a further fifteen troublesome periodicals out of business.

Encouraged by the effect it was having in England as well as by the revenue it raised, Parliament tried in 1765 to impose similar stamp duties on its American colonies. The immediate and violent reaction forced their repeal within a year, an ominous foretaste of the quarrel that would break out with the colonies during the next decade. England was less able to resist, and the stamp tax continued to be one of the most effective fetters on the freedom of the press for the rest of the century and halfway through the next. Increases were imposed in 1794, 1804 and 1815, when the tax had risen to a crippling 4*d* a copy. It was finally repealed in 1861 after a long campaign against this hated 'tax on knowledge'.

While the Stamp Acts served to procure a corrupt press, the law courts did their best to ensure a subservient one. They abandoned use of the cumbersome laws of treason, which were used to secure a conviction only once during the entire century when in 1720 a nineteen-year-old printers' apprentice called John Matthews was hanged at Tyburn for publishing a pamphlet which supported the Old Pretender's claim to the crown, the unfortunate youth being the last person ever executed in England for a printing offence.

The treason laws fell into disuse not only because the age considered itself more civilised, but because the courts had found a more effective weapon for use against the troublesome press. This was the common law crime of seditious libel, a device used against authors and printers throughout the eighteenth century. Its legal definition was brilliantly simple. Lord Chief Justice Holt had laid down in

1704 that publications which maliciously lessened the affection of the people for the government were criminal. 'If people should not be called to account for possessing the people with an ill opinion of the government, no government can subsist,' he said. 'For it is very necessary for all governments that the people should have a good opinion of it.' In another formulation, a seditious libel was defined as anything intended to 'disquiet the minds of the king's subjects'. This concept, so repellent to the modern mind, has been excused on the grounds that until well into the eighteenth century no government was so secure that it could disregard the attacks that were made on it, and after the expiry of the Licensing Act seditious libel was for a time almost the only remedy against factious attacks. Until the defeat of Bonnie Prince Charlie's army at Culloden in 1745, the exiled Stuarts' claim to their lost throne was an ever-present threat. In the knowledge of what had gone before, the courts placed the stability of the State over the freedom of the press.

The law of seditious libel was not only sweeping in its definition, it was all embracing in its scope. Once a charge had been brought, all the jury had to do was determine whether the person prosecuted was the publisher and whether the words he had published conveyed the meaning put upon them by the prosecution. The judge would then, as a matter of law, determine the extent of the criminal intent and the illegality of the published language. He alone determined whether the matter was seditious and whether there was any malice. Jurors were simply told, 'the question is not whether the papers are criminal, but whether the defendant is the author of the papers'. Truth was not a defence; on the contrary, it became a well-known legal maxim in sedition cases that 'the greater the truth, the greater the libel'.

In the early years of the century, journalists were routinely put in the pillory for publishing words held by a judge to have scandalised the government – among them the author of *Robinson Crusoe*, Daniel Defoe, who went to the pillory three times, once to have rubbish and dead kittens thrown at him for publishing a parody of Queen Anne's decree against religious dissent. He was, said the judge, 'a seditious man of diseased mind'. Sooner or later, the control of free speech by this form of 'legal terrorism' was bound to be challenged.

When the challenge came, it was coupled with an attack on the other main obstacle to the freedom of the English press, the rules that forbade the reporting of debates in Parliament. Any reference to what went on there was limited to what Parliament itself authorised. In the case of the Commons, this consisted of an official report of its votes, but not of its debates. The Lords hid behind an even more impenetrable curtain of secrecy. To print any of their proceedings was a breach of privilege under their standing orders, which covered both votes and debates.

The privacy of their debates had once been an important defence against the encroachments of the crown. So jealously had Parliament protected its privileges, it required all speeches to be oral and prohibited the use of written notes or manuscripts for fear they might later be used against the speaker. But by the eighteenth century Parliament was safe from monarchical intervention; it was shutting out the legitimate curiosity of the public. As Macaulay has said, between the time when Parliaments ceased to be controlled by royal prerogative and the time when they began to be constantly and effectually controlled by public opinion there was a long interval. A member could no longer be called to account for his harangues or his votes; he might arraign the whole foreign policy of his country; he might table articles of impeachment against all the chief ministers; and he ran not the slightest risk of persecution. But now, the defences designed to protect its members against the displeasure of the sovereign were being used to protect them against the displeasure of the people. One result was corruption. Another was a Parliament that grew more and more out of touch with its electors as the century progressed. It constantly refused to acknowledge that it owed them any account of the issues it discussed or the manner in which it reached its decisions. It was enough to tell them the result of its votes. Anything else was a breach of privilege. Newspapers in particular should not meddle in affairs which were none of their business.

Parliament kept up this obdurate attitude towards the press throughout the century. In February 1760, four newspapers reported what they supposed was the innocuous news that the Commons had voted to give thanks to Admiral Hawke for his victory over the French fleet at Quiberon Bay. The hapless editors were hauled before the bar of the House to beg pardon for this unconscionable breach of privilege and the Commons reaffirmed their earlier motion that to print accounts of their affairs was a 'high indignity' deserving the severest punishment.

Whichever way they turned, journalists and their publishers found themselves up against the Parliamentary restrictions on the one hand and the laws of seditious libel on the other. The man who now stepped forward to champion their cause was one of the most engaging and mistrusted men of the day: a wit, a rake, an MP soon to become an outlaw, and said to be the ugliest man in London. He also made a greater contribution to the liberty of the press than any man of his generation, and perhaps of the entire century. In 1762, John Wilkes launched a newspaper in London called *The North Briton*. The first sentence of the first number read: 'The liberty of the press is the birthright of a Briton, and is justly esteemed the firmest bulwark of the liberties of this country.'

Battle had been joined.

CHAPTER SEVEN

Wilkes and Liberty

John Wilkes was born in 1725 in Clerkenwell, then a leafy suburb of London, his father a prosperous malt distiller, his mother a devout non-conformist. He was educated privately, his father's influence ensuring that he was brought up as a gentleman, his mother's as a dissenter. His childhood was happy and uneventful, but shortly after leaving the then fashionable University of Leyden he made the greatest mistake of his life. 'To please an indulgent father,' he later recounted, 'I married a woman half as old again as myself – of a large fortune.' Mary might have been rich; but she was also bored and massively lethargic. Wilkes spent the most tedious years of his life in her company and that of his mother-in-law, his sole domestic comfort coming from his baby daughter Polly, to whom he was as devoted as his wife was indifferent.

Wayward adventures inevitably followed. Wilkes fell in with Thomas Potter, son of the Archbishop of Canterbury, and one of the most notorious sexual adventurers of the day. Together they frequented the low haunts and brothels of Bath and Tunbridge Wells, and led a life of debauchery that scandalised even that age of easy virtue. With a group of other acolytes of Dionysis they formed a dissolute order called the Medmenham Monks, also known as the Hell Fire Club, who met in a disused abbey on the banks of the Thames to conduct what were euphemistically described as 'nameless orgies'. While a member of this club, Wilkes wrote a mildly obscene parody of Pope's *Essay on Man*, entitled an *Essay on Woman*, which would later play an important part in his conflict with authority. It begins:

> Awake my Fanny, leave all meaner things;
> This morn shall prove what rapture swiving* brings
> Let us, since life can little more supply
> Than just a few good fucks and then we die.

Little more than a facetious rhyme written in an idle moment to amuse his private friends, Wilkes can have had no inkling of the troubles his *Essay* would bring down upon his head, as, having written the lines, he put them aside and settled down to enjoy the life of a country squire in his wife's home town of Aylesbury, where he was an active magistrate, a trustee of charities and a genial and popular member of local society. Through his friend Potter he was introduced to the most powerful Whig families in the country, finding a particular patron in Lord Temple, head of the Grenville family, and brother-in-law to William Pitt, the greatest statesman of the age, who spotted his talent and encouraged him to take up politics.

---

* A Chaucerian word for sexual intercourse.

Wilkes at once put himself forward as a candidate for the Scottish border seat of Berwick-upon-Tweed. Learning on his arrival there that his opponent had paid to bring a boatload of supporters up from London by sea to vote for him on election day, Wilkes bribed the captain to land his bewildered passengers on the coast of Norway. On this occasion his urge to turn everything into a joke failed in its purpose, and he lost the election.

About this time, too, he parted from Mary after a distressing episode involving their daughter Polly, who at the age of six had contracted smallpox while away at school. An agitated Wilkes rushed to her bedside and urgently summoned the little girl's mother; but Mary, whether through jealousy, indifference or a fear of infection, refused to come. Contemptuous and disillusioned, Wilkes applied for a formal separation. After that, the couple never met again.

As his marriage ended, his political career began. In 1757, three years after he had been defeated at Berwick, again at the urging of Pitt and after a great deal of backroom manoeuvring, he was elected Member of Parliament for Aylesbury. Pitt was at the height of his powers, and in the process of raising England to a glory previously undreamed of. In the following four years, she acquired the basis of the British Empire: vast new territories in North America, the conquest of India, the rebirth of the Royal Navy, ascendancy over the French and the supremacy of the seas from the Caribbean to the Indian Ocean. 'You would not know your country again,' wrote Horace Walpole to a friend overseas. 'You left it a private little island, living upon its means. You would find it the capital of the world.' Wilkes spent his political apprenticeship in a Parliament swept up in this tide of patriotic fervour under an administration in the hands of Pitt and the Duke of Newcastle. Nevertheless, his first four years in Parliament were uneventful. He played no part in government, though he had once been earmarked by Pitt to become governor of the new British provinces in Canada.

He was getting ready to move to Quebec, where he looked forward to reconciling the king's new subjects 'to the mild rule of laws over that of lawless power and despotism,' when fate intervened. In 1760, George II died unexpectedly. His 22-year-old grandson, the new King George III, took his place and in the ensuing election, Pitt fell from power.

The leader of the king's party who succeeded Pitt was the Earl of Bute, described by his mentor as 'a fine, showy man, who would make an excellent ambassador in a court where there was no business' – the first, though not the last in a long line of undistinguished prime ministers appointed by the new king. Wilkes at once joined the opposition. He was by no means a fluent speaker, but he could write. When the new administration blundered into a wholly unnecessary war with Spain, Wilkes responded with a devastating pamphlet, published anonymously. It rested on the premise that Pitt would have never let it happen, Bute's government was out of its depth, and the ministers were deliberately hiding the true facts. The pamphlet caused an immense commotion and the search was on for its anonymous author. Always unable to resist a practical joke, Wilkes solemnly informed an aspiring clergyman he happened to meet in the park that the clergyman himself was suspected of being the author. In a frenzy of perturbation, the poor man rushed around town spreading the rumour further as he tried to trace the slander to its source. 'I shall be strenuous in contradicting the report,' Wilkes told him. 'For, undoubtedly, the author has no chance of favour from any of the present powers.'

Wilkes had discovered his forte, pursuing his role as spokesman for the opposition not so much across the floor of the House but rather in the pages of the popular press, which was better suited to his style. His opportunity came when Bute used public money to bribe Tobias Smollett to produce a weekly newspaper, *The Briton*, whose sole purpose was to pour abuse on his great predecessor and all his works. The first edition came out at the end of May 1762. Within a week, Wilkes had written and published his response, the *North Briton*, a paper which ran for forty-five editions, the last of which was to make Wilkes the most notorious man in England.

The publication had been given its title as a satire both on Smollett's *Briton* and Lord Bute's Scottishness, the word 'Briton' having been revived by the king – as a sop, it was said, to his subjects in Scotland. The Scots and all their ways were at that time the butt of every English sarcasm, and sometimes of an even deeper distaste. Twice in the previous generation Scots had risen in armed revolt in support of the Stuart pretenders, now they swarmed over London, gaining preferment from the new administration and giving Wilkes a fund of jokes at the expense of Bute. No chance was lost to satirise Bute's homeland and Bute's own bad spelling, as in this imaginary 'Chronicle' of the future published in one of the paper's early numbers:

> Some time since died Mr. John Bull, a very worthy plain honest old gentleman of Saxon descent. He was choaked by inadvertently swallowing a thistle which he had placed by ornament on top of his sallad.

In an age when Parliamentary reporting was not allowed, the *North Briton* also served a serious journalistic and political purpose. While its rivals were largely filled with gossip and trivia, the *North Briton* contained a steady flow of political news and policy papers. Sweeping aside the timid convention of disguising all references to real people with a tiresome array of blanks and asterisks, or making living politicians appear as speakers in a world of fictional make-believe, Wilkes used their real names and, more dangerously, carried reports of their real words and actions.

He was helped in the endeavour by a new and equally rakish friend, Charles Churchill, a genial giant of a man, who had been pushed into the Church by his father, but as quickly out of it again by his bishop. A gifted satirist, Churchill proved the perfect foil for Wilkes's acid wit. He began by reading manuscripts and correcting proofs, and ended as the *North Briton*'s co-author and Wilkes's closest collaborator.

One of their editions was responsible for the epigram, 'Every person brought in by the Whigs has lost his post – except for the king.' Another retailed with great glee the story of an event that had occurred at the king's coronation. Young Lord Talbot, a dependent of Bute's, had spent many hours training his horse to carry him from the king's presence backwards. Unfortunately, when the great day came, the horse turned out to have been trained too well, so that Talbot *entered* the king's presence backwards. When Wilkes taunted him, he threw down a hot-tempered challenge to a duel. On this occasion, their bullets whistled harmlessly into the night, which was not the case when a few years later Wilkes was forced into another, more serious, combat.

He picked another quarrel with the celebrated artist William Hogarth, who, said Wilkes, 'possessed the rare talent of gibbeting in colours'. Short of funds, the old artist had taken money from Bute to produce a caricature of *The Times*, a less than distinguished work which showed Bute manning a fire engine while Pitt and Temple fanned the flames. Wilkes devoted the whole of the next edition of the *North Briton* to an attack on his old friend, criticising not only his malicious pencil but his new appointment as 'Serjeant-Painter' to the king. 'I think,' he wrote, 'the term means what is vulgarly called "house-painter"'. By holding the deformities of nature up to ridicule, Hogarth was squandering his talents for 'base purposes'. Hogarth never forgave Wilkes for this attack, and in due course took his revenge in one of the cruellest caricatures of the age.

Wilkes had always made light of his own deformities. It took him only half an hour, he said, to talk away his face. Born with a crooked chin, a drooling mouth and a hideous squint, he was in truth the ugliest of men. But what he lacked in looks, he made up for in charm and a lightning wit. His aphorisms remain justly famous. A young lady he encountered on the Steyne at Brighton told him she had come out for a little sun and air. 'I think, Madam,' he replied, 'you had better get a little husband first.' And most famously of all, when Lord Sandwich taunted him that his habits were so gross he would die either of the pox or on the gallows, Wilkes at once replied: 'That depends, my lord, on whether I embrace your mistress or your principles.'

In between the fun and games, the *North Briton* kept up its political attack on the government. With Pitt not only out of office but wracked by gout and in one of what Horace Walpole called his 'sullen and silent' moods, Wilkes became the chief, and in many ways the only, spokesman for the opposition. He came out against the terms of the peace treaty with France – 'the peace of God,' he called it – 'for it passeth all understanding'. Then, in the fortieth edition, he printed details of a scheme to bribe MPs by issuing them with government stock at a scandalously low rate. The distributor of the bribes, Samuel Martin, the Secretary of the Treasury, was denounced as 'the most treacherous, base, selfish, mean, abject, low-lived and dirty fellow that ever *wriggled* his way into a secretaryship'. In another edition, the paper exposed the profiteering that had taken place when someone spent government money to buy large quantities of mildewed and rotten oats for the army in Westphalia.

The government squirmed at these revelations, but did nothing. Emboldened by their silence Wilkes next launched series of satirical attacks on the monarchy, hinting at the rumoured liaison between Bute and the Dowager Princess of Wales,* which once again passed without comment from the government. Beginning to feel that the new administration did not have the nerve to touch him, he took himself off to France to see to Polly's education, meanwhile planning a new and even more daring attack on the government of Bute and the Tories.

* Symbolised by pictures of a boot and a petticoat hanging on inn signs.

While he was gone, Lord Bute resigned his office, without warning and without explanation, written out, said some, by the pen of Wilkes. Seeing a political crisis was imminent, the author of the *North Briton* hurried home. 'How far does the liberty of the press extend in England?' the governor of Calais asked him as he waited for his ship. 'I cannot tell,' replied Wilkes. 'But I am trying to find out.'

NUMBER FORTY-FIVE

Wilkes arrived back in London to learn that his patron's estranged brother, George Grenville, had been appointed prime minister, with Lords Halifax and Egremont as Secretaries of State, all three having served as Bute's faithful henchmen. Temple and Pitt, in great alarm, procured an advance copy of the king's forthcoming speech from the throne, which would outline the policies of the new administration. It confirmed their worst suspicions: Grenville had accepted office on the express promise of liberating the king from his dependence on the great Whig families, while his foreign policy was simply an echo of Bute's. Stung to fury, the two politicians communicated their views to Wilkes, who set to work to denounce the new administration in the next – and as it turned out, the last – edition of the *North Briton*, Number 45, published on 23 April.

Wilkes chose as his target the most hollow and artificial contrivance of the British constitution – the king's speech from the throne which opened every new Parliament. Everyone knew that the speech was the work of ministers and that the king's role was merely to act as their mouthpiece. If ministers put lies into his mouth, the responsibility was theirs, and not the king's. Wilkes himself took great care to spell out the doctrine in a clearly worded preface, the opening sentence of which read: 'The King's Speech has always been considered by the Legislature, and by the public at large, as the speech of the Minister.'

Wilkes then launched into a scathing attack on the speech from the throne.

> Every friend of his country must lament that a prince of so many great and amiable qualities, whom England truly reveres, can be brought to give the sanction of his sacred name to the most odious measures and the most unjustifiable public declarations from a throne ever renowned for truth, honour and unsullied virtue. [The honour of the crown was] sunk even into prostitution.

The idea of prosecuting the *North Briton* had been mooted before, but dropped when no one could come up with a strong enough reason. This time, George Grenville felt obliged to take a stronger line. Parliament might understand the conventions that lay behind the speech from the throne; the people at large decidedly did not. To them, it would come as a great shock to hear the king accused of falsehood. It amounted certainly to sedition, perhaps even to treason. The law officers were put to work and Halifax, as Secretary of State, issued a general warrant for the arrest of anyone connected with the *North Briton* – authors, printers and publishers, all un-named, together with the seizure of their papers. This document, infamous in the history of free speech, was put in the hand of the official messengers on 29 April, just six days after the publication of the offending newspaper. Over the next three days, forty-nine people were rounded up, one of them, Dryden Leach, dragged from his bed in the middle of the night, even though he had long since ceased to have any connection with Wilkes and the *North Briton*. They next arrested George Kearsley, the real publisher, with his workmen and papers, and the printer, Richard Balfe, though Wilkes himself was left untouched. All knew he was the author, but as he had written anonymously and had all the privileges of a Member of Parliament, Halifax and Egremont had proceeded against him with caution. At length, Kearsley and Balfe were brought before the two secretaries of State in person, and terrified of what might follow, confessed that they had printed Number 45 from a manuscript supplied by John Wilkes.

In came the law officers again. Treasonable or not, the paper was most certainly a libel, they advised, and since the publication of a libel 'tended towards a breach of the peace,' they considered that the author was not protected by his privilege as an MP. An order went out for his immediate arrest under the terms of the general warrant. 'Drag him out of his bed,' ordered the choleric Egremont, but the ever-cautious Halifax over-ruled him and told them to 'treat him with great civility'.

It made little difference what orders they gave; Wilkes had already made friends with the messengers sent to arrest him and knew exactly what to expect. That night when he came home they let him through on the feeble pretext that he was 'in liquor'. No doubt with the help of a little *douceur* they let him leave again next morning when he promised them he would be back for breakfast. What he in fact did was hurry to Balfe's printing works in the Strand, scatter the type of the paper's next edition and tear up the manuscript of Number 45. Then conspicuously dressed in the scarlet overcoat and cocked hat of the Bucks militia in which he served as a colonel, he strolled nonchalantly back home.

He was by now perfectly prepared for what was to follow and may, indeed, have set the trap himself. Outside his house in Great George Street he was met once more by the king's messengers, who said they had a warrant to arrest him. Wilkes demanded to see it. It was, as he already knew, the general warrant issued against the un-named 'authors, printers and publishers of the *North Briton*, No. 45'. This warrant was no warrant, Wilkes declared indignantly, putting his hand on his sword. 'I asked why he would serve it on me, rather than on the Lord Chancellor, or either of the Secretaries, on Lord Bute, or Lord Corke, my next door neighbour.' With this display of force and bluster, he inveigled the two messengers to enter his house, where he needed to keep them occupied until the courts were open and he could apply, through Lord Temple, for a writ of *habeas corpus* on the grounds that he had been illegally arrested and was now being held prisoner in his own house.

It had all been carefully planned. But then an accidental encounter nearly undid the whole scheme. Wilkes was still arguing with the messengers, his house by now filled up with a noisy crowd of friends, officials and lawyers, when in strolled the burly Charles Churchill, unaware that other messengers were at that very moment out searching for him. Before he could open his lips, Wilkes's quick wits saved the day. 'Good morning, *Mr Thomson*,' he remarked with heavy emphasis. 'How does *Mrs Thomson* today? Does she dine in the country?' Churchill paused, picked up the hint, and replied that Mrs Thomson was already waiting for him; indeed, so great was her need to dine in the country, he had merely time to pass by and enquire after Mr Wilkes's health, and then he must be on his way. He stayed just long enough to exchange a few pleasantries before making his excuses to leave, hurrying out of London that same day. The government never did discover where he had gone.

With time still to kill before the courts opened, Wilkes engaged in further heated argument with the messengers before Halifax finally lost patience and threatened to send a platoon of guards if Wilkes did not present himself immediately at Halifax's own house at the other end of Great George Street. Determined to wring every last drop of publicity from the ridiculous scene, Wilkes refused to leave except as befitted a gentleman and member of the House of Commons, in a sedan chair. This was duly brought, carrying him ceremoniously from one doorstep to the next, the prisoner peering through the glass at the crowds with a smile of derision on his face.

On reaching Lord Halifax's house, he was ushered into a large room overlooking Birdcage Walk where the two secretaries of State sat waiting to question him across a large polished table. Halifax spoke to him civilly, Egremont – the only man for whom Wilkes bore real rancour – addressed him with barely concealed contempt. 'Mr Wilkes, do you know Mr Kearsley?' they asked. 'Mr Wilkes, when did you last see Mr Kearsley?'

Wilkes replied they could ask him all the questions they liked, but 'all the quires of paper on their lordships' table should be as milk-white at the end of his examination as they were at the beginning'.

Lord Halifax said he was sorry a man of Mr Wilkes's rank and abilities should 'engage against his king and His Majesty's government'. Wilkes replied that the king had no more zealous subject than himself: it was his majesty's misfortune to be served by such ignorant, insolent and despotic ministers. They should be impeached for the outrage they had committed against the liberties of the subject in arresting him 'under a general warrant which named nobody'. Squinting across at Egremont, he added that even if he 'employed tortures', he would not utter a single word. 'Your lordship's verbal orders were to drag me out of bed at midnight,' he declared. 'Your lordship is very ready to issue orders which you have neither the courage to sign, nor I believe to justify.'

Getting nowhere, the secretaries committed their prisoner into custody. Where would he prefer to be held, asked the uxorious Halifax, in the Tower, in Newgate, or in his own house? 'Thank you, my lord,' replied Wilkes tartly, 'but I never receive an obligation but from a friend.'

They were about to commit him to the Tower when two MPs arrived with news that the court had issued a writ of *habeas corpus* demanding that their prisoner be delivered at once to the Court of Common Pleas in the corner of Westminster Hall. But the writ was made out when Wilkes was in the custody of the king's messengers; now he was in the custody of the two secretaries of state, who were advised that since it did not name them, the writ could be ignored. The sedan was summoned once more and Wilkes hurried off into the safe keeping of the governor of the Tower of London, where he was to be held close prisoner and denied the company of his friends. His house meanwhile was ransacked, locks picked, desks prised open and every possible piece of evidence thrown into a sack and taken by coach to the Treasury, where the case against him would be prepared. Invited to witness the seizure of Wilkes's papers, Lord Temple declined to be present at an act he declared 'too barbarous for any human eye,' and immediately took steps to procure his protégé's release. Meanwhile, the mean-spirited Egremont had Wilkes removed as colonel of the Buckinghamshire militia.

Four days later, Wilkes was brought from the Tower to appear in person before the Lord Chief Justice, Sir Charles Pratt. In a brief speech, Wilkes declared that the liberty of an English subject should not be 'sported away' with such impunity; he had, he said, an unparalleled grievance. Having listened to long legal arguments, the court censured the messengers for their trickery in avoiding the terms of the original writ of *habeas corpus* and ordered that Wilkes's friends should be allowed to visit him whenever they pleased. The case was adjourned for three further days as the hero of the hour was led back to his coach to cheers of 'Liberty! Liberty! Wilkes for Ever!'

Three days later, he was back for the hearing of the writ in the knowledge that the common people had rallied to his side. 'My lords,' he cried hoarsely. 'The liberty of all peers and gentlemen – and (what touches me more sensibly) that of all the middling and inferior sort of people, who stand most in need of protection – is, in my case, this day to be finally decided upon: a question of such importance as to determine at once whether English liberty is to be a reality or a shadow.'

The rest of his speech was a rehearsal of the indignities he had suffered: his home ransacked and plundered, his most private and secret concerns divulged, every vile and malignant insinuation made by his enemies, even of high treason. He finished in a frenzy of anticipation as the judge prepared to deliver the court's opinion. At first, it looked to be going badly for Wilkes. The judges ruled that the two secretaries had just as much power to commit a suspected person to prison as any other magistrate. Nor was it necessary for them to specify the particular passages alleged to be libellous. But while the judges found no fault with the warrant, it was becoming clear that Pratt was summing up in favour of Wilkes as he moved on to discuss a third question – that of Wilkes's privilege as a Member of Parliament. The only offences for which an MP's privilege could be suspended were treason, felony or a breach of the peace, and Wilkes was guilty of none of them. He was accused of libel, 'and we are all of the opinion that a libel is not a breach of the peace,' said the Lord Chief Justice. He raised his voice to declare: 'Mr. Wilkes is entitled to his privilege and must be discharged.'

Wilkes murmured his 'poor thanks' then turned around and made a low bow to the watching crowds. The loudest shout anyone had heard rang out through the ancient hall: 'Wilkes and Liberty! Wilkes and Liberty!'

Meanwhile, crouching behind a pillar, an old man with a pug nose and a round face was making a rapid sketch of the scene. It was Hogarth, taking his revenge. His cartoon of 'John Wilkes, Esq., Drawn From Life' showed his subject sitting on a chair, holding the Cap of Liberty precariously dangling atop the Staff of Maintenance, his face distorted into a cynical leer, his squint monstrously exaggerated, his wig fashioned to cover demonic horns. Charles Churchill retorted with a description of the old artist 'lurking most ruffian-like behind a screen' in an angry verse which concluded:

> Virtue, with due contempt, saw Hogarth stand,
> The murd'rous pencil in his palsied hand.

His friends were angry, but the mild-natured Wilkes, as always, took the insult in good part. 'I believe I grow more like Hogarth's cartoon every day,' he was to remark later in life. Hogarth was not the only one seeking revenge on that fateful day. From the moment of his discharge, a vindictive government determined that Wilkes must be destroyed – by fair means if possible, if not, by foul.

WILKES AND LIBERTY

In the country at large, Wilkes was the hero of the hour, crowds of disenfranchised workers gathering every time one of his cases was heard to cheer for 'Wilkes and Liberty!' A new movement, radical and democratic, was in the process of throwing off its ties to the two old parties of Whig and Tory, the revolution families still controlling the one and the king's friends dominating the other. The arrest of Wilkes had released all the pent-up frustrations of those he had called 'the middling and inferior sort of people,' who saw in the debonair, squinting champion of free speech, a man who was prepared to fight for the redress of their own grievances. They roared their appreciation and took him to their hearts, as he did them. From now on, he was an impassioned democrat, a conversion that has been described as sudden as St Paul's, and no less sincere. His support took on popular and wildly enthusiastic forms. The members of a working men's club in Wapping vowed to get drunk every year on Wilkes's birthday; when they discovered that no one knew when his birthday was, they resolved to get drunk every day for a year so as to avoid the charge of perjury. Vulgar and excessive though their support was, 'Wilkes and Liberty!' marked the birth of the British movement for democratic reform.

Everyone knew the test would come when Parliament reassembled for its winter session in November. Wilkes had prepared an elaborate plan to raise the breach of his privilege on the first day, but then offer to waive it and put himself on a jury of his countrymen, in the sure knowledge that in the current wave of democratic fervour, he could not lose. Meanwhile, discovering that no outside printer could be found to work for him, he set up a printing press of his own at Great George Street, disregarding the advice of Lord Temple, who saw great dangers in the plan. But Wilkes trusted his printers and pressed ahead, reprinting the whole of the *North Briton* in book form, including the now illegal Number 45. With spare capacity on his hands, he also ran off twelve copies of an extract from the *Essay on Woman*. Printed for private amusement, they were never published, and never intended to be. 'If I laughed, it was in private that I laughed,' he remarked later. Wilkes in fact had quickly abandoned the idea of printing the whole poem and kept what fragments remained under lock and key at home. But by now, government spies were watching him around the clock.

Once they got wind of it, there was no perfidy to which they would not stoop to lay their hands on the evidence that would enable them to damn Wilkes as a pornographer as well as the publisher of seditious libels.

Of all this Wilkes knew nothing as he took himself off to France on a visit to see Polly. Once he was gone, the government's paid agents set about their murky work. Several stories were subsequently put around as to how they finally got hold of a copy of the *Essay*. In one version, an apprentice printer had used a single proof sheet of the offending work to wrap up his dinner, which he then happened to eat in the company of one of the government's spies. However it was obtained, the copy was passed on to the Revd John Kidgell, a homosexual priest who was chaplain to Lord March, a government minister. Large sums were made available to obtain a full copy of this heaven-sent windfall and Kidgell used both bribery and blackmail to winkle a copy out of Wilkes's master printer, Michael Curry. Further copies were made 'for official use', during which it has been convincingly demonstrated that forgery took place to attribute the verses unassailably to Wilkes.* The government was preparing its assault with meticulous and utterly unscrupulous care.

Wilkes was unaware of any of this as he hurried home from France on the news that his old antagonist, Lord Egremont, had died of an apoplectic fit. His unlikely replacement was a fellow member of the Hellfire Club, Lord Sandwich, who offered to buy Wilkes off if he would only drop his opposition to the government. Wilkes indignantly refused and Sandwich joined the ranks of his enemies. Three days later, a full copy of the *Essay on Woman* fell into his hands. He was to put it to deadly use. Parliament met for its winter session in an atmosphere as tense as any since the days of the Glorious Revolution. Pitt took his place as unchallenged leader of the opposition, with every expectation of being recalled to office before the year was out. The Speaker swore in the new members and was about to open the session when Grenville and Wilkes sprang to their feet at the same moment – the prime minister to deliver a message from the king, Wilkes to raise the breach of his privilege, a matter which normally took precedence over everything else, especially messages from the king. Despite Pitt's vehement protests, the ministry forced through a motion to overturn this precedent with a majority of 300 votes to 111. The prime minister would be heard first.

The procedural wrangle had been both long and rancorous, and the day was far gone when Grenville rose to deliver his message from the king: John Wilkes had escaped punishment for sedition only by pleading the privilege of Parliament; his majesty now wished Parliament to resolve the matter. Lord North then obligingly proposed a motion that stigmatised the *North Briton* as a 'false, scandalous and seditious libel, tending to alienate the affections of the people . . . and to excite them to traitorous insurrections against his majesty's government'.

* It was thought at one time that the *Essay* was the work of Thomas Potter and that Wilkes had merely written the footnotes. Not until the nineteenth century were the forgeries uncovered by a Victorian connoisseur of pornography, H.S. Ashbee.

Wilkes objected to the word false, but the House chose instead to debate Pitt's shrewder amendment to leave out the words 'to excite them to traitorous insurrections'.

The debate on Lord North's motion raged for another eight hours, Pitt throwing his whole weight into the struggle, having seen more clearly than any of his colleagues that not only free speech but the supremacy of Parliament was at stake. Like one of Homer's heroes, we are told, he was omnipresent. Twenty-one times during the course of the debate he was on his feet to uphold the liberty of the press and the sacred right of criticism. Always impatient of legal views – he had once laid down as a maxim that 'lawyers are not to be regarded in matters of liberty' – he poured scorn on the government's definition of a libel. It was of no consequence that they disliked Number 45. He himself disliked all political pamphlets, but that did not make them libellous. In fact, he never could learn 'exactly what is a libel', but he would always maintain the liberty of the press and declared, 'he would die if a day were not appointed for hearing Wilkes.' Pitt had done all a Parliamentary genius could do, but it was not enough to overturn an entrenched majority of government placemen. When his motion came to a vote at two in the morning, the government had a majority of more than 150. Number 45 of the *North Briton* was condemned as a seditious libel and ordered to be burned by the common hangman.

It had been a bad day for Wilkes – and a bad one for free speech – but worse was still to come. While the government were condemning the *North Briton* in the Commons, they were attacking the *Essay on Woman* in the Lords. The instigator was the Bishop of Gloucester, Dr William Warburton, whose pedantic editing of Pope's *Essay on Man* had been satirised in the introduction to Wilkes's *Essay on Woman*. Since Warburton sat in the House of Lords, the poem was deemed to constitute a libel on one of its members. The minister picked to condemn the stolen verse was the former member of the Hellfire Club, Wilkes's friend the Earl of Sandwich.

The king had that day opened Parliament in person, but scarcely had he left the throne and the Commons trooped back to debate Number 45 in their own chamber when Sandwich was on his feet in the Lords. In tones of pious indignation he informed their lordships that a 'most scandalous, obscene and impious libel' had fallen into his hands and he proceeded to read out the whole of the *Essay on Woman*, pausing at the most salacious passages to express his utter indignation and revulsion that such things could be written. Lord Lyttleton protested at the disgusting spectacle and demanded that it should cease, but the rest of the House called out, 'Go on! Go on!'

Sandwich continued his recitation of the *Essay* to the end, and when he sat down, Bishop Warburton jumped to his feet, almost apoplectic with rage. He said, 'the hardiest inhabitants of hell would blush to hear such blasphemies,' and called God as his witness to deny – as if he had to – that he had written a single one of the words attributed to him by Wilkes.

One of the most odious displays of hypocrisy ever witnessed in the British Parliament ended with a resolution declaring the poem impious, profane, wicked and blasphemous. The House was about to declare that Wilkes was its author when Lord Mansfield pointed out that this would mean he would have to be heard in its defence. The matter was thereupon adjourned until the following Thursday, though it was of not the slightest concern what their lordships did next. The damage had already been done.

It was, of course, irreparable. 'Why do they not search the Bishop of Gloucester's study for heresy?' Pitt exclaimed indignantly when he heard the news in the lobby of the House of Commons. But he knew, and Wilkes knew, that the government had secured a crushing victory. No matter that they had used despicable and underhand methods to obtain their copy, no matter that the offending verses had never actually been published, no matter that honest people were indignant at Sandwich's treachery and despised the government he represented, Wilkes was condemned to odium as a pornographer. Nowhere was the damage more severe than among his most loyal followers, the rich and respectable nonconformist Churchgoers. Besides all that, Wilkes well knew he now faced even more terrible punishments for blasphemy than he had ever done for libel.

In the very hour in which he learned that all was lost in the Lords, yet another new blow fell upon him in the Commons. He had just finished his long delayed and now useless complaint that there had been a breach of his privilege when Samuel Martin, the former Secretary to the Treasury exposed in the *North Briton* as the 'mean, low, abject sort of fellow' who doled out the government's bribes, rose to complain that he had been grossly libelled. 'A man capable of writing in that manner without putting his name to it . . . is a cowardly rascal, a villain and a scoundrel,' he said. Wilkes sat by, smiling and imperturbable, but next morning, all caution cast aside, he got up early and wrote to Martin: 'You complained yesterday before five hundred gentlemen that you had been stabbed in the dark by the *North Briton*. I whisper in your ear that every passage . . . was written by your humble servant – John Wilkes.' Martin replied by return: 'I desire that you may meet me in Hyde Park immediately with a brace of pistols, to determine our difference.' The challenge arose from no heated passion of the moment. Martin had been practising with a pistol for months past. Wilkes's reckless courage had drawn him into another trap.

Despite the fact that it was his privilege to choose the weapons, and not Martin's, Wilkes accepted the challenge without protest and went at once to Hyde Park with a pair of pistols concealed beneath his scarlet overcoat. They fired at each other from a distance of fourteen yards, but in spite of his practice Martin's first shot missed, Wilkes's flashed in the pan. At the second attempt Wilkes missed again, but Martin's bullet glanced off a button on Wilkes's coat and wounded him severely in the groin. Wilkes fell on the ground, and, believing himself to be dying, urged Martin to make his escape. Martin made off and Wilkes was carried home, half delirious from the pain he was in, but sensible enough to instruct his servants to return Martin's letter before the authorities found it. He refused to speak further of the matter and told the surgeon he had been injured in 'a matter of honour'.

He was still on his back, recovering slowly, when Parliament resumed the debate on his breach of privilege. That they should resolve that 'the privilege of Parliament does not extend to writing and publishing seditious libels' came as no surprise. What was a surprise, and a hurtful one, was the insulting speech made in the debate by the man who had first encouraged his political career, William Pitt. While still defending Wilkes's privilege, Pitt declared that he knew 'no such author'. The king's subjects were one people, and whoever divided them was guilty of sedition. His majesty's complaint was 'well-founded, it was just, it was necessary'. The author did not deserve to belong to the human species – he was, said his old mentor, 'the blasphemer of his God and the libeller of his king'.

Pitt's gross and unforgivable abandonment of him wounded Wilkes deeply. Only two friends, he believed, had remained loyal during his time of trial: Lord Temple and Charles Churchill. And, of course there was Polly, to whom his thoughts now turned. He would, when he recovered sufficiently, go again to France, drawn there partly by his darling daughter, partly by his need for convalescence and partly, it is said, to hide his face. Courageous though he always was, the revelation of the infamous *Essay* had left him perplexed, unnerved, and not a little ashamed. At about the same time, the clergyman who had first betrayed him, the Revd John Kidgell, fled abroad to escape his creditors. The coincidence was too good for the satirists to miss:

> When faction was loud, and when party ran high
> Religion and Liberty joined in the cry:
> But, O grief of griefs! In the midst of the fray,
> Religion and Liberty both ran away.

In apparently running away, Wilkes had made a profound tactical mistake. He had meant to come back for the resumption of Parliament in January 1764, but the journey had opened the gash in his groin and he suffered a relapse, which prevented his return. His chance of another triumph was lost, his supporters disappointed, his opponents offered a golden opportunity to finish him off once and for all. On 20 January he was expelled from the House of Commons and stripped of his privileges as a member. A month later he was charged with reprinting a seditious libel on his private press, found guilty in his absence and a warrant issued for his arrest. When he failed to answer, the law took its course and by November he was formally pronounced an outlaw for failing to appear at the Court of the King's Bench, a legal *caput lupinum*, or wolf's head, being metaphorically placed upon his shoulders as a sign of his ostracism for all time. 'This completed the ruin of that unfortunate gentleman,' the *Annual Register* pronounced. Wilkes in fact stayed in exile for more than four years, but his contribution to the cause of English liberty was not over yet.

INTO EXILE

Abandoned by his allies, harried by his enemies, too ill to travel, all but forgotten by the fickle mob, and now even stripped of his nationality, Wilkes believed himself 'an exile for life'. There was indeed little to draw him home. Along with his membership of the House of Commons had gone his privilege against arrest for debt, and the creditors were already closing in. The house in Great George Street was repossessed, the manor in Aylesbury sold, his books, furniture and silver auctioned off to settle his debts. He was cruelly deprived of his faithful friend Charles Churchill, carried off by typhus while on a visit to see Wilkes in Boulogne. Wilkes could no longer sleep because of 'the idea of Churchill ever before my eyes'. In his absence abroad, the trials against him were being shamelessly fixed. The jury who condemned Number 45 had been hand-picked by the judge, who then proceeded to tell them that as a matter of law the paper *was* libellous. 'If you are satisfied that the defendant is the publisher of this paper, you will find him guilty,' he declared. 'If not, you will acquit him.' The defence never stood a chance.

What was he to expect, Wilkes asked, if he returned to England? 'Persecution from my enemies, coldness from my friends.' To go on to the public cause for which he was being persecuted – that of liberty – was there any point left to be tried? 'I think not,' he replied. 'The two important decisions have secured forever the Englishman's liberty and his property. They have grown out of my firmness in the case of the *North Briton*. But neither are our posterity nor we concerned whether John Wilkes or John à Nokes wrote the *North Briton* or the *Essay* on Woman. The public then has no call on me.'

With his spirits and his fortunes at their lowest ebb, he took off for Italy on borrowed money and in the company of a new and rapacious mistress, Gertrude Corradini, an Italian opera dancer. In Rome, they fell in with the Scottish historian, David Hume, and in Naples with Dr Johnson's biographer, James Boswell, where they received the news that one of Wilkes's workmen had been pilloried for printing the *North Briton*. The mob had carried the man to New Palace Yard aboard a hackney coach numbered '45' and decorated with sprigs of rosemary, just like the Puritan martyrs of the previous century. Crowds stood around the pillory roaring out 'Wilkes and Liberty!' and when the printer's ordeal was over they presented him with a purple purse containing over 200 guineas they had collected. Meanwhile, a jackboot and a Scottish bonnet had been symbolically hanged on an adjacent gallows. Wilkes's interest in home affairs began to revive.

The tempestuous Corradini held his heart captive for more than a year before she took off one day with his coach and most of his possessions. A chastened and even more heavily indebted Wilkes returned to Paris to rejoin the ever-faithful Polly. There, he found that another English government had fallen and the Whigs were back in office under Lord Rockingham. Wilkes at once began to petition for a pardon and even made a clandestine foray across the Channel, where the Church bells were rung at Dover when they heard their hero had landed. But the Rockingham government did not last and Wilkes returned to Paris, still in debt and still an outlaw.

At home, it was a period in which six weak ministries were swept from office in as many years. The sporting Duke of Grafton next became prime minister, a more unsuitable man for a crisis than ever. It is said that a search through his records revealed nothing in his favour except that he had once exhorted his vicar to preach a sermon against shooting foxes. Pitt meanwhile – the Great Commoner – had surrendered much of his popular esteem by entering the peerage as the Earl of Chatham and a pensioner of the crown. Wilkes sent a letter to the newspapers with a detailed account of his own persecution and a bitter attack on Pitt, in whom it was now apparent 'that private ambition was all the while skulking behind the shield of a patriot'.

'Friendship is too pure an emotion for a mind cankered with the lust of ambition,' Wilkes wrote as he exposed Pitt's hypocrisy over the *Essay on Woman*. Reminding him 'of the compliments he paid me on certain poems in the year 1754', Wilkes went on: 'If I were to take the declarations of himself and Mr Potter *à la lettre*, they were more charmed by those verses after the ninety-ninth reading than after the first. Was there not something peculiarly base and perfidious in Mr Pitt's calling me "the blasphemer of my God" for those very verses – and at a time when I was absent and dangerously ill from an affair of honour?'

The reason for Pitt's perfidy was plain. He was beginning to pay homage to Bute, and Wilkes had to be sacrificed at the shrine. History scarcely gave so remarkable a change. 'He was a few years ago, the mad, seditious Tribune of the People; now he is the abject, crouching deputy of the proud Scot. But I have done with Lord Chatham. I leave him to the poor consolation of a place, a pension and a peerage, for which he has sold the confidence of a great nation. Pity shall find and weep over him.'

It was an engraving etched in wormwood. 'I hear Lord Chatham is so provoked and storms so much that his friends talk of its driving him mad,' wrote the new prime minister. Pitt's reputation never recovered and Wilkes's highly charged account of his illegal arrest by Halifax and Egremont immediately placed him back at the centre of national attention. After a bad harvest, the price of bread was the highest ever known, the government was deeply unpopular, an unwanted war with the American colonies was likely over the Stamp Acts, and a general election was pending. Now that Pitt was seen to have taken his thirty pieces of silver, the country was without a credible leader of the opposition. Wilkes picked his moment and quietly returned home to fill the gap.

THE MIDDLESEX ELECTIONS

He came back in February 1768 a penniless outlaw with two criminal convictions and an indefinite prison sentence hanging over him. Under his sentence of *caput lupinum*, he could be legally shot on sight, like a mad dog. No one, therefore, could doubt his own cheerful courage – or the fervent support of 'the middling and inferior sort of people', who had taken him to their hearts. He laid low in the city for a week in the house of his sister and then declared his candidacy for the richest prize in the kingdom, the city of London.

'Good God!' exclaimed one city alderman when he heard the news. 'What is your qualification?'

'General warrants and the good nature of my fellow citizens,' was the genial reply.

But in spite of the enthusiasm of his supporters and the widespread cries of 'Wilkes and Liberty!' he came bottom of the poll. Undeterred, he immediately declared himself a candidate for the adjacent County of Middlesex, which was not due to cast its votes for another two weeks.

His new seat was better chosen. It had over 3,000 qualified freeholders, mostly small shopkeepers and artisans, the descendants of the Brentford lads who had joined with John Lilburne to halt Prince Rupert's march on London. Now they had another radical leader to whose cause they could rally. Lord Temple bought him a small freehold to qualify him to stand, and the government unaccountably left him alone, weakly concluding that the one thing certain to ensure his victory would be his arrest.

Wilkes had just twelve days in which to canvas for votes in what was to become one of the most famous elections in English history. There was the usual crop of *bons mots*. 'I'd rather vote for the Devil,' growled one opponent when asked for his support. 'And if your friend isn't standing?' Wilkes replied blandly. 'A pity about the squint,' another voter remarked. 'Mr. Wilkes squints no more than a gentleman ought to squint,' was the indignant riposte. 'Aye, there he hangs,' one woman remarked of his picture on an inn sign. 'Everywhere but where he ought to hang.'

His squinting likeness was indeed everywhere; sprouting up on inn signs, snuff boxes, punch bowls, medallions, milk jugs and clock towers. He had the most popular, as well as the ugliest face in England. Meanwhile, 40,000 notices were issued, a complete record kept of every doubtful voter, nearly 250 hired coaches decked out with blue favours, and an election headquarters set up in the Mile End Road. 'Register, register, register,' was Wilkes's motto, and the brief campaign owed its success as much to his own brilliant organisation as it did to the enthusiasm of his supporters.

When the results were declared on the morning after the poll, Wilkes came first in a field of four and was duly elected one of the two Knights of the Shire for the County of Middlesex. The constituency took in most of the London suburbs to the north and west of the city, and when it was known that Wilkes had won, the area erupted with joy. The celebrations went on day and night for forty-eight hours, led by the disenfranchised members of the working class, who found in 'Wilkes and Liberty!' a slogan to frighten the upper classes. Every carriage that passed through the streets was marked with 'Number 45', every house compelled to light its windows with candles in honour of the day, the Duke of Northumberland forced to open up his beer cellar to supply the crowds with ale, and every pane of glass in Lord Bute's stately house in Berkeley Square smashed by the mob. The Austrian ambassador was dragged from his coach and held upside down while the number 45 was chalked on the soles of his shoes. When troops were called out, the regimental drummers simply 'beat their drums for Wilkes'. And when the American emissary, Benjamin Franklin, rode out to Winchester, he observed that for fifteen miles out of town there was not a door or a window shutter unmarked with Number 45. As the pandemonium subsided, people found to their surprise that no one had been killed, hardly anyone injured, and the damage largely confined to panes of broken glass. Wilkes's election had been an occasion for rejoicing, not for revolution. But it gave the ruling classes their worst fright since Bonnie Prince Charlie had marched to Derby in 1745. In their eyes, Wilkes was not only an outlaw and a criminal, but worse than that, he was the hero of the lower orders – and once more an MP.

Wilkes left for Bath to flaunt himself for a few days before the *beau monde* before returning to the serious business of obtaining a pardon. He had already told the government he would surrender at the Court of the King's Bench on the first day of term, and, true to his promise, duly appeared before the court's chief justice, Lord Mansfield on 20 April. The court was in a state near to panic as Wilkes read out his carefully prepared speech, humbly submitting himself to the laws of his country. He had been found guilty on two charges, he said: he had accused the king of telling lies, and he had published a ludicrous poem. The first was untrue, the second may have justly offended people – 'but not with me', for he had taken care to see the poem was kept carefully concealed. If it had been published, it was not by him, but by Lord Sandwich. He had stood forth in support of the laws against the arbitrary acts of ministers, and because of it had been much misrepresented. He reaffirmed his reverence for the wise and mild system of English laws, its excellent constitution and its illustrious prince, and he asked the court for a pardon.

Everyone had expected the appeal to be summararily dismissed – it was Mansfield who had packed the jury at Wilkes's previous trial – but to everyone's astonishment, the Lord Chief Justice declared that since the prisoner was an outlaw, he did not legally exist. The court could therefore take no notice of him. Until the attorney general had him arrested under a properly drawn up writ, Mr Wilkes must please go away.

Benjamin Franklin concluded that Mansfield gave such a craven judgement so that the government and not the judges would have to answer to public opinion for Wilkes's imprisonment. What they had done between them, of course, was to make the whole apparatus of repression look ridiculous; not for the first time, nor as it turned out, for the last.

Wilkes amused himself ostentatiously for a week, then voluntarily gave himself up for arrest under the correct writ and entered an appeal against his outlawry. He was brought again before the court and swiftly remanded into the custody of the King's Bench Prison in St George's Fields to await his trial. The law officers even managed to bungle this simple order: the prison coach was hijacked by a mob on Westminster Bridge, the horses unharnessed and the coach and its prisoner carried off in triumph to the Three Tuns Tavern in Fleet Street. Wilkes appeared on the balcony to protest that he was the king's prisoner and must obey the law, but the crowd shouted him down and refused to let him go. Eventually, he slipped away in borrowed clothes and a private carriage, knocked at the door of the prison and desired to be allowed admission. The government's humiliation was complete: many people had previously disguised themselves in order to escape from prison; Wilkes was the first to have to disguise himself in order to enter it.

The appeal took place in Wilkes's absence, the court marshal cynically announcing that his officers were all busy and could not be spared to provide an escort. There was another cynical manoeuvre when Mansfield announced that the case was so knotty it would have to be deferred until the next term. As the next term did not begin until after Parliament had risen, this had the effect of preventing Wilkes from taking the seat he had just won. Fearing the wrath of the mob when they heard what had happened to their hero, Lord Weymouth, the secretary of state, called out troops to guard the prison. It was a fateful decision.

Wilkes's supporters were mystified and angry at the government's vacillation. When Wilkes had come home an outlaw, the government had ignored him. When he was elected to Parliament, they had clapped him in prison. When he appeared in court, they said he did not exist. Now they seemed unable to come to any decision. Would he, or would he not, be allowed to take his seat in Parliament? No one seemed to know, so on 10 May, the day Parliament was due to resume, a large crowd gathered outside the prison to find out. A group of sailors climbed up to his window and offered to help him escape, but Wilkes told them to go home: he had no doubt that the laws of his country would do him justice. Nevertheless, fearing an attempt to rescue him, the prison marshal followed his instructions and called up the troops, who happened that day to be a detachment of Scots guards, who were taunted by the cockney mob. Someone stuck a leaflet on the prison wall; one of the soldiers officiously tore it down. Stones were thrown, the Riot Act was read and the soldiers fired a volley of shots into the crowd, killing six and wounding some dozen others. A woman was bayoneted and a man in a red waistcoat was chased by a group of soldiers who believed him to be the ringleader. Around the corner working in an outhouse, a farmer's son, William Allen, was also wearing a red waistcoat, although he had been nowhere near the rioting. The soldiers shot him dead at point blank range.

Public opinion was horrified at the ghastly event, which immediately became known as 'the Massacre of St George's Fields'. A jury returned a verdict of wilful murder against the soldier who had shot Allen. An indiscreet letter of thanks written to the troops by the Minister of War found its way into the newspapers and convinced people that a Scottish regiment had been deployed deliberately to provoke bloodshed. The massacre drew the whole nation's attention to Wilkes's solitary battle against tyranny and oppression. His refusal to accept his liberty at the hands of the mob was widely admired, even in Parliament. The release on bail of the soldier charged with murder simply showed up the government's double standards, especially as Wilkes, who was charged with nothing in particular, had himself applied unsuccessfully for bail on the same day. It was less than four months since he had returned from his exile: four months which had seen the government's reputation sink so far it was despised throughout the country, while Wilkes, once the outlaw, was now the adored patriot.

Within a month, he had secured a new triumph when the judges of the King's Bench decided unanimously that his outlawry should be reversed, though on the most trumpery of legal technicalities. Lord Mansfield decided that the omission of the words 'of the County of Middlesex' from a sheriff's writ had rendered it null and void. Once again, the court had been frightened into its verdict. Opinion was so hostile, a decision to confirm Wilkes's status as an outlaw would with certainty have led to further riots, and perhaps even to revolution. As it was, once the country got over its astonishment at Mansfield's quibble, bonfires blazed in London and all the major cities. The government congratulated itself on a narrow escape. It was more expedient that the verdict should have been overturned on a minor procedural error by a sheriff's clerk than to have to admit to errors and oppression on their own part. They did not seem to care that the excuse was so flimsy it would bring them into even further contempt.

All that remained now was for Wilkes to receive his sentence for the two offences on which he had originally been found guilty. As he put on a show of careless nonchalance, the court sentenced him to a further ten months imprisonment and a fine of £500 for reprinting Number 45, and twelve months imprisonment and another fine of £500 for the *Essay*. Supporters paid the fines and raised the necessary recognisances. Wilkes responded by suing Lord Halifax for wrongful arrest. He then left the King's Bench for his twenty-two months incarceration while the government decided what to do about his membership of Parliament. King George had told his government, 'the expulsion of Mr. Wilkes appears to be very essential and must be effected'. For the ministers of the Grafton administration the perplexing question was 'how?'

For Wilkes, prison proved to be no great hardship. His quarters were comfortable, the service excellent, the jail itself said to resemble 'a neat little regular town'. It had its own shops, a coffee-house and tavern, and gifts of food began to arrive for Wilkes in embarrassing profusion. A firkin of rock oysters came from one admirer and a brace of fat bucks and twenty dozen bottles of the best wine from another. The borough of Richmond in Yorkshire sent a butt of ale, and in what was seen as an ominous warning of troubles yet to come, the American colony of Maryland sent him forty-five hogsheads of tobacco. On his birthday, Wilkes gave a turtle feast, and when two pregnant gentlewomen called on him, he raised his glass to 'a safe and speedy delivery to the three of us'. Women flocked to see him, some out of curiosity, some for more amorous purposes, though these casual amusements never diverted him for long. Hardly a week went by without some missive appearing in print of his endeavours to destroy 'all the remains of despotic power among our free-born countrymen'.

While still in jail, he was also elected a City of London alderman. With their typical contempt for public opinion, the government's placemen declared his election null and void on a technicality – the polls were found to have closed too early – but the only result was that he was re-elected a week later without opposition, further adding to the general obloquy in which the Grafton administration was now held.

By February 1769 Parliament was ready at last to confront the case of its most recalcitrant member. It would be 'a fair trial between faction and corruption,' Horace Walpole observed cynically – 'and of two such common whores, the richer will carry it.' In one dramatic week, Wilkes was denied his right to take his oath as a member on the grounds that he was still a prisoner, but then succeeded in calling his printer, Michael Curry, to admit he had been bribed to steal a copy of the *Essay on Woman*. The next day, Wilkes was himself called to the bar of the House to answer a charge that he had disclosed the contents of the war minister's memorandum on the St George's Fields massacre to the St James's *Chronicle*. In what was to be his last appearance in Parliament for more than five years, Wilkes not only acknowledged his role in the leak, he gloried in it.

The House thereupon voted to expel him for publishing three separate libels – Number 45 of the *North Briton*, the *Essay on Woman* and the attack on the war minister in the St James's *Chronicle*. His supporters protested in vain that libel was not a matter for the House of Commons, it was a matter for the courts; and in any case, Wilkes had already been sentenced and punished for two of the offences. Edmund Burke joined in with a devastating attack on the government's attempts to curb their freedom of speech. Some members had voted to expel Wilkes because they liked the strong roast beef of blasphemous libel, he said, others because they could not bear to see Christianity abused. One member would expel him for his article in the *North Briton*, another because, he says, 'in times of danger, I am afraid of doing anything that will shake the government'. The charges were all brought together to form an accumulated offence, which could lead to an expulsion of any other member of the House. Burke concluded: 'Is any man, when he takes up his pen, certain that the day may not come when he may wish to be a member of Parliament? This sir, will put a last hand to the liberty of the press.'

The debate was also the occasion of an eloquent speech in his defence by Wilkes's old enemy, George Grenville, who spoke so vehemently that when he sat down he spat blood. 'Let us look forward a little,' he suggested. 'Mr Wilkes will certainly be re-elected; you will expel again, and he will be again returned. What is to be done then, and how is so disgraceful a contest to terminate?'

How indeed. Rather than stand by and see the boasted constitution of England torn up by the roots, Wilkes offered himself for re-election, and within a week was returned unopposed. The result was hailed with fireworks and musical processions all over London – and amazement in the American colonies. It was the Middlesex election that first put the thought into American minds they too might win the right to elect their own representatives. From Boston, John Adams wrote on behalf of the Sons of Liberty to congratulate Wilkes on his brave struggle in the cause of freedom, and the people of South Carolina offered to pay off his debts. Much flattered, Wilkes replied that the interests of America should be 'the study of his life'. All over America his name was now honoured and revered. The towns of Wilkesboro and Wilkes-Barre were named after him, as were countless little children, the name lingering on into the next century, when by a curious irony of history the assassin of Abraham Lincoln bore the name of John Wilkes Booth.

There was one place, however, where Wilkes's re-election was received with little joy and much hostility: in the British Parliament itself. When they heard that Wilkes had celebrated his victory in St George's prison with 'a fine large swan' and that all evening long 'gentlemen on horseback, with drums beating, French horns playing, and colours flying rode close past his window', ministers met to discuss their dilemma. Next morning they sought to resolve it by introducing a motion that not only expelled Wilkes again, but declared that 'he is incapable of being elected a member.' Anyone who voted for him would be in contempt of the House of Commons and liable to be sent to jail. This spiteful and puerile action only served to make a bad situation worse. Wilkes at once stood again and was again returned unopposed. The government obstinately declared the election null and void and called yet another. This time they put up one of their own nominees to oppose him, a drunken ruffian called Colonel Luttrell.

Wilkes cast aside his light-hearted attitude towards the affair and addressed the electorate with the utmost seriousness. The matter had progressed beyond a personal struggle for liberty. It had become a struggle for the fundamental rights of the subject. This right was co-eval with the constitution. 'It began at the very first dawn of liberty on our island, and it will survive to the last convulsive pang of expiring freedom. It is part of the original compact between the sovereign of this nation and the subject, expressly stated in the Bill of Rights.' A representative elected without the consent of the voters was 'an insult to common sense, an absurdity scarcely to be paralleled, an injustice and insolence not to be forgiven'. The contest was between the present administration and all the electors of Great Britain. 'There is nothing personal in it. The cause is national and of the first magnitude.'

The result was an overwhelming vindication of his stand, 1,143 votes for Wilkes, 296 for Luttrell. A purblind government declared Colonel Luttrell duly elected. He was admitted to his seat in April 1769 on a day that the House of Commons would for ever after recall with shame.

REPORTING PARLIAMENT

Wilkes received his defeat with magnanimous good humour and on his release from prison later that same year plunged into the busy life of a city alderman. His supporters regularly petitioned to have the Middlesex election re-opened, but without success. The new prime minister, Lord North, was obstinate, the king insistent. Nothing short of civil war, it seemed, would prise Colonel Luttrell out of his ill-gotten seat. Wilkes, however, was not done with Parliament yet, nor with his contribution to the liberty of the press.

In 1771 he launched a daring coup to secure the freedom to report Parliamentary debates. The issue was initially brought up by the king, who had become irritated by the criticism of his government in the London press. Prosecutions for libel followed, which were invariably upheld by Lord Mansfield, who continued to adhere to the precept that it was for the bench alone to decide whether an article was libellous or not. The only function of the jury was to decide the question of printing. To Wilkes, Mansfield's ruling seemed to strike at the whole liberty of the press and was intimately bound up with the restrictions on reporting the affairs of Parliament. His experiences in Middlesex had convinced him that the people had the right to know what was said there in their name. It was unconstitutional to prevent it, and an outright scandal that critical reports of debates brought the publisher before a judge who was beholden to the government. Wilkes now set them a daring and ingenious trap. He promised his protection as a magistrate to any printer within his jurisdiction who published reports of Parliamentary debates.

Critical reports duly appeared, and on 26 February, Colonel George Onslow, the member for Guildford, lodged a complaint that the publishers of the *Gazetteer* and the *Middlesex Journal* had misrepresented members' speeches and that one of them had had the impertinence to call him 'little cocking George'. He put down a motion calling the two printers to attend at the bar of the House for punishment. On the advice of Wilkes, both men ignored the summons. The Commons forthwith called on the king to issue a proclamation for their arrest and offered a reward of £50 for anyone securing it. Onslow then announced he had 'three brace of printers more' – all, as it happened, outside the city's jurisdiction. Summoned to the bar, one apologised, two were granted leave of absence, two were reprimanded on their bended knees and one, John Miller of the *London Evening Post*, ignored the summons. An order was put out for his arrest also.

Wilkes's trap promptly snapped shut. John Wheble of the *Middlesex Journal* was arrested by one of his own workmen who was in on the plot and brought before the Guildhall Sessions, where Wilkes was sitting that day as a magistrate. Wilkes heard the case gravely and announced that the only grounds for arresting Wheble had been a royal proclamation – and no Englishman could be arrested simply by proclamation. There had to be a proper warrant, signed by a magistrate. Wheble was thereupon discharged and the workman who had arrested him despatched to the Treasury to claim his £50 reward. Wilkes wrote to his old enemy Halifax, who had once again become secretary of state, to inform him that he had discharged Wheble as his arrest had been in direct violation of his rights as a chartered freeman of the City of London.

Enraged by this defiance, the Commons sent a messenger that same evening to arrest John Miller of the *London Evening Post* at his home inside the city. Miller had also been coached, and the messenger sent to arrest him was himself arrested for assault by a city constable conveniently posted there for the purpose. All three proceeded to the Mansion House to be examined by the Lord Mayor, Brass Crosby, and Aldermen John Wilkes and Richard Oliver, the other two magistrates. Crosby solemnly declared that no power on earth had the right to seize a citizen of London without a warrant from himself or some other city magistrate. Miller was released and the hapless messenger committed to jail by the magistrates.

The Commons were beside themselves with fury. Goaded on by the king, they ordered the three magistrates to present themselves before the House the following day. Wilkes refused. He would not come unless he could take his place as the elected member for Middlesex. Crosby was ill with the gout and could not attend either. So Richard Oliver was left to face the wrath of the Commons on his own. He was young but resolute, and refused to apologise. The Commons sent him to the Tower.

Two days later, Brass Crosby, was drawn along to Westminster in his gilded coach by an enormous mob. Swathed in flannel and unable to stand, he waved the City's Charter in the Commons' face and bellowed out his defiance in the voice which gave him his name. He was the city's chief magistrate and the guardian of its charter. 'I could not have done otherwise without violating my oath and my duty, and shall always glory in having done so, be the consequences what they will!' He was denied the right to counsel, and the furious MPs ordered the offending records to be cut from the court's register before Crosby, too, was sent to the Tower for contempt.

Outside, the people of London were in a ferment of rage at this violation of their elected leaders. A mob dragged Lord North from his coach, smashed it up, pulled his hat to pieces and sold the buttons for souvenirs. The House of Commons was only saved from storming by the intervention of Wilkes and the chief reformers, who always held their supporters back from violence or any unconstitutional action. Their point had already been more elegantly made.

When it came to dealing with Wilkes himself, the government was in a quandary. The king had ordered Lord North to have nothing more to do with 'that devil Wilkes', but the Commons had already ordered him to appear before them on 8 April. They got out of their impasse by adjourning until the 9th. Then they passed another motion calling for John Miller of the *London Evening Post* to be taken into custody, though tamely failing to specify how, or by whom.

The process not only showed Parliament up as corrupt; it struck a blow for democracy and free speech. Burke and Chatham thundered in support of the press, Burke long-windedly in the Commons,* Chatham with more effect in the Lords. He warmly commended the City magistrates in the conscientious discharge of their duty and condemned the Commons for their gross and palpable act of tyranny in committing them to prison. Expunging the entry in the court register had been the act of a mob, not a Parliament. The government's actions, as violent as they were absurd, had made Wilkes the person of the greatest consequence and made the very name of Parliament ridiculous.

The Commons never did admit the right to print its debates, but the point was conceded nonetheless. While insisting on the sanctity of their privilege, they never again took arbitrary action to prevent accounts of their debates appearing in the press. They still complained of misrepresentation and were able to bring charges for libel for attacks on individual members, while journalists could always be cleared from the galleries under the House's Standing Orders. In 1775 most of the debates on relations with the American colonies were closed to the press, but orders to shut out the reporters were becoming rarer and it gradually became accepted that the public had a constitutional right to know what their elected representatives were up to. Petty restrictions continued until well into the next century – the reporters were given nowhere to sit and notebooks were not allowed in the chamber. But journalists are nothing if not resourceful, and in the session of 1772 William (Memory) Woodfall, editor of the *Morning Chronicle*, developed a remarkable ability to reproduce almost verbatim accounts of speeches delivered in the House. John Miller of the *London Evening Post* came back in spite of the outstanding motion calling for his arrest. Matters which concerned the community at large, he said, should be as free to circulate as the air they breathe. This significant step towards the liberty of the press was largely due to the challenge to an oligarchic and tyrannical regime thrown down and fought, almost single-handedly, by John Wilkes.

His own career still had many years to run. Towards the end of 1773 he was elected lord mayor, with Polly as his consort. By the time the first shots had been fired in the American War of Independence he was back in Parliament, fairly

---

* Burke's speeches are said to have emptied the Chamber like a dinner bell. 'Too deep for his hearers, he went on refining/And thought of convincing when they thought of dining.'

elected again for Middlesex, and a staunch supporter of the American rebels. 'Liberty I consider as the birthright of every subject of the British Empire, and I hold Magna Carta to be in as full force in America as in Europe,' he declared. In what is often regarded as his greatest speech, he warned the House that they were attempting the impossible. Massachusetts alone could hold out against Britain, Boston would become like Gibraltar, the colonists would make a stand at every Thermopylae, every Bunker Hill, while in the great scale of empire 'you will decline, I fear, from the decision of this day, and the Americans will rise to independence, to power, to all the greatness of the most renowned States, for they build on the solid basis of general, public, liberty'.

He even forecast that one day the Americans would celebrate 'the glorious era of the revolution of 1775 as we do that of 1688'. But his prophetic voice was crying in the wilderness. Britons, their own patriotism aroused, rallied stubbornly around their government, and Wilkes's influence, even among his own supporters, went into decline. Typically, and with his usual courage, he defended the American colonists to the end. In the midst of the war, he also found time to introduce a bill 'for a just and equal representation of the people of England in Parliament,' the precursor of the great reform bills of the following century. The meanest mechanic and the poorest peasant would be enfranchised, the rotten boroughs with only a dozen or so voters would be lopped off, and the rich new trading towns of Manchester, Birmingham, Sheffield and Leeds permitted to send their deputies to the great council of the nation.

Once again, he was ahead of his time. On the great issues of America and constitutional reform he went down to defeat. As a politician and statesman, he occupied no great offices of State. Posterity, too, has dealt with him severely. The upright reformers of the Victorian era disapproved of his morals and disparaged his achievements. 'A profligate spendthrift,' sniffed Lord John Russell, 'without opinions or principles, religious or political; whose impudence far exceeded his talents, and who always meant licence when he cried liberty.'

For all that, he was one of the great champions of English freedom. Without his stand over the Middlesex elections, future Members of Parliament might well have been elected not by their constituents but by their party. The great British tradition of loyal opposition and dissent would have been stifled. The press would have become docile, subservient and enfeebled. As it is, the liberty of the press became what he claimed for it on the very first page of the *North Briton*, 'the firmest bulwark of the liberties of the country'.

His own contribution to that liberty has never been surpassed. He established in the laws of all English-speaking nations the principles on which their freedom rests. In the *North Briton* he founded modern political journalism, free to comment, free to report and freed from concealing the names of the statesmen he mentioned. In Number 45 he asserted the right to criticise the king's speech without punishment. In his battles in the courts he exposed the repressive nature of seditious libel, and paved the way for Fox's Libel Act of 1792 which finally placed the liberty of the press under the protection of a jury. He won the right to report debates in Parliament, changing forever the relationship between the electors and their representatives. He led the way to the abolition of outlawry, which condemned a man in his absence, and to the protection of private property from unreasonable searches and seizures. He also did more than any other man of his age to prevent George III from overthrowing the 'principles of the Revolution', free speech now included among them. He is remembered today not only for the pluck with which he challenged the worn-out conventions of his own day, but also for the wit with which his challenge was conducted. Through all the vicissitudes of life, his humour never deserted him. Dining in old age with the Prince of Wales, then on very bad terms with his father, he raised his glass to wish the king a long life. 'Since when have you become so loyal to the king?' asked the prince. 'Ever since I have had the honour of knowing *your* royal highness,' Wilkes replied with a bow to the heir to the throne.

He lived on through the French Revolution, the violence of which he profoundly disapproved. By now, he was, he said, 'an exhausted volcano'. One day towards the end of his life he met a young stranger in a street in Bath who greeted him with the cry of 'Wilkes and Liberty!' 'Hush, my dear,' he replied. 'That's all long since over.' John Wilkes died on Boxing Day, 1797, at the age of seventy-two. Early in the next year he was laid to rest in the London parish in which he died, where a plain marble tablet carries an inscription written by himself:

> NEAR THIS PLACE ARE INTERRED
> THE REMAINS OF JOHN WILKES,
> A FRIEND TO LIBERTY.

Nowhere was his memory more revered or his influence on the future of free speech to be more profound than in the newly independent and now United States of America. From the moment of the British surrender at Yorktown, the cause of liberty, and with it that of free speech, was to advance more rapidly in the New World than it did in the old.

CHAPTER EIGHT

Tom Paine's Common Sense

In 1774, as Britain's relations with her American colonies were approaching their lowest ebb, an unknown 37-year-old Quaker staymaker set sail from London to begin a new life in Philadelphia. He was cut out to be neither a soldier nor a statesman, but as he would recall later, 'when the country into which I had just set foot was set on fire about my ears, it was time to stir. It was time for every man to stir'.

Tom Paine had found his vocation as a journalist. In little more than a year after settling in Philadelphia, he had written a pamphlet called *Common Sense*, which is generally agreed to have changed the course of American history. Its simple and dramatic call for the colonies to declare their independence provides perhaps the most vivid demonstration of the power of the printed word since Luther ran off his ninety-five theses on the university's presses at Wittenberg. In the judgement of George Trevelyan, the historian of the American Revolution, 'it would be difficult to name any human composition which has had an effect so instant, so extended, and so lasting' as Paine's *Common Sense*. 'It was pirated, parodied, imitated and translated into the language of every country where the new republic had well-wishers. It worked nothing short of miracles, and turned Tories into Whigs.' By the end of 1776, fifty-six editions of *Common Sense* had been printed and it played a decisive part in persuading the colonies to commit themselves to the break with Britain.

There was little in Paine's previous career to have prepared him for the astonishing success of his pamphlet. Born in 1737 in the Norfolk market town of Thetford, he was apprenticed at an early age as a staymaker in his father's business, spending his boyhood learning how to insert whalebone ribs into women's corsets. At sixteen he briefly ran away to sea, only to be fetched back by his father. Three years later, he left Thetford for good and spent the next seventeen years in a peripatetic assortment of jobs around the south and east of England.

He went first to the village of Sandwich on the coast of Kent, where he set up a shop of his own, but abandoned it two years later to become an excise man. He worked for a while looking out for smugglers on the coast of Lincolnshire, but was dismissed for allegedly stamping an assignment of goods he had not in fact examined. He returned to staymaking for a few months at Diss in Norfolk, then made his way to London to teach English at Kensington elementary school.

After writing a humble letter of apology for his previous misdemeanour, he was reinstated as an exciseman at Lewes, a well-known hive of smugglers on the Sussex Downs, where he stayed for the next six years collecting duty on such items as tea, tobacco and casks of beer. He had married a serving girl while still at Sandwich, but his young wife had died within the year, presumably in childbirth. In Lewes, he married his second wife, the daughter of a local storekeeper.

Lewes stirred an interest in both politics and self-education. He bought books, attended lectures, and became an active member of the local debating society. Here, he also discovered his talent for polemics, throwing himself into an ardent campaign to improve the lot of the underpaid excisemen. In 1772, he raided his meagre savings to publish a pamphlet setting out their grievances, arguing that, though they carried a heavy burden of responsibility, they were paid only £50 a year, which was reduced to £32 when the expense of maintaining a horse was taken into account. As this was less than a living wage, it was not surprising that bribery was so common or that the excisemen were so lax in the execution of their duties.

Paine ran off more than 4,000 copies of his pamphlet and went up to London to distribute them to people of influence. His career as a pamphleteer had begun, but at the expense of his job in the excise service. In 1774, he was dismissed for having left his post. In the same year he broke with his wife, the family store failed, and he was forced to sell his household goods and the contents of the shop. He returned to London bankrupt, alone and unemployed; his life seemed to have been a feckless and dismal failure. Like so many others of his kind, both before and since, he resolved to start afresh in America.

His campaign for the excisemen had brought him one stroke of luck. It had introduced him to Benjamin Franklin, the London agent for the American colonies. It was probably Franklin who persuaded him to emigrate, supplying him with a letter to a relative in Philadelphia recommending Paine as an ingenious, worthy young man capable of finding employment as a clerk, assistant tutor in a school, or an assistant surveyor. In this way, said Franklin, 'he may procure a subsistence, at least, till he can make acquaintances and obtain a knowledge of the country'.

Armed with this valuable if somewhat lukewarm recommendation, Paine set out on the two-month voyage to America, surviving an Atlantic storm and an outbreak of scurvy on the way. He arrived at New York in November, and made his way at once to Philadelphia, where after another lucky introduction he found a job on the *Pennsylvania Magazine*. He proved to be a brilliant polemicist in the direct, plainspoken style of Bunyan and Defoe. His political philosophy was equally down-to-earth and in advance of its time. And he had arrived in America at the most critical period in its history. The moment had found its man.

Britain and the American colonies had been at odds over taxes and customs' duties since the end of the Seven Years War in 1763. George III and his ministers were demanding that the prosperous colonies should bear their share of the cost of defending the vast new British territories in Canada and the Mississippi basin. To pacify the Indians, they had also imposed a ban on any further settlement west of the Appalachian Mountains. The Stamp Acts had come and gone, but during the 1770s new duties were imposed on such items as tea and paper and punitive taxes placed on imports not carried in British ships. Outraged that these measures had been imposed without their consent, the colonists took matters into their own hands. A series of protests culminated in the Boston Tea Party of 1773 when over 300 chests of tea were tossed into the harbour. Lord North, the prime minister, closed the port of Boston until the tea was paid for.

By the time Paine arrived in Philadelphia in 1774, the dispute was worsening by the day, though few had yet thought of open rebellion, still less of a complete break with England. The colonies were in the hands of prosperous merchants, planters and landowners, who, like their counterparts in England, had a strong sense of their own rights, but little taste for democracy or the prospect of civil unrest. Their wish was for compromise on terms favourable to themselves, with a Bill of Rights after the English model.

Paine himself later declared,

> I found the disposition of the people such, that they might have been led by a thread and governed by a reed. Their suspicion was quick and penetrating, but their attachment to Britain was obstinate, and it was at that time a kind of treason to speak against it. They disliked the ministry, but they esteemed the nation. Their idea of grievances operated without resentment, but their single object was reconciliation.

Moderate voices in Britain also spoke up for compromise. In the Commons, Edmund Burke poured ridicule on the idea that 'so paltry a sum as threepence in the eyes of a financier, so insignificant an article as tea in the eye of a philosopher' should shake the pillars of an empire that encircled the globe. In the Lords, Chatham urged the government to allay the Americans' grievances, while John Wilkes, as mentioned, wholeheartedly supported the colonists.

Sooner than compromise, the king and Lord North tried to bring their colonies to heel. When the Continental Congress boycotted the import of British goods, North's government blockaded the whole of New England. War followed within a few months. There were skirmishes at Lexington and Concord and a bloody retreat back to Boston by the British redcoats. When the second Continental Congress met at Philadelphia in 1775, the tide in favour of outright independence was rising fast, though it was far from certain it would prevail. It was Paine's *Common Sense* which struck the spark that engulfed a continent.

The plainest and most direct of all his pamphlets, it eschewed the ornamental and self-conscious literary style of the day and carried his readers along with great skill from one argument to the next. It opened not with an outright plea for independence, but with an attack on the 'much boasted constitution of England' with its careful balance of powers between king, lords and people. All through *Common Sense*, Paine is as much concerned to establish that America should become a republic as he is to argue for simple independence. Indeed, he was among the first to establish the notion that a republican form of government was inherently superior to a monarchy.

His condemnation of the British monarchy is savage. An 'exceedingly ridiculous' form of government, he called it, favoured by Englishmen as much from national pride as from reason. 'The plain truth is that it is wholly owing to the *constitution of the people*, and not the *constitution of the government*, that the crown is not as oppressive in England as in Turkey.' As to its rights of succession, 'no man in his sense can say that their claim under William the Conqueror is a very honourable one. A French bastard, landing with an armed banditti, and establishing himself king of England against the consent of the natives, is in plain terms a very paltry, rascally original. It certainly hath no divinity in it'.

To the royalist rulers of Pennsylvania, this was regarded as both heresy and treason. But Paine was beyond their reach as he went on to share his thoughts on the question most colonists still refused to confront – independence. 'The sun never shone on a cause of greater worth,' he declared.

'Tis not the concern of a city, a county, a province, or a kingdom, but of a continent – of at least one eighth part of the habitable globe. 'Tis not the concern of a day, a year, or an age; posterity are virtually involved in the contest and will be more or less affected even to the end of time, by the proceedings now. Now is the seed time of continental union, faith and honour. The least fracture now will be like a name engraved with the point of a pin on the tender rind of a young oak; the wound will enlarge with the tree, and posterity read it in full-grown characters.

Paine then turned to the arguments in favour of reconciliation, only to cast them aside 'as an agreeable dream which has passed away.' Some asserted America was dependent on maintaining her connections with Britain. Fallacious, said Paine, you may as well assert that because a child thrived on milk it is never to have meat. America would flourish on the commerce by which she had already enriched herself. She produced the necessities of life and would always have a market 'while eating is the custom of Europe.'

But Britain had protected us, said some. Yes, said Paine, but her motives were for the sake of trade and dominion and she would have defended Turkey from the same motive. 'She did not protect us from *our enemies* on *our account*, but from *her enemies on her own account*, [and] from those who had no quarrel with us on *any other account*.'

Britain is our parent country, said others. Then more shame upon her conduct, said Paine. 'Even brutes do not devour their young, nor savages make war upon their own families.' Europe, not England, was the parent country of America. 'This new world hath been the asylum for the persecuted lovers of civil and religious liberty from *every part* of Europe. Hither they have fled, not from the tender embraces of a mother, but from the cruelty of the monster'.

Much had been said about the united strength of Britain and the colonies, who might in conjunction bid defiance to the world. What have we to do with setting the world at defiance? Paine asked. Our plan is commerce, which, well attended to, will secure the peace and friendship of all Europe. 'I challenge the warmest advocate for reconciliation to shew a single advantage that this continent can reap from being connected with Great Britain,' he declared. There was not one; though the injuries and disadvantages were without number, and 'our duty to mankind, as well as to ourselves, instructs us to renounce the alliance'.

It was in America's interest to steer clear of European connections, because whenever war broke out between England and another foreign power, the trade of America would go to ruin because of her connection with Britain. Nothing but independence and a continental form of government could maintain the peace of the continent and keep it out of Europe's civil wars.

Everything that is right or natural pleads for separation. The blood of the slain and the weeping voice of nature cries, 'TIS TIME TO PART. Even the distance at which the Almighty hath placed England and America is a strong and natural proof that the authority of the one over the other was never the design of heaven. The time likewise at which the continent was discovered adds weight to the argument, and the manner in which it was peopled increases the force of it. The reformation was preceded by the discovery of America, as if the Almighty graciously meant to open a sanctuary for the persecuted in future years, when home should provide neither friendship nor safety.

He ended this section of his pamphlet on a ringing note:

O ye that love mankind! Ye that dare oppose, not only the tyranny, but the tyrant, stand forth! Every spot of the old world is over-run with oppressions. Freedom hath been hunted round the globe. Asia and Africa have long expelled her. – Europe regards her like a stranger, and England hath given her a warning to depart. O! receive the fugitive, and prepare in time an asylum for mankind.

America was overwhelmed by Paine's rhetoric. Edmund Randolph of Virginia noted that public sentiment, which a few weeks before its publication in January 1776 had 'shuddered at the tremendous obstacles with which independence was environed, now overleaped over every barrier'. General Washington found its reasoning so unanswerable he told the Continental Congress 'it would not leave members at a loss to decide upon the propriety of a separation'. A leading citizen of Massachusetts remarked that 'every sentiment has sunk into my well-prepared heart'; while a Connecticut reader told Paine 'your production may justly be compared to a landflood that sweeps all before it. We were blind, but on reading these enlightening words the scales have fallen from our eyes'.

All over New England 'it was read by public men, repeated in clubs, spouted in schools, and in one instance, delivered from the pulpit instead of a sermon by a clergyman in Connecticut'. Everywhere, the colonists spoke of it in terms of rapturous praise, save perhaps for the Boston radical, John Adams, who grumbled that Paine had merely offered a 'tolerable summary' of the arguments he had himself been putting forward for the past six months.

Adams was right to point out that Paine's arguments were not original. The separateness of America, the corruption they had left behind in Europe and the absurdity of hereditary government were the commonplace maxims of all American radicals. What Adams failed to see was the brilliant synthesis that Paine had provided in language which spoke straight to the hearts of the ordinary people and the relentless logic with which he demolished the arguments in favour of reconciliation. The fact that he had come to America as an outsider was a decided advantage. In the words of a recent biographer, his image of the new world 'could only be created by a man who knew Europe well enough to hate its society and who longed desperately enough for salvation to envision in a flash of illumination the destiny of the new world as liberation from the old'.

The impact of Paine's *Common Sense* is one of the most striking examples of the power of the printed word to sway the minds of man ever recorded in the English language. But how was it achieved? In any other country of the age, his words would have been suppressed and their author punished. In Britain, he would certainly have been charged with seditious libel and perhaps even with treason – which was to happen to him later for writing other pamphlets. At the time he wrote *Common Sense*, no coherent philosophy of free speech had been developed in America. Paine's triumph was unique, and may be said to have established the idea of a free press as one of the necessary bulwarks of the new country's constitution.

THE COLONIAL PRESS

The American press was different in kind from its British and European counterparts, having risen for commercial rather than intellectual reasons. Literature, in the form of books and *belles-lettres*, came in ready-made from the mother country. American printers served the more mundane needs of their own community and everywhere owed their first establishment to government subsidy. The first item ever printed in America was not a newspaper, a book of poetry or a copy of the Bible. It was a form, printed in 1639 to enable legal oaths to be sworn.

America's early publishers were essentially *printers*, ink-stained artisans striving to earn a living by offering a service to the general public, their work typically a mixture of advertising, official pronouncements, copies of documents needed to conduct everyday business and whatever private jobbing work they could pick up. Before the quarrel with Britain there were some thirty-one such presses scattered throughout the thirteen colonies, most of them run by a 'government man', answerable to the leaders of his colony. 'I do not know that the publication of newspapers was ever prohibited in Virginia,' Thomas Jefferson recalled many years later. 'Until the beginning of our revolutionary disputes, we had but one press, and that, having the whole business of the government, and no competitor for public favour, nothing disagreeable to the governor could be got into it.'

It is true that some of the attributes of free speech were present in colonial America – there was very little attempt at prior restraint, for instance – but by no means all of them were. Prosecution for seditious libel was still possible and printers were sometimes punished for the things they wrote. But the most effective control of all was the prospect of losing valuable business if the printer stepped too far out of line with those who provided him with his livelihood. Not until the break with Britain did he emerge as a leader of opinion, though by then he had acquired unique qualifications to take on the role.

Because the colonial printer often doubled as the local postman, his shop was usually a gathering place for the whole community, a forum for the exchange of news and opinions. He became a man who knew about public affairs, a person of influence, and often also the publisher of the local newspaper. To make his living, he had to discover sources of news within his own community, and in doing so he gradually acquired a status unknown to his English counterpart.

The American historian Daniel Boorstin observed that the 'Publick Printer' was an American institution, a printer-journalist-postmaster pursuing a new and distinctively American profession. He started as a craftsman and small businessman rather than as a man of letters, but he had an important function in government that kept him in touch with public affairs.

The most famous exemplar of this spirit was that personification of the successful artisan, Benjamin Franklin of Philadelphia. His *Poor Richard's Almanack* sold 10,000 copies a year, its celebration of self-improvement, hard work and thrift making him a rich man. 'Time is money,' he preached, and proved it in his own life to the full. Training a succession of apprentices and journeymen in his own printer's shop, Franklin sent them off to set up in another town, agreeing with his characteristic blend of idealism and practicality to pay a third of their initial expenses in return for a third of the profits. 'He that hath a trade, hath an estate,' he told them.

While Franklin's precepts inspired a whole generation of fiercely independent artisan printers, they had a hard struggle to make a living. Each of them was dependent for his raw materials – his ink and paper, even his lead type – on merchants who imported them from overseas. His economic survival was heavily reliant on credit and severely affected by the various tariffs that were imposed in the twelve rasping years of dispute that preceded the War of Independence. Those who survived were practical businessmen who knew how to cope in a competitive world. Until the quarrel with Britain turned them into ardent economic nationalists, they gave little thought to the liberties which underpinned their craft. Free trade had always been more important to them than free speech. Nevertheless, by the time America declared its independence, the spectacle had emerged 'not of the learned and the wealthy only, but of the great body of the people; even a large portion of daily labourers, having free and constant access to public prints'.

Inevitably, there had been conflicts with authority, and at least one notable landmark on the way towards a truly free press in America. Early in 1734, the German-born New York printer, John Peter Zenger, published a series of politically sponsored criticisms of the unpopular royalist governor, William Cosby, which were to lead to important changes in the law of seditious libel. Zenger's *Weekly Journal* had attacked Cosby as 'a governor turned rogue', accusing him of suppressing trial by jury and undermining the colony's fundamental laws. Having failed to persuade two grand juries to indict Zenger for these attacks, the governor had his council issue a warrant for the printer's arrest, charging him with 'tending to raise factions and tumults among the people'. The *Journal* was burned and Zenger spent ten months in jail, unable to raise the bail that Cosby demanded, and resolutely refusing to name the authors of the offending articles.

When the case came to court in 1735, it was expected to follow the common law process laid down by Lord Chief Justice Holt thirty years earlier, namely that it was for the judge to decide the libel and the jury merely the fact of publication. But to conduct the defence, Zenger's supporters (who may have included Benjamin Franklin) had hired one of the country's most distinguished lawyers, the elderly Andrew Hamilton of Philadelphia. It was an inspired choice.

After the formal indictment had been read and Zenger pleaded not guilty, Hamilton rose to admit that his client had indeed published the articles named in the charges. In that case, declared Richard Bradley, New York's Attorney General, the jury should bring in an immediate verdict of guilty.

'Not so, neither, Mr. Attorney,' Hamilton replied, 'You will have something more to do before you make my client a libeller. For the words themselves must be libellous – that is, false, malicious and seditious – or else we are not guilty.'

The judge intervened: 'You cannot be admitted, Mr. Hamilton, to give the truth of a libel in evidence. This court is of the opinion that you ought not to be permitted to prove the facts in the papers.'

Hamilton said that would make it a Star Chamber case. The flustered judge ordered him to mind his manners: 'you are not permitted to argue against this court.' The white-haired old lawyer bowed to him courteously. 'I thank you,' he said, and turned his back on the bench to address the jury. 'Then it is to you gentlemen that we must now appeal for witnesses to the truth of the facts we have offered.'

The judge again interrupted. Juries had no right under law to decide anything other than what Hamilton had already admitted, namely that Zenger had published the articles. It was for the judges, not the jury, to decide whether or not they were libellous.

Hamilton accepted that *false* charges against the authorities would merit punishment as a seditious libel; his argument was confined to the proposition that 'truth ought to be the whole affair of libels'. But after the judges again rejected this proposition he fell back on an eloquent plea for a free press. He put it to the jury – 'old and weak as I am' – that their one and only consideration should be liberty. The question before them was not the cause of a poor printer, nor of New York alone:

> No! It may in its consequences affect every freeman that lives under a British government on the Main of America. It is the best cause. It is the cause of liberty; and I make no doubt but that your upright conduct this day will not only entitle you to the love and esteem of your fellow-citizens; but every man who prefers freedom to a life of slavery will bless and honour you, as men who have baffled the attempt of tyranny; and by an impartial and uncorrupt verdict, have laid the noble foundation for securing to ourselves, our posterity and our neighbours, that, to which nature and the laws of our country have given us a right – the Liberty – both of exposing and opposing arbitrary power (in these parts of the world, at least) by speaking and writing truth.

Thanks to Hamilton's inspired pleading, the jury over-rode the judge's instructions and returned a general verdict of not guilty, an outcome that reverberated around the Anglo-Saxon world. Hamilton himself was made a Freeman of New York and forty years later, Gouverneur Morris, one of the signatories of the Declaration of Independence, traced the beginning of American liberty to the case – 'the morning star of that liberty which subsequently revolutionised America.'

While Zenger has subsequently become an American legend, the most singular aspect of his trial at the time was its isolation. 'The time had not yet arrived when the printers would act unitedly in behalf of their right to criticise public affairs,' wrote Arthur Schlesinger Sr, the historian of the pre-revolutionary newspapers. The case did, however, have two important consequences for the future development of free speech. It opened the way for the eventual admission of truth as a defence against seditious libel and it encouraged the idea that a jury of one's peers was an essential bulwark against the excesses of an oppressive government. When governments are unpopular and out of touch with public opinion, that is certainly true: juries are the guardian of individual liberties. What the libertarians of the day failed to see was that this is not a universal truth. Juries can be as prejudiced and intolerant of unpopular opinions as judges. All the Zenger case proved was that if the defendant in a case of seditious libel represents the voice of current public opinion, the jury are likely to acquit; but if not – if he threatens or challenges their own orthodox views – they will condemn him as readily as Lord Justice Jeffreys or the Spanish Inquisition. The libertarian fallacy was to be cruelly exposed before the century was out in both Britain and America, as indeed it had been two thousand years previously in ancient Athens.

Though the commercial press by and large remained aloof, the Zenger case had put the idea of free speech on the radical agenda. As the quarrel with Britain intensified, the works of two English journalists, Thomas Gordon and John Trenchard, who wrote under the name of 'Cato' had a huge vogue in America. Their essay *On Freedom of Speech* was quoted 'in every colonial newspaper from Boston to Savannah,' and was still being reprinted on the eve of the War of Independence. 'Whoever would overthrow the liberty of a nation must begin by subduing freedom of speech; a thing terrible to public tyrants,' they wrote. 'There can be no such thing as public liberty without freedom of speech, which is the right of every man, as far as by it he does not hurt and control the right of another. This is the only check which it ought to suffer, the only bounds which it ought to know.' Who was to determine those bounds Cato did not say. As for allowing the uncontrolled liberty to calumniate the government, Cato accepted that libels against authority were rightly unlawful and should be honestly punished as an abuse of liberty. Benjamin Franklin, too, often spoke up for the *principle* of free speech, holding the Miltonian view that all opinions ought to be heard, that truth would 'overmatch' error, but that vice and immorality should not be countenanced and that writers could be punished if they went too far. This widely held concept was drawn from the work of the influential English jurist, Sir William Blackstone, whose *Commentaries on the Laws of England* published in 1767 defined the limits to free speech in a way accepted on both sides of the Atlantic for more than a generation to come:

The *liberty of the press* is indeed essential to the nature of a free State; but this consists in laying *no previous restraint* upon publications, and not in freedom from censure for criminal matter when published. Every freeman has an undoubted right to lay what sentiments he pleases before the public: to forbid this is to destroy the freedom of the press; but if he publishes what is improper, mischievous or illegal, he must take the consequences of his own temerity.

Under Blackstone's definition, free speech lay solely in the absence of censorship. It left the will of individuals free and only punished its abuse. The fact that a man might be whipped or sent to jail for words deemed by a judge to be seditious never entered the argument, nor did the obvious fact that freedom of political discourse and the law of seditious libel were clearly incompatible. Despite Franklin's fine words and the acquittal of Zenger, the law remained in force even after the liberty of the press had been enshrined in the new country's constitution. Andrew Hamilton's proposition that truth should be a complete defence against a charge of seditious libel also turned out to be bulwark built on sand, since it soon became clear that truth was no more capable of an agreed definition than any other abstract concept, particularly when passions were aroused and patriotic truths became loyalist lies.

The boundaries of free speech in America consequently remained more or less static until the last decade of the eighteenth century. The orthodox definition taken from Blackstone was repeated as a comforting rubric on both sides of the great divide and both before and after the War of Independence. Chief Justice Hutchinson, the last royalist judge in Massachusetts, described the freedom of the press as 'doubtless a very great blessing.' But this liberty, he said, 'means no more than a freedom for every thing to pass from the press without licence from any authority'. To carry the notion to the lengths that some would have it – to print every thing that is libellous and slanderous – 'is truly astonishing and of the utmost dangerous tendency'. Radicals, too, accepted the principle that the State might be criminally undermined by mere words, even when their only demonstrable consequence was to cause the people to think less highly of their government. After the Zenger case, juries needed to be persuaded that the words were either malicious or false, but there was general agreement that seditious words, as well as seditious acts, constituted a crime. Until long after the revolution, the most advanced thinkers of the age could conceive of no freedom that went beyond the absence of prior restraints. And not until the crisis over free speech at the very end of the 1790s did anyone challenge the basic *concept* of seditious libel. The common sentiment of the age was that expressed by Francis Hopkinson, one of the signatories of the Declaration of Independence:

The liberty of the press hath been justly held up as an important privilege of the people. But when this privilege is manifestly abused, and the press becomes an engine for sowing the most dangerous dissensions, for spreading false alarms, and undermining the very foundations of government, ought not that government upon the plain principles of self-preservation, to silence by its own authority such a daring violator of its peace, and tear from its bosom the serpent that would sting it to death?

The patriotic Boston *Gazette* was even more explicit. 'Political liberty consists in a freedom of speech and action, so far as the laws of a community will permit, and no further,' it declared. 'All beyond is criminal and tends to the destruction of liberty itself.' They showed what they meant after the rebellion against the British had broken out: anyone who opposed their cause was denied access to the press. John Mein, publisher of the loyalist Boston *Chronicle*, was among those driven out of business for what he had written, his office windows smashed, his signs daubed with filth, and he was threatened with violence, forcing him to take refuge on a British ship in the harbour. The Adams cousins and their supporters were 'contending for an unlimited freedom of thought and action, which they would confine wholly to themselves', Judge Hutchinson acidly observed.

John Adams would not disagree. What he demanded for Massachusetts was not a 'free press', but a 'well-regulated' press. 'There is nothing in the world so excellent that it may not be abused,' he said. 'When a people are corrupted, the press may be made an engine to complete their ruin . . . and the freedom of the press, instead of promoting the cause of liberty, will but hasten its destruction.'

In Arthur Schlesinger's words, the patriots contended that 'liberty of speech belonged solely to those who spoke the speech of liberty'. So when a New York newspaper publisher acted on the principle that both sides should have a hearing and printed a loyalist rebuttal to Tom Paine's *Common Sense*, a gang of vigilantes dragged him from his bed and forced him to burn the manuscript. Next day, every printer in the city received the following communiqué: 'Sir, if you print . . . anything against the rights and liberties of America . . . death and destruction, ruin and perdition shall be your portion.' Nothing appeared thereafter but sentiments that were approved by the vigilantes.

Even after victory was assured, the same traits remained plainly in evidence. When the English journalist William Cobbett arrived in Philadelphia he was at first charmed with the liberty its citizens seemed to enjoy. 'I saw pamphlets in every window, and newspapers in every hand,' he wrote. 'I was, indeed, rather surprised to find that these pamphlets and these newspapers were all on one side: but I said to myself, this must be the fault of the authors and editors. Long did I hope to see something like a manly and effectual opposition, but I hoped and expected in vain.' The old myth that Americans of the revolutionary generation cherished and fought for the right to unfettered free speech is therefore seen to be a romantic illusion. The American people did not yet accept that freedom of thought and expression meant equal freedom for the other fellow, especially the one with hated ideas.

This is a phenomenon that goes a long way towards explaining the success of Tom Paine. He was able to write so freely because almost everyone in America agreed with him. When his writings were unpopular, as they became with his later attacks on organised religion, *The Age of Reason*, he would be reviled and shunned – especially in America. The new democracy proved to be no exception to the rule that the right to free speech is no right at all if it excludes the right to put forward unpopular, heretical, or even seditious ideas. The greatest tyrannies in the world have never curtailed the freedom to *agree* with them.

CHAPTER NINE

Revolution and The Rights of Man

Although France held the intellectual ascendancy of Europe, the concept of individual liberty – and with it, the freedom of speech – had never taken root there in the way it had done in the Anglo-Saxon world. Until the revolution, censorship was universal, free institutions unknown and the freedom of speech granted at the discretion of an absolute monarch. Society was rigid and hierarchical, the nobility set apart. Louis XVI chose his ministers from almost none but the aristocracy, all the bishops without exception were members of the nobility, while officers in the army were required to have at least four generations of noble blood. There was no representative national Parliament. The system of taxation was arbitrary and unjust. And yet for most of the eighteenth century the French bourgeoisie had prospered, their influence and independence growing rapidly alongside their contempt for the incompetence and extravagance of an absolutist form of government that seemed to intrude into every aspect of their lives but from which they were excluded.

The government of the later Bourbons has been described as not so much a tyranny as a ramshackle and fussy bureaucracy that seemed both more unenlightened and more despotic than it actually was. As a result, it lost the support of both conservatives and progressives, who became openly critical of its glaring faults. But under a system that lacked the means to reform itself, the freedom with which people began to criticise and complain about their government was spent in frustration. To the extent that free speech did exist in France under the monarchy, it was unwholesome and destructive, with no hope of making its effect felt and no audience but the disaffected and rebellious. Because of the censorship, it became sly and indirect, compelled to conceal its true aims in a variety of cunning subterfuges. Even Diderot, the compiler of the great *Encyclopaedia*, felt obliged to disguise his essay on the liberty of speech as an article on an obscure and otherwise unimportant Roman divinity.

Throughout its years of discontent, France had never enjoyed the benefits of a free press that was so praised in England. There was no inalienable right of the people to pursue reform or change their governments. The opposition was pent up, and worked unseen, but, as events soon proved, it was liable at any moment to burst forth in a destructive storm. In the 1780s it was actively helped on its way by the very people against whom it was directed. By flirting irresponsibly with ideas they only half understood, but found diverting, the old regime did as much as anyone to encompass their own undoing. Startling though it may seem, the court and the high nobility were the prime customers for the works that did most damage to their authority. In his seminal study on the causes of the French revolution, Simon Schama has shown that the proliferation of seditious and libellous material was openly encouraged by the court. Their appetite for daring literature – both political and erotic – was boundless. A number of shops surrounded the king's palace at Versailles, where professional hawkers, known as *colporteurs,* unloaded their stock. Similar outlets were found in towns to which the court seasonally moved, in particular Compiegne, Fontainebleau and St Cloud. The immunity of the nobility from search and seizure meant that the *colporteurs* used them shamelessly to smuggle their goods. Even the king's youngest brother, Artois, was said to be a protector of the hawkers of libels, while Marie-Antoinette was a persistent and enthusiastic spectator at the subversive plays of Beaumarchais and the other satirists, even though most of them were officially proscribed. The more outrageous the denunciations of the established order, the more the queen seemed to like it. As Schama said, it was not the disconnection, but the connection, between the world of monied patronage and fiery polemics that made the damage to the dignities of the old regime so serious.

The last decade of the monarchy saw a proliferation of banned literature of all kinds – from newspapers to polemical pamphlets, literary journals and printed ballads and poems. News came largely from abroad, with Holland, Brussels and Geneva all printing influential news-sheets in French. By the eve of the revolution, papers were openly published in Paris as well, the *Mercure de France* reaching a circulation of 20,000. One observer commented: 'This review has spread everywhere, to commoners as well as the nobles, in the salons of the aristocracy as well as the modest household of the bourgeois, delighting equally both court and town.'

All France was by now swarming with purveyors of forbidden literature, both high and low. They travelled on well-established routes, often using canals and rivers for their transport. By such means, Lyon, Rouen, Marseille, Bordeaux and most other major cities were well stocked with ostensibly forbidden works. Schama relates that in Paris, they could be had not only in the Palais-Royal but also from stands on the Pont Neuf and the quays. Though expressly prohibited, vendors hawked books in cafes and theatres, and even from stalls on the streets, all with the complicity of the authorities who seem to have concluded that since they had lost the ability to control the flow of ideas, they might as well keep themselves informed about what was going on.

Much of the illicit traffic was in 'low' literature: cheaply produced fantasies and fairy stories, gossip and scandal and subversively satirical works such as Beaumarchais' immensely popular *Marriage of Figaro.* But even those who drank only at the wells of ephemera were imbibing the pervasive message of innocence corrupted and the brutality of power. And along with the ephemera came serious works of philosophy and propaganda aimed directly at undermining the authority of the old regime. In many a fashionable salon, pink-ribboned parcels of forbidden writings by Rousseau, Voltaire and Montesquieu were excitedly unwrapped and secretly devoured, their readers little realising the extent to which they were sabotaging their own position. For just as the nobility was able to gain access to the forbidden works, so were other readers, the bourgeois intelligentsia, scornful of the privileges of the aristocracy, enraged by the abuses of the monarchy and wholly won over by the growing band of *philosophes* who for a generation past had been prophesying a new age of Enlightenment based on the modern concepts of reason and progress.

Though they were harried and often suppressed, the *philosophes* acquired enormous influence in France, and are justly remembered for starting the movement for intellectual and emotional emancipation now known as the European Enlightenment. To later generations, their faith in progress would seem naive, but at the time it came over as an exciting and tremendously powerful new concept. Their basic premise was that the ills that afflicted society were remediable and that the future ought always to be better than the past. Man could become the master of his own fate. The object of society was to secure the greatest happiness of the greatest number. Their cool, rational and essentially optimistic view of the world led them to reject as absurd those institutions that were hallowed by tradition and authority and allowed them to suppose they could apply the force of reason to their improvement. While such notions may have been simplistic – none of the *philosophes* foresaw the French Revolution, for instance, much less the Reign of Terror that followed it – there can be no doubt that they changed the course of western civilisation in ways that were intellectually beneficial.

In their war against dogmatic religion, they promoted the liberty of thought and in their passionate search for truth, they advanced the cause of free speech. Their optimistic belief in the perfectibility of human nature led them to oppose all forms of superstition, ignorance and tyranny and advocate the view that the diffusion of knowledge among the people was the means by which the improvement of their lot was to be effected. Their leaders prided themselves on being men of reason, less pedantic than the scholastic philosophers, better grounded in science and the humanities, and above all, more civic minded. And they showed more fully than ever before the power of the intelligentsia to shape public opinion.

Their most influential work – 'the great affair of the time' – was the *Encyclopaedia*, begun by Diderot in 1750 with the avowed intention of indoctrinating public opinion with the ideals of the Enlightenment. Twenty years of labour went into this inspired work of propaganda, as Diderot, like Galileo before him, ran rings around the official censors, insinuating his most radical ideas in the guise of an essay on some quite innocuous subject. Christian theology, for instance, was attacked under other headings, with cross-references to indicate the connection between pagan superstitions and Church doctrines. Conservatives charged the encyclopaedists with propagating materialism, destroying religion and inspiring an unwelcome spirit of independence, and when the authorities moved in to suppress them, Frederick the Great – the patron saint of the Enlightenment – invited them to finish it in Prussia.

The most famous freethinker of the age was of course Voltaire, whose influence was perhaps greater even than the *Encyclopaedia*. Born of bourgeois parents in 1694 and educated by the Jesuits, he tempered his faith in reason with the typically French virtues of scepticism and irony. His legacy to the liberty of thought and conscience is encapsulated in his legendary phrase: 'I disagree with everything you say, but will fight to the death for your right to say it.' For Voltaire, more than any other thinker of the Enlightenment, freedom of thought was his primary objective and he spent his long lifetime striving to bring it about, much of it in exile from his native land, where his works were banned. But while

France could shut out Voltaire, they were unable to shut out his ideas. No man of his day was better known, more widely admired, more deeply feared – or, it might be added, more widely read. In spite of his exile and censorship, illegal copies of his pamphlets sold by the thousand and his best-known work, *Candide*, was read in every literate salon in Europe.

He had immersed himself in literature after leaving college and became a famous Paris wit until he went too far and mocked the regent of the young Louis XV, the Duke of Orleans, for which he was imprisoned in the Bastille for nearly a year. He became an aggressive deist and learned English in order to study Locke, ending up in England as an exile for two years after a quarrel with the chevalier de Rohan. It was England that stirred his interest in the freedom of thought, and he became convinced that it was because of their freedom of speech that the English had been able to develop liberal political institutions and, with Newton and Locke, were at the forefront of scientific thought. 'See into what horrible decadence the liberty of the press has brought England and Holland,' he once said. It had merely enabled them to 'possess the commerce of the whole world'. Even in literature, he concluded that France had something to learn from England, and he became a lifelong admirer of the plays of Shakespeare, though he was shocked by the barbarism of the productions and always had a fastidious French dislike of the partisan violence of English political life.

His visit to England convinced him that law was the source and basis of all civilisation. In a free country, he had enjoyed 'the greatest benefit I know and humanity's most glorious right, which is to depend only upon men's laws and not upon their whims'. To him, the essential aspects of English society were freedom of speech and the press, religious toleration and popular power as expressed in an elected House of Commons. He saw that the fundamental principle of freedom of thought determined a long series of other liberties. Break that link, and the whole system collapsed. Reason, he argued, was a vital discipline for every individual. But it became useful to society only when its findings were communicated; hence freedom of expression was an indispensable corollary of freedom of thought. Man must be free; freedom depended on law; hence the best government was that which guaranteed to all, without distinction, the utmost liberty he could enjoy without harm to his fellows.

Returning to France in 1729, he held up England as a model for his compatriots to follow and began to write plays in the style of Shakespeare, though with little success. Shakespeare was at that time quite unknown in France,* where, then as now, it was akin to high treason to seek for light beyond their own frontiers. But by shrewd speculation, Voltaire built up a vast fortune, which assured his independence for the rest of his life and allowed him to turn to the writing of history and philosophy. In one of his *Lettres Philosophiques*, published in 1734, he affirmed that the purpose of life is not to reach heaven through penitence, but to assure happiness to all men through progress in science and the arts.

---

* Readers who turned to 'Shakespeare' in the famous *Encyclopaedia* found there was no such entry.

Scandal followed, and a warrant was issued for Voltaire's arrest, which led him to take refuge in the chateau of Mme de Châtelet, with whom he began a liaison that lasted for fifteen years. Controversy was never far away and Voltaire had to go into hiding again for exercising too freely his belief in free speech while standing at the queen's gaming table. After Mme de Châtelet had lost large sums, he whispered to her in English: 'You are playing with card sharpers.' The remark was understood and Voltaire exiled in disgrace.

On a personal level these were the happiest days of Voltaire's life, though the liaison with Mme de Châtelet ended tragically when he discovered her love affair with the poet Saint-Lambert and then witnessed her death in childbirth. Voltaire returned in despair to the house where they had lived together in Paris, wandering around in the darkness calling out the name of the woman who had not only been his mistress and companion, but his intellectual equal and counsellor.

The loss of his life's love, the failure of his plays and his disenchantment with the new literary fashions which favoured sentiment and passion over enlightenment and reason, caused Voltaire to take off for the court of Frederick the Great at Potsdam, where he became a kind of philosopher in residence. After three years there, he quarrelled with Frederick over another pamphlet and left in a huff. Frederick had him detained at an inn in Frankfurt, Louis XV forbade him to approach Paris, and for more than a year Voltaire literally had nowhere to turn. A spell at Geneva ended in further quarrels over an outspoken essay on Calvin in the *Encyclopaedia*, which he was said to have inspired. Finally, in 1758, he settled in Ferney, just inside Switzerland, with another property over the border in case the police should harry him from one country to another.

In Ferney, Voltaire entered the most productive period of his life. *Candide* mocked the optimistic philosophy of Condorcet that 'all was for the best in the best of all possible worlds' – a work of satire that caused many to suppose Voltaire himself was a pessimist. He in fact shared the Enlightenment's believe in progress; but a progress which could only be achieved by the rigorous application of science and reason and which took as its starting point the view that if man already lived in the best of all possible worlds 'then God help man'.

For someone already in his sixties, Voltaire displayed prodigious energy. He turned Ferney into a model estate, renovated the local Church under the motto *Deo erexit Voltaire* (Voltaire built this to God) and took an active part in local politics, abolishing the customs barrier outside the village and taking on unemployed *natifs* to work in a stocking factory and watchworks on his estate. He entertained Boswell, Casanova, Gibbon and countless others and became known as the 'Innkeeper of Europe'. He made up his quarrel with Frederick the Great and entered into correspondence with the Empress Catherine of Russia, whom he called the 'Semiramis of the North'. Meanwhile, his literary output was greater than it had ever been. Works of history, philosophy, drama, political economy and low polemics flowed from his pen. He wrote his *Treatise on Tolerance* and developed his famous battle-cry *ecrasez l'infame*, by which he meant the organised Church.

Like most men of the Enlightenment, Voltaire was a deist. His famous aphorism that 'if God did not exist, he would have to be invented', is a mark of the cool and rational nature of his religious beliefs, as was his remark that 'doubt may be uncomfortable, but certainty is ridiculous'. Voltaire's God was so unspiritual that Newton's watchmaker might have invented him; passion he reserved for hatred of the excesses of the established Church. This was an age in which Protestants were still broken on the wheel for preventing their children's conversion to the Catholic faith and a nineteen-year-old *chevalier* beheaded for insulting a religious procession and damaging a crucifix. On each occasion, Voltaire was there with an active protest or a devastating broadside, constantly preaching the benefits of tolerance, free thought and the application of reason.

It was to supervise the production of his best-known play *Irene* that he returned to Paris in 1778 after a break of twenty-eight years. On his arrival, he embraced that other venerable sage, Benjamin Franklin, and enjoyed his final triumph. More than 300 people called to see him the next day, and when *Irene* was performed at the Theatre-Français he was crowned in his box. The excitement over-taxed his strength – he was by then 84 years old – and he died in May with a jest on his lips at the expense of the Church. To the very last, a Catholic confessor had attempted to persuade him to accept the rites of absolution, and when asked to renounce the devil, Voltaire is reputed to have opened one eye and replied, 'Is this the time to make enemies?' At the height of the revolution, in 1791, the remains of the wicked old deist were transferred to the Pantheon in a ceremony of great pomp.

His legacy is mixed. The revolution, when it came, caught the enlightened *philosophes* wholly by surprise. Yet it was they as much as anyone who had brought it about. Their repeated and thoroughly justified attacks on a rotten system of government and their equally justified criticism of organised religion fatally undermined both Church and State. But they offered nothing practical to put in their place and had shown little concern for the political institutions that are needed to secure a balance between order and freedom. Neither Voltaire nor any of the other *philosophes* of the French Enlightenment worked out any systematic theory of government or drew up a constitution, as the American radicals had done. Few of them believed in democracy – Voltaire repeatedly referred to the common people as a 'rabble' and on the whole put his trust in an enlightened and educated monarchy, his ideal being a 'benign despot' like his friend Frederick the Great. Freedom, in which he passionately believed, would be imposed from above by the few enlightened men who were capable of thinking for themselves. Free speech was reserved for the educated élite, and still considered to be too dangerous to entrust to the masses.

THE CONSERVATIVE REACTION

When revolution engulfed France in 1789, a wave of fear coursed its way through the entire civilised world. America enacted its Alien and Sedition Acts, England a series of measures that threw free speech and a free press into the severest jeopardy since the collapse of the licensing laws. The victories of John Wilkes and the American revolutionaries seemed to have gone for nothing. Their battles would have to be fought all over again; though this time the old order was not just fighting for supremacy, it was fighting for survival.

Their call to arms was sounded late in 1790 by the Irish politician Edmund Burke in his seminal *Reflections on the Revolution in France*, a brilliant and savage attack on all the radicals stood for and an eloquent defence of the *status quo*. Burke's pamphlet, the foundation-stone of modern conservatism, viewed society as a complex amalgam of tradition and established institutions which man cast aside at his peril. The accumulated wisdom of the past was a far surer guide to politics than abstract 'prattling about the rights of man' which, as France had shown, had a dangerous tendency to upset the stability on which every successful State was founded. Burke revered tradition, admired the hierarchical and hereditary social order and believed in the 'principles of natural subordination' that stable government required of the body of the people. If society was a contract, it was not one that could be dissolved at pleasure. It was one which spanned the generations, a partnership not only between those who are living, but also with those who are dead, and those who are yet to be born. As such, it had to be looked upon with reverence.

Burke's *Reflections* not only foresaw that the revolution would end in discord, but that it would lead to the emergence of 'some popular general' who understood the true spirit of command. The moment in which that event shall happen, wrote Burke, the person who commands your army becomes your master – 'the master of your king, the master of your assembly, the master of your whole republic'. It is on that singular flash of foresight that Burke owes his modern reputation as a political philosopher of the first rank, as much as on his reverent acceptance of traditional institutions. Events seemed to bear him out.

Burke's *Reflections* were published in November 1790. Within two months they were countered by Tom Paine, who had been drawn back to his homeland convinced that the spirit of political reformation that had already swept through America and France would now 'sweep over Britain like a tidal wave'.

His dialogue with Burke brought a classic confrontation between the conservative view of politics and the radical, between hierarchy and equality, tradition and reform, and ultimately between order and revolution. It also precipitated the most notorious of all trials for seditious libel and forced Paine into lifelong exile.

In the plain but powerful English that so contrasted with Burke's 'spouting rant', Paine laid into his former friend's veneration of royalty, and in particular his high-flown passages on the plight of Marie-Antoinette, who had been compelled to forsake Versailles, taunted by a mob as she followed a procession into Paris behind the severed heads of two of her murdered guards, held up on spikes. With deadly effect, Paine pointed out the contrast between Burke's sympathy for Marie-Antoinette and his indifference to the sufferings of the prisoners in the Bastille:

> Not one glance of compassion, not one commiserating reflection that I can find throughout his book, has he bestowed on those who lingered out the most wretched of lives, a life without hope, in the most miserable of prisons . . . He is not affected by the reality of distress touching the heart, but by the showy resemblage of it striking his imagination. He pities the plumage, but forgets the dying bird.

Burke had lamented that 'The age of chivalry is gone!' that 'The glory of Europe is extinguished for ever!' But what did this quixotic nonsense mean? Only that in the rhapsody of his imagination, Burke had discovered a world of windmills. It was not against Louis XVI but against the despotic principles of government that the nation had revolted. These principles did not have their origins in him, but in their establishment many centuries back. There were not one, but 1,000, despotisms to be reformed in France, which had become rooted between the Monarchy, the Parliament and the Church, besides the feudal despotism operating locally, and the ministerial despotism operating everywhere.

In a theme he would develop later, Paine went on to consider the distinction between the natural rights of man and his civil rights, and demonstrated how the one grew out of the other. Man did not enter society to have fewer rights than he had before, but to have those rights better secured. His natural rights as an individual were the foundation of his civil rights as a member of society. By this, Paine explained that a man's natural rights were those that appertained to him in right of his individual existence. Of this kind were the entire intellectual rights, or rights of the mind, including religion and the freedom of thought. Civil rights were those that appertained to a man in right of his being a member of society, and which had for their foundation some pre-existing natural right, that were shared in order to give, for instance, greater security or protection. By his natural rights, a man had a right to judge in his own cause; and so far as the right of mind is concerned, he never surrendered it. He might choose to deposit this right in the common stock of society, of which he was a part, and so take society's arm, as it were, for support; but he remained the proprietor of the capital he has invested. It therefore followed that the power produced from the aggregate of pooled individual rights could not be used to invade the natural rights that were retained in the individual. From this philosophical platform, Paine was to build up his theory of the rights of man, which importantly included the right to free speech, a natural right, with which society had no locus to interfere, save where it was injurious to the natural rights of others.

THE RIGHTS OF MAN

Paine had intended to publish *The Rights of Man* in time for the opening of Parliament in February 1791, but his printer took fright and another had to be found. Paine meanwhile left for France, leaving the work to be done under the supervision of his friends William Godwin and his wife, the loquacious feminist Mary Wollstonecraft, in whose presence Paine was said to lapse into a persistent shy silence. The couple found him a braver printer, J.S. Jordan, whose first run of 10,000 copies sold out overnight.

Paine by now was back at work on a companion volume, in which he intended to combine 'principle and practice'. Regarded today as his greatest work, part two of *The Rights of Man* appeared in February 1792 and immediately caused an immense sensation. For not only did the pamphlet set out an ambitious programme of social and constitutional reform on the lines that had been established in America and France, it called, in effect, for revolution in England.

The pamphlet began by declaring that what Archimedes said of the mechanical powers may be equally applied to reason and liberty: 'Had we a place to stand upon, we may move the world.' The war of independence in America had provided such a place. As a result of the example it had set, Paine did not believe that monarchy and aristocracy would continue seven years longer in any of the civilised countries of Europe. The English monarchy had its origins in 'a band of ruffians', while the House of Lords was no more qualified to govern than a House of Brewers or House of Bakers, or any other separate class of men. From there, he went on to introduce his readers to a new concept of democracy – hitherto thought of as the anarchic rule of an entire people – repeatedly using it in the favourable modern sense of *representative* democracy on the lines being established in his beloved America.

Paine had said much the same before, though never more cogently; but suddenly, six chapters into his pamphlet, he unveiled an entirely new vision of the State as an agent of social reform. To do away with poverty, he asserted, more was needed than a simple overthrow of the monarchy. The basis of taxation should be changed from the poor law rates and excise duty on the articles of consumption to direct progressive taxation on property, especially land. The revenue would be used to educate the children of all classes, there would be State pensions for the old, unemployment relief for the 'casual poor' and burial money for the 'tramping artisans' who roamed the country in search of work and frequently died 'at a distance from their friends'. He produced tables of figures to support his proposals and argued for the abolition of the laws that regulated and limited workmen's wages. 'Why not leave them as free to make their own bargains as the law-makers are to let their own farms and houses?' he asked. 'Personal labour is all the property they have.'

The response to the pamphlet was overwhelming. The English radical movement had been presented with a programme, the labouring poor with a sense of hope and reformers everywhere with a cause to which they were ready to commit themselves. With a year, 200,000 copies of Paine's work had been distributed and avidly read throughout the British Isles, particularly in the rapidly growing, though still disenfranchised, manufacturing towns of Scotland and the north of England. The principles it laid down are commonplace enough today, but at the height of the French Revolution were regarded as wildly radical, and it is said that no reputable bookseller would admit to stocking copies, although on demand would always be able to produce one from under the counter. By the time it had been reprinted in France and America, it is estimated that more than 2 million copies of his work were in circulation, though Paine, typically, pocketed none of the profits.

The Rights of Man did not in itself create the radical movement in England, any more than *Common Sense* had created the independence movement in America, but it gave it a voice and articulated its grievances at a decisive moment. For the second time in his life, Paine had been the right man in the right place at precisely the right time. The astonishing success of his second volume inspired the creation of a new political class in Britain and offered them the prospect of a 'living alternative' to the oppressive and hierarchical society in which they lived. It also led the government to conclude it was time to take action. The popular success of the second instalment of *The Rights of Man* provoked Pitt to impose censorship of a kind England had not known since the lapse of the licensing laws a hundred years earlier. In the following five years, his government suspended *habeas corpus* and suppressed the freedom of speech through the systematic prosecution and imprisonment of publishers of radical works that lasted almost without a break for over thirty years.

Paine had not only misjudged Pitt's determination to silence and discredit him, he had underrated his fellow countrymen's fear of revolution. The mobs that burned him in effigy may not have been entirely spontaneous, but they represented a xenophobic strain in the English that he never fully understood. At any rate, Pitt concluded that the radical movement must be suppressed. 'Tom Paine was quite right when he wrote *Rights of Man*,' he observed cynically to Lady Hester Stanhope, 'But what am I to do as things are? If I were to encourage his influence, we should have a bloody revolution.' Consequently, in May 1792, after Paine's pamphlet had been in circulation for three months, Pitt's government arranged the issue of a royal proclamation against seditious writings and less than three hours later used it as the basis for a summons against both Paine and J.S. Jordan his printer. Jordan pleaded guilty in exchange for a verdict 'to the author's prejudice', and Paine made it clear that he alone was responsible for *The Rights of Man* and was prepared to stand by his every word. He sent a note to the court pleading not guilty and appeared before them on 8 June, confident that he would soon be acquitted.

To Paine's disappointment, the case was adjourned until December, ostensibly in order to give the prosecution more time to prepare its case, but also to give the government time to launch a coordinated campaign of propaganda. Mass rallies roared their approval of the royal proclamation against free speech and men were hired at 5s each to roam the streets chanting anti-Paine slogans. In Chelmsford, it was reported that

> on Wednesday last, the effigy of that infamous incendiary, Tom Paine, was exhibited in this town, seated in a chair, and borne on four men's shoulders; – in one hand, he held *The Rights of Man* and under other arm he bore a pair of stays; upon his head a mock resemblance of the Cap of Liberty, a halter round his neck and a banner proclaiming:
>
> Behold a Traitor!
> Who, for the base purposes of Envy, Interest and Ambition
> Would have *deluged* this Happy Country in
> BLOOD!'

The effigy was hanged on a gibbet 40 feet high and burned to the sound of muffled drums beating out the Dead March. By the end of the year, Paine's effigy had reportedly been hanged in every town of more than 3,000 persons in the British Isles. In Scotland the young exciseman, Robert Burns, watched an anti-Paine bonfire in angry silence, having been warned to keep his radical sentiments to himself. Meanwhile, seeing they had failed to check sales of Paine's pamphlet, the government moved at last to silence him.

How far Paine had under-estimated the official hostility against him now became clear. By the early part of September he was making fiery speeches almost every night to a radical club called 'The Friends of Liberty', in which he demanded the abolition of monarchy and the establishment of a British republic. On the night of 12 September 1792, he was about to leave when the visionary William Blake, who alone among the company had the wit to realise that Paine had put himself into imminent danger, took him aside and said 'You must not go home, or you are a dead man'. His warning was reinforced by the American minister to Britain, Thomas Pinckney, who had concluded that Paine was in danger of imprisonment or even hanging. Seeing they were in earnest, Paine packed a few belongings and set out next day for Dover with a guide who knew the safest route. That same afternoon, bailiffs appeared at his lodgings with a warrant for his arrest, and, realising he had gone, sent a horseman to stop him leaving Dover. Paine had been detained there by customs officers, but had overawed them by showing them letters from his eminent friends, including President Washington, and they had let him pass. The warrant for his arrest reached Dover just twenty minutes after his ship had left for France. He never set foot in his homeland again; his trial took place *in absentia*.

ON TRIAL FOR SEDITION

Paine's trial opened before a special jury at the Court of the King's Bench in the London Guildhall on 18 December 1792. There, Thomas Paine, late of London, was arraigned as 'a wicked, malicious, seditious, and ill-disposed person', who had 'most unlawfully . . . contrived to write and publish a scandalous and seditious libel', which libel 'did traduce and vilify the late happy Revolution, providentially brought about and effected under the wise and prudent conduct of [King] William', and which had insulted the Bill of Rights as a Bill of Wrongs – 'a most wicked, cunning and artful insinuation'.

Brevity was not the essence of eighteenth century lawyers' wit, and the attorney general too made a speech of much reiteration as he spun the web that was meant to seal Paine's fate. He finally got to the point and declared, 'I impute then to this book, a deliberate design to eradicate from the minds of the people of this country that enthusiastic love which they have hitherto had for that constitution, and thereby to do the utmost work of mischief that any human being can do to this society.' Paine had laid out all the objections which could be possibly urged to monarchy and aristocracy, but had never chosen a single syllable to state the objections to what the attorney-general termed 'that worst of all governments, an unbalanced democracy, which is necessarily pregnant with democratical tyranny.'

And to whom was Paine's book addressed? To the ignorant, to the credulous, to the desperate, the people to whom all government was irksome. Paine's artifice was merely gross to those who could observe it, but it was dangerous in the extreme 'to those whose minds perhaps are not sufficiently cultivated and habituated to reading to enable them to discover it'. The government had chosen not to prosecute the first part of *The Rights of Man*, because it had circulated only among the judicious part of the public, who possessed an antidote to the poison; but the second part of the pamphlet had been forced into every corner of society: had been printed and reprinted for cheapness 'even upon whited brown paper, and had crept into the very nurseries of children, as a wrapper for their sweetmeats'. Having established that the government was prosecuting Paine as much for appealing to their social inferiors as for what he actually wrote, the attorney-general sat down after congratulating himself at having done his duty 'in bringing before a jury an offender of this magnitude'.

Paine's defending counsel, Thomas Erskine, then rose to make one of the most cogent speeches in defence of a free press ever heard in an English court. The question before the jury was not whether the British constitution was or was not preferable to the constitution of the United States or France, or any other human constitution. Nor was it a test of whether they agreed or disagreed with the propositions put forward by the defendant, or even whether the propositions tended to alienate opinion. The charge upon the record was a naked charge of libel, 'the cause resolves itself into a question of the deepest importance to us all: THE NATURE AND EXTENT OF THE LIBERTY OF THE BRITISH PRESS.' He continued:

> The proposition which I mean to maintain as the basis of the liberty of the press, and without which it is an empty sound, is this: – that every man not intending to mislead, but seeking to enlighten others with what his own reason and conscience, however erroneously, have dictated to him as truth, may address himself to the universal reason of a whole nation, either upon the subject of governments in general, or upon that of our own particular country: – that he may analyse the principles of its constitution, – point out its errors and defects, – examine and publish its corruptions, – warn his fellow-citizens against their ruinous consequences, – and exert his whole faculties in pointing out the most advantageous changes in establishments which he considers to be radically defective, or sliding from their object by abuse. – All this every subject of this country has a right to do . . .'

A free press detected and examined the errors of governments and so let the people reform them. 'This freedom alone made our government what it is; this freedom alone can preserve it; and therefore, under the banners of that freedom, today I stand up to defend Thomas Paine.'

Under the settled laws of England, no legal argument could shake the freedom of the press to pursue the great unalienable right of the people to reform or change their governments. Other liberties were held *under* governments, but the liberty of opinion kept governments themselves in due subjection to their duties. This, he said, had produced the martyrdom of truth in every age, and the world had been only purged from ignorance with the innocent blood of those who had enlightened it.

Their melancholy history passed like a shadow before them. The saviour of mankind, the fountain of all light, had expired upon a cross, the scoff of infidel scorn, and his apostles had followed him in the train of martyrs. Erskine traced the history of the martyrs of free speech down to Milton's visit to the aged Galileo. In Britain he supposed the court of the Star Chamber had marked the first restriction of the press, and declared that 'from that moment, no man could legally write without an *Imprimatur* from the State'. Truth and freedom had nonetheless found their way with greater force through secret channels, and the unhappy Charles, unwarned by a free press, had been brought to his ignominious death. The conclusion was that 'when men can freely communicate their thoughts and their sufferings, real or imaginary, their passions spend themselves in the air, like gunpowder scattered upon the surface: – but pent up by terrors, they work unseen, burst forth in a moment, and destroy everything in their course. Let reason be opposed to reason, and argument to argument, and every good government will be safe'.

At the Restoration of Charles II the Star Chamber ordinance was made into an act of Parliament and was followed up in that reign, and in the short one that followed it, by the most sanguinary prosecutions: and who could doubt that this blind and contemptible policy had hastened the revolution? At that great era, he said, 'these cobwebs were all brushed away, the freedom of the press was regenerated, and the country, ruled by its affections, has since enjoyed a century of tranquillity and glory.' In proportion as the press had been free, English government had been secure.

In their own day, licensing was no longer contended for. But if every work were to be adjudged a libel that was adverse to the wishes of government, the revival of a licenser would be a security to the public. 'If I present my book to a magistrate appointed by law, and he rejects it, I have only to forbear from the publication,' he said. 'But upon the argument of today, a man must print at his peril, without any guide to the principles of judgement upon which his work may be afterwards prosecuted and condemned.' Milton's argument therefore applied, and was meant to apply, to every interruption in writing, which, while they oppress the individual, endangers the State. Bad books served in many respects to discover, to confute, to forewarn, to illustrate, their very errors of assistance towards the speedy attainment of what was truest.

The danger of touching the press lay in the difficulty of defining its limits. In prosecuting Paine the attorney-general had drawn no line and unfolded no principle: 'he has not told us if *this* book is condemned, *what* book may be written. If I may not write against the existence of a monarchy, and recommend a republic, may I write against any part of the government? May I say we should be better without a House of Lords, or a House of Commons, or a Court of Chancery, or any other given part of our establishment?'

Arbitrary power has seldom been introduced into any country all at once; it is usually introduced by slow degrees, lest the people see its approach; and some plausible pretences have to be found for removing or hoodwinking, one after the other, those sentries posted by the constitution of a free country, for warning the people of their danger. Once these preparatory steps have been made, the people may then see slavery and arbitrary power taking over their land, indeed with regret, but too late to think of preventing or avoiding the impending ruin. Of the sentries that stand guard over a country's freedoms, the most vigilant is the press. If it is removed, or hoodwinked, or thrown in fetters, the enemy may surprise them.

Engage the people by their affections – convince their reason – and they will be loyal from the only principle that can make loyalty sincere – a conviction that it is in their truest interest, and that the government is for their good. Constraint is the pregnant proof that reason is not on the side of those who use it. When Jupiter appealed to his thunder, it was always when he was in the wrong. This, said Erskine, 'is the case with me: I can reason with the people of England, but I cannot fight against the thunder of authority'. Paine's opinions may indeed be adverse to the British system of government: 'but I maintain that OPINION is free, and that CONDUCT alone is amenable to the law.'

Erskine had done what he could for Paine, even to the extent of having to defend himself against libellous attacks sponsored by the government for undertaking the defence. But it was loaded case, heard by a loaded jury at a time when the country's deepest prejudices had been aroused not only by the revolution in France but by a government campaign of vilification against the defendant. For all of Erskine's eloquence in laying down the enduring principles of a free press, Paine stood little chance of acquittal. At the end of Erskine's long speech, the Attorney-General rose again to reply, but the foreman of the jury, a Mr Campbell, interrupted: 'My Lord, I am authorised by the jury to inform the attorney-general that a reply is not necessary for them.' At this, the court record reports that the attorney-general sat down and the jury gave in their verdict – guilty. The judge, Lord Kenyon, pronounced the sentence of *caput lupinum* passed twenty years before on John Wilkes. Like his predecessor in the cause of English liberty, Tom Paine had been declared an outlaw.

It is ironic that the first important test of Fox's new libel act should end in such injustice. For a generation, libertarians had been arguing that it should be the jury and not the judge who should be empowered to decide the question of libel – on the assumption that juries could be relied upon to champion the cause of individual liberty. This assumption was now shown to be cruelly mistaken. Within a year of the new law's enactment, the attorney-general declared that he had on file 200 informations for sedition, and in the following two years more people were convicted of seditious libel in England than in the whole of the eighteenth century before that time. Pitt's determination to crush the radical ideas that were spreading across the Channel from France ensured that for the next thirty-five years, the mildest criticism of the government was taken to be subversion and ruthlessly suppressed. A lawyer who declared while tipsy that he was for equality, no king and a better constitution was disbarred from his profession and put in the pillory; a minister who preached against oppressive taxes was jailed for four years, and juries regularly returned verdicts of guilty for words, oral or printed, that were harmless and hardly intemperate. The day was coming when hawkers would be whipped for distributing radical pamphlets on market day and agitators transported to Australia for urging the people to read Tom Paine's *Rights of Man*. From being hailed as an inalienable human right on the point of becoming enshrined in every civilised country's constitution, the concept of free speech had come, in the space of barely three years, to be regarded in both England and America as a dangerous and subversive doctrine that threatened the stability of the State. And in France, the initial euphoria, which had brought the abandonment of all forms of censorship, lasted less than four years after the fall of the Bastille. Free speech and the liberty of the press died with the Terror and were not to revive again until after the overthrow of Napoleon.

EXILE IN FRANCE

In the seeming safety of his French exile, Paine now entered the most enigmatic and controversial period of his life. There were two great pamphlets still to come, but ahead of him lay also a decade and a half of disappointment and ultimately of despair. His hopes of inspiring a peaceful and democratic revolution evaporated in the violence of the Terror, while his own career collapsed into bitterness and isolation.

He had at first been welcomed in France as 'the most formidable of all experts on constitutions', and elected to the National Assembly. But in truth both he and his *coterie* were out of touch with the mood of the French lower classes and never understood the destructive thirst for vengeance of the Parisian *sans-culottes*. On the constitutional issues, such as the formation of a republic, the right of free speech and universal suffrage, he was more consistently radical than they were. But in the crisis of 1793, he took the side of the more moderate Girondists, unable to abandon his commitment to *laisser-faire* economics and the sanctity of private property, while his Quaker beliefs led him to try to persuade the Assembly to spare the life of Louis XVI.

The bloodlust which was consuming the new republic filled Paine with 'disgust and anguish'. As he later wrote to Jefferson: 'Had this revolution been conducted consistently with its principles, there was once a good prospect of extending liberty throughout the greater part of Europe, but now I relinquish that hope.' To Danton, he confided, 'I despair of seeing the great object of European liberty accomplished, and my despair arises not from the combined foreign powers, not from the intrigues of aristocracy and priestcraft, but from the tumultuous misconduct with which the internal affairs of this revolution are conducted'. It had delivered a blow to liberty from which it would not quickly recover.

'Man is born free, but is everywhere in chains,' Rousseau had written, but it was his insistence that man must be *forced* to be free in obedience to the infallible 'general will' that became the rubric of the revolutionaries. '*Our* will is the general will,' said Robespierre. 'To permit vice when one has the right and the power to suppress it, is to be oneself vicious.' Arguing from such logic, the revolutionaries, while piously invoking the principles of liberty, equality and fraternity, imposed a kind of democratic tyranny on the entire nation. The general will prevailed. Dissent amounted to treason. People were put to death simply for being born into a particular class, or for being foreigners or simply on suspicion of being disloyal to the revolution. 'You must entirely refashion a people whom you wish to make free,' the Committee of Public Safety had decreed. 'You must destroy its prejudices, alter its habits, limit its necessities, root up its vices, purify its desires.' Under the so-called 'Law of Suspects' people were condemned if either their conduct, their conversations or their writings showed them to be 'partisans of tyranny or federalism and enemies of liberty'.

As a foreigner, Paine now found himself in great danger. In October, his name was added to the list of deputies publicly accused of treason, and in December he was placed under arrest and put in the Luxembourg Palace, which had become a prison. The reign of terror had begun, and Paine saw all his closest friends murdered, and only escaped death himself by a fluke. According to his own account, 'one hundred and sixty-eight persons were taken out of the Luxembourg in one night, and a hundred and sixty of them guillotined next day, of which I now know I was to have been one'. He had been suffering from a severe chill and had been placed in a cell with three other prisoners, all of whom had been marked for death by a large chalked cross on the cell door. This happened, unobserved by the occupants, when the door was open and flat against the wall. Thereby, he said, the chalk mark 'came on the inside when we shut it at night, and the destroying angel passed us by'.

Paine remained in the Luxembourg for ten months. The American ambassador in Paris, his old critic Gouverneur Morris, did nothing to help, and when a group of American citizens petitioned for his release, the President of the Convention replied that Paine was a citizen of England, an enemy country, while his genius had failed to understand the revolutionary fervour, which had regenerated France. He remained in jail even after the fall of Robespierre, and was only released after the intervention of the new American ambassador, James Monroe.

Paine had fallen seriously ill in prison, severely chilled, half-starved and with an abscess in his side. When he was released in November 1794, the Monroes took him into their own home and nursed him back to health. The news that their old adversary was still alive came as an unwelcome surprise to the government in England, who thought he had been guillotined. Paine took considerable pleasure in reading a pamphlet that quoted from the speech he was supposed to have made on the scaffold: 'I am determined to speak the truth in these my last moments, tho' I have written nothing but lies all my life.' The English government never shook off the idea that Paine's radical views had fomented not only the revolution but the terror to which they supposed he had himself fallen victim. Before his own execution, Brissot observed that 'the grievance of the British cabinet against France is not that Louis has been executed, but that Thomas Paine wrote *The Rights of Man*'. His name was raised so often during the debates that led to the declaration of war, that Fox demanded of Pitt, 'Can you not prosecute Paine without an army?'

After his release from the Luxembourg, Paine found himself in a country experiencing a conservative reaction against the excesses of the Jacobin rule of the previous year. A *sans-culottes* insurrection in May 1795 was ruthlessly suppressed and a new constitution adopted which abandoned the principle of universal suffrage in favour of stringent property qualifications for both voting and office holding. Reinstated as a member of the Convention, but now virtually alone, Paine denounced the new constitution and the abandonment of universal suffrage, standing up, as he always did, for the principles of individual liberty and political equality. Despite his efforts, the new constitution was approved by the Convention, a new legislative body was elected, and Paine's hopes of seeing individual liberty extended throughout the continent of Europe had come to an end.

In answer to the English reformer Henry Redhead Yorke, who expressed a platitudinous hope that much might yet be done for the Republic, Paine despaired. 'Republic! Do you call this a Republic? This is not a country for an honest man to live in. They do not understand anything at all of the principles of free government, and the best way is to leave them to themselves.' There was no country in the world for men such as they were, he said – except America, the one nation that had stayed true to its republican principles. In 1802, at the age of sixty-five, he finally got his wish and returned to the only place in the world where he had ever truly felt at home and there began the final and tragic chapter of his career.

AMERICAN NEMESIS

After fifteen years' absence, Paine had looked forward to receiving a warm welcome from the country he had done so much to bring into existence. But America had changed profoundly since he first arrived in Philadelphia at the start of the revolution. The radical enthusiasm of its early youth had been replaced by a conservative ideology which for the past ten years had put political and social power into the hands of the well-to-do and still largely aristocratic federalists. In their eyes, Paine was identified with the excesses of the French Revolution and no longer with their own Declaration of Independence. *Common Sense* belonged to the distant past. They knew Paine now as the author of the godless assault on Christianity, *The Age of Reason*, a deist pamphlet he had begun in the Luxembourg Prison and completed at the Paris home of the Monroes.

Far from the joyous homecoming he had expected, Paine was greeted on his arrival in Baltimore by a barrage of vituperative attacks in the federalist press. A Boston newspaper described him as 'a lying, drunken, brutal infidel'. Others called him 'a loathsome reptile', 'a lily-livered rogue', and an 'object of disgust, of abhorrence, of absolute loathing to every decent man except the President of the United States'. *The Age of Reason* was the work of the devil; blasphemous and inclined to atheism.

The attacks were as unjust as they were untrue. Far far from being an atheist, Paine was in fact an ardent deist. What he was not was a Christian. 'I do not believe in the creed professed by the Jewish Church, by the Roman Church, by the Greek Church, by the Turkish Church, by the Protestant Church, nor by any Church that I know of,' he declared. 'My own mind is my own Church.' He had taken up his pen in the Luxembourg for fear that the anti-clericalism of the French revolutionaries was leading them into godless atheism. As he said in his introduction to *The Age of Reason*, the total abolition of everything appertaining to formal religion in France had rendered his work 'exceedingly necessary', lest in the general wreck of superstition 'we lose sight of morality, of humanity, and of the theology that is true'. With simple sincerity and frankness, he enunciated his deist creed:

> I believe in one God, and no more, and I hope for happiness beyond this life. I believe in the equality of man; and I believe that religious duties consist in doing justice, loving mercy, and endeavouring to make our fellow-creatures happy.

Dedicated to the citizens of the United States of America, the pamphlet begins with a bold appeal for the freedom of speech:

I have always strenuously supported the right of every man to his own opinion, however different that opinion might be to mine. He who denies to another this right, makes a slave of himself to his present opinion, because he precludes himself the right of changing it. The most formidable weapon against errors of every kind is reason. I have never used any other, and I trust I never shall.

The two volumes that followed consisted of a sustained attack on the grosser absurdities of Christian theology and a minute chapter by chapter analysis of the contradictions, the false chronology, the barbarism and the illogicality displayed in both the Old Testament and the New, starting with the story of Adam and Eve, in which most Christians still implicitly believed. 'When I am told that a woman called the Virgin Mary said, or gave out, that she was with child without any cohabitation with a man and that her betrothed husband Joseph said that an angel told him so, I have a right to believe them or not.' Paine wrote. 'Such a circumstance requires a much stronger evidence than their bare word for it.'

To the claim of orthodox Christians that the scriptures were the revealed word of God, he asked: who told us so? No one could tell, except that we told one another so. The historical fact was that the founders of the Early Church collected all the writings they could find and decided by *vote* which of them should be the word of God, and which should not. Had they voted otherwise, all the people calling themselves Christian would have believed otherwise. Who the people were that did all this, we knew nothing of; they called themselves by the general name of the Church, and that is all we knew of the matter.

Jesus Christ was a virtuous and an amiable man. The morality that he preached and practised was of the most benevolent kind. But Christ had written no account of himself. The history of him was altogether the work of others; and the accounts they gave, from the virgin birth to the resurrection and ascension, were simply hearsay upon hearsay, and had every mark of fraud and imposition stamped upon them. The ascension through the air was a 'wretched contrivance', an event that would have admitted of public and oracular demonstration 'like that of the ascension of a balloon, or the sun at noon-day, to all Jerusalem at least'. Yet no evidence of it was ever given. Instead, a small number of persons, not more than eight or nine, were introduced as proxies for the whole world to say they saw it, and all the rest of the world were called upon to believe it. But the apostle Thomas did not believe it, and neither, said Paine, do I.

Too absurd for belief, too impossible to convince and too inconsistent for practice, organised religion was an engine of power to serve the purposes of despotism and the avarice of priests. Apart from the book of Job, which he admired, almost the only biblical passage for which he had a good word to say was the opening verse of the nineteenth psalm – and that because it reflected his own deist belief: 'The Heavens declare the glory of God and the firmament sheweth his handiwork.'

Although Paine failed to see that an attack on the religious beliefs of his fellow citizens was different in kind from an attack on their political views, making no allowances for the fact that religion is a matter of faith, not of reason, and therefore not subject to correction by argument in the same way a political view would be, he felt obliged to tell his readers what he conceived to be the plain truth of the matter. In refusing to compromise, he composed what has been called the last great work of the Enlightenment.

As an exercise in free speech, *The Age of Reason* had a number of interesting consequences. Although it was the boldest, and for its day the most reckless, attack on orthodox religion, the only country in which he was not free to publish was atheist France. In Britain and America, Paine's ideas, however unpopular with the Church establishment, achieved an enormous circulation – helped, unwittingly, by the Anglican Church, which commissioned scores of printed pamphlets refuting Paine's deist ideas. One of them, *An Apology for the Bible*, written by Bishop Richard Watson, was distributed free of charge to virtually every literate man and woman in the British Isles. Watson, however, made frequent and lengthy references to *The Age of Reason*, which had the effect of stirring a lively interest in the real thing. Seeing their opportunity, a deist organisation, the London Corresponding Society, sponsored a cheap reprint of *The Age of Reason* itself, which spread Paine's deist philosophy to every corner of the country.

The damage had therefore already been done when, in 1797, its printer, Thomas Williams, was brought before the High Court charged with publishing a blasphemous work. By an ironic coincidence, the prosecution was led by the eloquent defender of the *Rights of Man*, Thomas Erskine. When he heard of it, Paine wrote to Erskine asserting that every man's religion was a private matter between himself and his creator. No third party had a right to interfere. It was, above all, not a matter for the government or a prosecutor.

Erskine responded with all the eloquence he had previously deployed in defence of Paine's freedom to criticise the British constitution to argue *against* his freedom to criticise its established religion. He told the jury he had risen from his reading of *The Age of Reason* with 'astonishment and disgust'. It was a work as cruel and mischievous in its effects as it was manifestly illegal in its principles. The poor and humble, whom it affected to pity, would be stabbed to the heart by it. He went on:

> I can conceive a distressed but virtuous man, surrounded by his children, looking up to him for bread when he has none to give them; – sinking under the last day's labour, and unequal to the next, – yet still, supported by confidence in the hour when all tears shall be wiped from the eyes of affliction, bearing the burden laid upon him by a mysterious Providence which he adores, and anticipating with exultation the revealed promises of his Creator, when he shall be greater than the greatest, and happier than the happiest of mankind. What a change in such a mind might be wrought be such a merciless publication!

However hypocritical it might seem, the evidence suggests that Erskine's attack on his old client was sincerely meant. Indeed, he argued that this was not a case of free speech at all. Every man had a right to investigate, with decency, controversial points of the Christian religion – without it, there would have been no reformation – and the English constitution permitted every man, even publicly, to worship God according to his own conscience. But, for all the purposes of human happiness and improvement, this was sufficient. 'How any man can rationally vindicate the publication of such a book, in a country where the Christian religion is the very foundation of the law of the land, I am totally at a loss to conceive.' Under what oath would witnesses give their evidence, without which there could be no justice? The whole judicial fabric, from the king's sovereign authority to the lowest magistracy, owed its allegiance to God. 'What God?' he asked. 'That God, undoubtedly, who has commanded the king to rule, and judges to decree justice and . . . who has said to witnesses in revealed commandments, "Thou Shalt Not Bear False Testimony Against Thy Neighbour".'

Erskine's silver tongue persuaded the jury to convict, and Lord Kenyon, the judge, sentenced Williams to a year's imprisonment. When he heard of it, Paine's response was terse, but withering: 'It is difficult to know when a lawyer is to be believed.'

The trial had demonstrated that in England then, and in theory down to this day, the word of God is exempt from rational argument; free speech does not extend to works that are deemed by a jury to be blasphemous. In America it was different. The Bill of Rights forbade Congress to make any law limiting the freedom of speech or of religious belief. But while Paine was protected from prosecution in America, he had no such protection against the obloquy and ostracism that afflicted him during the last ten years of his life. *The Age of Reason* sent his reputation into a steep decline from which it has only recently recovered.

The ageing Paine spent his last years in what has become Greenwich Village in New York City or on his farm in New Rochelle, 25 miles away, which had been presented to him by a grateful nation for his services to the revolution. For a while, he took in as lodgers the wife and children of Nicholas Bonneville, an old American friend who had looked after him in Paris on his release from prison; but with no family of his own, he became cantankerous and argumentative, left alone to dwell on his bitter reflections at having been forgotten or ignored. In 1805, he wrote to a friend:

> I am master of an empty house, or nearly so. I have six chairs and a table, a straw-bed, a feather-bed, and a bag of straw for Thomas, a tea-kettle, an iron pot, and an iron baking-pan, a frying pan, a gridiron, cups, saucers, plates and dishes, knives and forks, two candlesticks, and a pair of snuffers. I have a pair of fine oxen and an ox-cart, a good horse, a Chair, and a one-horse cart; a cow, and a sow and 9 pigs . . . I live upon tea, milk, fruit-pies, plain dumplins, and a piece of meat when I get it; but I live with that retirement and quiet that suit me. Mrs Bonneville was an encumbrance upon me while she was here, for she would not do anything, not even make an apple-dumplin for her own children . . .

Paine had come full circle. From his beginnings as an unknown and bankrupt staymaker, he had risen to become one of the most influential men of his generation. He had been the friend of two great presidents. He had mixed on equal terms with the finest minds of his day. He had changed fundamentally the way men thought about their political institutions and their religion. Now he was once again ignored or mocked, the solitary occupant of a simple farmhouse. It was a fate he found hard to bear, though he kept on writing until the end, turning for solace more and more to the brandy bottle. When he died in 1809, only a handful of New Rochelle neighbours gathered around his fieldside grave. Madame Bonneville recorded the scene as they committed Paine's body to its obscure resting place:

> Before the earth was thrown down upon the coffin, I, placing myself at the east end of the grave, said to my son Benjamin, 'stand you there, at the other end, as a witness for grateful America.' Looking round me, and beholding the small group of spectators, I exclaimed, as the earth was tumbled into the grave, 'Oh, Mr Paine! My son stands here as testimony of the gratitude of America, and I, for France!' This was the funeral ceremony of this great politician and philosopher!

Outlawed from his homeland for writing *The Rights of Man*, ostracised by his much loved adopted country for writing *The Age of Reason*, and denied his proper place in the pantheon of Founding Fathers, in spite of his earlier services in writing *Common Sense*, Paine had in a real sense died as a martyr to free speech. His American reputation remained in eclipse throughout the nineteenth century, largely because of the reaction against freethinkers in the pious post-enlightenment world. In England, *Common Sense* and *The Age of Reason* have been largely forgotten, and the egalitarianism of *The Rights of Man* was considered too radical by the middle classes who came to power after the great Reform Acts. Only in the later decades of the twentieth century did the rehabilitation of his reputation begin. Over the safe distance of two centuries, he can now be claimed as one of the most influential forces that ever helped to free the minds of human beings.

Though he died forgotten, his story has a curious postscript. When William Cobbett, another English champion of free speech, fled to America to escape prosecution for the radical pamphlets he had written, he sought out the grave of Thomas Paine and in 1819 returned to England with his hero's bones, which he kept in a box. Having failed to raise sufficient money to erect a memorial around them, the bones were offered for auction on Cobbett's own death in 1835, but a court ruled that human remains should not be regarded as a marketable asset. It is said that Paine's skull was acquired at some stage by a Brighton phrenologist, though it has subsequently been lost. All that remains is a badly disfigured fragment of Paine's tombstone.

CHAPTER TEN

The Jefferson Enigma

America ended its own revolutionary decade still without a formal commitment to the freedom of speech. Even the new republic's crowning achievement – the constitution of 1789 – made no mention of it. Because the federal government possessed only the powers they had enumerated for it, the framers of the constitution saw no need to build in guarantees for civil liberties that were, by definition, outside its jurisdiction. 'Why declare that things shall not be done which there is no power to do?' asked the arch-federalist, Alexander Hamilton. 'Why, for instance, should it be said that the liberty of the press shall not be restrained, when no power is given by which restrictions may be imposed?'

When the new constitution was sent to the individual states for ratification, many of them did not trust this reasoning. Civil rights, they argued, were something that should not rest solely on inference. Citizens and states needed formal protection against the encroachments of central government. Virginia went so far as to draft its own Declaration of Rights as an addendum to the federal document.

Seeking to resolve the impasse, James Madison, the young, soft-spoken constitutional theorist whose influence was pivotal, let it be known that when the new government had settled in he would work to have a Bill of Rights introduced as a constitutional amendment. He did not himself believe that its omission made much difference one way or another, but he saw that concessions were vital if the federal constitution was to be secured. Though opponents dismissed his work as 'little better than whip-syllabub, frothy and full of wind, formed only to please the palate', they won acceptance in the House of Representatives, which voted to send seventeen of his proposed amendments up to the Senate for approval as a single Bill of Rights. The Senate accepted fifteen of them and out of conference came twelve, which were submitted to the states for approval. By December 1791 ten of Madison's amendments had been ratified by the necessary majority of states, starting with the beguilingly simple rule that 'Congress shall make no law . . . abridging the freedom of speech, or of the press.'

And that seemed to be that. The Bill of Rights had put it within the power of the judiciary to interpose its authority whenever free speech was endangered. 'The right of freedom of speech is secured,' Madison announced. 'The liberty of the press is expressly declared to be beyond the reach of this government.' Political truths declared in so solemn a manner would acquire, by degrees, the character of fundamental maxims.

Solemn and fundamental though Madison's catalogue of first principles may have been, it was soon shown up to be short on specifics. People began to ask what the first amendment to the federal constitution actually meant. Why, for instance, did it say merely that *Congress* shall make no laws abridging the freedom of the press? Did that mean the individual states were free to enact restrictions? Did it mean the executive branch of government could institute prosecutions for the common law offence of seditious libel? Did the common law itself still exist at federal level? If so, did the Bill of Rights in fact offer any worthwhile protection at all?

No one seemed to know. Indeed, it was widely agreed that an abstract concept like free speech defied precise definition. 'Few of us, I believe, have distinct ideas of its nature and extent,' wrote Benjamin Franklin. John Adams thought it meant the press was free 'within the bounds of truth'. Like most politicians who had voted for the Bill of Rights he believed that the common law crime of seditious libel was still in force, though he thought cases should be heard by a jury of the state where the offence had been committed. Others found it inconceivable that the framers of the first amendment had not intended to do away once and for all with the obnoxious concept of putting people on trial for expressing political dissent. It was clear that a more precise definition of free speech would only emerge from the crucible of experience.

The test was to come sooner than anyone expected. By the turn of the century, the freedom of speech and of the press – far from being immune from abridgement – was as gravely menaced in the United States as it had become in Europe.

ALIEN AND SEDITION ACTS

When the French Revolutionary Wars broke out, some Americans took the Burkean view that a gang of bloodthirsty fanatics were threatening the foundations of civilised society; others shared the liberal conviction that they heralded the dawn of a heroic new order based on liberty, equality and fraternity. These divisions dovetailed all too neatly with the Federalist-Republican split over the constitution and led to one of those paroxysms of intolerance that have punctuated American history ever since.

Over the indignant protests of the first president (who had been elected unanimously) his administration began to rend itself asunder on party lines: Hamilton and his supporters favoured reconciliation with Great Britain; Thomas Jefferson and his allies held to their allegiance to the nation that had helped them in their own hour of need.

When Washington insisted on retiring at last to Mount Vernon, his farewell address was seen as a signal, 'like the dropping of a hat,' for the party races to start. Jefferson became the inevitable candidate for the Republican* cause, Adams for the Federalists'. The first contested presidential election in American history soon became a bitter ordeal by slander, with Republicans portraying the vice-president as 'the blind, bald, toothless, querulous ADAMS', the 'blasted tyrant of America'. Federalists responded with equally extravagant attacks on Jefferson's

---

* Not to be confused with the modern Republican Party, which evolved later. Jefferson's Republicans were, in fact, the forerunners of the modern Democratic Party.

supposedly Jacobin and atheist views. If he were to be elected to the presidency, the people must expect not only 'the just vengeance of insulted heaven', but 'dwellings in flames, hoary hairs bathed in blood, female chastity violated, children writhing on the pike and halberd'.

Perhaps because of his uncritical enthusiasm for the French revolutionaries, Jefferson's views did not prevail. Adams beat him in the Electoral College by three votes, with Jefferson, as runner-up, elected vice-president and, effectively, leader of the opposition.*

Although John Adams had an outstanding record as a patriot of courage and integrity, he had a prickly personality and was a virulent anti-democrat. While vice-president to George Washington, he had striven to surround the government with a regal 'dignity and splendour', and had proposed that the head of state should be referred to as 'His Highness, the President of the United States'. Ever afterwards, the dumpy little Massachusetts lawyer was jocularly referred to as 'His Rotundity'. More seriously, he shared the high federalists' patrician disdain for the 'swinish multitude' and believed that mankind in the mass was incapable of rational thought and dangerously susceptible to the wiles of the demagogue. There is a story, recorded in Jefferson's diary, that on his second election as vice-president, when there were several votes cast for Governor George Clinton of New York, Adams said in the Senate chamber, gritting his teeth, 'Damn 'em, damn 'em, damn 'em, you see that an elective government will not do'.

Democracy did have a role to play in the Federalist scheme of things, but only in its allotted place in the House of Representatives. It was emphatically not the whole of government, for where the people ruled, liberty perished, as had been so amply demonstrated by events in France and Athens – and, for that matter, in the original Confederation of American States. In opposing an all-powerful democracy, the Federalists sincerely supposed they were upholding the cause of freedom, or what they preferred to call 'temperate liberty'. Like the English Whigs, their leaders tended to be men of wealth and social prominence, who fell easily into the assumption that they alone possessed the talent to govern. Wise, sober and public spirited, they made no pretence to be other than what they were: upper-class grandees who had arrogated to themselves the right to rule. They held that America's peace, happiness and prosperity depended upon a strong national government administered by those best qualified to do so.

All too aware that they did not command the support of the majority of Americans, the Federalists lived in constant fear that they were about to 'perish miserably on the shoals of democracy'. Theirs was not a happy or an optimistic creed. Gouverneur Morris lamented that it was as futile to attempt to instil wisdom in the people as to preach religion to unbelievers – 'they are to be

---

* Until the reform of 1804, the runner-up in the election automatically became vice-president. Following the dead heat between Jefferson and Burr, it was laid down that candidates could not run for the Presidency and the Vice-Presidency at the same time.

converted only by suffering'. Federalists were for ever instructing the people in these 'salutary truths' or trying to 'rectify' common errors. They argued that true freedom could not be enjoyed unless some rights were curtailed, that it was necessary to maintain a fastidious distinction between liberty and licentiousness, and that 'honest men must submit to the force that is necessary to govern rogues . . . To make a nation free, the crafty must be kept in awe, and the violent in restraint'. In their eyes, democracy only aroused the jealous passions of the mob and set the poor against the rich. Federalists, by contrast, prided themselves on their disdain for 'the vile love of popularity'. Even if political office depended on it, they would not truckle to the people and would always rather be right than popular. But they were perceptive enough to see that the people *en masse* could be just as great a threat to individual liberty and the freedom of expression as the single tyrant. 'The fundamental article of my political creed,' announced John Adams, 'is that despotism, or unlimited sovereignty, or absolute power is the same in a majority of a Popular Assembly, an Aristocratic Council, an oligarchical Junto and a single Emperor.' It was a sentiment used again and again in the ensuing debates about free speech and individual liberty.

The Federalists owed their decade-long ascendancy to the fact that in an age of turmoil they represented the forces of order and stability, and had rescued the nation from the crisis of 1787/8 when the old confederation of States had collapsed. But above all, they remained in power because they were led by George Washington, the father of his country, a Federalist above party. It was Adams's prestige as Washington's chosen successor as much as the country's suspicion of Jefferson's extreme pro-French views that carried him into office. But he was never permitted to forget that he was 'President by three votes'.

With the nation divided against itself as never before, the insolence of revolutionary France precipitated an international crisis that widened the rift still further. Provoked by Jay's Treaty, which had restored America's links with Great Britain, the Directory under Talleyrand began seizing American vessels on the high seas and confiscating their cargoes. Over 300 merchantmen flying the Stars and Stripes were sunk or captured. When Adams sent three distinguished emissaries to Paris in an attempt to negotiate a settlement, the Directory at first refused to see them. Then they let it be known through agents mysteriously referred to as X, Y and Z that they would deal with the mission only if they agreed to offer suitable apologies for unfriendly remarks made about them in the president's message to Congress, pay a bribe of $250,000 to Talleyrand and advance the French government a loan of $12 million. 'No, no,' came the indignant American reply. 'Not a sixpence.'

The crisis deepened. When the three envoys reported back to their government in April 1798, the entire correspondence was published and laid before the American people by order of the Senate. The so-called XYZ despatches stirred up a patriotic fervour not seen since the war of independence. The Federalists were acclaimed as national heroes, the *Marseillaise*, once so popular, was hissed off the American stage, and the spirited national hymn *Hail to Columbia!* played at every entry of the President (as it still is).

President Adams himself appeared in full military regalia as 12,000 patriots paraded past his house in Philadelphia to the sound of martial music.

Everywhere, there was talk of invasion, subversion and revolution. General Washington was drafted from retirement to command an American army, should the need arise. 'Watch, Philadelphians, or the fire is in your houses and the *couteau* at your throat,' said the high-Federalist *Porcupine's Gazette.* 'When your blood runs in the gutter, don't say you weren't forewarned.'

There was no declaration of war for all the talk of one, but the Federalists used the supposed treachery of the 'democrats, mobocrats and all other kinds of rats' to whip up a hurricane of intolerance which gravely menaced freedom of speech and of the press. In the summer of 1798, Congress passed four measures known as the Alien and Sedition Acts, all of them violating the new Bill of Rights. It became a crime to criticise the government. Words deemed to be 'false, scandalous or malicious' were punishable by fine and imprisonment. Editors could go to jail for disseminating 'unfounded calumnies'. Jefferson found the Alien Act 'worthy of the eighth or ninth century'. One of its provisions, for instance, required the vice-president to send a messenger 70 miles for the written permission of a federal judge before he could sit down to dinner with a foreign guest at Monticello.

The measure that bore most severely on the press was the Act for the Punishment of Certain Crimes, commonly known as the Sedition Act, which in its original form had proposed the death penalty for citizens found giving aid and comfort to the French. The House of Representatives sent it up for consideration by the Senate on Independence Day, 4 July, when any serious discussion of its merits was drowned out by the noise of passing drums and trumpets. 'The military parade so attracted the attention of the majority that much the greater part of them stood with their bodies out of the windows, and could not be kept in order,' reported Stevens Thomson Mason, the Senator from Virginia.

Despite these distractions, the Senate eventually passed the bill, though removing the provisions for a death penalty, instead prescribing heavy fines and imprisonment for those found guilty of writing, publishing or speaking matter deemed to be of 'a false, scandalous and seditious nature' against the government or its officers, or either House of Congress. The high federalist Harrison Gray Otis declared during the debate that 'to punish licentiousness and sedition is not a restraint or abridgement of the freedom of speech or of the press' – there could be no absolute right to publish what one pleased. Judge Addison of Pennsylvania declared that Americans could no longer afford the luxury of discussing both sides of a question. 'Truth has but one side,' he said, 'and listening to error and falsehood is a strange way to discover it.' Indeed, 'all truths are not useful or proper for publication: therefore all truths are not to be written, printed, or published'. The Federalist *Gazette of the United States* refined this to mean, 'it is patriotism to write in favour of our government – it is sedition to write against it'.

Only seven years after its enactment, the Federalists seemed to have declared war on the Bill of Rights itself. The Republican *Journal* of New Jersey declared that the Alien and Sedition Acts were 'the most diabolical laws that were ever attempted to be imposed on a free and enlightened people'. Madison wrote to Jefferson, it is to be hoped . . . that any arbitrary attacks on the freedom of the press will find virtue enough remaining in the public mind to make them recoil on the wicked authors. No other check to desperate projects seems now to be left. The sanguinary faction ought not, however, to adopt the spirit of Robespierre without recollecting the shortness of his triumph and the perpetuity of his infamy.

Jefferson himself found the measures

so palpably in the teeth of the constitution as to show they mean to pay no respect to it.

The Federalists who had forced through the legislation claimed they had done no more than affirm the authority of the government to defend itself against subversion. Since seditious and defamatory words were a crime at common law, there could be no breach of the constitution in providing punishments for such crimes. Indeed, the acts provided many liberal improvements not to be found in common law: truth was allowed as a defence, the jury and not the judge would decide on the facts of the libel, and proof was required of malicious intent.

These were legal sophisms. In practice, the act was a wholly partisan measure aimed at silencing the opposition press. The Federalist politicians who enacted the provisions cast their protective mantle exclusively over President Adams and his cabinet. Not the slightest attempt was made to include the vice-president in its provisions. But then, Thomas Jefferson was a Republican. What is more, he was a Francophile.

THE FREE SPEECH DEBATES

The Federalists' efforts to create a one-party press forced their embattled opponents to focus their minds on the real meaning of free speech in a way Americans had never done before. Just what were the 'inalienable rights' protected by the First Amendment? Was there a legitimate distinction to be drawn between liberty and licence, and if so, what was it? Did the notion of seditious libel have any place in the laws of an elective system of government? Was its punishment constitutional or unconstitutional? As the election drew closer, an intense debate took place to define just how far the freedom of speech should extend in the United States and under what circumstances it might be limited.

Republican thinkers began to realise there could be no satisfactory way of distinguishing between liberty and licence without abridging liberty itself. The same arguments applied to the distinctions between truth and falsehood, since any offensive criticism of the government would invariably be denounced as false. George Hay declared that there were many truths important to society, which were not susceptible to the full, direct and positive evidence which alone can be exhibited before a court and a jury. As a result, printers 'would not only refrain from publishing anything of the least questionable nature, but they would be afraid of publishing the truth, as, though true, it might not always be in their power to establish the truth to the satisfaction of a court of justice'.

The old measures of liberty were, on this theory, no longer valid. The prosecutions under the Sedition Act had brought the realisation that 'truth' and 'facts' were no more helpful guides to what was permissible than a determination of what was meant by 'malice' or 'licentiousness'. Indeed, John Thomson of New York argued that the terms 'licentious' and 'false' were 'destitute of any meaning' and were used only by those who wished no one to enjoy the liberty of the press, save those who shared their own opinions. But the truth of opinions could never be proved. It was an abstract concept no more capable of absolute definition than asking a jury to decide which is the most palatable food, agreeable drink, or beautiful colour. If the administration prosecuted a citizen for his opinion that the Sedition Act itself was unconstitutional, would not a jury, picked by that administration, find the opinion ungrounded, or, in other words, false, scandalous and malicious? And by what kind of argument, in the present climate of opinion, could the accused convince them that his own opinion was true? If the trial was political, a jury was incapable of giving an impartial verdict.

Out of this torrent of questioning, a new, libertarian, theory of free speech can be seen emerging, not yet fully coherent, but already offering bold and original new definitions of the meaning and scope of political discourse. Those engaged in the debate made two lasting contributions to the legal theory that underpinned the right to free speech: they rejected the notion of seditious libel as inappropriate in a two-party republic and they finally broke away from the old Blackstonian concept of freedom based on the mere absence of prior restraint.

In Congress, Albert Gallatin of Pennsylvania made a powerful argument against the doctrine that no prior restraint was the sole test of a free press. It appeared to him preposterous to say that to punish a certain act was not an abridgement of the liberty of doing that act. It was an insulting evasion of the constitution to say,

> We claim no power to abridge the liberty of the press – *that* you may enjoy unrestrained; you may write and publish what you please, but if you publish anything against us, we shall punish you for it. So long as we do not prevent, but only punish your writings, it is no abridgement of your liberty of writing and printing.

It was absurd to contend that the First Amendment only prohibited laws laying prior restraints on publication, for what those could be, he was at a loss to conceive – 'unless gentlemen chose to assert that the constitution had given Congress a power to seal the mouths or to cut the tongues of the citizens of the Union' – which were the only means he knew of laying previous restraints on the freedom of speech.

As George Hay saw it, the old 'British' definition of free speech meant that a man might be mutilated or put to death for what he published provided that no notice was taken of him before he published: a concept that did not deserve to be transplanted into America. Hay, who was later to sit on the US Supreme Court, was one of the first to publish a reasoned analysis of the meaning of the first amendment and its implications for political expression. In a pamphlet that was to influence Jefferson's own thinking on free speech, he went further towards taking an absolutist stance than any influential jurist had done before. To Hay, the whole concept of a verbal political crime was abhorrent. 'A man might say anything which his passions suggest,' he wrote. He may, without fear of prosecution, 'employ all his time, and all his talents, if he is wicked enough to do so, in *speaking* against the government matters that are false, scandalous and malicious.' The first amendment provided that from 'within the sanctuary of the press' one was safe to condemn republican institutions, censure the government and its officers, ascribe its measures and their conduct to the basest motives, and lie outright in doing so. All were matters of public concern, affecting the rights and interests of the people, and were therefore in the 'open field of discussion' without any limits. Those who had framed the constitution knew 'that this field would be often occupied by folly, malignity, treachery and ambition; but they knew too that intelligence and patriotism would always be on the spot in the hour of danger, and to make *their* entrance at all times easy and secure, if it was left open to all'.

Truth should be offered no greater protection than falsehood. To attempt to distinguish between them was to ignore the fact that opinions were unprovable. Any harm that resulted from unfettered publication would be far less than the evil that would result from an attempt to restrain it. The only line that Hay was prepared to draw was to protect private reputations from libel. And even that was not a matter for the criminal law. If an injury had been sustained, the proper redress was a civil suit for damages.

As the arguments intensified, the so-called Father of the Constitution joined the debate. Early in 1800, James Madison wrote a lengthy official report for the Virginia House of Delegates on the Alien and Sedition Acts, in which he deployed all of his authority to show what the Bill of Rights should mean in practice. In a learned and brilliantly argued summary he advanced the proposition that the United States possessed no jurisdiction over common law crimes; that a popularly elected republican government cannot be libelled; that the freedom guaranteed by the first amendment was absolute, and could not be abridged by any federal authority. The Sedition Act was therefore unconstitutional.

Since it was drawn from the sovereign authority of the people, the constitution was paramount over the legislature as well as the executive. The press was accordingly free, not only from the prior restraint of the executive, but from legislative restraint also; 'not only from the previous inspection of licensers, but from the subsequent penalty of laws'. Madison then posed a crucial question: 'Is then the federal government destitute of every authority for restraining the licentiousness of the press, and for shielding itself against the libellous attacks which might be made on those who administer it?' He replied:

The Constitution alone can answer this question. If no such power is expressly delegated, and if it be not both necessary and proper to carry into execution an express power; above all, if it be expressly forbidden by a declaratory amendment to the constitution – the answer must be, that the federal government is destitute of all such authority.

The Death of Socrates, by Jacques-Louis David. (Metropolitan Museum of Art, Wolfe Fund, 1931)

Desiderius Erasmus of Rotterdam, by Quentin Massys or Metsys. (Palazzo Barberini, Rome, Italy/Bridgeman Art Library)

Martin Luther. (Photo Archive Marburg)

'The Martyrdome and Burning of Master William Tindall in Flanders, by Filford Castle', from Acts and Monuments by John Foxe. (Private Collection/Bridgeman Art Library)

Galileo Galilei, by Justus Sustermans. (Galleria degli Uffizi, Florence, Italy/Bridgeman Art Library)

John Locke, by John Raphael Smith. (AKG Photo, London)

John Wilkes, the vengeful cartoon by William Hogarth. (AKG Photo, London)

An engraving of Thomas Paine, French school, nineteenth century. (Private Collection/ Bridgeman Art Library)

'The Life of William Cobbett written by himself', by James Gillray, London, 29 September 1809. (AKG Photo, London)

John Stuart Mill, by George Frederic Watts, 1873. (National Portrait Gallery, London)

Horace Greeley, 1870. (AKG Photo, London)

C.P. Scott. (*Manchester Guardian* Archives)

Oliver Wendell Holmes (1841–1935).
(National Portrait Gallery,
Washington DC)

A body of opinion was emerging, later to be called Jeffersonian, that articulated the case for the freedom of expression with an intellectual clarity and legal authority that was uniquely American. What was the preferable way to counter an injurious opinion in a free society, they asked, by fair and argumentative refutation, or by the terrible dissuasive of a statute of sedition? By the convincing and circumstantial narrative of the truth, or by the terrors of imprisonment and the singular logic of the pillory? Only a government whose policies cannot survive investigation had need to resort to the punishment of seditious utterances. And while coercion might compel, it could never persuade. That could only be achieved by representation of the truth, the open publication of government transactions, a good record, and reliance upon public opinion.

The debate reached its height just as the prosecutions under the Sedition Act were in their fullest spate and the election campaign of 1800 beginning to warm up. Free speech and the operation of the Sedition Act became central issues of the campaign.

JEFFERSON AND THE PRESS

The challenge to the freedom of the press thrown down by the Sedition Act brought Jefferson to the most serious crisis of his career. Not only was he looked upon as the great apostle of American liberty, his party was the principal target of measures he regarded as unconstitutional. Without the freedom of thought, freedom of speech and of the press, the republican experiment seemed to him to be insupportable. The strength of his faith in the proposition can be gauged by a letter he wrote to a young college student in the year the prosecutions began: 'To preserve the freedom of the human mind . . . and freedom of the press, every spirit should be ready to devote itself to martyrdom, for as long as we may think as we will and speak as we think, the condition of man will proceed in improvement.'

Those were his private thoughts. In public, this most enigmatic of men said nothing; he certainly showed no sign of offering himself up to the martyrdom he had urged on his young friend. A politician to his fingertips, he saw that with war in prospect an open challenge to the acts was unlikely to succeed. Besides, his own political survival was at stake. 'I am very much inclined to think that the patient must find his own disorder,' advised his friend, James Monroe. 'The physician must not appear.'

Jefferson heartily agreed. All his life, he had shrunk from open confrontation. To some, this was the mark of a consummate politician. To others, it was a sign of cowardice. His opponents called him a 'shifty-eyed southerner' – Jefferson seldom looked directly at people when he spoke and was always pained by any sort of censure. Hamilton called him 'the most intriguing man in the United States . . . cautious and sly, and wrapped up in impenetrable silence and mystery'. His modern biographers find him equally impenetrable and elusive, a mass of bewildering conflicts and contradictions. His affirmation of the principles of liberty have nourished the American spirit for over two centuries, and the words inscribed on his memorial in Washington reflect his own enduring spirit – 'I have sworn upon the altar of God eternal hostility against every form of tyranny over the mind of man' – yet in the words of one modern study, his ardent defence of liberty rarely required him to make a personal display of courage. 'Thomas Jefferson never once risked career or reputation to champion free speech, fair trial, or any other libertarian value,' wrote Leonard Levy. On this, as on so many other occasions, he trimmed his sails and remained silent, saving his complaints about the government's abridgement of freedom for his private correspondence. His open affirmations of liberty would have to wait until he had attained office.

This impenetrable man was an archetypal child of the Enlightenment and a prodigy of talents. He yearned for the contemplative life of an intellectual yet could not resist the attractions of active politics. The tributaries of his mind, it is said, ran in all directions. He hated idleness. He kept detailed accounts of the minutest phenomena and in the early part of his life took meteorological readings three times a day, regularly, over several decades. He knew when each of the vegetables in his garden was planted, and when they would be ready for the table. He built his own home at Monticello, full of ingenious contrivances that he had designed himself. Nothing seemed to be beyond the versatile grasp of a man who, in James Parton's memorable description, 'could calculate an eclipse, survey an estate, tie an artery, plan an edifice, try a cause, break a horse, dance a minuet and play a violin'.

His father had been a native born Virginian, brought up on the edge of the wilderness along the James River. A slave owner, like most southern planters, he had raised a large landed family, Thomas, the tall sandy-haired eldest son, going on to college, politics and the law. He was thirty-three when he wrote the Declaration of Independence, and had since served as the American emissary in Paris – which kept him out of the country during the debate on the Bill of Rights – returning to become Washington's first Secretary of State before his brief retirement and recall as Adams's vice-president in the election of 1796. To his great distress, he had been widowed before he was forty and now lived the enforced life of a bachelor, returning whenever he could to be with his two surviving daughters at his beloved Monticello.

Jefferson's contribution to the development of the Republican Party had been conducted in his favoured sphere of operations – behind the scenes. As a political leader, it was said he always preferred to work through others rather than permit his own hand to appear, to write a letter rather than make a speech, and to remain outwardly every man's friend rather than to engage in open controversy.

His response to the passage of the Alien and Sedition Acts had been typically enigmatic. He withdrew to Monticello to write a history of Anglo-Saxon grammar. Suspecting that his mail was being spied upon, he warned his friends they would seldom hear from him, because of 'the infidelities of the post office and the circumstances of the times'. He counselled Monroe always to examine the seal of his letters to see if they had been tampered with, adding, 'I know not which mortifies me most, that I should fear to write what I think, or my country bear such a state of things'. Then, as was his custom in times of crisis, he called on his old friend James Madison to discuss what action they might take secretly to mitigate the effect of the noxious acts. Between them, they concocted two resolutions to be put before the State legislatures of Kentucky and Virginia, denouncing the two acts in the name of the Bill of Rights and asserting that, in the last resort, the individual States had the right to decide whether or not they were constitutional.

Most other States were unconvinced by this argument. Massachusetts pronounced the acts to be 'not only constitutional, but expedient and necessary'. Maryland found them 'wise and politic', and seven others pointed out that their interpretation was a matter for the Supreme Court.

Rebuffed by their northern and eastern neighbours, some of Jefferson's supporters began hinting at more radical measures. Secession from the union was openly spoken of; rumours spread that Virginia was making military preparations. The State government declared this was to guard against invasion by the French, but most others assumed – correctly – that the measure was directed to guard against troops of the federal government. From New York, it was known that Hamilton was urging military action to curb the rebellious southerners. A crisis of free speech was threatening to become a crisis of the Union.

When he realised that the Union was in danger, Jefferson's essential caution re-asserted itself. While he did not go so far as to renounce the Kentucky Resolution that he himself had secretly drafted, he counselled his radical followers against violence. 'This is not the kind of opposition the American people will permit,' he said. 'In every free and deliberating society, there must, from the nature of man, be opposite parties, and violent dissensions and discords; and one of these, for the most part, must prevail over the other for a longer or a shorter time . . . But if on a temporary superiority of one party, the other is to resort to a scission of the Union, no federal government can ever exist.' Where would the process stop? One confederacy would become two, then three, and then four, with no end in sight. 'Seeing therefore . . . that we must have somebody to quarrel with, I would rather keep our New England associates for that purpose, than to see our bickerings transferred to others.' He philosophically concluded that the 'reign of witches' would soon be over and their spells dissolved; the mass of the people were suffering only a temporary distemper, and the doctor was already on his way. They were wise words, eventually to be justified, although the worst of the storm was still to come.

Prosecutions under the Alien and Sedition Acts proceeded throughout election year. Twenty-five persons were arrested in all, fourteen indicted, and ten tried and convicted. All were Republican printers and publicists. The first victim was to have been the publisher of the pro-French *Aurora*, Franklin's grandson, Benjamin Bache, described as 'an ill-looking fellow who looks as though he had just spent a week or ten days on a gibbet'. But while in jail awaiting his trial, Bache succumbed to one of Philadelphia's regular epidemics of yellow fever. In his place, Adams's attorney-general, Timothy Pickering, tried to have Bache's successor as editor of the *Aurora*, William Duane, deported as a 'wild Irish alien', but he was saved from this fate by his American birth.

The first defendant actually to come to court was a democratic congressman, Matthew Lyon of Vermont, who was known to his opponents as 'Ragged Matt, the

Democrat'. He was indicted on charges arising out of the publication in a local newspaper of a statement which he had already uttered under the protection of privilege in Congress, protesting against President Adams's 'unbounded thirst for ridiculous pomp, foolish adulation and selfish avarice'. Lyon based his defence on the argument that the act was unconstitutional, but the judge over-ruled him. He was found guilty, fined $1,000, sentenced to four months in jail, and hustled straight from the courthouse into a cell used for horse thieves, counterfeiters and runaway slaves.

Another prominent victim was Thomas Cooper, one of William Duane's counsel before the Senate, who also edited a Pennsylvania newspaper, the *Northumberland Gazette*. An immigrant from England, he had written a number of philosophical works about the liberty of the press and was known to be a friend of Jefferson's. In April, he was tried on a charge of seditious libel for remarks he had made on an election handbill attacking Adams for enlarging the armed forces. The shockingly partisan Justice Samuel Chase declared that because Cooper had intended to mislead the ignorant and influence their votes in the forthcoming election, he must go to jail.

A quite ludicrous case then came before the courts – Luther Baldwin of New Jersey was sentenced for stating while drunk that he hoped a cannon shot fired in salute to Adams might find its way up the presidential posterior. But it was the trial of a Scottish hack called James Callender that touched the Republican candidate most directly. The woebegone Scot had come to America on the run from a charge of seditious libel in Edinburgh, and was later to be described by Jefferson himself as 'a poor creature . . . hypochondriac, drunken, penniless and unprincipled'. But he was a useful tool in the war against the Federalists, and the vice-president had been paying him subsidies ever since his feud with Hamilton in the 1790s.

Callender had first come to prominence when Hamilton, then treasury secretary, fell into the hands of a pair of blackmailers, James Reynolds and his wife, Maria, with whom Hamilton had been lured into a brief affair. Reynolds was given cash to soothe his injured feelings, but when he was later arrested on another charge, he swore to three members of Congress that he could prove Hamilton was speculating illegally in government stock. Confronted with the allegations, Hamilton admitted the affair, but denied the corruption. Callender got hold of the story, and published it in a pamphlet entitled *The History of the United States in 1796*, which made Hamilton appear guilty not only of adultery, but of stealing from the Treasury. The story effectively ended Hamilton's hopes of high office.

Fearing he would become an early victim of the Sedition Act, Callender had quit Philadelphia in 1798 and was working now as a writer for the Richmond *Examiner*, Virginia's leading Republican newspaper. He had meanwhile continued to sponge off Jefferson, on the grounds that 'an assistant writer' of a party was entitled to support. As the next election approached, Callender wrote to Jefferson, promising to give his readers 'such a tornado as no government ever got before'. Jefferson sent him $50 on account, disguised as a purchase. After seeing the page proofs, he wrote, 'such papers cannot fail to produce the best effect. They inform the thinking part of the nation'.

Friends were already beginning to warn the vice-president about his protégé, who no one seemed to like and many feared. 'The wretch has a most thief-life look,' wrote one. 'He is ragged, dirty, has a downcast with his eyes, leans his head towards one side, as if his neck had a stretch, and goes along working his shoulder up and down with evident signs of anger against the fleas and lice.' He was not the candidate the Republicans would themselves have chosen to champion the liberty of the press, but when Justice Samuel Chase rode into Virginia in May 1800 to preside over the Sedition Act trials, they were given no options. Callender was hauled before him and charged with publishing the pamphlet that had been approved by Jefferson, *The Prospect Before Us.*

The trial was a travesty of justice. The prosecution was based on a marked copy of the *Prospect*, in which Callender had done no more than describe Adams as 'a hoary-headed incendiary'. Most people would regard this as mere vulgar abuse, common currency in an election year, and certainly no worse than the vilification of Jefferson to be found in the Federalist press. But Judge Chase was set on conviction. After declaring he would allow no atheist to give evidence – a sideswipe at Jefferson – he harangued the privately subsidised defence lawyers so persistently they were forced to withdraw. The all-federalist grand jury found the now defenceless Callender guilty as charged. Chase sentenced him to nine months' imprisonment and fined him $200. The embittered Scot was later to turn, not on those who had sentenced him, but on the man he believed had betrayed him, Thomas Jefferson, by then the Republican candidate for President.

By now it had become obvious that the Federalist Party would be hard pressed to hold on to office. The hysteria of the XYZ affair had died away, while Nelson's defeat of the French at the Battle of the River Nile had removed the fear of invasion. The use of the military to put down a minor rebellion in eastern Pennsylvania, the ever-present bogey of the high Federalists' 'monarchism', rising taxes and the unpopularity of the partisan and now quite unnecessary prosecutions under the Alien and Sedition Acts all played into the hands of the Republicans. Peace was in the air, and the Federalist heroes who had seen the country through the XYZ crisis of 1798 were now perceived as warmongers.

Jefferson characteristically stayed at home and conducted the campaign from his study at Monticello. Among the fundamental doctrines he put forward was a somewhat abstract attachment to the freedom of religion and the press coupled with the sovereign right of the people to oppose and criticise the governing authorities.

While Jefferson had a deep and sincere belief in the *concept* of free speech, and a conviction that the Sedition Act represented a mortal danger to the liberty of the press, he was not yet ready to go as far as outright libertarians like Madison and Hay. He did not reject the substantive law of seditious libel, or find it incompatible with a Republican form of government. He still accepted without question the dominant view of his generation that governments could be criminally assaulted by mere words. His understanding of the issues had not advanced beyond eloquent and felicitously phrased abstractions. Throughout the election campaign he intoned 'freedom of the press', as if by merely pronouncing the words, he had offered a sovereign remedy.

Jefferson admittedly had an election to fight. He was also on the defensive against the most abusive attacks from the Federalist press. Indeed, it was mainly through propaganda against his Jacobin and atheist views that they counted on keeping him from the presidency. Indiscreet words Jefferson had written privately about George Washington leaked out just at the moment the first president had been unexpectedly carried to his apotheosis by streptococcal laryngitis. With the country draped in black crepe, it was thought the prestige of the one Federalist who seemed genuinely to be above party might yet carry Adams into the President's House in the new capital city being cleared from the wilderness on the banks of the Potomac. 'Our campaign will be as hot as that of Europe,' Jefferson forecast. 'But happily indeed in ink only; they in blood.'

The campaign ran on throughout the summer and into the autumn, though it was never a national election in the modern sense. What was known as 'Election Day' – 3 December – was simply the day on which the members of the electoral college cast their votes in their respective States, having themselves been chosen by a variety of means during the months of October and November. Jefferson meanwhile moved into a boarding house in the new capital and waited for the results to come in with a growing sense of optimism.

At last, on 12 December, on the basis of the count in South Carolina, Jefferson believed himself safely elected. He was now sure of seventy-three votes in the Electoral College, Adams a maximum of sixty-five. 'The Jig's Up!' pronounced the *Baltimore American*. No more 'gags, inquisitions and spies', no more 'herds of harpies'. It was said that dismayed Federalists wore such long faces the barbers doubled their prices. For the jubilant Republicans, the election seemed to be in the bag. 'Be Glad America!' cried the *Readinger Adler*.

They rejoiced too soon. Over the next few days, as the final results trickled in from the new western States of Kentucky and Tennessee, a distressing flaw was revealed in the electoral system. Jefferson had beaten Adams sure enough, but he had polled exactly the same number of votes as his own Republican running mate, Aaron Burr. Under the rules, a tied election had to be decided in the House of Representatives, voting by states. With Burr's unscrupulous connivance, the Federalists gave him their votes in a desperate attempt to keep Jefferson from the presidency. The crisis ran on from December until the middle of February. In the final frenzied week Congressmen sent home for their pillows and night-caps as the balloting continued night and day, until finally, on the thirty-sixth ballot, the absurd process came to an end and Jefferson was duly elected.

A few days later, John Adams left town without waiting for the inauguration of his successor, with whom he was no longer on speaking terms. Later that same day he was seen passing 'like a shot' through New York on his way home to Boston. He had left behind him the Judiciary Act of 1801, which reorganised the Supreme Court and appointed Federalist supporters to several other judicial posts. The appointment of what became known as Adams's 'Midnight Judges' was the Federalist Party's final act of government, for they never held high office in the United States again. With their oligarchic philosophy, their vindictive persecution of their opponents and their contempt for public opinion, they had condemned themselves not only to defeat in the election of 1800, but to their own extinction as a party.

Jefferson took his oath of office in the chamber of the US Senate, the only part of the new Capitol building then completed, which stood, we are told, 'in shining contrast to the dismal scene around'. The new president had walked to his inauguration through a swampy wilderness infested with snipe and wild turkeys. When he rose to give his inaugural address, he was able to look out over the wide Potomac to a breathtaking panorama of rolling virgin forests and distant heights. While the views were majestic, the ceremonies were carried out with republican simplicity, and though Jefferson's predecessor had absented himself, what was happening here represented a revolution in human affairs as momentous as that of 1776: the peaceful transfer of power from one political party to another – the moment at which representative democracy might fairly be said to have come of age.

The address itself was delivered in a low, inaudible mumble, for Jefferson was no orator. Indeed, as far as is known, this was the only public speech he made during the whole of his first term in office. But his words had been as carefully crafted as anything he ever wrote and intended to be studied and re-read on the printed page. It rates today as one of the finest statements of the American ideal ever delivered, a pellucid survey of the essential principles on which the republic had been founded. 'Peace, commerce, and honest friendship with all nations – and entangling alliances with none,' was just one of the phrases for which it would be remembered. The simple plea for national harmony was another – 'we are all federalists; we are all republicans' – written by Jefferson without capital letters to emphasise that he was speaking of abiding principles and not of passing political attachments. And finally, his declaration in favour of the freedom to dissent: 'If there be any among us who would wish to dissolve this Union or change its republican form, let them stand undisturbed as monuments of the safety with which error of opinion may be tolerated where reason is left free to combat it.'

Within a few weeks, the words of the inaugural address had spread the length and breadth of America. Printers vied with each other in distributing it, teachers taught their classes to commit it to memory, Republicans hailed it as an American Magna Carta, even Federalists found it conciliatory. All that remained now was for the high idealism of the new president's inaugural address to be translated into deeds.

Jefferson's first term as president was among the most notable in American history, as the nation reached out from its straggling base along the eastern seaboard to its destiny as a continental power stretching from 'sea to shining sea'. His own expectations were high. 'It is impossible not to believe we are acting for all mankind,' he wrote during his first administration. 'Circumstances denied to others, but indulged to us, have imposed on us the duty of proving what is the degree of freedom and self-government in which society may venture to leave its individual members.'

In most matters, he was fastidious – and sometimes downright pedantic – about putting his principles into practice. Unlike his two predecessors he consistently refused to designate national days of prayer, fasting or thanksgiving. Civil power alone, he insisted, was vested in the president of the United States. He therefore did not possess the authority to direct events of a religious character. To do so would be in violation of the constitutional prohibition against the establishment of religion.

In matters of free speech, the Sedition Act was declared a nullity, and Jefferson found himself scolded by his old friend, Abigail Adams, for pardoning the 'scoundrels' convicted under its provisions during her husband's administration. One of the first of these 'scoundrels' was James Callender, whose prison term for libelling President Adams in the Richmond *Examiner* was just coming to an end. Jefferson gave him a retrospective pardon and ordered remission of the $200 fine imposed on the writer by Judge Chase.

When the money was not immediately forthcoming – the Richmond marshal was an uncooperative Federalist – Callender turned nasty. He had gone to jail for the Republican cause, he complained, but the only result of his martyrdom was that 'I have been equally calumniated, pillaged and destroyed by all parties'. Now without job, money or prospects, the very least he deserved was a government appointment – the Richmond post office was the vacancy he had in mind. Instead of a job, Jefferson sent him another $50. Callender thereupon appeared in Washington with threats of blackmail, intimating to the president's private secretary that he was asking for the money, not as charity, but as a due; in fact, as hush money.

At this point, it came out in public that Jefferson had been paying money to Callender, who he had once regarded as 'a man of science fled from persecution' – words he now renounced. His gifts to Callender, he said, were 'mere charities . . . no more meant as encouragement to his scurrilities than those I give to the beggar at my door are meant as rewards for the vices of his life'. Jefferson's motives had become hopelessly entangled, and the use he made of the feckless Scot had involved him in what would become the most damaging personal relationship of his career.

Sent back to Virginia empty-handed, and animated by his natural bent for muck-raking, Callender saw fit to revive a scandalous story he had unearthed while in jail in Virginia – namely, that the new president had fathered several mulatto children on one of his own slave girls, Sally Hemings, described by Callender as 'the African Venus said to officiate as housekeeper at Monticello'. The malodorous little histoire was given a seeming authenticity by being cleverly interspersed with the letters Jefferson had sent to Callender, encouraging his own nefarious work. It was a sorry episode which has cast a cloud over Jefferson's reputation to this day. But in the country as a whole, and especially among those who read the Federalist press, the scandal was regarded as one more example of Jefferson's hypocrisy. A spate of bawdy songs flew around, one of which begins:

> Of all the damsels on the green
> On mountain or in valley
> A lass so luscious ne'er was seen
> As Monticello Sally.

There were further revelations, too, about a challenge to a duel the president had received from a neighbour whose wife Jefferson had attempted to seduce many years previously, while he was still a bachelor. In public, he maintained a stoic silence about these disclosures. In private he went through a profound crisis of the spirit. It was one thing for him to express a high-minded belief that truth would always triumph over falsehood; that was an argument that applied to disagreements over politics and philosophy. It was quite another thing to have to endure a campaign of personal smear, scandal and innuendo. In such matters, falsehoods might run 1,000 miles while truth was still putting on her boots. 'Our printers ravin on the agonies of their victims as wolves do on the blood of the lamb,' Jefferson wrote. 'Nothing can now be believed that is read in a newspaper. Truth itself becomes suspicious by being put into that polluted vessel.' In later life, he himself read only one newspaper, the Richmond *Enquirer*, 'and in that chiefly the advertisements, for they contain the only truths to be trusted on in a newspaper'. All this was a world away from the famous statement he had made as a young man in Paris: 'The basis of our government being the opinion of the people . . . were it left to me to decide whether we should have governments without newspapers, or newspapers without a government, I should not hesitate a moment to choose the latter.' Like so many of Jefferson's high-flown statements of principle, the abstract concept did not always match the harsh reality.

Jefferson's involvement with Callender haunted him throughout his two terms of office. In 1803, it led him to support an assault on the liberty of the press that showed up the double standards he applied to matters involving the freedom of speech. The New York *Evening Post* had accused the president of having paid Callender to call George Washington a traitor and John Adams 'a hoary-headed incendiary' – the offence for which Callender had been convicted under the Sedition Act. The *Post* had close connections with Hamilton, and probably for that reason was left alone. But when an obscure upstate newspaper called the *Wasp* reprinted the article, its editor, Harry Crosswell, was arrested and charged with the common law offence of seditious libel.

The tables had been turned with a vengeance. The Republicans who had protested so vehemently against the sedition laws when they were used against them, were now arresting editors for the same offence. When defence lawyers tried to *subpoena* Callender to testify that the allegation was true, the Republican judge disallowed the request on the grounds that a libel did not depend on whether it was true or not. Ignoring the precedent set in the Zenger case, he followed Lord Justice Holt's ancient precept that the jury must concern itself only with the fact of publication, and not of its truth or intent. Crosswell was found guilty.

The case at once went to appeal, where the defence was led by Alexander Hamilton, now privately practising law in the State of New York. The scene was set for a famous trial on the right to free speech, with Jefferson sitting uncomfortably on the side of the prosecution – the subject, it was claimed, of the libel, if, indeed, there had ever been a libel.

Hamilton was at his brilliant best. 'The liberty of the press consists in publishing free remarks, with truth and good motive, on men and measures,' he declared. He did not mean by this an unchecked press – he remembered too well the calumnies heaped on the head of George Washington. The distinction between a free press and an unchecked press lay in the truth of the publication and the good motives that lay behind the exposure, though he readily admitted that truth in itself was insufficient; the publication must also not be malicious. Guilt or innocence depended upon circumstance and motive. But all that was for a jury to decide. Judges, he argued, were not competent to pronounce on such matters.

Hamilton then made what one of the judges described as 'a most masterly and eloquent digression' on the indispensable necessity for permitting truth as evidence and the historical role of the jury as the bulwark of British liberties. From there, he moved with great skill from defence to attack. If it was necessary to impugn the measures introduced by government, it was equally necessary in a free society to impugn the authors of those measures. Otherwise, a party once in control 'may go on from step to step, and . . . fix themselves firmly in their seats, especially if they are not to be reproached for what they have done'. To watch the progress of such endeavours was the office of a free press – 'to give us early alarm, and put us on our guard against the encroachments of power.' This, he said, 'is a right which, instead of yielding up, we ought rather to spill our blood . . . Our worst danger comes not from a few provisional armies, but from *dependent* judges – from *selected* juries – from *stifling* the press and the voice of leaders and patriots – from devoting a wretched but honest man as the victim of a *nominal* trial. We ought to *resist – resist – resist –* till we hurl the demagogues and tyrants from their imagined thrones'.

He ended with an impassioned eulogy of his old hero and mentor, George Washington, which led one of the judges to declare he had never heard eloquence so pathetic and sublime. Hamilton had delivered a speech in support of a free press at least a match for that made by Thomas Erskine in support of Tom Paine's right to publish *The Rights of Man*.

But, like Erskine before him, Hamilton lost his case. The judges were all politicians and voted on party lines: two for and two against. Under the rules, Crosswell's sentence stood, though Hamilton had won a great moral victory, showing up the Republicans' hypocrisy in attempting to suppress the truth of a most serious – and subsequently proven – allegation. He had also won the wider legal argument. Within a year the libel laws in New York were amended so that, seventy years after the Zenger trial, truth might at last be admitted in evidence and the jury given the duty to determine both the law and the fact in cases of libel. Crosswell was unanimously awarded a new trial and the State's constitution was eventually amended. The other States followed suit, and Hamilton's position, eventually successful, finally settled the law of libel across America.

What was arguably Hamilton's greatest speech was also his last. Later that same year, he had his fatal encounter on the banks of the Hudson with Jefferson's vice-president, Aaron Burr, who shot him dead in a duel over remarks he had made about Burr's political honour. By then, the author of the charges that had led to Crosswell's trial was also dead. In July 1803, James Callender had drowned, while drunk, in the James River.

Jefferson's role in the case that was brought against Crosswell was never made clear, though he continued to support the notion of seditious libel in the individual States throughout his term of office. Indeed, in the same year that Crosswell was charged, he personally prompted the prosecution of a journalist in Pennsylvania who had reprinted the rumours about his liaison with Sally Hemings. In another example of Jefferson's ambivalent standards, he sent a private note to the state governor complaining that the Federalists, having failed to destroy the freedom of the press through their gag law, now sought to attack it from the opposite direction, 'that is by pushing its licentiousness and its lying to such a degree of prostitution as to deprive it of all credit. I have therefore long thought that a few prosecutions of the most eminent offenders would have a wholesome effect in restoring the integrity of the press. Not a general prosecution, for that would look like a persecution, but a selected one. The paper I now enclose appears to me to offer as good an instance in every respect to make an example of, as can be selected.'

The paper he enclosed was the *Port Folio*, which had published many of the ballads about Monticello Sally. Soon afterwards, its editor, Joseph Dennie, was indicted for seditious libel – though not for mocking Jefferson, but for a tirade he had written against democracy. 'No wise man but discerns its imperfections,' Dennie had written. 'No good man but shudders at its miseries, no honest man but proclaims its fraud, and no brave man but draws his sword against its force.' The indictment served on him for publishing these words was as intolerant as that served on Harry Crosswell. Dennie was charged with maliciously intending to 'revile, deprecate and scandalise the characters of the revolutionary patriots and statesmen, to endanger, subvert and totally destroy the republican constitutions and free governments of the United States'.

When the case came to trial two years later, the judge – a Federalist – more or less instructed the jury to acquit. While Dennie was answerable for any abuse of his constitutional right to speak freely, they should also bear in mind that 'the enlightened advocates of representative republican government pride themselves on the reflection that the more deeply their system is examined, the more fully will the judgements of honest men be satisfied that it is the most conducive to the safety and happiness of a free people'. Dennie was set free, though the case did nothing for Jefferson's subsequent reputation. While the trial was brought under common law in the State of Pennsylvania, his open encouragement of it was hardly compatible with his inaugural pledge to let those who wished to dissolve the Union's Republican form 'stand undisturbed as monuments of the safety with which error of opinion may be tolerated'. We are driven, once again, to the conclusion that Jefferson's glittering declarations of principle were not always matched by his actions as a practical politician. It always seemed to depend on whose ox was being gored.

By the time of his second inaugural address in 1805 so embittered had he become at the licentiousness of the press that he hinted he would not be displeased if its abuses were corrected 'by the wholesome punishments reserved and provided by the laws of the several States against falsehood and defamation'. But, however regrettable were the abuses of an institution so important to freedom, and however much they lessened its usefulness, he was still able to hold to a rhetorical, though by this time decidedly rueful, defence of free discussion. 'Since truth and freedom have retained their ground against false opinions in league with false facts, the press . . . needs no other legal restraint,' he said. The only permissible censorship was the censorship of public opinion. On a full hearing of all parties, the public judgement would correct false reasonings and opinions: no other definite line could be drawn between 'the inestimable liberty of the press and its demoralising licentiousness'.

It was one of the most eloquent defences of a free press he ever uttered. But like almost all his ringing declarations against tyranny over the minds of man it was a rhetorical statement of first principles. And while rhetorical first principles may suit the needs of moralists and philosophers, they rarely decide hard cases. In the realm of practical politics, as Jefferson himself recognised, 'a government held together by the bands of reason only, require much compromise of opinion; that things even salutary should not be crammed down the throats of dissenting brethren', as the high-Federalists had tried to do.

The fact is that Jefferson bestrode two worlds. As an eloquent exponent of first principles, he has had few equals; as a President in office, he was a consummate, and if needs be, a ruthless, politician. In all the hard political decisions of his presidency he was never wracked by the self-doubt and agonies of conscience that affected, say President Lincoln, during a crisis. There was never any sign, in Jefferson, of an inner struggle or an admission that his deeds sometimes ran counter to his conscience. There was no room for doubt. The biographer of this 'darker side' of Jefferson, Leonard Levy, believes the explanation lies in his belief that the great experiment in self-government that he led was in almost constant danger, so that 'he completely identified with that experiment, to the point that an attack on him or on the wisdom of his policies quickly became transmuted in his mind as a threat to the security of the tender democratic plant'. But it did so at the expense of a belief in individual liberty. In Thomas Jefferson's mind, democracy and liberty had parted company, as it has done so often, both before and since.

The argument about free speech was not settled in Jefferson's day, any more than it has been thereafter. What does abide as a guide to human conduct are his own words in favour of liberty in his first inaugural address and what have been called the 'studied imprecisions' of Madison's Bill of Rights. Its simple statement that 'Congress shall make no laws abridging the freedom of speech or of the press' has endured now for more than two centuries, even though the argument about what it should mean has been renewed in every generation. Within seven years of its adoption, its objectives had been subverted by the Alien and Sedition Acts. In the years between Jefferson's second administration and the civil war, they were to be subverted again, when the right of free speech was suppressed, in both north and south, over the great issue of the abolition of slavery. By then, it was found that the Bill of Rights protected American citizens only against the encroachments of the federal government, and could do nothing to stop the infringement of liberty by the individual States. Abolitionist newspapers were suppressed throughout the south, while the southern view of the argument never found a voice in the north. In the following century, Congress passed another Sedition Act, and in our own era, the Bill of Rights afforded scant protection to the dissidents persecuted by those such as Senator Joseph McCarthy in the 1950s. The argument about free speech is never over. Each succeeding generation must find its own definition. But in the American Bill of Rights, the nation had at least found a beacon to guide it back from an errant course, a political truth, in James Madison's words, that has acquired by degrees the character of a fundamental maxim.

CHAPTER ELEVEN

Twopenny Trash

In America, the hysteria that had led to the sedition laws gradually died away after Jefferson's election, and the press settled down to a period of relatively peaceful progress. In England, the oppression intensified. Far from reducing the fear of domestic upheaval, victory over Napoleon seemed to increase it. The governing classes became possessed by a spirit of intolerance that caused them to stamp on the least sign of dissent for another generation to come. In Parliament, in the Church, in the workplace, in the administration of justice, as well as in the press, the ordinary Englishman was steadily losing his ancient rights, with no champion to speak up for him.

The cause of this state of affairs was masked for a while by the epic struggle against France. But once the war was over, people began to realise that the country was in the grip of a profound upheaval. Population was on the move from the country to the newly industrialised towns. A new class of capitalist entrepreneur was emerging, and alongside it, a new underclass of dispossessed, ruthlessly exploited workers, who found themselves reduced by the peace to a state of abject poverty.

It was an age which saw Luddite riots sweep across the Midlands and the North, the introduction of the infamous Speenhamland system of poor relief on the land, the massacre of workers at Peterloo, and the deportation of the Tolpuddle martyrs for forming a trade union. As the government struggled to hold down this seething cauldron of discontent, it was an age that also saw the introduction of the most repressive laws against free speech and free assembly since the rule of the Stuarts a century and a half earlier. 'No means can be more effectual for checking the intolerable licence of the press but that of making transportation the punishment of its abuse,' declared the government-sponsored *Quarterly Review* of 1812.

With Tom Paine by this time dead and buried, a new voice at last emerged to take up the cause of the poor and the dispossessed. Looking on England from his own American exile, William Cobbett was the first influential man of his generation to understand what was happening to a homeland he loved with a fierce and devoted passion. 'A revolution of the most extraordinary kind has taken place in our country,' he wrote. 'The Revolution of 1688 was as nothing . . . compared with that which we now witness. In England, in that same England which was the cradle of real liberty and just laws; in that same England where justice and freedom were preserved while despotism reigned over the rest of the world, what do we now behold?' He answered his own question:

We behold Acts passed by [the] House of Commons which have taken from the people all liberty of the press, all liberty of speech, and all the safety which the laws gave to their very persons, it now being in the absolute power of Ministers to punish any man whom they may please to punish, in the severest possible manner short of instant death, not only without any trial by jury, but without any trial at all; without hearing him in his defence; without telling him who are his accusers; and without any appeal, now or hereafter, from their decisions!

Cobbett would hammer away at this theme for the next twenty years. Twice, his exercise of free speech would bring him to trial for seditious libel, once to be thrown into jail as a felon, once to a period in exile, and, at the end, to a triumphal acquittal and election to Parliament in the wake of the Reform Bill he had done so much to bring about. He also wrote an enduring English classic, *Rural Rides*, in which he painted an unforgettable portrait of a land in transition.

A more unlikely radical can scarcely be pictured. Born in 1763 at Farnham, in Surrey, his father a smallholder and landlord of *The Jolly Farmer*, young Cobbett was a Church-going conservative, a loyal supporter of King George and a vehement opponent of the French Revolution. All through his life, he was, in the words of G.K. Chesterton, eminently and emphatically a respectable man. It is his great virtue that he preferred to be reviled. It is to his great glory that he used his self-made success to make something better than himself.

Though born, as he liked to say, 'in old England', and deeply rooted in the Surrey countryside, Cobbett was possessed by a strong and sometimes impulsive desire for change. He had spent his boyhood on the farm, and could not remember the time 'when I did not earn my living'. His job as a small child was to scare away the birds from the turnip seeds. From there, he progressed to weeding wheat, hoeing peas and following the plough. It was a time, he would say, of 'honest pride and happy days'. He had learned early on to read and write, and at the age of eleven, an adventurous impulse saw him walk from Farnham to see the new royal gardens at Kew. Wearing a blue smock-frock and red garters, and with 3*d* left in his pocket, his eyes fell on a little book in a shop window in Richmond, on the outside of which was written TALES OF A TUB; PRICE 3*d*. His curiosity overcame his need for the 3*d* he had put aside for his supper, and he spent the rest of the afternoon under a haystack in the corner of Kew Gardens absorbed in the work of Jonathan Swift. A lifetime's passion for literature had been precociously aroused. He read on until it was dark, slept in the open, and for the next nine and a half years carried the precious book with him wherever he went, until to his great sorrow it was lost overboard while disembarking in the Bay of Fundy on the coast of Canada.

His next adventure was equally impulsive. Dressed one day in his holiday clothes and on his way to Guildford Fair, he was startled by a stagecoach rattling down the turnpike with LONDON written on its side. The coach drew up close to where he stood, and without a second thought young Cobbett clambered aboard, arriving at the foot of Ludgate Hill at 9 p.m. The money he was carrying 'melted like snow', but good luck was with him, and a chance acquaintance he had met on the coach took him in, wrote to his father, and found him work in the city as a clerk in an attorney's office.

He laboured away at his uncongenial task for eight or nine months, hating the gloom of Gray's Inn and the tedium of his work, before acting on another impulse and enlisting as a private soldier in a regiment bound for Nova Scotia at a salary of 6*d* a day. Canada he found a land of 'bogs, rocks and stumps, mosquitoes and bullfrogs', but he stayed there until 1791 and rose steadily through the ranks to become the regiment's much respected sergeant major. His habits of industry, his egotism and assertiveness enabled him to endure the tedium and toil of the army, while he found time, too, to read and educate himself. He learned a grammar textbook off by heart, repeating it to himself while standing on guard duty, so acquiring not only the rudiments of plain English but also the benefits of a well-trained memory. The edge of his bed was his seat to study in, his knapsack his bookcase, a bit of board lying on his lap was his writing table, and to buy a pen or a sheet of paper, he had to go without food. With nothing left over to purchase candles or oil, he had to read and write by firelight amid 'the talking, laughing, singing, whistling, and brawling of at least half a score of the most thoughtless of men, and that, too, in the hours of their freedom from all control'.

In this hard school, he trained himself to become one of the most forceful stylists in the English language. He took charge of the regiment's reports and accounts and most of its administration, while at the same time discovering the profound and surprising ignorance of his well-born officers. In his own words, 'I should have been broken and flogged for fifty different offences had they not been kept in awe by my inflexible sobriety, by the consciousness of their inferiority to me, and by the real and almost indispensable necessity of the use of my talents'. So while his officers swaggered about, getting roaring drunk on the 'profits of their pillage', the self-righteous Cobbett got on with the task of developing his talents.

His contempt for his officers was based as much on their corruption as it was on their boorish behaviour. Most had obtained their commissions through social connections spiced with peculation; few of them knew or much cared about their duties in the army, and Cobbett discovered that the regimental quartermaster was making money on the side by keeping back about a fourth part of the men's rations for sale on the black market. When he mentioned this to the older sergeants, they told him it had been going on for many years, and were quite astonished and terrified that he should think of complaining about it.

The incident marked Cobbett's first clash with authority and had a profound influence on the development of his political thought. For when he got home and obtained his discharge, he did lodge a complaint, only to discover that the authorities took no notice of it. The practice, it seems, was not peculiar to his regiment in New Brunswick, but was widespread throughout the army, and was indeed, an integral part of the system under which the public services as a whole were at that time conducted. Suffused with indignation at his discovery, Cobbett withdrew from the fray, first to France and, later in the same year, to begin a new life in America with his young wife. His impulsive nature had once more got the better of him.

AMERICAN SOJOURN

America – where he remained for the next seven and a half years – stirred an interest in journalism. The Federalists were in power, Britain and France were at war, and feelings in America were running high. In between teaching English grammar to French émigrés, who had fled to the new world after the fall of the Gironde, Cobbett wrote and published a pamphlet in defence of his native country. This apparently came about as the result of an argument with one of his students about a newspaper article reporting the attacks on the English monarchy made by Dr Joseph Priestley, the radical English scientist, who had recently moved to Philadelphia. Stirred by patriotic ire, Cobbett wrote a coruscating counter-attack on France and its revolutionary ways, found a publisher, and, it seems, a receptive audience. 'Thus sir, it was that I came to be a writer on politics,' he proclaimed later.

It was a task into which he threw himself with huge and obvious enjoyment. He loved a good hot dispute and developed an unsurpassed talent for writing invective. In pamphlets with such titles as *A Kick for a Bite, A Bone to Gnaw, A Little Plain English Addressed to the People of America*, and, above all, the letters of *Peter Porcupine*, Cobbett quickly became the best and most vehement of the Federalist pamphleteers. He stoutly defended George Washington, criticised the pro-French views of Thomas Jefferson, launched a rousing attack on the works of Tom Paine and proudly proclaimed the virtues of his homeland. In the middle of republican Philadelphia he opened a shop of his own and displayed in the window an imposing portrait of the most provocative personage he could think of: King George. On the day he opened for business, a huge mob gathered outside, threatening violence; friends warned him his house would be burned down, though no actual violence was done, and Cobbett's audacity made him famous.

Eventually, he over-stretched himself with an attack on Dr Benjamin Rush, a well-known physician and politician. Dr Rush had developed a new treatment for the Philadelphia yellow fever based on copious bleeding and mercurial purges known as 'Rush's powders'. When the fever returned in 1797, Rush's treatment was energetically boosted in the American press, Cobbett and a very few others dissenting. In his *Porcupine's Gazette*, he criticised the unorthodox treatment and nicknamed Rush 'Doctor Sangrado' after the bleeding physician in *The Adventures of Gil Blas*, a popular contemporary novel. Dr Rush sued him for libel.

The case dragged on for a full two years, delayed deliberately, Cobbett thought, in order to check his freedom of utterance; but when the trial finally took place in 1799, a democratic jury found the libel proved and awarded Dr Rush $5,000. Within a few days, Cobbett's property in Philadelphia was sold up, copies of the next *Porcupine's Gazette* disposed of as waste paper and a collected edition of his American writings destroyed. Angry and financially embarrassed, Cobbett withdrew to New York and eventually made his way home to England.

That he had libelled Dr Rush was not in doubt, though the truth of his criticism received an ironic confirmation on the very day the jury returned its verdict. George Washington, the father of his country, lay dying at Mount Vernon of streptococcal laryngitis, hastened on his way, it later transpired, by Dr Rush's regimen of bleeding and mercurial powders.

Under threat of deportation as a debtor, and refusing to become an American citizen, Cobbett set sail for home in the summer of 1800 with his wife and growing family, leaving behind a bittersweet farewell in the last of his American letters written under the name of *Peter Porcupine*.

To my friends who are also the real friends of America, I wish that peace and happiness which virtue ought to ensure, but which I greatly fear they will not find; and as to my enemies, I can wish them no greater scourge than that which they are preparing for themselves and their country. With this I depart for my native land, where neither the moth of *Democracy* nor the rust of *Federalism* doth corrupt and where thieves do not, with impunity, break through and steal five thousand dollars at a time.

THE *POLITICAL REGISTER*

Back home, Cobbett's taste for polemics led him to start up a newspaper, the *Political Register*, which with one short interval while he was crossing the Atlantic, he wrote, edited and published from 1802 until his death in 1835. It was at once a huge success, thanks largely to Cobbett's vivid and assertive prose, and it became by far the most influential publication of the age. Cobbett had in fact invented a new kind of journalism, the forerunner of the modern political review, though at first its contents were hardly distinguishable in tone from those of his vehemently anti-Republican *Porcupine's Gazette*. The early editions of his *Register* are filled with attacks on the recently concluded Peace of Amiens and sonorous calls for a resumption of the war. Every sentiment was stoutly Tory; there were even, it has to be said, articles in defence of the slave trade and the cruel country sport of bull baiting.

The success of the *Register* made Cobbett affluent and it made him famous. He settled his growing family at a farm near Botley in Hampshire and divided his time between town and country. His fame opened the fashionable salons, so that in 1804 he was able to report that he had dined the day before with the secretary of state in the company of Mr Pitt, and had been waited on by men in gaudy liveries. 'When I came to reflect,' he wrote, '*what a change*! I looked down at my dress. What a change! What scenes I had gone through! How altered my state! . . . I had had no one to assist me in the world. No teachers of any sort. Nobody to shelter me from the consequences of bad, and no one to counsel me to good behaviour. I felt proud. The distinctions of rank, birth and wealth, all became nothing in my eyes; and from that moment . . . I resolved never to bend before them.'

His farm at Botley gave him new insights into what was happening in the countryside and in the years from 1804 he began to write critically of the enclosure of the common land which was dispossessing the poor and turning his beloved yeomen into landless labourers. Based on the evidence of his own eyes, Cobbett was on the way to becoming an outright radical.

At the age of thirty-seven, he was still the tall, stout, florid-faced English peasant he had always been, and still an impassioned and devoted patriot.

What opened his eyes was the social transformation that had taken place in England during his almost continual absence over a period of more than fifteen years. The degradation of the labouring poor and the breakdown of a popular sense of honour set him in an agony of reforming zeal that he would never lose. In the next two years, his severance from orthodox politics was complete. He launched vigorous attacks on all manner of abuses in the Church and State, he woke up to the fact that corrupt pensions and sinecures underpinned the whole system of government, and that radical reform was the only cure. He attacked the wrongs of British rule in Ireland and exposed the scandalous fact that promotions in the army were being sold for money by the Duke of York's mistress. Then, in 1809, he printed an article in the *Register* that gave the government the excuse to move against him.

The occasion was the punishment given to five soldiers from the garrison at Ely, who had been court-martialled for throwing their knapsacks on the ground, surrounding their officers, and demanding payment of their arrears of pay. The ringleaders were each sentenced to receive 500 lashes. What was worse, the sentence was to be carried out by a detachment of mercenary German troops who were paid to garrison towns in England while British soldiers were away fighting in Europe.

The news brought Cobbett to a paroxysm of fury. Remembering the cheating and cruelty of his own army days and the incredible brutality of floggings where, he said, he had frequently seen seven or eight stout and hardy men 'fall slap upon the ground, unable to endure the sight, and hear the cries without swooning away', he launched an attack in the *Register* made all the more violent because of his patriotic indignation that English soldiers had been flogged by foreign mercenaries. 'It was not in the power of man to express indignation too strongly,' he later wrote.

In the *Register* he directed his wrath against Lord Castlereagh, the minister responsible for the Militia Act, and Mr Huskisson, a Treasury minister who had advanced the hated cause of paper money. He took as his motto the article he had read in the government's *Courier* which had praised the floggings. 'See the motto, English reader!' Cobbett wrote. 'See the motto and then pray recollect all that has been said about the way in which Bonaparte raises his soldiers. Well done, Lord Castlereagh! This is just what it was thought your plan would produce. Well said, Mr Huskisson! It was really not without reason that you dwelt, with so much earnestness upon the great utility of the foreign troops.' Napoleon's lashings were often cited as evidence that, in their hearts, the people of France hated their dictator, and would willingly rise against him. What became of that argument now? Did it apply to Great Britain as well? What would loyal Britons say now that they see that our 'gallant defenders' not only require physical restraint, in certain cases, but even a little blood drawn from their backs, and that, too, with the aid and assistance of German troops.

Five hundred lashes each! Aye, that is right! Flog them! flog them! flog them! They deserve a flogging at every meal time. 'Lash them daily! lash them daily!' What! shall the rascals dare to *mutiny*? And that, too, when the German legion is so near at hand? Lash them! lash them! lash them! They deserve it. Oh, yes! they merit a double-tailed cat! Base dogs! What! mutiny for the *price of a knapsack?* Lash them! flog them! Base rascals! Mutiny for the price of a goat's skin; and then, upon the appearance of the German soldiers, they take a flogging as quietly as so many trunks of trees!

The passage showed Cobbett's unparalleled mastery of the art of invective. It also goaded the government past enduring. The attorney-general filed an information against him for seditious libel. His long legal battle for the right to free speech was about to begin.

For almost a year, nothing more happened. Governments commonly issued writs for sedition merely in order to silence their critics. Cobbett meanwhile prepared his defence and put his affairs in order. He eventually came to trial in June 1810 before Lord Ellenborough, but made the mistake of mounting his own defence. He attempted to introduce speeches which had been made in the House of Commons quoting material he had written, but Ellenborough ruled that they were privileged and therefore inadmissible. Thrown off his stride, Cobbett made a bad defence, so poorly delivered that at one point the judge and jury all laughed at him. The respectable property owners who sat on the jury took no more than five minutes to find him guilty. Before sentence was passed, the prisoner was given time to go home to Botley to settle his affairs.

There then followed an episode which was used ever afterwards to blacken Cobbett's name. The truth is still unclear, but before sentence was passed some sort of negotiation took place with the government. Cobbett made arrangements to wind up the *Register* and retire quietly to his farm, and drafted a *Farewell Address* to his readers saying, 'I never will again, upon any account, indite, publish, write, or contribute towards, any newspaper, or other publication of that nature, so long as I live'.

The *Farewell Address* was never published, and the *Register* did not die. Cobbett came to the conclusion that the government had been playing with him. Once they had his *Address* safely in print, he believed they would renege on whatever promise they had made about his sentence and send him to jail. Without a firm promise, he refused to yield. Orders to wind up the *Register* were rescinded and the *Address* withdrawn. In later years, when the story came out, Cobbett firmly denied he had entered into any negotiations with the government. His position was that of a soldier surrounded by a superior force: he had offered to surrender. His terms had not been accepted, so he had no choice but to fight on.

However deviously he had arrived at it, it was a decision that may have saved the cause of Parliamentary Reform. The liberty of the press, too, would have received a crippling blow if Cobbett had meekly surrendered and abandoned his vocation as a journalist. As it was, he appeared for sentence in July together with his printer and publisher. His printer, Hansard (with whom Cobbett had launched the famous record of Parliamentary proceedings), got three months' imprisonment, his publishers, Budd and Bagshaw, two months' each. Cobbett himself was sent for two years jail in Newgate and, in effect, financially ruined. He was fined £2,000, and at the end of his sentence was to post a further £3,000 in bail and find two further sureties of £1,000 each for his keeping the peace for a further seven years. It was a crushing and vindictive sentence, passed solely for the crime of speaking his mind. It marked a melancholy moment in the history of English liberty and the severest setback of the century for the rights of a supposedly free press. If ever proof were needed that free speech consists of more than the mere absence of prior restraint, it is provided by the sentence passed on William Cobbett.

The savage sentence also missed its aim. Far from silencing a dissident voice they did not care for, the foolish men who sent Cobbett to prison had created a rebel. And they had done so out of the most loyal and unrebellious material that could have been found anywhere in the kingdom. Newgate put Cobbett into a rage he was unable to contain, a more furious rebel because he was a reluctant rebel. As Chesterton said, 'the man in that cell was no Stoic, trained in the Latin logic of a Condorcet or Carnot, seeing his own suffering . . . as part of the inevitable system of kings. He was no Irish martyr, schooled to breathe the very air of tragedy and tyranny and vengeance, and living in a noble but unnatural exaltation of wholly spiritual hate'. He was an angry and bewildered Englishman, fond of his happiness – which meant practical things to him, like his own farm, family and children – but on whom the sky had just fallen in. He was a patriot, punished for being patriotic, a plain man condemned for speaking plainly. All he had ever asked for was that things should become what they always used to be. 'We want nothing new,' he would often say, 'we want only what our forefathers enjoyed, what the stock-jobbers, the place-hunters and the Pittites and the cotton lords have taken away.' The world has rarely seen a more conservative rebel. Yet rebel he now became.

Conditions in Newgate were not onerous, and Cobbett was able to receive visitors, hire his own suite of rooms, and continue to work on the *Register*. His loyal wife and family divided their time between Newgate and Botley, and Cobbett was able to see to his children's education and look over affairs on the farm. He continued to read, of course, among other things the works of Tom Paine, who won him over to his own radical views on finance and much troubled Cobbett's Christian conscience with *The Age of Reason*. Cobbett also quarrelled with his agent, John Wright, who had allowed his financial affairs to get into a tangle. He described how, faced with ruin, 'everyone to whom I owed a shilling, brought me sighs of sorrow, indeed; but, along with these, brought me his bill'.

But his financial plight appeared as nothing when his wife, insisting on taking lodgings in Smithfield so she could be as near to him as possible, lost the child she was carrying: the result, thought Cobbett, of the incessant rattle of coaches and butchers' carts outside her rooms, and the noise of cattle, dogs and bawling men. Even this did not prevent him working, and during the two years of his imprisonment, he tells us he wrote and published 364 essays and letters and was visited by persons from 197 cities and towns, many of them deputations from the growing number of political societies and clubs.

Outside the walls of the jail, the economic crisis was growing worse. America had closed its ports to British goods, the Luddite riots were at their height, and one edition of the *Register* carried reports of violent unrest from a score of towns throughout the North and the Midlands. By 1812, frame-breaking had been made a capital offence and the government was pouring troops into the troubled districts. From his prison cell, Cobbett wrote that 'measures ought to be adopted, not so much for putting an end to riots, as to prevent the misery out of which they arise'.

To his great anger and distress, the Whigs in Parliament said little and did less to oppose the repressive measures being introduced by the Tory government against what they called the 'treasonable activity' of the Luddites. Looking on from Newgate, Cobbett responded sarcastically, 'Far be it for me to attempt to justify people in the commission of unlawful acts. I do not wish to justify the woman who, according to the newspapers, committed *highway robbery* in taking *some potatoes out of a cart at Manchester,* and, who, according to the newspapers, was HANGED FOR IT. I do not pretend to justify her conduct. But there is, I hope, no harm in my expressing my compassion for her.'

The distress of the northern textile workers had extended his sympathy beyond the agricultural poor to the working classes as a whole, and he left jail in July 1812 to take up their cause. Dinners were held to celebrate his release and large crowds of well-wishers escorted him home to Botley. He at once resumed his political activities. The coming of peace after the victory over the French at Waterloo brought him to his most impassioned cause – and once again into conflict with the government over his right to free speech.

The peace brought on the most severe economic slump the country had ever known, and with it, disaster for the labouring poor. The wages of the Lancashire spinners were cut to less than 5s a week, and their working day mercilessly extended, but still the rate of unemployment went up. On the land, the price of corn collapsed; hardly anyone could earn a living wage, while poor law relief was reduced to starvation levels as magistrates struggled to bring down the cost to the community. Because of the national debt, taxation was high, the burden of it falling almost entirely on the poor – all of these consequences of the peace having been prophesised by Cobbett, who attributed them all to the hated 'Thing'. 'The play is over,' the government's *Courier* had said when the war ended. 'We may now go to supper.' 'No,' replied Cobbett. 'You may not go to supper. You have not yet *paid for the play.*'

As the crisis deepened, the pages of the *Register* were filled with accounts of working-class risings, riots and rick burnings, and the shootings, deportations and hangings that the government used to suppress them. Well-meaning attempts at charity were worse than useless, Cobbett said, aiming a venomous dart at Bishop Wilberforce, whose attitude towards the poor he likened to the old couplet:

> Open your mouth and shut your eyes.
> And God will love you, and send you a prize.

The labourers needed higher wages not charity. They also needed to be rallied to the cause of reform. But how could they be reached? How could the radicals get their message across? How, in short, could Cobbett put his *Register* into the hands of the poor? The *Register* had at first been issued fortnightly, but it sold so well it soon became a weekly, which, thanks to the outrageously high stamp duties, he was obliged to price at 10*d* a copy, and put this up in 1812 to 1*s*. Paradoxically though, it was the stamp duties which helped Cobbett to his early success, since they put the price of daily newspapers beyond the reach of all but a privileged few. At this time, the two main newspapers, *The Times* and the *Morning Post*, sold no more than 1,250 copies each and Cobbett's weekly *Register* came out at just the time to fill the gap, though it was still well beyond the spending power of a working man. In many places, workers now clubbed together to share a copy, which would be read out loud in an alehouse or reading room. But the authorities constantly harassed the publicans who allowed their premises to be used for this purpose, and many were threatened with having their licences taken away for encouraging sedition.

Cobbett at first hit on the idea of allowing other journals to make free reprints of his articles in the *Register*, but this failed when the government inspired imitations, putting forward ideas under Cobbett's name which were really the government's, and sometimes ransacking Cobbett's own earlier writings for examples of his then Tory views. At last, towards the end of 1816, he found the solution. He had written a lengthy *Address to the Journeymen and Labourers* for the *Register*, which he had reprinted as a separate pamphlet priced at twopence. Its instantaneous success led him to print every edition of the *Register* in this form: an expensive edition containing news as well as opinion, and a cheap edition containing only the opinions.

The ruse was necessary because the repressive and complicated rules imposed by the Stamp Act required a 4*d* stamp to be attached to every copy of a publication containing news, while opinions, for the moment, remained free. The penalty he had to pay was that unstamped publications could not be sent by post, and Cobbett had to set up his own network of agents, who were asked to send a regular weekly order to the London publisher, with 'very plain' directions as to the coach on which it was to be despatched, and the name of the inn at which the coach would drop it off. With every parcel sent into the country, a placard was enclosed for display in the shopkeeper's window, so that the public would know where the *Register* was on sale. Cobbett pointed out to his distributors that, at the wholesale price of 12*s* 6*d* a bundle, the profit on the sale of a few hundred copies was sufficient to support a small family.

The scheme was brilliantly successful. Sales of the 2*d Register* soared to 40 or 50,000 a week, a single copy often serving for scores of readers. Within two months, 200,000 copies of the *Address to the Journeymen* were in circulation. He was at last reaching his working-class constituency. According to Samuel Bamford, a Lancashire radical,

> at this time, the writings of William Cobbett suddenly became of great authority. They were read on nearly every cottage hearth in the manufacturing districts of South Lancashire, in those of Leicester, Derby, and Nottingham, also in many of the Scottish manufacturing towns. Their influence was speedily visible; he directed his readers to the true cause of their sufferings – misgovernment; and to its proper corrective – Parliamentary Reform. Riots soon became scarce, and from that time they never obtained their ancient vogue with the labourers of this country.

Cobbett had not only achieved striking success as a journalist, he had helped to launch England on the inexorable road to reform.

He was engaged, however, in a dangerous trade. The London press was bribed to 'write him down', and when that failed, harsher measures were employed. A Shropshire magistrate – the local rector – had two men apprehended under the Vagrants Act for distributing the *Register* and ordered them 'well-flogged at the whipping post', since when, he reported, the pestilence had ceased, at least in his neighbourhood. That same year, *The Times* warned that 'such is the poverty of the more humble classes of the community . . . that if they do read, or know anything about public affairs, it must be in the cheapest forms: and hence they become dupes, to a certain extent, to the basest and most profligate of men'. Public houses were disliked by frightened Tories as dens of sedition and dissent, with Cobbett's *Register* now 'read aloud in every ale-house'.

Everywhere they looked, the government saw nothing but conspiracy and treason, where the reality was starvation and despair. 'They sigh for a plot,' Cobbett wrote. 'Oh, how they sigh! They are working and slaving and fretting and stewing; they are sweating all over; they are absolutely pining and dying for a plot!' They did not have to stew for much longer. Early in 1817, the Prince Regent was attacked in his coach as he was returning to Carlton House after the opening of Parliament. The panic-stricken government had found their plot.

Their response was to introduce more repression. The Habeas Corpus Act was suspended, with the result that anyone considered to be an agitator was liable to imprisonment without trial. Public meetings required the consent of the magistrates, who were empowered to order the arrest of any speaker uttering words 'calculated to stir up the people to hatred or contempt of the government'. The penalty for resisting arrest was death. All public reading rooms, lecture halls, and places of assembly were to be licensed by the magistrates. Licenses would be refused to premises which allowed irreligious, immoral or seditious material to be read. Lord Sidmouth, the home secretary – who had found Cobbett's *Address to the Journeymen* 'one of the most diabolical publications that ever issued from the English press' – sent a circular letter to magistrates around the country telling them that they might issue a warrant for the arrest of any person selling radical literature, and compel them to give bail.

The Times protested that this extra-judicial decision would make it impossible 'in this land of liberty' to conduct a newspaper except on sufferance. There was not a newspaper in England that was not obliged, while having a scrupulous regard for truth, to publish oftener than once a week matter which some aggrieved person or other would swear was libellous. 'We should prefer a censorship to such a state of things,' *The Times* said.

Believing the measures were aimed directly at him, Cobbett made plans in the greatest secrecy to set sail to the United States. 'The laws which had just been passed forbade me to entertain the idea that it would be possible to write on political subjects according to the dictates of truth and reason, without drawing down upon my head certain and swift destruction,' he wrote. From America, he could at least continue to write; indeed, he edited the *Register* from there and wrote *The Last Hundred Days of English Freedom* quoted at the beginning of this chapter.

For more than two years Cobbett stayed on a farm he acquired on Long Island, but took no part in American affairs and wrote only for his English readers. He kept up with the *Register*, compiled a book about gardening and fulminated against the loathsome potato as 'a root worth than useless'. He denounced the popular cult for the works of Milton and Shakespeare – the plot of *Paradise Lost* he found 'absurd and immoral' and Shakespeare was good only for 'bombast, puns and smut'. He was appalled by American drinking habits, and records a conversation he had with a Long Island tavern-keeper, who asked him how it was he looked so fresh and young, considering what he had gone through in the world. 'I'll tell you,' Cobbett replied. 'I rise early, go to bed early, eat sparingly, never drink anything stronger than small beer, shave once a day, and wash my hands and face clean three times a day, at the very least.' The American told him 'that was *too* much to think of doing'.

In 1819, Cobbett deduced that it was safe to go home again, but before he left he took the action for which his period of exile in America would be best remembered: his absurdly romantic decision to bring home the bones of Tom Paine. It was intended as an act of atonement for his earlier criticisms of a man he had grown to admire, though it brought him only ridicule. Gillray teased him over it in a cruel cartoon, and when he arrived in Liverpool with the sacred relics, he had trouble getting them through customs. He never did build the marble mausoleum he had planned and was reduced to storing his hero's bones in a wooden box, where they remained until his own death sixteen years later.

THE SIX ACTS

Cobbett arrived home just as the government was passing the infamous Six Acts, which outlawed the combination of workers and put tighter controls than ever on the rights of assembly and free speech. Among the six new laws was the Blasphemous and Seditious Libels Act which gave the authorities the power to search out and seize libellous pamphlets and provided for the transportation of offenders to the penal colonies in Australia for a period of up to fourteen years. In the period from 1819 to 1824, scores of otherwise obscure and respectable men and women were sentenced to imprisonment, fines or deportation for resisting the persecution. Gilbert Macleod, editor of the radical Glasgow periodical *Spirit of the Union* was sentenced to transportation for five years for seditious propaganda, Joseph Swann, a hat maker, was sentenced to four and a half years' imprisonment for publishing a blasphemous and seditious libel, and Richard Carlile spent nine years in jail for various publishing offences, among them reprinting extracts from the works of Tom Paine, which he sold from his shop at 55 Fleet Street through a hole in the wall – customers had to turn the hands of a dial to the publication they wanted, drop their payment through the hole and receive the work *incognito* so as to conceal the identity of the bookseller.

The act which bore most heavily on the press and put an end to Cobbett's cheap edition of the *Register* was the renewed Stamp Duties Act, whose avowed purpose was to smash the cheap radical newspapers and pamphlets. All pamphlets containing any public news, *or comment*, printed more often than once a month, and smaller than two sheets, were liable to pay the stamp duty of 4*d* a copy. Their printers and publishers were required to deposit sureties of several hundred pounds, which would be forfeit if they printed a libel. During the debate on the measures in the House of Lords, the judge who had sent Cobbett to Newgate, Lord Ellenborough, now the Lord Chief Justice, observed that 'it was not against the respectable press that this Bill was directed, but against a pauper press, which, administering to the prejudices and the passions of a mob, was converted to the basest purposes, which was an utter stranger to truth, and only sent forth a steady stream of falsehood and malignity'. For the next seventeen years, until its partial repeal in 1836, the Stamp Duties Act was used by successive governments as the principal means under which the British press was regulated, and was, in fact, applied more vigorously by the Whigs who came to power in 1830 than it had been by the Tories who introduced it.

The large circulation of what Castlereagh had disparagingly called Cobbett's 'Twopenny Trash' was immediately cut away. Cobbett defiantly proclaimed, 'I was born under a King and Constitution; I was not born under the Six Acts', and did what he could to keep his journal going. An unstamped edition came out at 6*d*, and a stamped edition at 1*s*, though with much reduced circulations. Then he took to the road and for ten years conducted the larger part of his propaganda campaign by word of mouth. He stood in the 1820 general election for Coventry, but lost. He also lost his farm at Botley when he was declared bankrupt because of the mounting cost of the debts, fines, sureties and damages he had incurred. In 1821, the family moved into four acres of rich land at Kensington, now a residential suburb but then in the country, where Cobbett started a seed farm and settled down to serious literary and political writing.

A year earlier, the Prince Regent had come to the throne as George IV, and Cobbett energetically took up the cause of his estranged queen, Caroline, whose conduct before the coronation had been subject to what was euphemistically termed 'the delicate investigation'. When she came back to claim her crown, she at once became the heroine of the radicals, less because of her own virtues than because of the widespread hatred they felt for the new king. The Queen's case monopolised space in the *Register* for months on end, culminating with coverage of her attempt to force her way into Westminster Abbey during the coronation service. When, shortly afterwards, she died, the *Register* was printed with thick black borders, and only after that did the affair gradually fade from view.

These were the years which saw some of Cobbett's finest writing – *Cottage Economy*, his grammar of the English language, the splendid *Advice to Young Men*, and finally, the book for which he is best remembered today, *Rural Rides*. He was now well over sixty, as vigorous as ever, and with his busiest and most productive years still to come. With the fall of Wellington's government in 1830 and the return of the Whigs, he threw himself into the cause of Parliamentary Reform, and at the same time became involved in the last revolt of the agricultural labourers in the southern and western counties, an episode that led him to another trial for seditious libel.

The distress in the country was as widespread as ever, but inspired by the example of the great Irish leader, Daniel O'Connell, working people had begun to organise themselves on a large scale. Their campaign was helped by the publication of a large number of cheap papers circulated without the hated stamp: the *Pioneer*, the *Poor Man's Advocate*, and, most influential of all, Henry Hetherington's *Poor Man's Guardian*. All were sold 'in defiance of authority' at 1*d* or 2*d*.

For some time, Hetherington had attempted to evade the stamp by publishing his pamphlets at irregular intervals, under different titles, but always signed at the end 'The Poor Man's Guardian'. When this was prohibited, he resorted to outright defiance, and in 1831 openly published his pamphlet under the title: '*The Poor Man's Guardian*: a weekly newspaper for the people. Established contrary to Law, to try the power of "Might" against "Right". Price *One Penny*.' Where the government's red stamp should have been was a black one inscribed 'Liberty of the Press'.

The paper lasted for more than four years, and had an immense influence on its readers, though Hetherington had twice to suffer six months' imprisonment for publishing it. His presses were more than once seized and confiscated and parcels of the *Guardian* taken by the authorities (who were sometimes entrapped into seizing bogus ones). Hundreds of hawkers were imprisoned for obstructing the thoroughfares by selling it, some of them again and again, but somehow the paper survived and played its part in achieving the emancipation of working people.

Far from undermining Cobbett's own influence, the new working-class journals seem to have enhanced it. He always obeyed the law and published the *Register* duly stamped, but he catered for the people's thirst for radical polemics, both by reprinting many of his articles in pamphlet form and by starting a new publication that he could legally publish unstamped once a month, but not oftener, on payment of a small tax. Inspired by Castlereagh's disdainful sneer, he entitled it *Twopenny Trash*.

The object of what he called 'this little cheap work' was to explain to the people what it was that in spite of their own industry and frugality kept them poor. 'This *was*,' he said, 'the happiest country in the world; it *was* the country of roast beef; it *was* distinguished above *all* other nations for the good food, good raiment, and good morals of its people; and is now as much distinguished for the contrary of all of them.'

Reform was the question of the hour, and Cobbett was its best-known and best-loved advocate. Reform Societies and Political Unions were springing up everywhere, and Cobbett was indefatigable in addressing them. Age had not dimmed his energy, nor reduced his capacity for pugnacious prose. When Earl Grey became prime minister after the fall of Wellington in the election caused by death of George IV, Cobbett constantly warned his readers not to put their faith in the Whigs. They were aristocrats, not democrats; they would look after their own, and would always put the interests of the property-owning classes above those of the ordinary people. His words were quickly born out, when, after the election, an epidemic of rick-burnings and machine-breakings swept the southern and western counties in protest against the steam-driven threshing machines that were causing widespread unemployment on the land. No one was killed, but the gentry took fright. Troops were rushed into the countryside and Special Commissions set up in each of the disturbed counties to mete out exemplary punishments to the ringleaders.

Cobbett did not praise or encourage the burnings, but he stood up, as he always did, for the workers. He could not believe that the Special Commissions would cause blood to be shed. Lord Melbourne, the new home secretary, was 'not a ferocious fellow'; surely, the Whig government would think rather of redressing grievances than punishing offenders; would slay no one; would visit none of them with the terrible punishment of transportation. Working people had always been told that their acts of burnings and violence could do no good, but they now knew better: they knew that one threshing machine took the wages from ten men; and they knew also that *they* were getting none of the extra food produced. Ninety-nine hundredths of men supported the dissidents' call to make parsons reduce their tithes. This would probably now come about – but only because of the terror caused by the fires. From Cambridgeshire it was reported that '*since the terrible* fires that have taken place in that county, "the magistrates have met, and resolved *immediately* to make enquiry into the actual *state* and *condition of the poor in every parish of this county.*"' Very wise, very just, said Cobbett; 'but never so much as talked of, much less resolved on, until the labourers rose, and the *fires* began to blaze.'

Cobbett's hopes that the new Whig government would respond leniently to the burnings were now cruelly dashed. In Hampshire, a nineteen-year-old ploughboy was hanged for causing serious damage to a banker, Mr Bingham-Baring's hat. In the country as a whole, 9 persons were hanged, 400 imprisoned, and 457 transported to Australia, of whom more than a quarter died of the hardships of the voyage. Cobbett himself was to be silenced by imprisonment.

He was first condemned in the Commons for his attack on the Church and for writing an article 'subversive of the laws and conducive to anarchy and delusion'. Then he was indicted for sedition on the basis of a speech he had made in one of the disturbed counties. A labourer of eighteen who had been convicted of setting fire to a barn near Battle in Sussex, and thinking he was about to be hanged, was visited in his cell by the local curate, who extracted from him the following confession:

I, Thomas Goodman, never should of thought of douing aney sutch thing if Mr Cobet had never given aney lactures; i beilieve that their never would have bean any fires or mob in Battel nor maney other places if he never had given aney lactures at all.

Based on evidence such as this, everyone knew that the trial, when it came, would be as much a trial of the government as it was of Cobbett. The punishments meted out to the rioters had roused him into a grand passion against the Whigs and the pitiful state of people in the countryside. They were committing crimes for the purpose of getting into jail so that they might be better fed than they were at home. They were living only on bread or potatoes; children had been stealing food from hog-troughs; men were found lying dead under a hedge with nothing in their stomachs but sour sorrel; in the coal mines they were harnessed like horses and made to draw carts and wagons; they were made to work with bells around their necks; they had drivers set over them, just as if they had been galley slaves; and when, all across the south, they began breaking the threshing machines that had robbed them of their wages, well-fed soldiers were ready to shoot or cut them down.

Now Cobbett was to stand trial alongside them, and face going to prison again himself, his only crime to have spoken out against the conditions to which his countrymen had been reduced by a system, as he saw it, of usury, monopoly and grinding taxation.

There were the usual delays before he was brought to court, and he once again chose to defend himself, but with this difference: in the twenty-one years that had elapsed since his trial in 1810, Cobbett had acquired vast experience as a public speaker. He now knew how to speak as pungently as he wrote; he understood the value of humour, and he knew that, this time, the people of England were behind him. On the morning of his trial, he rose at four o'clock, went into his garden to give instructions for the day, ate a good fat leg of mutton for his breakfast, without bread or salt, and had nothing to drink all day until after the conclusion of his speech, when he drank two stone bottles of milk out of a horn given to him the previous summer by a pretty young American lady.

The court was crowded, and he had to struggle to get in through a cheering and clapping throng of supporters. When he got to his place, he turned to them and said, 'Be patient, gentlemen, for, if truth prevail, we shall beat them'. Uncomfortably ranged before him were six Whig ministers he had subpoenaed, including Lords Grey, Brougham, Melbourne and Palmerston, who were to be questioned about their handling of the riots. Lord Melbourne, the home secretary, was asked to explain his reasons for pardoning Cobbett's accuser, Thomas Goodman. Though the judge disallowed the question, Cobbett had made his point to the jury simply by asking it. Next came Lord Brougham, the Lord Chancellor, who, to his colleagues' great embarrassment, was forced to admit that, in his capacity as president of a learned society, he had written to Cobbett in the midst of the disturbances asking for permission to reprint his *Letter to the Luddites*. Far from regarding him as an incendiary, Brougham was thus seen to have called for his advice in coping with the troubles. The trial was almost ended there and then, but the Lord Chief Justice was hostile to Cobbett and allowed it to continue. With the government's most senior ministers looking on, Cobbett then spoke for four and a half hours in defence of his right to free speech, concluding: 'If I am compelled to meet death in some stinking dungeon, to which they have the means of cramming me, my last breath shall be employed in praying God to bless my country and to curse the Whigs to everlasting; and revenge I bequeath to my children and to the labourers of England.'

The Lord Chief Justice then summed up in favour of the prosecution and had the handpicked jury locked away for the night. When they came back to deliver their verdict in the morning, they were evenly divided: six for conviction, six for dismissal. The prisoner was accordingly acquitted. Cobbett had won a notable victory for his freedom of speech. 'Well might I say it was a day of joy to me!' he wrote. 'It was a reward going ten thousand times beyond all that I have ever merited.' It was perhaps the only modest statement he had made in his life.

LAST YEARS

The year after his acquittal, the so-called Great Reform Act was passed, though the aristocracy continued to dominate British politics until after the end of the century. But the franchise was widened to include most freeholders, and Cobbett urged his supporters to accept the measure since nothing more radical stood any chance of success. In the election of 1832, he was himself returned as MP for Oldham, together with the radical manufacturer from Todmorden, John Fielden. By this time sixty-eight years old, Cobbett spent the two and a half years of his Parliamentary life as leader of the tiny group of radicals in the House, supported sometimes by Daniel O'Connell and his Irish members, but always fighting for forlorn hopes. He worked harder than ever, but his Parliamentary career is not generally accounted a success. His health was failing, and he was troubled by a persistent cough, though, characteristically, he spent the last months of his life campaigning for the repeal of the Whigs' new poor law, which had been enacted in 1834.

He took part in one last debate in May 1835, when he attempted to speak to a motion on agricultural distress, but his throat was inflamed and he could not make himself heard. He went down next morning to his farm in Surrey and imprudently drank tea in the open air. That night, he fell violently ill, but the following day still insisted on being carried to see the work going on in his fields, and there ran across a little boy in a blue smock-frock, to whom he gave a laughing look. His son, John, recorded that 'he seemed refreshed at the sight of the little creature, which he had once precisely resembled, though now at such an immeasurable distance'.

That night, he grew more and more feeble, but continued to answer every question that was put to him with perfect clarity. 'In the last half-hour,' wrote John, 'his eyes became dim; and at ten minutes after one o'clock he leaned back, as if to sleep, and died without a gasp.'

Cobbett's reputation as a great radical reformer and writer has endured. He was that rare thing, an articulate peasant and a rebellious patriot, uniquely English, with a keen eye for the changes taking place in his native land and an unparalleled sense of indignation at the hardships they had brought. In matters of free speech, Hazlitt said he was a fourth estate all to himself. His two great trials for seditious libel stirred the conscience of the nation and showed up the injustice of measures brought in by frightened, foolish men with the sole purpose of suppressing liberties which were soon to be accepted as an essential component of any civilised and self-governing community.

He had also, and almost single-handedly, transformed the practice of journalism. When Pitt was in Downing Street and Cobbett just launching his *Political Register*, newspapers were primarily vehicles for public notices and advertisements, spiced with information often corruptly provided by the government, and with a circulation measured in the hundreds. At one time, Cobbett himself had believed the press to have become perverted by bribery, favouritism and abuse of the Stamp Acts, which put independent views beyond the reach of the general public. Instead of enlightening the people, a kept press was being paid to hold them in ignorance, a willing instrument in the hands of all those who oppressed, or wished to oppress them. 'Some truths, and valuable truths, get abroad through the means of the press,' he wrote in 1808, 'but these are infinitely outnumbered by the falsehoods; and, if the people were left without any press at all, matters would be much better, because they would then judge and act from what they *saw* and what they *felt*, and not from what they read.'

It was Cobbett himself who broke the old corrupt system of journalism. He made his newspapers popular, he was the first to use them to address the common people and he practically invented the weekly review. His battles in the courts, and the example he set to others, gradually taught newspapermen to value their independence and break away from their previous subservience to government. After Cobbett, they learned to make their publications pay, and preferred, on the whole, to represent what they considered to be public opinion rather than simply to reflect the opinions of their paymasters in Parliament.

In fact, Cobbett's lifetime saw the gradual reversal of the process whereby politicians controlled the press, and with it, much of public opinion, until, by slow degrees, public opinion began to control the politicians. The ancient rights of petition and meeting played its part in bringing the pressure of opinion to bear, as indeed did the constant threat of rebellion. But the most persistent and in the end the most powerful instrument of public control was the political press. The freedoms it had slowly and often painfully established during the previous century had taken root, and proved impossible to eradicate, even during the repressive rule of Ellenborough and Sidmouth. Even at the depth of the crisis over the Six Acts, outright censorship was never restored, and it is always worth remembering that England was the sole country in Europe where liberty of the press in this sense existed.

The notion of a free press – if not always the reality – had by now entered the national consciousness. 'Give me but the liberty of the press', Sheridan exclaimed during a debate in 1810, 'and I will give to the minister a venal House of Peers – I will give him a corrupt and servile House of Commons – I will give him the full swing of the patronage of office – armed with the liberty of the press, I will go forth to meet him undismayed'.

The liberty of the press was not immune from attack, of course. In the first thirty years of the nineteenth century there is no doubt that it lost some ground. Legislation had been put in place to curb writing that incited hatred or contempt of the king or the government; the anonymous publication of newspapers was prohibited; journalists could be prosecuted on *ex officio* informations and tried by a biased 'special jury'; the Newspaper Stamp Duties Act was reinforced; truth was not yet a defence against libel; and Parliamentary debates were still difficult to report, in spite of the victories won by John Wilkes.

By the end of Cobbett's life, however, more had been gained than was lost. His own trial had rebounded against the government and he had the honour of being the one of the last persons of significance to be prosecuted in England for a seditious libel.* The concept remained intact, but actual prosecutions

---

* There were a few cases against the Chartists in the 1840s, though mostly associated with actual rioting, and in 1886 John Burns, one of the founders of the Labour Party, was prosecuted for uttering seditious words at a rally of the unemployed in Trafalgar Square which was followed by rioting and the smashing of windows in the Pall Mall clubs.

gradually faded from use. Even his earlier trial had achieved precisely the opposite effect to that sought by the prosecution: the publicity it generated brought the scandal of barbarous floggings in the army to the attention of the whole nation.

This colossal egoist was, of course, never in any doubt himself about the importance of his own influence on the events of his age. In a passage in the *Register*, as remarkable for its conceit as it is for its faith in the power of a free press, he wrote:

> For more than twenty-five long years I was the great and constant and only really sharp and efficient thorn in the side of that system which, at last, brought this country to the edge of convulsive ruin. I was the evening and the day star, the moon and the sun and the aurora of the press; all other parts of it have come twinkling behind me, shining now and then, indeed, but shining with borrowed light. I always led the way at a great distance forward; I foresaw, foretold every event, every effect; my predictions in due succession became history; I was the teacher of the nation; the great source of political knowledge, and of all those powerful arguments by which so many hundreds of thousands were able to combat the nefarious and desolating system of sway.'

After his death, there were battles aplenty still to come – the stamp duties, for instance, were not finally abolished until the 1860s – and the law remained as uncertain a friend to liberty as ever, but the force of public opinion and the liberty of expression, at least in a political sense, were now more or less secure. Many questions still remained: just what was meant by free speech, and what were its legitimate frontiers? To what extent was it possible to define the boundary between liberty and licence? And who should be the ultimate arbiter of the degree of free speech permitted by society? These and other philosophical conundrums were to be answered in the next generation by an English thinker as unlike William Cobbett as it is possible to imagine. John Stuart Mill, the great Victorian philosopher of liberty, was twenty-eight at the time of Cobbett's death in 1835, and had already embarked on his glittering intellectual adventure. What Cobbett's earthy pugnacity achieved for free speech in practice, Mill's soaring imagination was about to justify in principle.

PART FOUR

A Principle Defined

Everyone has the right to freedom of opinion and expression;
This right includes the right to hold opinions without interference
and to seek, receive and impart information and ideas
through any media and regardless of frontiers.

Article 19, Universal Declaration of Human Rights, 1948

CHAPTER TWELVE

John Stuart Mill On Liberty

By any standards, John Stuart Mill had an extraordinary upbringing. Born in London in 1806, he was the eldest son of the philosopher, James Mill, a friend and intimate of Jeremy Bentham, the last of the great eighteenth-century *raisonneurs* and the founder of the English utilitarian movement. Between them, the two philosophers conceived the notion of rearing the perfectly rational man in accordance with Bentham's belief that he had mastered the science of human behaviour. They drew up a carefully distilled intellectual diet for the boy, compounded of natural science and classical literature, which was fed to him at home under the daily supervision of his father in isolation from all other children. At the age of three, he began to learn Greek, starting with Aesop's *Fables*. By the time he was seven he had read most of the early dialogues of Plato, and the next year took up Latin, having already read the whole of Herodotus, Xenophon's Memorials of Socrates, much of Diogenes and Laertius, and part of Lucian. Between the ages of eight and twelve he went through the works of Virgil, Horace, Livy, Sallust, Ovid, Terence, Lucretius, Aristotle, Thucidides, Sophocles, Euripides and Aristophanes, took up geometry, algebra and differential calculus and read Pope's English translation of the *Iliad* twenty or thirty times through.

At twelve, Mill was studying logic and the works of Hobbes, and the following year wrote out his own survey of political economy. A little music was included in his syllabus, but no religion, no metaphysics, and little poetry, since these had been stigmatised by Bentham as tending to produce superstition and error. In his painfully candid autobiography, Mill tells us that no holidays were allowed, 'lest the habit of work should be broken, and a taste for idleness acquired'. He was carefully kept from having much to do with other boys for fear that he would be exposed to the contagion of what his father termed vulgar modes of thought and feeling. The only companions of his own age were his brothers and sisters, and his only exercise long country walks with his father, during which he was earnestly catechised on his day's intellectual endeavours.

The experiment has been called 'an appalling success'. By the time Mill was sent to spend a year in France at the age of fourteen it was with the learning of an especially erudite man of thirty, though he was himself innocently unaware that his attainments were anything out of the ordinary. 'If I thought anything about myself,' he says, 'it was that I was rather backward in my studies.' His father's expectations were always a step ahead of his own accomplishments.

This remarkable education was far from the mere learning of facts by rote. He was taught to think, to reason and to find things out for himself. There were many failures, and his father was a stern taskmaster, but by the time young Mill was ready to start his career, he had, as he tells us, an advantage of a quarter of a century over his contemporaries.

In work, too, he followed in his father's footsteps, taking up a post under his direct supervision as a clerk in the office of the examiner of correspondence in the East India Company, the body that effectively governed the sub-continent. The job gave him enough leisure to pursue his intellectual activities, and he was soon helping to launch the *Westminster Review,* and meeting a group of friends on his way to work in the morning for long cerebral discussions on such subjects as political economy, Ricardo's theory of international values and syllogistic logic. 'Our rule,' he says, 'was to discuss thoroughly every point raised, whether great or small, prolonging the discussion until all who took part were satisfied with the conclusion they had individually arrived at; and to follow up every topic of collateral speculation . . . never leaving it until we had untied every knot which we found.' His wider ambition was to become a reformer, a leader of the new breed of 'philosophical radicals' who were growing up in reaction to the complacency that had dominated English politics for so long.

To his father, it seemed as though Bentham's views on education had been triumphantly vindicated. They had produced the perfectly rational man, with a brain so far ahead of his contemporaries' that its powers of reasoning would soon soaringly surmount the ignorance and weaknesses of a superstitious age. He was the utilitarians' heir-presumptive, clear-headed, highly articulate, utterly serious, and without any trace of vanity, fear or base ambition. But he was also spiritually crippled, and at the age of twenty, Mill paid the inevitable psychological price of an education that had violently over-developed his mind, but starved his emotions. He suffered an agonising nervous breakdown.

He had been feeling in a dull state at the time and later recognised that he was going through a crisis of faith much like converts to Methodism smitten by their first 'conviction of sin'. Feeling a lack of purpose and a paralysis of the will, his well-trained analytical mind posed itself a simple question: suppose Bentham and his father's noble ideal of reason leading to universal happiness were to be instantly realised? Would this be a source of fulfilment and joy to him? To his horror, an irrepressible inner voice answered 'No!'

'My heart sank within me,' he wrote. 'The whole foundation on which my life was constructed fell down.' He saw no purpose in his existence; he had nothing left to live for. In vain he sought relief from his favourite books, but they had lost their charm. Hardly anything had power to give him even a few minutes oblivion of his woeful state. For months the cloud seemed to grow thicker and thicker. He thought himself devoid of all feeling, a monster whose normal human nature had atrophied, leaving him stranded at the commencement of his voyage through life with a well-equipped ship and rudder, but no sail, and no desire to set out for the destination for which he had been so carefully prepared. He wished only for death.

He went through the tasks of life mechanically, thinking he would not last beyond a year. Then one day he began reading the memoirs of a now almost forgotten French writer called Marmortel, who related the story of how his own father's death had inspired him as a mere boy to make his family feel he would fill the place of all they had lost. The passage moved Mill to tears. From that moment, his burden began to grow lighter. The thought that all feeling was dead within him was gone. 'I was no longer hopeless,' he wrote. 'I was no longer a stock or a stone.'

With the discovery that he was capable of emotion, the long slow psychological recovery began. At first reluctantly, for he loved and admired his father, but with an increasingly profound conviction, he began to distance himself from the cold rationality of the Benthamite view of life. A lesser mind might have found solace in religion, but Mill stayed true to his own basic tenets and continued to reject all forms of dogma and superstition. What changed was his view of the nature of man and the importance of diversity, individuality and spontaneity. He read Goethe and the poetry of Wordsworth and Coleridge and found pleasure again in sunshine and sky, in conversation and music – though he became neurotically tormented by the thought that the possible musical combinations must soon exhaust themselves. The octave, he reasoned, consisted of only five tones and two semi-tones, which could be put together in only a limited number of ways; most would surely soon be used up, leaving no room for a long succession of Mozarts and Webers to strike out into new veins of musical beauty. His neurosis, he wryly admitted, resembled that of the ancient philosophers who worried lest the sun should burn out. But in worrying about tones and semi-tones, Mill had come alive again. In music and poetry, he had discovered beauty, and things that spoke to his heart, and with them came a new meaning to his existence.

Mill's escape from a crisis that had nearly killed him was to have a profound effect, not only on the development of his own processes of thought, but on the intellectual climate of his age. First of all, he discarded the Enlightenment's notion that the pursuit of happiness was the chief aim of mankind. His experience had taught him that happiness was only to be attained by not making it the direct end. Those only are happy, he thought, who have their minds fixed on some object other than their own happiness; on the happiness of others, on the improvement of mankind, even on some art or pursuit, followed not as a means, but as itself an ideal end. Aiming thus at something else, they find happiness by the way. The enjoyments of life were best taken *en passant*. Once make them a principal object, as Bentham and his father had done, and they were immediately felt to be insufficient. They will not bear a scrutinising examination, said Mill. 'Ask yourself whether you are happy, and you cease to be so.' The only chance was to treat, not happiness, but some end external to it, as the purpose of life. If you are lucky, you will inhale happiness with the air you breathe. This theory, he said, now became the basis for his philosophy of life.

His discovery, so obvious to a psychologically aware generation such as our own, would lead him in due course to his great tract *On Liberty*, with its emphasis on the supremacy of the individual and his theory of free thought and discussion which swept the Victorians off their feet. He never renounced the intellectual culture developed by the Benthamites, but had found through his own bitter experience that it must go hand in hand with another prime necessity of human well-being, the 'internal culture of the individual' which the utilitarians had so fatally ignored.

Though Mill experienced several later bouts of depression, none was as deep or unsettling as his initial crisis of faith. By 1829, when he was twenty-three, he was more or less fully recovered and immersed again in the study of philosophy and economics. Then he fell head over heels in love with a married woman.

Harriet Taylor was the mother of three young children. Divorce in those days was out of the question, so for almost twenty years, Mill and Harriet wrote love letters to each other, travelled abroad together, even spent their weekends under the same roof together, all in a relationship that went no further than 'strong affection, intimacy of friendship and no impropriety'. Harriet called herself Mill's '*Seelenfreundin*', and Mill assured his father 'he had no other feelings towards her than he would have towards an equally able man'.

Temperamentally and intellectually, Harriet appeared to be everything Mill was not: intuitive and romantic, a free spirit who wrote poetry and held decidedly advanced views on the status of women. She was said to possess a stooping, swan-like beauty with large dark eyes, a complexion like a pearl, and a low sweet voice which emphasised the effect of her engrossing personality. Subconsciously, she seems to have been in revolt against the social conventions which had trapped her into a too early marriage with a man she regarded as her intellectual inferior. The infatuated Mill compared her to Shelley, but went on to add that in thought and intellect Shelley 'was but a child' compared to what Harriet ultimately became.

Mill himself was at this time an innocent young creature with thick auburn hair and a small clear Roman-nosed face, described by his friend Thomas Carlyle as 'modest, remarkably gifted with precision of utterance, enthusiastic, yet lucid, calm; not a great, yet a distinctly gifted and amiable youth'. Having grown up in the absence of love, his feelings for Harriet, however innocent, were all the more intense, and their relationship soon became the subject of gossip. One of his friends, John Roebuck, an early morning debating companion, reported that once at a dinner party he saw 'Mill enter the room with Mrs Taylor hanging on his arm. The manner of the lady, the evident devotion of the gentleman, attracted universal attention, and a suppressed titter went round the room'. Seeing the relationship was bringing ridicule on his friend, Roebuck determined, 'most unwisely', to speak to him on the subject. When he did so, Mill broke off their friendship.

As early as 1831, a 'reconciliation' had to be arranged with the long-suffering Mr Taylor, and Carlyle teased them by calling Harriet 'Platonica'. He wrote to his brother: 'They are innocent says Charity: they are guilty says Scandal: then why in the name of wonder are they dying broken-hearted?' The humourless Mill was not amused and this friendship also cooled.* Harriet was by now feeling ill used by everyone, and the couple withdrew even further into their own intense relationship with each other. 'Adieu my only & most precious,' Harriet once wrote to Mill, 'till Saturday – Dear Saturday!' For almost twenty years they lived this double life, Mill residing at home with his parents, and Harriet with her husband, leaving from time to time to travel abroad together, sometimes in secret, sometimes with one or other of Harriet's children, but always persuading themselves that their intimate friendship was one of perfect innocence.

Then, in 1849, John Taylor died, having been nursed for the last two months of his life with great tenderness and genuine anxiety by his wife. Two years later, Mill and Harriet Taylor were married and moved to live together in Blackheath, a then remote suburb in south-east London, safely beyond the reach of their former friends. Mill defensively justified their isolated mode of life by claiming that English society had become insipid. Anyone of really high-class intellect, he said, should only enter into unintellectual society as an apostle: 'those persons of any mental superiority who do otherwise are, almost without exception, greatly deteriorated by it.' Not to mention the loss of time, the tone of their feelings was lowered; they became less in earnest about their more advanced opinions and tended to look upon their most elevated objectives as unpractical or merely visionary. Their feelings of isolation intensified when it was found that both he and Harriet were suffering from tuberculosis and convinced they had only a short time to live. Travels abroad were now undertaken mainly for the purpose of convalescence, though Mill's illness did not prevent him from going on prodigiously long walks and, on one occasion, riding across Sicily on the back of a mule.

During the long years of their 'perfect friendship' Mill and Harriet had forged a formidable intellectual partnership, and in the short time they believed remained to them began to apply their minds to what they conceived would be a lasting work of philosophy. Mill was already the leading economic philosopher of the day, with his seminal work on the *Principles of Political Economy* published in 1848, which had brought him an international reputation. Now, in a curiously self-conscious echo of Edward Gibbon's *Decline and Fall*, which had been conceived on the same spot, they developed an idea that had come to Mill while ascending the steps of the Capitol in Rome: Mill's tract would be called *On Liberty*, and was to be a distillation of their ideas on the importance of the individual, their rejection of conformity, the central importance of free thought and discussion and their distrust of public opinion. Harriet had already written that the opinion of society was a 'phantom power', yet as often was the case with phantoms, of more force over the minds of the unthinking mass than all the flesh and blood arguments which could be brought to bear against it. It was a combination of the many weak against the few strong; an

---

* Though doubtless also affected by the fact that Mill (or perhaps Harriet) accidentally burnt the manuscript of Carlyle's *History of the French Revolution* that he had been lent.

association of the mentally listless to punish any manifestation of mental independence. It led to a spirit of conformity, which was the root of all intolerance, and whether it was religious, political, moral or social conformity, they were alike hostile to individual character. Not until they were destroyed would envy, hatred, uncharitableness and all their attendant hypocrisies also be destroyed. This, in essence, became the central tenets of Mill's philosophy, too, the origins of which, in his case, can be traced back without difficulty to the circumstances of his own life – the long drawn out revolt against some aspects of his father's upbringing and the unconventional nature of his relationship with Mrs Taylor.

At the age of fifty-two, Mill retired from his post with the East India Company on a generous pension and set to work on the book. 'None of my writings have either been so carefully composed, or so sedulously corrected as this,' he said. 'After it had been written as usual twice over, we kept it by us, bringing it out from time to time, and going through it *de novo*, reading, weighing and criticising every sentence.' It was, he always insisted, a joint work. 'When two persons have their thoughts and speculations completely in common; when all subjects of intellectual or moral interest are discussed between them in daily life and probed to greater depths . . . it is of little consequence which of them holds the pen.'

The final revision of the volume was to have been the work of the winter of 1858/9, which after Mill's retirement they had planned to spend in southern Europe. They travelled by easy stages to Montpellier, where Harriet's health began to cause concern. By the time they arrived at Avignon, she was seriously ill with bronchitis, brought on by her underlying tuberculosis. The medical men in Avignon were able to do nothing for her, and before the physician called from Nice could arrive, Harriet Mill was dead. 'The hopes with which I commenced this journey have been fatally frustrated,' Mill wrote to a friend in London. 'My Wife, the companion of all my feelings, the prompter of all my best thoughts, the guide of all my actions, is gone!' In another letter, he added: 'It is doubtful I shall ever be fit for anything, public or private, again. The spring of my life is broken.' Unable to bear parting from his beloved Harriet even in death, he bought a cottage overlooking the English churchyard at Avignon where she was buried and in which he was to spend the greater part of the rest of his life cared for by Harriet's daughter, Helen, who was as devoted to him as her mother had been.

Gradually, interest in his work returned, and arrangements were made to publish *On Liberty* in the spring of 1859, with an extravagantly worded dedication to 'the beloved and deplored memory of her who was the inspirer, and in part the author, of all that is best in my writings – the friend and wife whose exalted sense of truth and right were my strongest incitement, and whose approbation was my chief reward'. Because of her influence, Mill said, *On Liberty* far surpassed anything else he had ever written and was likely to survive longer because the conjunction of their two minds had rendered it a philosophical textbook of a single truth. Although it had never undergone her final revision, he gave instructions that it was to appear exactly as it had been left on Harriet's death. 'I have made no alteration or addition to it,' Mill wrote, 'Nor shall I ever. Though it wants the last touch of her hand, no substitute for that touch shall ever be attempted by mine.' *On Liberty* was published in February 1859 and was accepted immediately as one of the most important works of the age. It has been in print ever since.

ON LIBERTY

The argument Mill put forward addressed the central question in politics: who governs me? For the sake of what, and in the name of what? His answer was bold and absolute, and, for its day, very radical. In his own words, it asserted 'one very simple principle':

> That the only purpose for which power can be rightfully exercised over any member of a civilised community, against his will is to prevent harm to others. His own good, either physical or moral, is not a sufficient warrant. He cannot rightfully be compelled to do or forbear because it will be better for him to do so, because it will make him happier, because, in the opinion of others, so to do would be wise or even right. These are good reasons for remonstrating with him, or reasoning with him, or persuading him, or entreating him, but not for compelling him or visiting him with any evil in case he do otherwise . . . The only part of the conduct of anyone for which he is answerable to society is that which concerns others . . . Over himself, over his own body and mind, the individual is sovereign.

In the rest of the book, Mill elaborates and illustrates his 'one very simple principle', holding up the liberty of the individual as the touchstone against which any actions sanctioned by the majority should be tested, whether in thought, deed, or discussion. In every sphere, individual liberty was the supreme principle governing social relations, subject only to the exception where liberty caused harm to another. With that one very important qualification, liberty and individualism should prevail, even where they appear to conflict with other desirable ends.

The liberty of expression was so important to Mill that it over-rode the question of truth. Like Milton before him, he had faith that in a free and equal encounter with falsehood, truth would emerge victorious. The peculiar evil of silencing the expression of an opinion was that it robbed the human race, posterity as well as the existing generation – those who dissented from the objection, still more than those who held it. If the opinion was right, they were deprived of the opportunity of exchanging error for truth; if wrong, they lost what was almost as great a benefit, the clearer perception and livelier impression of truth, produced by collision with error.

His faith in the proposition was absolute. Though English law, on the subject of the press, was as servile in his day as it had been in the time of the Tudors, there was little danger of its being actually used to suppress political discussion except during some temporary panic when fear of insurrection might drive ministers and judges from their propriety. But let us suppose, Mill said, that the government was entirely at one with the people, and never thought of exercising any power of coercion unless in agreement with what it conceived to be their voice. Even in that case, 'I deny the right of the people to exercise such coercion, either by themselves, or by their government. The power itself is illegitimate'. Indeed, it was a more noxious power when exerted in accordance with public opinion than when in opposition to it. He went on from there to formulate his well-known precept that 'if all mankind minus one were of one opinion, mankind would be no more justified in silencing that one person than he, if he had the power, would be justified in silencing mankind'.

To the argument that judgement was given to men so that they may use it and that it was the duty of governments to make the best judgement they could about doctrines they thought were pernicious or dangerous to society in order to prevent them from being scattered abroad without restraint, Mill had his own clear answer: to prohibit even dangerous doctrines was illegitimate. His opponents might say that men and governments must act to the best of their ability; that it was not conscientiousness, but cowardice, to shrink from acting on their honest opinions. And while there was no such thing as absolute certainty, there was assurance sufficient for the purposes of human life. They might, and must, assume their opinions to be true for the guidance of their own conduct; and it was assuming no more when they forbade bad men to pervert society by the propagation of opinions which they sincerely regarded as false and pernicious.

'I answer,' said Mill, 'that it is assuming very much more. There is the greatest difference between presuming an opinion to be true because . . . it has not been refuted; and assuming its truth for the purpose of not permitting its refutation.' Complete liberty to contradict and disprove an opinion was the only justification for assuming the truth of that opinion. On no other terms could anyone hold a rational assurance of being right.

Ages were no less fallible than individuals. Every age had held opinions that subsequent ages deemed not only false but also absurd. Just as certainly, many opinions general in Mill's age would be rejected by future ages. Mankind could therefore never be sure that an opinion they were attempting to stifle was a false opinion; and if they were sure, stifling it would be an evil still. In his own age, nothing could be surer than that the theories of Newton were true. But if it were forbidden to question them, mankind would feel no more complete assurance of their truth than they already did. The best safeguard for even the most warranted beliefs was an invitation to the whole world to prove them unfounded. If the lists were kept open, if there were a better truth, it would be found when the human mind was capable of receiving it; and in the meantime, they might rely on having attained as close an approach to truth as was currently possible.

In their own age – an age Carlyle had described as 'destitute of faith, but terrified of scepticism' – the claims of an opinion to be protected from public attack rested not so much on its truth, as on its importance to society. There were thought to be certain beliefs so indispensable to social well being that it was the duty of the government to uphold them: not because they necessarily believed them to be true, but because they believed them to be useful. It was often argued, and still oftener thought, that none but bad men would desire to weaken these salutary beliefs; and there could be nothing wrong in restraining bad men. To Mill's mind, this was the sort of thinking that had led men to commit those dreadful mistakes which excited the astonishment and horror of posterity. There were too many instances in history where the arm of the law had been deployed for the most respectable of motives to root out those who were later seen to be the best men and the noblest doctrines.

He reminds his readers of the death of Socrates, condemned by a tribunal who honestly found him guilty, though of all men then living, he least deserved it. In Jerusalem, the high priest who rent his garments when he heard Christ speak in the Temple was no doubt quite as sincere in his horror and indignation as the generality of respectable and pious Englishmen who shuddered at his conduct, but would in all probability have acted precisely as he did. Perhaps the most striking historical example of all was that of the Roman Emperor, Marcus Aurelius, who had the finest mind and the tenderest heart ever to occupy the imperial throne. Yet he persecuted Christianity, believing it was his duty to put it down as a threat to the morals of Roman society. No Christian more firmly believed that atheism was false and tended to social dissolution than Marcus Aurelius believed the same things of Christianity. Therefore, said Mill, 'unless anyone who approves of punishment for the promulgation of opinions flatters himself that he is a wiser and better man than Marcus Aurelius – more deeply versed in the wisdom of his time, more elevated in his intellect above it, more earnest in his search for truth, more single-minded in his devotion to it when found – let him abstain from that assumption of the joint infallibility of himself and the multitude which the great Marcus Aurelius made with so unfortunate a result'.

When hard pressed, the enemies of religious freedom argued with Dr Johnson that the persecutors of Christianity were in the right, that persecution was an ordeal through which truth ought to pass, and always passed successfully, and that the only method by which religious truth could be ascertained was by martyrdom.* Mill dismissed this argument as not supported by the facts. The idea that truth always triumphed over persecution was one of those pleasant falsehoods that were refuted by history. Christianity had spread and become predominant because the persecutions were only occasional, lasting but a short time, and separated by long intervals of almost undiluted propagandism. It was a piece of idle sentimentality to say that truth, merely as truth, had any inherent power denied to error of prevailing against the dungeon and the stake. Men were no more zealous for truth than they often were for error, and determined penalties generally succeeded in preventing the propagation of either. It was true that the present age no longer put heretics to death, though it still penalised dissenters. Under the pretence that all atheists must be liars, English courts denied justice to those brave enough to confess a detested creed rather than affirm a falsehood. But Mill was not so much concerned with these 'rags and remnants' of persecution as he was with a new and more pernicious form of intolerance that had taken root in his own age: the intolerance of public opinion, or what, in a phrase borrowed from de Tocqueville, he termed 'the tyranny of the majority'. Majority rule was a far more insidious form of despotism than that of the absolute rulers of old, for it entered into every nook and cranny of life, impossible to escape, and was even in danger of 'enslaving the soul itself'. It set itself up as the arbiter of right and wrong, of propriety and impropriety; it presumed to tell people what to think and read, how to dress and behave, what

---

* Dr Samuel Johnson is quoted by Boswell as saying 'I am afraid there is no other way of ascertaining truth but by persecution on the one hand and enduring it on the other.'

they could say and write. It obliged them to conform; it discouraged originality
and it disapproved of unconventional ideas. It was fatal, in short, to the
individuality that Mill so prized.

He was writing, of course, against the *mores* of a claustrophobic age. In its
overweening self-confidence, mid-Victorian England had grown respectable,
bourgeois and stuffy. Even the most enlightened people felt themselves in the grip
of a social and intellectual conformity unknown in our own age. Mill was among
the first to call for more air and more light. He saw before him the spectacle of
highly intelligent and civilised human beings feeling themselves stifled and
silenced by the prejudice, the mediocrity and the stupidity of conventional
morality. Believing that all human progress rested on the preservation of
originality, he called for the liberty that alone could ensure that it survived. The
evil of conformity, the fallibility of conventional judgement, the right to err, the
right to dissent, and a passionate belief in the virtues of individual choice are
themes that recur throughout the essay and take many forms.

Mill noted that European civilisation owed its predominance to having followed
'a plurality of paths'. This had led to toleration, variety, humanity, progress, the
very qualities that were in danger of being extinguished by the grey, conformist,
middle-class congregations of England who held to the principle that it was one
man's duty to see that another should conform. Mill, by contrast, asserted
'mankind are the greater gainers by suffering each other to live as seems good to
themselves, than by compelling each other to live as seems good to the rest'.

In political life too, people needed to be protected from the deadening
conformity of the mass. It used to be thought that, when democracy came, the
nation would not need to be protected against its own free will. There would be
no fear of its tyrannising over itself. Let the rulers be answerable to the ruled,
and promptly removable by them, and they could safely be trusted with power.
For the power of the rulers would be but the nation's own power, concentrated
in a convenient form. Mill had the insight to see that this was not the end of the
process. Now that democracy occupied a large portion of the earth's surface,
people had begun to realise that 'self-government' meant not the government of
each by himself, but of each by all the rest. The will of the people meant the will
of the most numerous, or the most active. The people may consequently desire
to oppress a part of their number, and precautions were just as much needed
against this as any other abuse of power.

Though obvious to us, Mill's insight came as a revelation to a nation that had
been familiar with truly representative government for less than a generation.
There was a receptive audience for his call for the freedom to dissent from the
sometimes oppressive views of the majority. Now that public opinion ruled the
world, Mill taught them the need to preserve individuality and protect
independent thought. The mere example of non-conformity, the mere refusal to
bend the knee to custom, was itself a service.

What was it, then, that made the diversity of opinion so advantageous? It was
not just that the received opinion might be false, and some other opinion true,
and that an open conflict between them was necessary to establish the truth.
A commoner case was that, instead of one being true and the other false, the
conflicting opinions shared the truth between them. The non-conforming

opinion was then needed to supply the remainder of the truth. Popular opinions were often true, but seldom or never the whole truth. They were part of the truth, sometimes a greater, sometimes a smaller part, but exaggerated, distorted, and disjointed from the truths by which they ought to be accompanied and limited. Similarly with political opinions, it was necessary for the health of society that there should be both a party of order or stability and a party of progress or reform. Each of these modes of thinking derived its utility from the deficiencies of the other; and it was in great part the opposition of the other that kept each within the limits of reason and sanity. Unless all the antagonisms of practical life were expressed with equal freedom and defended with equal energy, a balance between them would not be secured. Very few had minds sufficiently capacious and impartial to arrive independently at a correct opinion on all issues; in the world of practical politics, that had to come through the rough process of a struggle between combatants fighting under hostile banners.

From this necessary conflict of opinion, Mill distilled another of his famous aphorisms – 'if either of the two opinions has a better claim than the other, not merely to be tolerated, but to be encouraged and countenanced, it is the one which happens at the particular time and place to be to be in a minority'. Only through ensuring diversity of opinion was there a chance approaching the whole truth. 'When there are any persons to be found who form an exception to the apparent unanimity of the world on any given subject, even if the world is in the right, it is always probable that dissentients have something worth hearing to say for themselves, and that truth would lose something by their silence.' So convinced was he of the need to keep truth, as it were, on her toes, that he believed that if opponents of an important truth did not exist, it would be necessary to conjure them up, and arm them with the strongest arguments of a skilful devil's advocate.

Mill goes on in this vein for over forty tightly packed pages of argument on the subject of thought and discussion, asserting again and again the absolute supremacy of liberty. Even in those cases where the received opinion was wholly true and the dissenting opinion wholly false liberty came first. For without the competition and collision of opinion, truth would degenerate into 'dead dogma'. A thinker's first duty was to follow his intellect to whatever conclusions it may lead. Truth gained more by the errors of one who thought for himself than by the true opinions of those who had taken their views from others. To permit the dissemination of error was therefore necessary if truths were to retain their vitality.

He then moves to apply his arguments to human behaviour, but before he does so, he recapitulates the four distinct grounds on which freedom of speech is necessary for the mental well-being of mankind. First, if any opinion is compelled to silence, that opinion may, for aught we can certainly know, be true. To deny this is to assume our own infallibility. Secondly, though the silenced opinion may be an error, it may, and very commonly does, contain a portion of truth; and since the prevailing opinion on any subject is rarely or never the whole truth, it is only by the collision of adverse opinions that the remainder of the truth has any chance of being supplied. Thirdly, even if the received opinion be not only true, but the whole truth, unless it is suffered to be, and actually is, vigorously and earnestly contested, it will be held by most people merely as a prejudice, with little comprehension or feeling of its rational grounds. Fourthly, the meaning of a doctrine that is not challenged will be in danger of being lost or enfeebled, and so descend into mere dogma – 'inefficacious for good, but encumbering the ground and preventing the growth of any real and heartfelt conviction from reason or personal experience'.

When Mill finally put down his pen, it was apparent that he had written one of the most influential books of the age, an abiding statement of high liberal principles and the most passionate defence of the freedom of speech since Milton wrote his *Areopagitica*. He had also started a debate which has lasted to this day.

MIXED RECEPTION

With its publication in 1859, *On Liberty* became an instant classic, giving Mill an authority in the English universities that has been compared to that wielded in the Middle Ages by Aristotle. From Cambridge, one tutor wrote: 'In our little circle, the summary answer to all hesitating proselytes is, "read Mill".' John Morley, then a student at Oxford, declared: 'I do not know whether then or at any other time so short a book ever instantly produced so wide and so important an effect on contemporary thought.' Charles Kingsley chanced on a copy in a bookshop and announced that it had made him 'a clearer-headed and braver-minded man on the spot'. Mill himself thought *On Liberty* was likely to survive longer than anything else that he had written. Nothing, he believed, could better show how deep were the foundations of the 'simple principle' it illustrated than the great public impression it made at a time, which, to superficial observation, did not seem to stand much in need of such a lesson. 'The fears we expressed, lest the inevitable growth of social equality and of the government of public opinion, should impose on mankind an oppressive yoke of uniformity in opinion and practice, might easily have appeared chimerical,' he wrote in his *Autobiography*. But the danger of intellectual conformity was no chimera, and unless mankind woke up to that fact they would end up being 'stunted' and 'dwarfed' by it. The teachings of *On Liberty*, he feared, would retain their value for a long time.

And so it at first seemed. Gladstone described Mill as 'the Saint of Rationalism', and to liberal thinkers everywhere his book became 'a sort of gospel'. 'It was the code of many thoughtful writers and several influential politicians,' wrote Frederic Harrison, himself an influential historian of ideas. 'It undoubtedly contributed to the practical programmes of Liberals and Radicals for the generation that saw its birth; and the statute book bears many traces of its influence over the sphere and duties of government.'

Yet along with the almost universal acclaim came the first doubts. No one denied that Mill had fashioned one of the most influential doctrines of the time, or even of all time. But even those critics who took him as seriously as he always took himself began to question the basic intellectual premise on which he had built so impressive an edifice. Was it true that individualism was in danger? The historian, Lord Macaulay, was one of those who did not think so. Thought and invention had never in fact been bolder than it was in their day: look at the development of the steam-ship, the steam engine, the electric telegraph, the gas-lights. And whatever one thought of the theology, the metaphysics, the political theories of their time, boldness and novelty were not what they lacked. Their literature was eccentric enough, every writer seeming to aim at doing something odd in style or metre. 'I therefore do not like to see a man of Mill's excellent abilities recommending eccentricity as a thing almost good in itself – as tending to prevent us sinking into that Chinese, that Byzantine, State,' said Macaulay. 'He is really crying "fire!" in Noah's flood.'

Other critics picked up the same point. Certainly the preservation of individuality was important and the denial of liberty was an evil. But had Mill not exaggerated the threat they were under, possibly because of the peculiar circumstances of his own upbringing? In the areas which mattered, man had hardly ever enjoyed so much freedom as he did in their own day. There was no censorship, at least not of any serious work of scholarship or political controversy. Man could read what he pleased, think how he liked, worship God in his own way – or not worship God at all. He could educate his children in the manner of his own choosing. Even in the trivial matters of life, he was free to wear a coat of his own cut, smoke tobacco, wear a beard, travel abroad, and argue freely with his friends, while in dozens of ways, eccentricity was becoming so commonplace it was ceasing to be eccentric. 'There probably never was a time when men who have any sort of originality of character had it in their power to hold the world at arm's length so cheaply,' wrote the *Saturday Review*. Mill's book read as though it had come from the prison cell of some persecuted thinker bent on making one last protest against the growing tyranny of the public mind rather than from the study of a writer who had perhaps exercised more influence over the thinking of cultivated Englishmen than any other man of his generation.

These criticisms culminated in a book-length attack by Sir James Fitzjames Stephen, who pointed out that it did not seem to be true that self-expression depended on complete intellectual freedom. History showed that fierce integrity, a passion for truth and fiery individualism flourished just as well in severely disciplined communities as they did in tolerant democracies. Calvinist Scotland, Puritan New England and Tsarist Russia had all produced thinkers and philosophers at least the equal of England. If this were so, Mill's argument that liberty was a necessary condition for the growth of individual genius must fall to the ground.

Published in 1872, a few months before Mill's death, Stephen's critique took issue with several of the essay's central assumptions. Mill's assertion that the removal of restraints tended to invigorate character was the very opposite of the truth. In perhaps the most telling of his criticisms, Stephen argued that Mill had drawn an unfounded distinction between what philosophers call 'self-regarding' acts and those which affect others. Such a distinction was like trying to draw a line between time and space, for every action happened both at a particular time and in a particular place. They were impossible to separate. Mill's doctrine was based on a similar fallacy: it applied to the formation and publication of opinions about matters connected with politics, morality and religion, and the doing of acts which may, and do, and are intended to influence other people's opinions upon those subjects. The exercise of free speech on matters of public controversy was therefore not a self-regarding act, since it inevitably affected others, often in unforeseen and damaging ways. Luther would never have justified the publication of his theses at Wittenberg on the grounds that it was an act which concerned himself alone. Mill would himself have hardly written his essay in order to show that it was wrong to interfere with his neighbour's hours or with his diet.

In advocating moral *laisser faire*, Mill had failed to distinguish between good and bad. History did not show that progress sprang from liberty; it showed that the progress of civilisation depended on the expedient use of moral, religious and legal coercion. If coercion were used wisely and judiciously, a civilisation would be stabler and more progressive than if every member of it were left to do as he pleased. Mill's prescription of unrestricted liberty, if pursued to its logical conclusion, would lead merely to anarchy. Liberty, said Stephen, was like fire, neither good nor bad in itself, but 'both good and bad, according to time, place, and circumstance'.

That *On Liberty* was flawed, both in logic and practice, was apparent from the first. Yet, as John Morley argued, its flaws seem inconsequential when set against the force of its moral arguments. Modern scholars have added that its moral arguments are made all the more appealing precisely because of its flaws: its overbold simplicity, its denial of complexity, its assertion of a single powerful principle which has exerted a hold over man's imagination for almost a century and a half.

But Mill was no prophet and foresaw none of the upheavals which convulsed the world in the generations following his death. He had no inkling of the impending world wars of the twentieth century, the rise and subsequent overthrow of totalitarianism, the collapse in many areas of social order and discipline, the creation of the welfare State and the concomitant extension of government into almost every aspect of personal life – or, for that matter, the discoveries of Freud and Darwin, the social theories of Marx and Lenin, the techniques of mass propaganda perfected by Goebbels, or the invention of the powerful new mediums of radio, television and the internet. Yet, for all that the world has been transformed almost beyond recognition since Mill wrote *On Liberty*, it still continues to be read and admired. Is there, then, a message in it for the modern world; and, if so, what is it?

Isaiah Berlin, one of the foremost intellects of the last century, put forward a compelling argument to show that Mill's views on liberty were as relevant and controversial in his day as they were when he first wrote them. Like Mill's contemporary critics, Berlin accepted that the tract *On Liberty* was not of the highest intellectual quality; most of Mill's arguments could be turned against him; certainly, none was conclusive enough to convince a determined or unsympathetic opponent. From the days of James Stephen to the conservatives, socialists, authoritarians and totalitarians of their day, the critics of Mill had, on the whole, exceeded the number of his defenders. Nevertheless, the inner citadel – the central thesis – had stood the test. It might need elaboration, or clarification, but it was still the clearest, most candid, persuasive, and moving exposition of the point of view of those who desire an open and tolerant society.

The reason for this was not merely the honesty of Mill's mind, or the moral and intellectual charm of his prose, but the fact that he was saying something true and important about the fundamental aspirations of human beings. He had perceived the unintended effects of the otherwise successful experiment in modern democracy and the fallaciousness and practical dangers of the theories by which some of the most destructive of these consequences were (and still are) defended. That is why, despite the weakness of the argument, the loose ends, the dated examples, the touch of the finishing governess so maliciously noted by Disraeli, despite the lack of that boldness of conception that marks true genius, his essay had educated a generation and was controversial still. Mill's central propositions were not truisms, and were not at all self-evident. They were statements of a position which was still resisted and rejected by the modern descendants of his contemporary critics, and they were still assailed because they were still contemporary.

Where Mill's doctrine has been less helpful in solving the modern dilemmas of free speech is his failure to define what its limits should be. He accepts at the outset of his essay that there should *be* limits. His 'simple principle' allowed that society was justified in imposing its power over any one of its members in order to prevent 'harm to others'. It is, indeed, the only purpose for which he believes such power can rightfully be exercised. But nowhere in his discussion of free speech does Mill define what he meant by 'harm to others'. It is equally unclear whether he is talking only about harm to other individuals or some unspecified harm to society as a whole. He does not even tell us whose task it should be to decide on the 'harm' or what steps they should be allowed to take to prevent it. On the all-important exception to his doctrine of absolute liberty, Mill is silent. Nowhere does he draw a line between what is permissible and what is impermissible. We are left with the vague generalisation that mankind may interfere with an individual's freedom of speech solely for the purpose of 'self-protection', a concept capable of a myriad different interpretations. It is 'self-protection', after all, that was used to justify the concept of seditious libel (and Sidmouth's introduction of the infamous Six Acts), and which is used today by any hard-pressed government to excuse the suppression of free speech and the censorship of the press.

Now it seems obvious that acts that might appear purely self-regarding can have indirect and harmful consequences for the rest of society. Does this permit society to forbid such acts? Mill does not say. At one point in his essay he does ask what should be the rightful limit to the sovereignty of the individual over himself, and where the authority of society should begin. But he answers the question by saying that while society has jurisdiction over conduct that prejudicially affects the interests of others, it is simply 'open to discussion' whether the general welfare will be promoted by interfering with it. He is much more concerned to make the point that in most such cases there should be perfect freedom, legal and social, to 'do the action and stand the consequences'. What those consequences are, or ought to be, he does not say. Who defines harm, and where to draw the line are questions he left for others to argue. For all its huge moral authority, Mill's doctrine does not provide us with a handbook for use on all occasions when free speech seems to be under attack. What, without doubt, he did leave behind was comparable to the legacy that James Madison left to America: a universal truth, declared in a solemn manner, that has, by degrees, acquired the character of a fundamental maxim. For all its flaws, *On Liberty* stands as the pre-eminent statement in defence of free speech ever written.

MEMBER OF PARLIAMENT

In 1865, six years after his success with *On Liberty*, Mill stood for Parliament in the constituency of Westminster. He characteristically refused to canvas, or incur any expense, and told his constituents that, if elected, he would spend no time and labour on pursuing their local interests. He would stand on his own views, or he would not stand at all, and among those views was his conviction that women were entitled to representation in Parliament on the same terms with men: the first time, he thought, that such a radical notion had ever been mentioned to English electors. Nothing, he said, appeared more unlikely than that a candidate whose professions and conduct set so completely at defiance all ordinary notions of electioneering should ever be elected. A literary friend told him that the Almighty himself would have no chance of being elected on such a programme. Mill nevertheless adhered to it, neither spending money nor canvassing, answering all questions from the electors with his usual candour, refusing only to speak about his religious views.

At one meeting, he was asked about a remark he had made in a pamphlet that the English working classes, though different from those of some other countries, in being ashamed of lying, are yet generally liars. An opponent had the remark printed up and read out at the meeting. Had he written and published it? Mill at once answered, 'I did'. 'Scarcely were these two words out of my mouth, when vehement applause resounded throughout the whole meeting,' he wrote. So accustomed had the electorate become to expect equivocation and evasion from politicians, they concluded at once that here was a man they could trust. They wanted friends, not flatterers, and the most essential of all recommendations to their favour was complete straightforwardness. To his great surprise, Mill was elected by a comfortable margin.

He served as their MP for almost four years, speaking with authority in support of Gladstone's Reform Bill, which extended the franchise to almost all male adults. He was instrumental in exposing the appalling cruelty with which black plantation workers were treated in Jamaica, and spoke, with less effect, for the abolition of capital punishment, the enfranchisement of women and Irish Home Rule, but made a further lasting contribution to the English respect for free speech by establishing the right to hold meetings in Hyde Park at the place now known as Speakers' Corner.

He continued in this mode until his death in 1872 at the age of sixty-six, always 'sober, censorious and sad', something of a goose, in Isaiah Berlin's words, something of a prig, afflicted in his later years by a constant facial tic, but loved by his followers as the authentic voice of high liberal values and the guardian of the English tradition of free speech. He lies buried in the graveyard at Avignon beside his beloved Harriet, whom he had laid to rest there fourteen years earlier.

CHAPTER THIRTEEN

The Fourth Estate

DELANE OF *THE TIMES*

As democracy in the English-speaking world thrust down its roots, a subtle change took place in the debate about free speech. Until the lifetime of John Stuart Mill, the arguments had been mainly about the right to hold unorthodox or unpopular opinions. Thereafter, it was increasingly about the right to disseminate facts. News, independently gathered and impartially conveyed, was seen to be an indispensable commodity in a society where the people ruled themselves. To enable them to choose between the different opinions that were canvassed, the voters needed to weigh the various facts on which those opinions rested. Universal suffrage and a free press were therefore seen to be entirely correlative things. Without the free circulation of news, there could be no true democracy. As Rebecca West put it, people need news for the same reason they need eyes – to see where they are going.

As early as the 1840s, Alexis de Tocqueville was startled to find that what Anglo-Americans looked for in a newspaper was not only hotly disputed opinion, it was knowledge of facts. Their Argus-eyed press laid bare the secret shifts of politics and forced public figures to appear before the tribunal of opinion. He even thought that newspapers did not just guarantee liberty; in a democracy, they maintained civilisation. No longer did a country's rulers all know and mingle with each other; in a democracy the rulers were lost in the crowd, brought together only by their newspapers, which came to them every day of their own accord and talked to them briefly about public affairs without distracting them from their private business. Newspapers were the cement of democracy; their freedom from censorship was essential to the health of society.

As the century progressed, this principle was reinforced by the steady advance of technology, first through the steam-driven cylinder press and the development of automated paper-making and then through the arrival of the electric telegraph, the mail train and the invention of the linotype machine, which together revolutionised the production and distribution of newspapers.

The new technology brought increased circulation. Increased circulation attracted advertisers. With advertising revenue came financial security, and with security came editorial independence. The old subservience of the press to political subsidy gradually came to an end, and a generation of fiercely independent editors enthusiastically shook off the last shackles of government control.

In Britain, these developments were masked for a while by the continued imposition of stamp duties which stunted and distorted the development of the press until the mid-1850s. In America, a free press based on the principles of capitalist *laisser faire* was by then already well established. Long before the British press did so, American newspapers served a popular readership, having grown up for trade rather than literary reasons. Men like Horace Greeley could flourish in New York, Joseph Pulitzer in St Louis, and George Hearst in the burgeoning new State of California, but their influence was still confined to their own neighbourhood. The age of the national newspaper editor and its ruling tycoon lay in the future. This was the age when the individual editor ruled supreme.

While America led the way, it was in mid-Victorian Britain that newspapers acquired their greatest influence and where the power of an independent press grew so great that it 'could make ministers of State tremble and crowned heads feel disquiet'. What was even more extraordinary, this power was largely confined to a single newspaper, and for much of the time held in the hands of a single man. The newspaper was the London *Times* and the man its editor for thirty-seven years, John Thaddeus Delane, who became perhaps the most powerful journalist of the age as well as the most important and eloquent defender of the liberty of the press. Under his rule, *The Times* assembled a formidable team of reporters and established the primacy of news. 'It has ears everywhere,' wrote Ralph Waldo Emerson from across the Atlantic. 'Its information is earliest, completest, and surest.' And President Lincoln could say, 'I don't know anything which has more power, except perhaps the Mississippi River'.

The Times owed its pre-eminence to another of those paradoxes that punctuate the history of free speech: it grew to maturity under the shelter of the Stamp Acts. With duty imposed at 4*d* a copy, only the well to do could afford to read newspapers, and it was serving this market that *The Times* first established itself. When the flood of unstamped newspapers threatened the monopoly in Cobbett's day, the government reckoned it could undercut their influence by reducing the duty from 4*d* to 1*d*. Sure enough, the unstamped press died away, their profits no longer worth the risk of prosecution. But the stamped press was now within the reach of the respectable bourgeoisie, who not only read newspapers but also bought the new consumer goods they advertised. The main beneficiary of the process was what Cobbett called 'that cunning old trout' – 'that brazen old slut' – 'the bloody old *Times*'.

By the time Queen Victoria came to the throne in 1837, *The Times* was already the country's predominant newspaper, its circulation twice that of all its rivals put together. It had grown to prosperity under the enterprising Walter family, who had introduced steam and the rotary press and established the paper's independence under the first of its great editors, John Barnes, who ran the paper for twenty-five years, but who died suddenly in 1841 while still at the height of his powers. The succession fell on a young man only a year out of university who had caught the eye of the paper's proprietor. 'By Jove John, what do you think has happened?' the young man exclaimed as he burst in on his flatmate in St James's Square. 'I am editor of *The Times*!'

John Walter had made a shrewd choice. Although only twenty-three and without any previous literary or academic distinction, John Delane was a heaven-sent editor, with the most prescient news sense in London. Again and again during his thirty-seven years in the editor's chair, he showed an uncanny ability to foresee the outcome of developing events. As early as 1845, he realised the railway-building boom would collapse and ran a series of articles to 'expose the knaves and warn the dupes'. John Walter stood by him when the railway companies withdrew their advertising, and Delane was triumphantly vindicated when the bubble burst, exactly as he had forecast. A few months later, he pulled off an even bigger coup by revealing that the government of Sir Robert Peel was about to do away with the Corn Laws, an historic event that paved the way for the era of free trade on which industrial Britain built its prosperity. A decade later, on the eve of the Crimean War, the Tsar was astonished to read in *The Times* that the British government was sending him an ultimatum, which owing to some accident to the official courier had not yet reached St Petersburg. As the political crisis deepened, Queen Victoria was even more furious to read an account of her private audience with Lord Granville after he had turned down her invitation to become Prime Minister. 'Who am I to trust?' she wailed. 'These were my very own words.' Perhaps most famously of all, it was Delane's *Times* that exposed the disgraceful state of the army's hospital camps outside Sevastopol after the Crimean war had broken out.

'How do you get to the secrets?' someone once asked him. 'By sticking to the centre of them,' he replied. Indefatigable in pursuing his sources, he was to be seen everywhere, dining out every night of the week during the London season and spending weekends in the great country houses, hunting with his hosts and conversing with their guests. Like many journalists, he was an inveterate snob who relished mingling with the titled and mighty. The radical politician Richard Cobden disapproved of a newspaper editor dining at tables where 'every other guest but himself was an Ambassador, a Cabinet Minister or a Bishop', but it was from such gatherings that Delane gleaned his news and his paper gained its authority. He went regularly to the races, enjoyed gambling with the aristocracy and on one occasion became so engrossed in conversation with the Prince of Wales that before he left the room the prince had shaken hands with him four times. He was in the habit of riding around London on horseback, being observed one day riding down Whitehall earnestly engaged in conversation with a pair of dukes walking humbly alongside. He sought news wherever it was to be found, 'awake to one aspect only of the events of his exciting world', in the words of the *History of The Times*. 'Wars, the discoveries of science, movements in literature, painting and music, the catastrophes of nature, railway disasters, crime, famine, the fall of dynasties interested him little and only in so far as they needed recording in *The Times*.'

Perhaps because of the tragic nature of his private life – a few years after their marriage his wife had a mental breakdown and was confined to an asylum – he lived almost exclusively for his paper. After his round of social engagements in the evenings, he would arrive at Printing House Square around 10 p.m. and stay there until 5 the next morning, supervising every detail of the paper's production – reading through the voluminous Parliamentary reports, selecting the influential letters to the editor, supervising the content of the leading articles – although rarely writing them himself – revising despatches from his correspondents, sub-editing, rewriting, and reading his proofs as if they were holy writ. 'I believe not a column has been published in *The Times* which has not some of my handwriting in the margin,' he wrote once.

Every inch the professional editor, nothing seemed to escape his eagle eye whether he was railing at 'those devils of printers' who would try to save space by taking out his cross-heads at the expense of disfiguring the whole paper, or muttering 'excrement! excrement!' at an inappropriately phrased review. At five in the morning, the paper having been safely put to bed, Delane would walk home to his apartments at Serjeants Inn, not far from *The Times* office, seeing in the course of his life 'more sunrises than almost any man alive'. He rose again at noon, ate a combined breakfast and lunch, took a ride on horseback in Hyde Park, then returned to his apartment to deal with his correspondence, read documents and decide on the subjects for next morning's leading article.

His social life began again at dusk, his frock-coated, mutton-chop bewhiskered figure gliding smoothly around the circles of influence, deploying his persuasive gift of getting politicians to confide their secrets to *The Times*. 'What do you intend to do with this information?' a cabinet minister who had just revealed a State secret once asked him. 'Why, publish it, of course,' Delane replied. In the days of his ascendancy, there was practically no decision he was not told about within a few hours of the cabinet meeting that took it. The secrets he usually revealed; the sources he always protected. Indeed, so extensive were his contacts he always refused to listen to information 'off the record'. 'I don't much care to have confidential papers sent to me at any time,' he said, 'because the possession of them prevents me from using the information which from one source or another is sure to reach me without any such condition of reserve.'

His greatest hour came when Britain went to war in the Crimea in 1854. Delane, as always, had kept himself informed about developments, and even had the foresight to visit the area himself before war broke out. By the time the British army set sail, *The Times* had assembled its own glittering corps of war correspondents, led by the gifted Irish reporter, William Howard Russell, the man who coined the phrase 'the thin red line' to describe a regiment of British infantry. In the days before either censorship or public relations officers, Russell began sending home a series of brilliant but coruscating war despatches, including his exposé of the hopeless inadequacy of the commissariat and medical services and the terrible suffering of the wounded soldiers in the hospital camps. His fearless reporting 'saved the remnants of an army'. It also inspired the mission of Florence Nightingale and overturned the ministry of Lord Aberdeen.

Russell's gifts were brilliantly backed up by Delane, who as the war progressed fought battle after battle for the liberty of the press not only to express opinions, but to report the facts. In an age when despatches from the front took days, and sometimes weeks, to appear in print, Russell's description of the Battles of Inkerman and Balaclava can have revealed little that the enemy did not already know. But they had an enormous impact on public opinion at home and cruelly showed up the shortcomings of the aristocratic high command and the manner in which they exposed their men to unnecessary suffering. 'Custom and an acquired sentiment of reticence tied the tongues and pens of our chiefs,' wrote the official historian of the war. 'William Howard Russell dared to tell his employers, and through them the English-speaking peoples, that our little army was perishing from want of proper food and clothing.'

While Russell thundered from the front, Delane held the line against a battery of complaints from the government at home. 'Your friend Mr Delane seems to be drunk with insolence and vanity,' said the foreign secretary, Lord John Russell. '*The Times* aspires not to be the organ, but the organiser of government.' Queen Victoria demanded to know by what right the editor of *The Times* tried her officers. And when Lord Derby, later to become prime minister, complained that Delane was revealing cabinet secrets, their dispute led to a series of classic exchanges on the liberty of the press and its role in an open society.

Early in the war, *The Times* disclosed that the cabinet had discussed a proposal from the Tsar to partition Turkey. Lord Derby was outraged that the news had appeared in print, and Lord Aberdeen took the timid politician's easy way out – he blamed his staff. The leak, he suggested, had come from a disaffected clerk in the Foreign Office. Delane replied next day with a magisterial riposte in *The Times*. His journal never was, and he trusted never would be, the journal of any minister. It was the 'executor of the public will' and a check against the abuse of power. 'We aspire, indeed, to participate in the government of the world,' he said. 'But the power we seek is exercised solely and freely by way of language and reason over the minds of men . . . As long as we use the information we obtain and the influence we possess for the honour and welfare of the country, the people of England will do us justice.'

This thunderclap from Olympus was repeated the following week when the debate resumed and Lord Derby complained that the cabinet's decision to send an ultimatum to Russia had appeared *in extensio* in *The Times* on the next morning but one after the meeting of the cabinet. 'How is it possible,' he asked, 'that any honourable man, editing any public paper of such circulation as *The Times*, can reconcile to his conscience the act of having made public that which he must have known was intended to be a cabinet secret?'

Delane, who had been listening from the public gallery, answered genially that 'to accuse this, or any other journal, of publishing early and correct intelligence, is to pay us one of the highest compliments that we can hope to deserve'. *The Times* kept correspondents in all the capitals of Europe for that very purpose. As for the ultimatum, 'we hold ourselves responsible, not to Lord Derby or the House of Lords, but to the people of England, for the accuracy and fitness of that which we think proper to publish'. In deciding what was proper to publish – 'we ourselves and the public at large are quite as good judges on that point as the Leader of the Opposition.'

Delane spoke for the educated middle-classes who read his newspaper and not for the unlettered masses that *The Times* has always held in snobbish disdain. But within their class-bound limits, his verbal duels with Lord Derby led to some of the most trenchant defences of an independent press ever penned. On one occasion, when Napoleon III tried to bribe *The Times* into silence – the French regularly buying up their own opposition newspapers in order to keep them under government control – he was rebuffed with an onslaught so fierce it made the Emperor dance around the room with rage. He sought to bring pressure on the paper through his friends in Britain, and Lord Derby again obliged. He said in the House of Lords that if the press aspired to exercise the influence of statesmen, they should regard it as 'a sacred duty' to maintain a tone of 'moderation and respect'.

Delane delivered his rejoinder only after the most careful discussion with the chief proprietor, John Walter III, and Henry Reeve, the leader-writer assigned to pen the words. In two leading articles published on successive days, *The Times* sought to define the permanent principles of a free press. The duty of a journalist, it said, was to obtain the earliest and most correct intelligence of the events of the time, and instantly by disclosing them to make them the common property of the nation. This function was separate, independent and sometimes diametrically opposite to that of the statesmen. The article went on, in words engraved on the heart of every young journalist:

The Press lives by disclosures. Whatever passes into its keeping becomes a part of the knowledge and history of our times. It is daily and forever appealing to the enlightened force of public opinion – anticipating if possible the march of events – standing on the breach between the present and the future, and extending its survey to the horizon of the world. . . . We are bound to tell the truth as we find it, without fear of consequences – to lend no convenient shelter to acts of injustice and oppression, but to consign them at once to the judgement of the world.

It was arrogant. It was presumptuous. But it set standards that have guided honest journalists ever since. At the time it was written, it won the respect even of his opponents. For all the pugnacity of his prose, he never lost the confidence of the ministers of the day, who continued to seek out his company and feed him their secrets. They knew they could trust him, and were beholden to his influence. Rivals might grumble at *The Times*'s 'extraordinary and dangerous eminence', but in mid-Victorian England it was an eminence not to be gainsaid. The press had acquired an authority that allowed it to rise above all criticism – and, said some, into hubris. When the manager of *The Times*, Mowbray Morris, was called before a select committee of the House of Commons to explain the paper's claims that all Irish members took bribes, he refused to answer their questions. Asked if he extended his idea of the privilege of the press to facts as well as opinion, he loftily replied, 'To everything whatever'. And to the question whether he was willing to offer any explanation or justification of the charges *The Times* had made, he answered, 'I am not'. After which, reported the *Manchester Guardian*, 'the gentleman bowed, retired, and went home to dinner, convinced no doubt that the Tsar of Russia, the Member for Bucks (Benjamin Disraeli) and *The Times* newspaper can defy the whole of mankind'.

Indeed, so powerful had Delane's *Times* become, and so regularly the recipient of government secrets, it was often, but erroneously, seen abroad as the voice of the British government. When Queen Victoria complained about this, Lord Palmerston sent her a private memorandum explaining that 'the newspapers on the Continent are all more or less under a certain degree of control, and the most prominent among them are the organs of political parties, or of leading public men; and it is not unnatural that Governments and parties on the Continent should think that English newspapers are published under similar conditions'. But such a view was mistaken. 'In this country, all thriving newspapers are private and commercial undertakings.' They were critical, because criticism is popular and therefore good business. Palmerston spoke as a cynical politician – his morning habit was to throw his copy of *The Times* into the fire (though only after he had read it). But he also put his finger on the central truth that editors are free and independent only in so far as their newspapers are commercially successful. And *The Times* was so commercially secure it was above all bribes or blandishments; at least one prime minister was heard to complain that there was nothing the damned fellows wanted. But its success was a strictly middle-class phenomenon. In no other country in the world was a democratically elected government confined to such an ingrown, tightly knit oligarchy as it was in class-ridden Victorian Britain. It owned the land, it ruled the country, and, without exception, it read *The Times*. That is what gave it its extraordinary power.

The main problem with *The Times* in Delane's day was not that it was commercially independent, but that it held a virtual monopoly. Nothing else could grow under its massive shade. To Richard Cobden, *The Times* had itself become an obstacle to the freedom of expression – a view unhappily confirmed when Mowbray Morris told another select committee he had 'very little opinion of the sagacity of uneducated people'. The production of newspapers should be confined to educated and enlightened people like himself. In which case, Cobden said drily, Delane's lofty talk of the freedom of the press was arrant nonsense. So long as *The Times* was protected by the stamp duties there could be no daily press for the middle or working class. How could they afford to take in a daily newspaper at 5*d*?

At this time, *The Times* accounted for practically 80 per cent of all daily newspaper sales, not only in London, but throughout the British Isles. In vain did the *Morning Chronicle*, the *Morning Herald* and Charles Dickens's *Morning News* try to break into the market. Without Delane's access to confidential information, not one of them could command a circulation of even a tenth that of *The Times*. And without the circulation, they could never become commercially viable. The stamp duties merely reinforced the *The Times*'s supremacy, since it could afford to pay the daily tax while other London papers could not. Against its provincial rivals, the tax was a positive asset, for stamped papers were carried free through the post. Local papers, compelled to pay the tax even though they had no need for the free postage, were forced to go on sale at the same price as *The Times*, although quite unable to match its twelve or sixteen daily pages and the associated advertising revenue. In some cities, subscription libraries loaned *The Times* out for 1*d* an hour, further adding to the competitive pressures on its potential rivals.

The long campaign against the stamp duty ran on into the 1850s when Delane was approaching the height of his powers – and honourably putting principle above profit in arguing that, even though *The Times* would be the main loser, 'there is something positively ridiculous in taxing that intelligence which really constitutes the great medium of a civilised country'. The tax on news was 'a tax on light, a tax on education, a tax on truth, a tax on public opinion, a tax on good order and good government, a tax on society, a tax on the progress of human affairs, and on the working of human institutions'.

But the government needed the revenue and were frightened by the spectre of mass democracy, the then prime minister, Lord John Russell, shuddering with horror at the prospect of such abominations as popular newspapers, or, come to that, popular education. In Richard Cobden's words, 'the governing classes will resist the removal of the penny stamp, not on account of the loss of revenue – *that* is no obstacle – but because they know that the stamp makes the daily press the instrument and servant of the oligarchy'.

The oligarchy resisted to the end, but by now the tide of reform was running too strongly. After what Gladstone termed 'the severest Parliamentary struggle in which I have been engaged', the stamp duties were finally repealed in 1855 and the remaining taxes on paper and advertisements removed six years later. Not only was *The Times*'s monopoly at an end, the government had given a vicious little twist to its tail – in revenge, said some, for its exposure of the military debacle in the Crimea. Under the new legislation, newspapers that went by post had to pay a surcharge if they weighed more than 4oz. The weight had been carefully set to catch only *The Times*.

Delane responded with a long and angry tirade against the hypocrisy of the politicians. Everyone knew, he said, that *The Times* was being victimised for 'our honest exposure of favouritism, incapacity, and inertness in the conduct of the war, and our evident determination to be bound to no party. We know, too, that there are men in the House of Commons who are opposed not only to us, but to any independent and respectable press'.

Now at a disadvantage against its untaxed rivals, *The Times* was compelled either to reduce its size or put up its price. Being *The Times* and convinced of its unique role as a public institution it chose to increase its price in order to maintain its character. It was a decision that would lead later on to the paper's long, slow decline and its eventual rescue by Lord Northcliffe, an entirely different kind of newspaper tycoon to the Walter family who had owned it in the years of its greatness.

For the rest of the press, the abolition of stamp duties had an immediate and invigorating effect. A great psychological barrier had been removed, and daily newspapers sprang up practically overnight in cities and towns all across the British Isles. On the very day the tax was repealed, a group of London entrepreneurs launched the 2*d Daily Telegraph*, destined to overtake the circulation of *The Times* within six years and eventually become the first British newspaper to sell more than a million copies a day. But so long as Delane remained its editor, *The Times* maintained both its commercial and its moral ascendancy. Even after he had gone, his editorial creed of untrammelled independence lived on, an abiding contribution to the development of free speech and the liberty of the press.

He stayed in the editor's chair until 1877, when he retired at the age of only fifty-nine, worn out and rheumy-eyed through years of relentless nightly toil in putting to bed some 7,000 editions of his beloved *Times*. 'I may or may not live a few months,' he wrote on his last day in the office, 'but my real life ends here; all that was worth having of it was devoted to the paper.' Two years later he was dead, the best-informed man in England and charioteer of what Hazlitt called 'the greatest engine of temporary opinion in the world'.

HORACE GREELEY: AMERICA'S 'HOLY FOOL'

While Delane was defending the liberty of the press in the sonorous cadences of mid-Victorian England, Americans were saying the same thing in earthier language. The Englishman saw the business of a newspaper as obtaining 'the earliest and most correct intelligence of the events of the time, and instantly, by disclosing them, to make them the common property of mankind'. To William Storey's *Chicago Times*, its job was to 'print the news and raise hell'.* In that age, American newspapermen were more in touch with ordinary folk than their English counterparts, especially those of them who worked for the London *Times*.

The public who bought their wares was more varied, too, as Americans became a people on the move, with fresh immigrants pouring in every year from Europe and others reaching out to find new opportunities beyond the Appalachians and across the Great Plains. 'Go West, young man,' urged Horace Greeley, the archetypal, oddball editor who practically invented the campaigning, mass-circulation daily paper and in doing so developed a formula for serving up the news that transformed the journalist's trade on both sides of the Atlantic. Brought up a tatterdemalion New Hampshire farm boy, his newspapers made him so famous the Democrats chose him to run against President Ulysses S. Grant in the election of 1872. After a typically quixotic campaign, he was soundly trounced, and later that same year he died in an asylum mouthing oaths.

Greeley's beginnings were as unpropitious as his end was inglorious. Born of drunken and impoverished parents of Ulster descent, he was given a minimal education and put out to work for a printer at the age of fourteen. Morbidly sensitive to noise, with sheet-white albino skin, watery blue myopic eyes and a piping voice than even in manhood grew to nothing higher than a falsetto squeak, his employer called him 'the Ghost' and the other apprentices took him for an idiot and threw ink at him. In later life, his appearance became even more outlandish, his huge moon face set atop a sea of flaxen whiskers that grew from his throat, his low-crowned hat sporting a brim double the size of his head, odd boots on his feet and the boundary between them and his trousers said to be in a state of constant litigation. His shambling sailor's gait made him appear to be walking down both sides of the street at once, and when he got good news he turned somersaults in the office. He was a man of ideas, he said of himself, and to spend any time in front of a looking glass 'would be robbing the public'.

On his way to maturity, he had become a precocious reader with a passion for acquiring factual information. He devoured the Bible from Genesis to Revelation, the *Arabian Nights* and *Robinson Crusoe*, a large part of Shakespeare and any other book or newspaper he could lay his hands on. He acquired a hit-and-miss knowledge of history, literature and economics which left his brain 'crammed with half-truths and odds and ends of ideas which a man inevitably accumulates who scrapes knowledge together by fits and starts on his way

---

* Though he rather spoiled the effect when he added in a cynical instruction to one of his correspondents, 'When there is no news, send rumours'.

through life'. This turned out to be the ideal background for a campaigning journalist and gave him a new hobbyhorse to ride in every edition.

His father's eighty stony acres were seized by creditors before young Greeley had finished his apprenticeship, the family evicted from the farm and their goods sold off to the highest bidder. His parents ended up in a log cabin in the Pennsylvania wilderness while Horace set off for New York at the age of twenty with ten dollars in his pocket and a Bible in a bandana over his shoulder. He found a job on the first penny paper in New York, the *Morning Post*, but it closed down three weeks later. Moving on to a new literary magazine, the *New Yorker*, he became a Liberal Whig, met and married a schoolteacher who was as eccentric as he was, and by the time he was thirty had saved up enough to launch his own newspaper, the New York *Tribune*, which was dedicated to reform, economic progress and the elevation of the masses. The *Tribune* became the first of the great crusading popular newspapers, pressing causes practical and impractical, from impassioned anti-slavery to the prohibition of alcohol, from the abolition of capital punishment to the promotion of trade unions, from spiritualism to vegetarianism, all of them pursued with equal energy and sincerity.

Greeley had the gift, essential to any editor, of attracting and nurturing talent, however different it was from his own. By 1854, he had a staff of fourteen reporters in New York and thirty-eight regular out-of-town and overseas correspondents, one of them the relatively unknown Karl Marx (who dismissed Greeley as a bourgeois humbug). Backing them up were ten associate editors working on features, leading articles and reviews, including the only man Greeley ever rebuked for working too hard, Henry Jarvis Raymond, who went on to found the even more influential *New York Times*. Between them, Greeley's team made the *Tribune* of the 1850s a forum for the popular discussion of politics, religion, philosophy and literature on a scale that had never before been attempted. To this mix he added the infallible insight that what the readers of any newspaper most like to read about is themselves. Next to that, Greeley explained in a letter to 'Friend Fletcher' who was about to start a country newspaper, give them news about their neighbours – Asia and the Tonga Islands came a long way behind these in most people's regard. His advice went on:

Do not let a new Church be organised, or new members added to one already existing, a farm be sold, a new house raised, a mill set in motion, a store opened, nor anything of interest to a dozen families occur, without having the fact duly, though briefly, chronicled in your columns. If a farmer cuts a big tree, or grows a mammoth beet, or harvests a bounteous yield of wheat or corn, set forth the fact as concisely and unexceptionally as possible.

By such means, casually and almost spontaneously, the popular press was born. It was based on no fine theories of free speech or high-minded attempts to bring truth to the voting masses, yet the public very quickly accustomed themselves to expect a daily cornucopia of facts to arrive in their own homes, and, on Sundays, an illustrated encyclopaedia to accompany it. For this 'daily miracle', as it was quickly called, they expected to pay the smallest copper coin from the mint. Nobody thought for a moment that they ought to pay the cost price for their news, even when they recognised it as one of the fundamental guarantors of a free society. In the words of the American journalist Walter Lippmann, 'they expect the fountains of truth to bubble, but they enter into no contract, legal or moral, involving any risk, cost or trouble to themselves'. They paid their penny when it suited them, stopped paying whenever it suited them, would turn to another paper when that suited them. The newspaper editor had to stand for election every day of the year.

As de Tocqueville had found, the press played quite as vital a role in American society as the school, the Church or the learned professions. News was the cement of their democracy. Yet the citizen expected it to come to him practically *gratis*. This was made possible because, while unwilling to pay for his news, he *was* ready to pay to have others read the advertisements that sold his products. As a result, a newspaper's circulation became a means to an end. Whatever its Jeffersonian role as a beacon of truth, in economic reality it existed in order to sell its readers to its advertisers. This in turn led to the paradox that newspapers became more beholden to their readers, who paid them little, than to their advertisers, who paid them fortunes. A newspaper that could rely on the loyalty of its readers discovered that it had a power greater than that which any individual advertiser could wield and a power great enough to turn away even a combination of advertisers. Editors could thus afford to flout or ignore the views of their advertisers, they could flout or ignore the wishes of government, but they ignored the views of their readers only at their peril.

The day was in sight when the popular press would learn the cynical trick of tailoring its news and trimming its views to cater for the vulgar prejudices of the largest possible mass of readers. Even the best of such newspapers can never lead or create public opinion, they exist simply to reflect it, and the worst of them merely pander to it. In doing so, they surrender their own integrity, and with it, much of their authority. Horace Greeley, who started all this, would appear at first sight to be a spectacular exception to his own rule. He disdained those who published only to sell, comparing them to parsons who only preach to fill the pews. He often stood out against the tide. He advocated unpopular causes. He was threatened with violence for the *Tribune*'s campaign against slavery, he railed against convention and resisted the orthodox. He rejected the old notion that a newspaperman's principles ought to be as 'negotiable as a promissory note', and of himself he once wrote:

> My critics evidently assume that I am a mere jumping-jack, who only needs to know what others think to insure my instant conformity – in short, that a journalist is no higher than a waiter at a restaurant expected to furnish whatever is called for.

For all his quirkiness and odd ideas, Greeley had an almost uncanny knack of earning the respect of his readers, his immense influence stemming from the manifest independence of his views. He wrote at a time when people were beginning to learn that *laisser faire* capitalism brought injustice and exploitation as well as wealth and power, when waves of economic depression were bringing distress and bankruptcies to decent hard-working farming folk, when Marx was declaring that the proletariat had nothing to lose but its chains and Europe was convulsed by revolution. Greeley had a panacea for every ill and it gave him an almost reverential following in the small towns and cities of America. His formula of domestic news mixed with homespun philosophy proved to be a phenomenal success, not only in New York but in the rural States across the Appalachians, where the weekly edition of the *Tribune* became known as the Bible of the Mid-West, 'doing all the farmers' thinking for them', in Emerson's patronising phrase, and for a subscription of only $2 a year.

The paradox was that Greeley's early years as a journalist had been anything but independent. In fact, he had spent most of them as a mercenary in the service of the Whig Party, then strong in New York under its political boss, Thurlow Weed, and the State governor, William H. Seward, later to become President Lincoln's secretary of state. But Greeley was never at ease in a subordinate role, and the politicians he worked for found him mercurial, obstreperous and unreliable. He became an influence in the land only when he started up on his own. He still supported the Whigs, but in doing so from a manifestly independent base he immediately acquired an authority that no paid hack could ever hope to match.

The *Tribune* was founded partly on his own savings, partly on borrowed money, and Greeley launched its first edition in April 1841 with a doleful account of the funeral of President Harrison, who had died of a chill caught at his own inauguration. He had to give away a good proportion of the 5,000 copies he had printed, but before long the *Tribune* caught on, holding up a mirror to the world, at once a political paper and a family paper, a paper with an eye on its profits and a dedication to reform – 'Anti-Slavery, Anti-War, Anti-Rum, Anti-Tobacco, Anti-Seduction, Anti-Grogshops, Brothels, Gambling Houses' – though profits triumphed over ethics when it came to accepting advertisements for cancer cures and disreputable playhouses. Nor did its high-minded slogan against 'seduction' prevent it reporting the lurid details of a double rape on Broadway. So long as they were prefaced by suitable expressions of horror, Greeley's nose for news got the better of his sense of propriety and such stories became one of the ingredients that made the *Tribune* so successful. But above all, it was the fact that the *Tribune* stood for progress and an optimistic belief in American values that most appealed to its aspiring and pioneering readers.

Greeley spent each day in the office from noon until midnight, reading every word that went into his paper, scolding, chiding, and railing at his staff in his high piping voice, writing his own articles standing up at a painted pine desk, paste always at hand, a pair of scissors dangling from his belt and a pile of cuttings in a hatbox by his side. Once in a while, the staff would find him curled up asleep on a pile of old newspapers – though not very often, for his energy was inexhaustible. And just as he imposed his engaging and eccentric personality on the office, he imposed it also on his readers and on the nation.

It did not seem to matter that his nostrums were often a bundle of contradictions; they were expressed in such pungent language they came over as nuggets of plain common sense, with a turn of phrase as memorable as Cobbett's. During the Mexican wars, he was a pacifist who described armies as 'journeymen throat-cutters'. But when the Civil War broke out, he was the first to

cry, 'Forward to Richmond!'. He criticised the labour laws as an infringement of
the employer's freedom, but later damned it as a freedom 'so extreme that those
who have no shoes are at perfect liberty to go barefoot'. He was a follower of the
idealist French philosopher Fourier, who advocated organised labour communes,
yet he could say, 'you may praise the Dignity of Labour until doomsday without
making a bootblack's calling as honourable as that of an engineer'. He employed
the best-educated editorial staff in New York, yet thought that 'of all horned
cattle, a college graduate in a newspaper office is the worst'. The *Tribune* carried
tobacco advertising, while its editor regarded cigars as 'a fire at one end and a
fool at the other'. He believed sincerely in extending the rights of women, yet
regarded the idea of female suffrage as 'preposterous'. And when it came to free
speech, Greeley told a friend, progress was best served by open discussion and
full exposition, rather than by suppression and concealment. But this did not
mean the paper always printed both sides of an argument, or that its obstinate,
didactic editor was above occasionally distorting the news to suit his own views or
letting his devotion to truth stand in the way of a moral good. Challenged once
about the report of a strike he had doctored, he replied testily, 'Well, I don't
want to encourage those lawless proceedings'.

To Andrew Johnson he came across as a holy fool, 'a sublime old child', to
others he had 'zeal, untempered by prudence', but for almost three decades he
held his readers in his spell, a champion of the masses who had risen from their
own ranks. To the new settlers in the west, Horace knew everything. They
thought he wrote every word of the *Tribune* himself, and when he went on his
tours they were apt to come up to him after a lecture in Oshkosh or Kalamazoo
in order to enquire when their subscriptions ran out.

His flaw as a journalist – and it was to prove a fatal one – was that he was never
content with his influence as an editor and propagandist. He had an itch for
public office that as the years went by grew into an all-consuming passion. Not
content with exercising the privilege of free speech as an observer, or as a
commentator and persuader looking on from the outside, he wished also to
guide affairs from the inside. It is a temptation to which later press barons have
succumbed, though the combination has never been successful. A newspaperman who seeks high office at once loses his most precious asset as a
journalist – his editorial independence. He is bound to betray either his readers
or his electors. A few have successfully made the transition, though only by
leaving their earlier career behind. Greeley thought he could carry out both
roles at once, and in the end the attempt destroyed him.

Ever since he arrived in New York he had played a prominent part in Whig
politics. In 1848, he ran for office himself and spent a single term in Washington
as a US Congressman. But his reporter's instincts got the better of him and he
began a campaign in the *Tribune* against the scandal of the 'mileage elongators' –
a practice, then almost universal, for Congressmen to claim they had travelled to
town by the most circuitous route possible, when they had in fact come direct.
The *Tribune* published tables showing the mileage actually claimed by each
member, and the amount he should have claimed. The total came to many
thousands of dollars, and even Congressman Abe Lincoln was shown to have
pocketed nearly $700 more than he ought to have done. It was a first-class news

story and the *Tribune* made the most of it. But it destroyed Greeley's career as a congressman. 'I have divided the House into two parties,' he wrote to a friend, 'one that would like to see me extinguished and the other that wouldn't be satisfied without a hand in doing it.' Every time he rose to speak he was shouted down as a demagogue, and there was talk of impeachment and expulsion for a breach of the House's privilege. They came to nothing, but when his two-year term was over he was not invited to stand again. He went back to the *Tribune*, developed the use of the telegraph to speed up delivery of the news and sent a reporter out to cover the western gold rush.

By the mid-1850s he had broken with the Whigs and under his guidance the *Tribune* helped to bring together the disparate strands of opinion that made up the modern Republican Party, endorsing the dashing young explorer John Fremont in the election of 1856 under the slogan,

> Free Speech, Free Press,
> Free Soil, Free Men,
> Fre-mont and Victory!

But James Buchanan went on to win the White House, and as the nation drifted towards civil war the pacifist Greeley dithered between letting the southern States secede and virulent anti-slavery. The decisive moment came with the Supreme Court's judgement in the Dred Scott case, where a runaway slave was denied his freedom on the grounds that his master had been deprived of his property without due process of law. No wonder old Chief Justice Taney had delivered the court's majority opinion in an almost inaudible voice, Greeley wrote in the *Tribune*. For 'however feeble his voice might have been, what he had to say was still feebler'. Downright and barefaced falsehood was the judgement's main staple. 'Any slave-driving editor or Virginia bar-room politician could have taken the Chief Justice's place on the bench,' he said, 'and with the exception of a little bolder speaking up nobody would have perceived the difference.'

The *Tribune* hammered away at the moral viciousness of the Dred Scott decision for months to come, bringing the wrath of the south down upon Horace Greeley, a man, said Sam Houston, 'whose hair is white, whose skin is white, whose eyes are white, whose clothes are white, and whose liver is in my opinion of the same colour'. The *Tribune's* editorials did almost as much as the decision itself to define the differences which five years later turned the States against each other.

When the Civil War came, Greeley was as quixotic as ever. The once-pacifist *Tribune* cried 'Forward to Richmond!' the rash cry that helped to bring on the Union's early military disasters. Afterwards, Greeley prodded Lincoln towards emancipation, but then earned enormous unpopularity throughout the north by running a campaign to free the imprisoned rebel leader, Jefferson Davis. The effect on the *Tribune* was catastrophic – showing once again that no newspaper can afford to cross its loyal readers in however worthy or courageous a cause. Greeley's well-meaning attempt to heal the breach between the States brought him to the edge of bankruptcy; the result, said Andrew Johnson, of running 'to goodness of heart so much as to produce infirmity of mind'.

But the hatreds gradually subsided, and Greeley felt vindicated as he watched the Grant administration sink into corruption, the wounds of war unhealed and the south exploited by ruthless northern carpetbaggers. By the 1870s, the old itch was back and Greeley yearned again for office. Through an odd combination of circumstances and the lack of any suitable alternative, his supreme ambition was fulfilled: after six ballots in their convention at Cincinnati in 1872 the new Liberal Whigs nominated him to run for president on a platform of reconciliation with the south, free land in the west and a railroad link to the Pacific. A month later, the Democrats adopted him as their candidate too, hoping cynically that even yet 'a crooked stick might beat a mad dog'.

Greeley at once resigned as editor of the *Tribune* and threw himself into the campaign with his usual innocent fervour, but it was a hopeless quest, and in his heart he knew it was. Cruel cartoons mocked his ambition, then his queer, cantankerous wife fell ill of dropsy and Greeley had to leave the campaign trail to tend her as she died. He buried her on election eve and wrote to a friend, 'I am not dead, but I wish I were. My house is desolate, my future dark, my heart a stone.' The next day he went down to a crushing defeat at the polls, and a week later returned to the *Tribune*, worn out in mind and body, though still hoping to pick up the reins he had relinquished 'on embarking on another line of business six months ago'. But through his neglect the *Tribune* was now in decline, its type old, its presses worn out, its Dickensian warren of offices on the verge of tumbling down, its authority gone. Greeley had made the cardinal journalistic error of using his paper as a footstool to public office. He had learned the hard way that the liberty of the press can never cohabit with the exercise of power. One cannot be both the gadfly and the thoroughbred horse it is meant to goad into action.

He did not have long to reflect on this melancholy lesson. By the time he got back to the *Tribune*, Greeley was losing his grip on reality. 'I stand naked before my God,' he wrote in one last frenzied cry, 'the most utterly, hopelessly, wretched and undone of all who ever lived.' And he begged God to take him from a world in which all he had done had turned to evil. He was put into a private asylum rambling incoherently, and before November was over, he was dead of despair. He had created no empire and left no dynasty – seven of his nine children had predeceased him – and his end had been tragic. Before long the influence of the *Tribune* would be overtaken by that of Raymond's staid grey *New York Times*, which dedicated itself to 'all the news that's fit to print,' and grew to become one of the great newspapers of the world. Greeley's legacy was less tangible, though no less influential. He had brought free speech to the masses.

C.P. SCOTT'S *MANCHESTER GUARDIAN*

Good journalism takes many forms. All of them flow from a spirit of independence, a belief in free speech and an editor of character and courage. John Delane established the primacy of hard news. Horace Greeley invented the popular crusading newspaper. After their deaths a hitherto obscure provincial daily showed the importance of newspapers as a moral force. C.P. Scott, editor of the *Manchester Guardian* for fifty-seven years, can be acclaimed without irony as 'the man who made righteousness readable'. High-minded as any bishop, serious as any judge, Scott took to journalism with a stern sense of duty to his readers, to the community, and above all to the truth. He was the author of the most famous of all newspaper aphorisms, 'comment is free, but facts are sacred'. He wrote that at the peril of its soul a newspaper must see that its supply of news is not tainted; 'neither in what it gives, nor in what it does not give, must the unclouded face of Truth suffer wrong'. Comment, too, was justly subject to a self-imposed restraint. It was as well to be frank; it was even better to be fair.

When it came to moulding public opinion, Scott had no peer. When it came to gathering the facts on which those opinions rested, the *Guardian* was – and has remained – less reliable than some of its more prosaic rivals. For all his long years in the editor's chair, 'CPS' was not much interested in news for its own sake. When the *Manchester Guardian*'s correspondent rode with the column of British soldiers that relieved the siege of Mafeking, his exclusive eye-witness account of the most dramatic news story of the decade was despatched by sea mail in order to save the cost of a telegram. Scott himself drove his news editor to distraction by withholding stories he had been handed privately. 'That's not news,' he remarked of an item reporting the impending resignation of a cabinet minister, 'I knew it a fortnight ago.' He even omitted to tell the paper of a cabinet rift over the 1914 navy estimates on the grounds that the chancellor had sought his advice personally – a case, wrote a colleague, where comment was free, but facts were evidently taboo.

In the view of at least one distinguished editor, Scott's unconscious denigration of his reporters helped to reduce the quality and independence of a good deal of essential news-gathering – a mistake never made by the American press, where the greatest journalists have always been proud to think of themselves, and describe themselves by, the honourable title of reporter.

It was not for its exclusive disclosures or its well-organised news service that the *Manchester Guardian* grew to fame. It was for the unique sense of moral authority bestowed on it by C.P. Scott, a journalist regarded by President Woodrow Wilson as 'one of Europe's great men'. He was an editor with the courage of his convictions, ready to stand against the popular tide if he had to, even when it brought his paper into obloquy, and on one occasion to the brink of bankruptcy. He might drive his staff to distraction, but he always commanded their affectionate loyalty, even when he was at his most exasperating. Seeing his editor pass him in the street on his famous upright bicycle, white hair flying in the wind, the *Manchester Guardian*'s obituary writer shook a sorrowful head and muttered, 'There he goes, the silly old bugger. And not a word written about him'.

Charles Presley Scott was born in 1846, the eighth child of a family whose ancestors had been 'zealous in the cause of Protestant Dissent and Civil and Religious Liberty'. Educated at a minor Oxford college – the major ones did not take dissenters – he was engaged at the age of twenty-four as a leader writer on the *Manchester Guardian* by his cousin, John Edward Taylor, who owned it. A year later, he was invited to become its editor and grew a beard to give him authority over staff who in some cases had worked for the paper since before he was born.

Until Scott became editor, the *Manchester Guardian* had been a conventional provincial paper of a moderate Whig tendency, founded in the 1820s to serve the fastest growing city in the north, but which did not yet have its own Member of Parliament. When that was put right in the Reform Act of 1832, reporters from the provinces were still not allowed into the House of Commons press gallery and the *Manchester Guardian* had to buy in its Parliamentary reports from London newspaper reporters, who, with the connivance of the Serjeant-at-Arms, operated what was in effect a profitable black market. Stamp Duties were another handicap the provincial press had but recently overcome. It was only with their final abolition in the 1860s that the *Manchester Guardian* was able to compete at last on equal terms with its great London rival, *The Times*.

Like Greeley, Scott had the gift of attracting and nurturing talent, and soon after he arrived the *Manchester Guardian* acquired a reputation for good writing, intelligent reviews and a civic pride in Manchester as northern capital of the arts, music and the theatre. It took longer to find its political voice, which sounded in earnest only after the ruling Liberal Party split over the issue of Irish Home Rule in 1886. As Gladstone's government fell and the country swung sharply to the right, the *Manchester Guardian* moved equally decisively to the left. The conversion was slow and often painful, but by the time Irish Home Rule went down to defeat the *Manchester Guardian* had moved from cool scepticism to warm advocacy, Scott converted by his own correspondent's warning that 'either Ireland must be free or else she must be more thoroughly conquered than ever'. Scott concluded there and then that whatever the disadvantages of Home Rule they were far outweighed by the evils of the alternative.

The *Manchester Guardian* now became the radical conscience of the north. In the dock strikes, the pit strikes and the engineering lock-outs of the 1880s and 1890s, Scott stood firm for the workers' cause. On women's suffrage too, Scott took a radical line. But it was his opposition to the wave of jingoistic fervour that led Britain into the Boer War that brought him to the test. Britain was then at the height of her imperial glory and Scott's opposition to its darker aspects brought down a storm of hatred that nearly killed the paper. The events began in 1898 when General Kitchener's forces annihilated an army of Dervish tribesmen at the Battle of Omdurman, notable as the occasion of the last cavalry charge in military history. Afterwards, the *Manchester Guardian* discovered that Kitchener had ordered the Mahdi's tomb to be opened, his body thrown to the crocodiles and his severed head sent in a crate to Cairo en route for London. The outrage which greeted the news was directed not at the author of the barbarous act but at those who had reported it. 'How bitterly I regret that you did not give me some note of warning as to the way in which the public would take it,' wrote the mild Oxford don persuaded by Scott to write a critical article on the affair.

But this was as nothing next to the storm which broke over the paper when it exposed the shameful treatment of the defeated enemy, whose wounded were left untended on the battlefield, their dead looted and many who were still alive shot or bayonetted where they lay. The atrocities were subsequently confirmed by young Winston Churchill in his eye-witness account of the battle in *The River War*, but it was against the pacifist *Manchester Guardian* that the public's wrath was directed, its charge that British soldiers had killed wounded men begging for quarter excoriated as a slur on the nation's honour that fell not far short of treason.

While the *Manchester Guardian*'s allegations were substantially true, the paper found it difficult to prove them, having fallen into its old habit of relying too much on second-hand sources, and too little on direct enquiry. Quotations from others are no substitute for a professional eye-witness account from its own reporters, however well its sub-editors presented them. The trouble was compounded when Scott succumbed to Horace Greeley's itch for active politics and spent much of his time away in London serving as an MP. Though he never accepted office and afterwards claimed that his spell as an MP had given him fresh insights as a journalist, his absence from the helm at a crucial period for the paper added to the impression that the *Manchester Guardian*'s approach to the gathering of hard news could sometimes seem amateur.

No one could doubt its courage, though, or its commitment to radical causes. In 1899, when the London press were almost without exception rabidly in favour of going to war with the Boers in South Africa, the *Manchester Guardian* stood alone against it. It took all of Scott's constancy – and Taylor's backing – to stick to a line that grew ever more unpopular as the war-fever grew. Shaky as ever on its reporting and parsimonious in its spending on telegrams, the *Manchester Guardian* won no prizes for its news stories from the war zone, but its analysis was steadfast, cool, and immensely well-informed. At a time when all of the South African papers and many of those in London were controlled by imperialist speculators like Cecil Rhodes, the channel was very narrow through which news that was hostile to this lobby could reach England. The chronicler of the *Manchester Guardian* wrote that even if the paper had been wrong in its facts and its diagnosis 'it would have served the public interest in asserting the freedom of the press – not from official "doctoring" or, as yet, from censorship – but from the power of great capitalists.' In the paper's own words, 'the mischief of it is that though nine plain men out of ten feel rightly when they see plainly, it is the hardest thing in the world to make them see plainly when it is in the interest of a very strong and rich party that they should not see at all'. Scott took it upon himself to ensure that Manchester readers, at least, should be given the chance to see plainly. England had made a promise to respect the independence of the Transvaal; all that stood in the way of the Transvaal's annihilation was the desire of Englishmen to keep that promise.

But the promise was broken, and when war came, the *Manchester Guardian* switched from criticism of its objectives to even more unpopular criticism of the methods by which the war was waged – from the mass evictions of the Boers and the burning of their farms to the building of concentration camps for their displaced inhabitants. The paper's attacks on 'the methods of barbarism' split the Liberal Party almost in two, the London press was universally hostile and police had to be called to protect the paper's staff as they arrived for work. None deserted, even in 'the darkest days when to be a *Guardian* man was to be labelled an enemy of one's country, a pro-Boer'.

To many, Scott himself seemed to have taken leave of his senses. A respected neighbour wrote that he was breaking off friendly relations since 'the course which you took respecting Mr Gladstone's proposals for Home Rule, and still more the course which you have taken respecting the controversy about education, and most of all the course which you have taken about the Transvaal War, force me to believe that either political life has partly deprived you of reason or that you have preferred the supposed advantage of a political party to the good of the country'. There was no respite when the owner of the main Liberal paper in London, the *Morning Chronicle*, took fright at the drop in sales and ordered his editor to support the war. The *Chronicle*'s editor, H.W. Massingham, resigned with almost the whole of his staff, many of them taking refuge in Manchester, where the *Guardian*'s chief leader writer offered to share his salary with his displaced opposite number. By this time, the *Guardian* itself was under siege, losing one seventh of its readers and seen to be in such trouble that rivals hired a brass band to parade around its headquarters in Cross Street playing the 'Dead March' from *Saul*.

The nadir came when the paper's only remaining correspondent in South Africa was discovered to have taken money to do public-relations work for a Dutch-owned railway company – a gift to the jingo press in London who used it to throw doubt on the *Manchester Guardian*'s exposure of the concentration camps. Northcliffe's *Daily Mail* carried the story under the headline 'How the pro-Boer Press was Hoodwinked'. Right though it had been about the concentration camps, the *Manchester Guardian* felt betrayed, writing of its own correspondent that he had committed a grave offence against the code of honour with which its journalism was governed and which in the court of his own conscience he could not be acquitted. The damage to the paper was, without doubt, severe. 'We must remember,' the general manager wrote to Scott, 'that of about a hundred and fifty thousand daily readers some sixty or seventy thousand are Conservatives and others are Liberals who are in favour of the war or at least less opposed to it than the *Guardian*.' To be unpopular in what seemed to be a wrong cause could lead only to disaster.

But the editorial staff stuck by their story, and as time went by it became not only clear that it was true but that thousands of women and children had died in the camps of hunger and disease. Using great skill and ingenuity to decipher the official mortality figures, the *Manchester Guardian* wrote at the close of 1901:

> Take the population of greater Manchester roughly at a million. In a year, at the rate of camp mortality, there would be in this area 250,000 deaths. Every day there would be about 680 funerals. The deaths would outnumber the births by about nine to one, and everywhere in a few months there would be houses standing empty . . .

Britain had blundered into a crime against humanity. But only the *Manchester Guardian* and a few radical MPs found the courage to say so. The paper stood vindicated, though at a grievous cost to its prosperity. Unpopular because of its stand against the war, facing fierce competition from the new ½d press, and struggling against an economic depression, it hovered for several years on the brink of bankruptcy. Then in 1905 John Edward Taylor died, leaving a will of extraordinary vagueness. After complicated legal manoeuvres, Scott risked his entire family fortune to buy the paper outright, and served until his retirement in 1929 as the chief proprietor, governing director and editor. He worked for a fixed salary, was paid no dividends and ploughed all the profits back into the paper to ensure that it operated as a public service.

The Taylor family accused Scott of running the paper 'as a hobby and not purely upon a commercial basis', but after his experience in the Boer War the new proprietor knew very well that the paper could fulfil its public service role only if it stood on sure foundations. 'A newspaper has two sides to it,' he wrote. 'It is a business, just like any other business, carried on for profit and depending on profit for prosperity or existence.' He would never sacrifice the paper's integrity in order to ensure its commercial success and had shown that over issues like Irish Home Rule and the Boer War he would rather face extinction than surrender his principles. Yet he never neglected the paper's trading position nor deceived himself that a newspaper could sustain its independence 'on the charity of a rich man or the favour of a political party'. As well as a great editor, Scott was a thrifty man of business, and through the careful accumulation of his reserves he was eventually able to buy the profitable *Manchester Evening News*, which became a useful buffer against the years when the high-minded *Manchester Guardian* might run again into deficit.

He took the paper reluctantly through the First World War – 'I am strongly of opinion that the war ought not to have taken place and that we ought not to have become party to it,' he wrote to a friend, 'but once in it the whole future of our nation is at stake and we have no choice but to do the utmost we can to ensure success.' He played his part in the manoeuvres which led Lloyd George to succeed Asquith as prime minister, though all-out war was not a notable time for the exercise of free speech, nor for independent-minded journalism. But it meant more work for Scott since his chief leader writer, C.E. Montague, had dyed his silver hair and enlisted in the Sportsmen's battalion at the age of forty-seven – a man, it was said, whose hair had turned black with courage. By the time the war was over, Scott was turning out 117 long leaders a year, a figure that rose in 1920 to 123.

In his seventies by this time, he was still whizzing dangerously bareheaded around the streets of Manchester on his upright bicycle. Returning home one night after putting the paper to bed, he had to explain to a watchman that he had been kept late at his work. The watchman, he reported, was properly indignant at such treatment of old age. It was not until he was over eighty that Scott yielded to the remonstrances of his friends and kept his bicycle for the daylight. To the end, his life was simple and Spartan, starting every morning with a cold bath; in middle age he had endured the loss of his wife with a dignified stoicism, living like Delane and Greeley almost wholly for his paper. 'What a work it is!' he once exclaimed. 'How multiform, how responsive to every need and every incident of life! What illimitable possibilities of achievement and of excellence!' He made sure the *Manchester Guardian* kept up with the times, though he characteristically referred to the products of Hollywood as the kinema, insisting on the 'k' because that is how the Greeks would have spelled it.

He would arrive in the office around 6 p.m. and hand over to a messenger two eggs, salt wrapped in a screw of paper, milk and sometimes an apple. Then, as one of his successors, W.P. Crozier tells it, 'no interruption, no visitor, no office conference was allowed to delay the sacred task of fixing for the night the subject of the Long,' – the main leading article – 'the prime instrument of policy, the voice, persuasive or protestant, for whose utterance more than for any other single purpose, he believed the paper to exist'. An American visitor who once called in at the office wrote 'his secretary, thinking that I was wanting to talk with Scott personally, said in a tone of horrified remonstrance, "But he's *writing*," and I knew that Scott writing was not more to be interrupted than the Bishop of London at prayers.'

Not for him the conception of the new press barons that it was their papers' business to reflect public opinion not to direct it. To C.P. Scott, as Montague wrote,

> to exploit popular ignorance, to play up to the vices or weaknesses of half-formed characters and half-filled minds would have seemed a policy no more worth considering than a policy of living on the proceeds of disorderly houses. With eyes perfectly open to the new forces at work in journalism, he determined to maintain his previous course and endeavour only the more resolutely to give the public, not what it was currently rumoured to desire, but what he believed to be true.

It was a policy that gave him an influence and authority far beyond the reach of those cynical manipulators of opinion who counted their circulation, not in thousands, as he did, but in millions.

He wrote in a plain, muscular style of English, without much beauty or wit, but always with an immense power, and a prescience that on reading it more than eighty years later can be startling, as in this leader on the British policy towards Ireland written in 1918, the terrible answer to which is with us to this day:

> The constitutional party in Ireland is dead; more than any man, Mr Lloyd George has helped to kill it. Now he is faced by a dire problem. By the ordinary law, Ireland is now ungovernable, and, unless by some supreme act of statesmanship aid be forthcoming, she is likely to remain permanently and increasingly ungovernable. But from Mr George, it is to be feared, we can look for no such act. Nothing in his recent career suggests the remotest hope of it. What then?

Such writing brought him a reputation that had spread far beyond Manchester and the north of England. Over the whole world, the *Manchester Guardian* was now looked upon as a moral force; a paper which, in the words of J.L. Hammond, was guided, whether it went right or wrong, whether it praised or blamed, by a large view and not a small view, by generous and not a narrow spirit, by a desire to treat truth as the first need of good politics, valued for a quality that men prized more as they missed it more.

Scott's weakness as a journalist was his disdain for hard news and his view that the leader writer, the creator of opinion, was more worthy than the reporter, the purveyor of the facts on which opinion must rest. For all that newsgathering was a blind spot, Scott's conception of the role of a free press was as consistent as it was clear-headed. In the words again of C.E. Montague, without any skill in the study of his readers' prejudices, with unfashionable policies and a cold side to the strongest emotions of crowds, he pursued his own slowly chosen and frankly declared line in total indifference to what people might say about it or about him. And yet the further he went the more influence did he gain over those to whom he made so few concessions, so strong is the instinctive feeling – in England at any rate – that the friend who in all friendliness and for no worldly motive, will withstand you to your face must be worth listening to anyhow.

Free speech and the liberty of the press has had no more upright a champion.

CHAPTER FOURTEEN

'A Clear and Present Danger'

SCHOLAR, SOLDIER, JUDGE

In 1867, a few years before his death, John Stuart Mill received a letter of introduction from a well-known American author, Dr Oliver Wendell Holmes, recommending his eldest son as 'a presentable youth with fair antecedents and more familiar with your writings than most fellows of his years'. Mill was then at the height of his fame, having laid down the abiding principles of free speech with an unmatched moral authority – though failing to define with sufficient clarity what its limits should be. His young American visitor, Oliver Wendell Holmes Jnr, was to spend a long lifetime in the law trying to discover those limits. In doing so, he made as important a contribution to the theory of free speech as Milton or Mill himself.

Sixty-three years later, when Mr Justice Holmes stepped down from the Supreme Court of the United States at the age of ninety-one, he was acclaimed as the guardian of the first amendment and the author of legal opinions which had become classics in the literature of the law. 'This is how to stop,' wrote the journalist Walter Lippmann, 'with every power used to the full, like an army resting, its powder gone but with all its flags flying. Here is the heroic life complete.'

Holmes was born a Boston Brahmin, a phrase coined by his father to describe his own circle of Bostonian friends, among them Henry and William James, Henry Adams, Ralph Waldo Emerson and the poet Henry Wadsworth Longfellow. Like Mill, the junior Oliver Wendell Holmes learned Greek and Latin early in life, and on the eve of his ninetieth birthday was still reading Thucydides, in order, he said, to freshen up his mind. Born in 1841 soon after the election of the ill-fated President Harrison, Holmes spent his youth in the then genteel heart of Boston, a city still dominated by the descendants of the Puritan settlers who had come to Massachusetts two centuries earlier. The future Justice of the Supreme Court went on to study at Harvard College, where initially he read philosophy. He graduated in the Class of '61, which he would describe as one of the two most powerful influences of his life.

The other formative experience followed almost immediately. Together with forty-seven of his classmates, Holmes went off later that same summer to fight for the Union in the Civil War, enlisting as a lieutenant in the 20th Massachusetts Volunteers – which at once became known as the Harvard Regiment. Ten of his classmates never came back, and Holmes himself was seriously wounded on three separate occasions. In the skirmish at Ball's Bluff, on the banks of the Potomac, he was hit by a sharpshooter's Minnie ball, which passed between his lung and his heart, nearly killing him. He had been in action for only one month. After a winter's convalescence at home in Boston, he was back in action in the spring of 1862, taking part in McClellan's disastrous Peninsula campaign against the Confederalists' capital at Richmond. In the battle of Antietam Creek, his regiment found itself outflanked by the rebel army. During a bloody retreat, the 21-year-old Holmes, now a captain, was shot through the neck by a bullet, which narrowly missed both his aorta and his windpipe. Summoned by telegram, the elder Holmes set out for Virginia in search of his wounded son, incidentally noting on his travels the 'soft, sallow, succulent, delicately finished' mouths of southern women, which he found 'quite distinguishable from our New England pattern'. After scouring hospitals, churches, camps and private homes through three States and hundreds of miles, Dr Holmes finally found his son embarked on a hospital train travelling north from Hagerstown.

'How are you, Boy?'

'How are you, Dad?'

Such, said the elder Holmes, were 'the proprieties of life observed by us Anglo-Saxons of the nineteenth century, decently disguising those natural impulses that made Joseph weep aloud so that the Egyptians and the house of Pharaoh heard – nay, which had once overcome his shaggy old uncle Esau so entirely that he fell on his brother's neck and cried like a baby'.

The reticent father and son made their way home to Boston for a second convalescence, where Dr Holmes's 'white Othello' was tended by a 'semicircle of young Desdemonas'.* But he was back with his regiment in time for the Battle of Fredericksburg, in which his battered unit fought with Lee's Confederate Army from street to street, and cellar to cellar. By May, the Union Army had fallen back on Chancellorsville, commanded now by Ambrose Burnside, the general famously said to have placed his headquarters where his hindquarters ought to be.† It was here that the Confederate Army lost Stonewall Jackson, accidentally shot by his own pickets. It was here, too, that the Union Army suffered its worst defeat of the war, losing 17,000 dead and wounded men, among them Captain Oliver Wendell Holmes, whose heel was shattered by a piece of flying shrapnel, his third and final wound of the war.

His regiment went on to fight at Gettysburg, but Holmes was still recovering from his wounds, and so missed the decisive battle of the war. His father reported that his patient was 'very reasonably tractable, avoids stimulants, smokes *not* enormously, feeds pretty well, and has kept tolerably quiet until today'.

By the time his wound had healed, the war was over, though the memories of it grew increasingly precious and noble to him, and left him with a philosophy of life based on the value of courage, endurance and selfless sacrifice. The Civil War was America's formative experience, and nowhere is that experience better exemplified than in the speeches of Oliver Wendell Holmes. 'War, when you are at it, is horrible and dull,' he said. 'It is only when time has passed that you see that its message was divine.' Addressing a memorial day ceremony, he once declared:

---

* A 'white Othello' was Dr Holmes's term for an abolitionist.

† In the saddle.

If you have been on the picket line at night in a black and unknown wood, have heard the spat of bullets upon the trees, and as you moved have felt your foot slip upon a dead man's body; if you have had a blind fierce gallop against the enemy, with your blood up and a pace that left no time for fear . . . you know that man has in him that unspeakable somewhat which makes him capable of miracle, able to lift himself by the might of his own soul, unaided, able to face annihilation for a blind belief.

For the rest of his life, Holmes held to the soldierly virtues that had seen him through the war. What he lost were the fervent 'blind beliefs' that had impelled him to enlist in the army in the first place. More even than that, the experience caused him to lose his belief in all beliefs. After the war, the idea grew steadily in his mind that nothing led more certainly to violence than the inflexible attachment to an ideology.

His own certainties had dissolved even as he lay in hospital after the engagement at Ball's Bluff, watching his comrades dying around him and believing that he, too, had been mortally wounded. In the midst of an experience his previous life had not prepared him for, he calmly examined his own philosophy in order to discover if there was anything he might wish to revise. He found he had no need of a religious faith, nor did he draw comfort from the knowledge that he was dying in a noble cause. 'I am to take a leap in the dark,' he told himself. It was consolation enough to know he had done his military duty 'up to the hub'.

The experience led him to conclude that even the most strongly held beliefs can only ever be conditional. Ideas are not something solid and permanent, waiting to be discovered. They are a temporary and tentative response to particular circumstances, their survival dependent entirely on their adaptability to the environment in which they find themselves. It follows that ideas should never be allowed to become ideologies, used to impose an inflexible system of compliance on others. Later in life, such views gave Holmes a certain reputation for cynicism. It also profoundly affected his attitude towards the free speech cases that came his way while serving on the Supreme Court.

After his active life as a soldier, Holmes found plunging into the thick fog of the law a bewildering experience in which there were no flowers, no spring, and no easy joys. He added, 'one heard Burke saying that law sharpens the mind by narrowing it. One heard in Thackeray of a lawyer bending all the powers of a great mind to a mean profession. One saw that artists and poets shrank from it as from an alien world.' And yet, he found, the law was human – part of man, and of one world with all the rest.

In 1866, this already remarkable young man took his degree as a Bachelor of Laws and the following year made his visit to England where he met John Stuart Mill who, rarely for an Englishman, seemed to possess 'the democracy of intellect'. Holmes felt at home among the London intelligentsia, though he thought the old country ran 'more on its regrets than on its hopes'. On his return to Boston he was admitted to the bar, and practised briefly with his brother, Edward. But he soon abandoned casework in order to rejoin Harvard as a lecturer in constitutional law. He wrote for the *American Law Journal*, edited the classic edition of Kent's *Commentaries on American Law*, and by 1881 had written the definitive American work on *The Common Law*. At thirty-one, he married Fanny Dixwell, the daughter of his first Latin teacher, and embarked on what has been described as 'a fifty-six year honeymoon'. The pair became noted wits and conversationalists and enjoyed the high-spirited fun of running to fires together, a habit they kept up even after he was dignified as Mr Justice Holmes of the US Supreme Court and over sixty years old.

In 1882, faced with making a choice between a professor's chair at Harvard or elevation to the Supreme Court of Massachusetts, he chose – to the great chagrin of his college – to go to the bench. 'To *think* of it,' wrote Dr Holmes, who never lost a chance to deprecate his grown-up son – 'my little boy a Judge, and able to send me to jail if I don't behave myself!' The doctor's 'little boy' sat on the Supreme Judicial Court of Massachusetts for the next twenty years, the last three of them as Chief Justice, where he became famous for his witty and lucidly written judgements as well as for his wonderful searching eyes and dramatic white moustache. The life of the law was to him not logic, it was experience, and what he called 'the felt necessities of the time'. 'The law embodies the story of a nation's development through many centuries,' he wrote. 'It cannot be dealt with as if it contained only the axioms and corollaries of a book of mathematics.' His approach to the hundreds of cases he dealt with in Massachusetts was always worldly, always timely and always eclectic, but also aware that the degree to which the law was able to work out desired results depended very much on its past.

Then in 1902, the call came from President Theodore Roosevelt to join the Supreme Court of the United States. In his farewell address to his local bar association, Holmes spoke of his 'mighty joy' at being asked to help shape the laws of the entire country, adding, characteristically, that it spread over him the hush he used to feel forty years earlier on the eve of battle. 'We will not falter,' he said. 'We will not fail. We will reach the earthworks if we live, and if we fall we will leave our spirit in those who follow, and they will not turn back. All is ready. Bugler, blow the charge.'

Already over sixty years old, Mr Justice Holmes was to sit on the Supreme Court for another thirty years. Much of his early work was spent on the trust-busting cases of the day, and his great contribution to the legal definition of free speech came only after the United States had entered the First World War against Germany in 1917, when Congress began to enact a series of sedition laws which had uncanny parallels to the panic measures introduced under President John Adams more than a century earlier. But this time, the Supreme Court had found its voice. And that voice was increasingly that of Holmes who penned opinion after opinion in defence of the freedom of speech, the freedom of assembly – and the freedom of the press.

HOLMES'S SUPREME COURT

The court Mr Justice Holmes had joined was an institution unique in the western world, an élite and sometimes mysterious body set in a populist country, with a role in relation to the president like that of the Church to a medieval monarch. At once the guarantors of change and the guardians of tradition, its nine elderly judges needed to be not only jurists, but statesmen as well. In de Tocqueville's words, 'the peace and prosperity, and the very existence of the union are placed in the hands of the judges'. This made them a mightier judicial authority than any other tribunal known to man, both by the nature of their rights and by the categories subject to their jurisdiction. Without them, the constitution would be a dead letter; for it was to them that the executive appealed to resist the encroachments of the legislature, the legislature to defend itself against the assaults of the executive, the Union to make the states obey it, and the States to rebuff the pretensions of the Union. It was here that the public interest strove against the private, the spirit of conservation against the instability of democracy. The power of the nine judges was immense, said de Tocqueville, though it was a power that sprang entirely from opinion. So long as the people consented to obey the law, they were all-powerful; when they scorned it, the judges could do nothing.

The pattern had been set by the great John Marshall of Virginia who presided over the court from 1801 to 1835 and drew up the lines which strengthened the fledging central government against the States, furthered its growth, and protected the property rights of individuals. His successor, Roger Taney, who served for another thirty years, sought to redress the balance in favour of the States, ending with the disastrous Dred Scott decision, which, in upholding the legal ownership of slaves, helped to precipitate the Civil War. The long era which followed the war was primarily concerned with the regulation of commerce and defending the sanctity of property as the growing nation rapidly industrialised itself. The court became conservative and resistant to change and at one point even condemned the income tax as 'communistic in its purposes and tendencies'. By the time Holmes was summoned to the bench, the court had become identified with the protection of the rights of those Roosevelt called 'malefactors of great wealth,' the capitalist entrepreneurs who used the law to gather the industrial resources of the nation into their own hands. Holmes's appointment was intended, in part, to restore the balance.

Cases involving the constitutional right to free speech rarely came before the Supreme Court during the nineteenth century. This was in part because the Bill of Rights only placed limitations on its abridgement by Congress, and not by individual States. As early as 1833, Marshall's court had ruled that the Bill of Rights contains no expression indicating an intention to apply them to the State governments. Therefore, he said, 'this court cannot so apply them. It has no jurisdiction.'

Free speech judgements under the first amendment were, therefore, very rare. In those cases that did come before the court, it was asked to do little more than place obvious cases on one side of a line or another. 'They told us, for instance, that libel and slander were actionable, or even punishable, that indecent books were criminal, that it was contempt to interfere with pending judicial proceedings, and that a permit could be required for street meetings,' wrote the Professor of Law at Harvard University, Zechariah Chafee. They ruled, on the other hand, that some criticism of the government must be allowed, that a temperate examination of a judge's opinion was not contempt, and that honest discussion of the merits of a painting caused no liability for damages. But, says Chafee, 'when we asked where the line actually ran and how they knew on which side of it a given utterance belonged, we found little answer in their opinions.'

There were, therefore, practically no satisfactory precedents for the judges to go on when, in 1917, the United States entered the First World War on a wave of anti-German hysteria whipped up by improbable rumours. It was widely believed that 'submarine captains landed on our coasts, went to the theatre, and spread influenza germs; a new species of pigeon, thought to be German, was shot in Michigan; mysterious aeroplanes floated over Kansas at night', and a man changing the electric light bulb in his hotel room at the seaside was arrested on suspicion of sending signals to a lurking U-boat.

Public opinion demanded that something be done, and Congress duly passed the Espionage Acts of 1917 and 1918, with an amendment tacked on by the Senate, later called the Sedition Act, which would stamp out the printing, writing or utterance of statements deemed disloyal, profane, scurrilous or abusive of the government of the United States, its constitution, flag or military uniforms. Offenders were liable to twenty years' imprisonment, or a fine of $10,000, or both.

The acts have been excused on the grounds that they prevented patriotic lynch mobs taking the law into their own hands, though, as the historian of the acts has pointed out, twenty years in prison seems a queer sort of protection. The fact is that, in an echo of the anti-French panic of 1798, the measures, even if lawful on their face, were construed in ways that the first amendment had been designed to prevent.

Prosecutions followed almost as soon as the legislation had been enacted, some of the cases tragic, some merely comic, and almost all of them unnecessary. Not one of them can, with hindsight, lay claim to have rescued the United States from subversion, or to have saved its citizens from being seduced from their patriotic duty. The chief characteristics of the prosecutions which took place in this wave of xenophobic zeal were the trivial nature of the crimes that were alleged and the excessive severity of the sentences that were handed out. Over and again, people were sent to prison not for any overt criminal act, but for the utterance of words that a patriotic judge and jury thought might tend to injure the State. For the two years the acts were in force, America turned the clock back to the bad old days of Lord Justice Holt, who had decreed that words that diminished respect for the government must perforce be seditious.

One of the first cases to come to trial stopped the distribution of a movie about America's own revolution entitled *The Spirit of '76*. Produced by Robert Goldstein, who had collaborated with D.W. Griffiths in making the Civil War epic, *Birth of a Nation*, the movie contained reconstructions of Paul Revere's ride, the signing of the Declaration of Independence, and Washington's winter travails at Valley Forge. After its preview in Los Angeles, Goldstein was indicted on the grounds that one of the scenes portrayed British soldiers bayoneting American women and children in the so-called Wyoming Massacre. The court ruled that the scene was intended to arouse hatred and enmity between the United States and their British allies and 'to make us a little bit slack in our loyalty to Great Britain in this great catastrophe'. The film was seized, the business forced into bankruptcy, and Goldstein sentenced to ten years in the federal penitentiary for attempting to cause insubordination in the armed forces. In Montana, a man was charged with sedition for resisting the attempts of a mob to make him kiss the flag. 'What is this thing anyway?' he said of the hallowed stars and stripes. 'Nothing but a piece of cotton with a little paint on it and some other marks in the corner there. I will not kiss that thing. It might be covered in microbes.' He was convicted of using language calculated to bring the flag into contempt and sentenced to not less than ten years hard labour. A Vermont clergyman was sentenced to fifteen years in prison for distributing pacifist pamphlets that argued that it was wrong for a Christian to go to war. In other cases, it was judged illegal to argue that a referendum should have preceded America's declaration of war, or to discourage women from knitting by the remark, 'No soldier ever sees these socks'. D.H. Wallace, a former British soldier living in Iowa, was prosecuted for saying that when a soldier went away, he was a hero, but when he came back flirting with a hand-organ he was a bum. The asylums would be filled with them, he said, the soldiers were giving their lives for the capitalists, and 40 per cent of the allies' ammunition, or their guns, was defective, because of graft. The poor man was sentenced to twenty years in prison, where he died insane.

There are some 1,900 such cases on record, almost all of them leading to conviction and a savage sentence. Each one of them proved once again that, when popular passions are aroused, the old belief that juries would protect the right to free speech is an illusion. In his seminal study of the prosecutions, Professor Chafee has shown that so long as the war hysteria lasted, the human machinery of the law broke down. He quotes Judge C.F. Amidon of North Dakota saying that only those who had administered the Espionage Act could understand the danger of such legislation. When crimes were defined in generic terms, instead of by specific acts, the jury became the sole judge of whether men should, or should not, be punished. Most of the jurymen had sons in the war. They were all under the power of the passions which war engenders. Judge Amidon tells how he tried war cases before jurymen whom he had known for thirty years as candid, sober, intelligent businessmen, but who looked back into his eyes in court with the savagery of wild animals, saying, by their manner, 'Away with this twiddling, let us get at him'. The only verdict in a war case that could show loyalty was a verdict of guilty.

The result was a series of savage acts of vengeance worthy of England under the Six Acts. At least 11 persons went to prison for ten years, 6 for fifteen years, and 24 to twenty years, not counting more than 100 other unreported cases where the judges sent people to jail for the most trivial or inconsequential breaches of the act. Judge Van Valkenburgh summed up the bench's attitude when he said that freedom of speech meant the protection of criticism that was 'friendly to the government, friendly to the war, and friendly to the policies of the government'.

Once again, the freedom of speech and the rights supposedly enshrined in the first amendment had been put into the severest jeopardy by panic measures as ministers and judges were, in Mill's phrase, 'driven from their propriety'. As one district judge ruefully admitted when the delirium had passed, 'There was no conspiracy to overthrow the government and no evidence was ever produced which excused the action of the government. The safeguards of the constitution were ignored and any true American must blush at what was done and at the indifference in which he and all but a handful of his countrymen, tolerated it.'

The question now was whether the Supreme Court could redress the grievous damage that had been done. But with the war already fought and won, it seemed, in Professor Chafee's phrase, that the justices were being asked to bolt the doors of freedom after the Liberty Bell had been stolen. Nor were their judgements of much help to the hapless defendants since in case after case the Supreme Court upheld the original convictions. But tardy in correcting individual injustices though they were, the judgements they delivered would eventually set bounds to free speech which survived more or less intact for the following half century.

THE GREAT DISSENTER

It was Mr Justice Holmes who set the tone, aided by a new ally on the bench, the formidable jurist and intellectual, Louis Brandeis, appointed by President Woodrow Wilson in 1916 and destined to serve until the eve of the Second World War in 1939. At first, they were in a minority, and the verdict 'Holmes and Brandeis dissenting' became a byword. Brandeis was a genuine liberal, Holmes a pragmatist, but from their widely differing starting points their opinions usually converged on the same conclusion. In time, they won over the whole court, and their originally dissenting views are today enshrined in constitutional law. It has been said that the majority decided the cases, but the opinions of Holmes and Brandeis decided the future.

It was an alliance based on intellectual respect and mutual bantering affection. 'I am afraid Brandeis has the crusading spirit,' Holmes once told his secretary. 'He talks like one of those upward-and-onward fellows.' On another occasion, when the more earnest Brandeis sent him a crate of statistics he thought he ought to study, Holmes took one look at the box and told the deliveryman, 'Just nail it up and sent it right back to him.' Then, with a sigh of relief, he immersed himself again in Plato.

Ironically enough, the court's first judgements under the Espionage Acts happened to be unanimous. *Schenck v. the United States* was one of the rare cases where there had been an undisputed attempt to incite conscripts to resist the draft, a clear and dangerous interference with the right of Congress to raise armies. No real issue of free speech was at stake, but in expressing the unanimous verdict of the court, Holmes laid down for the first time the precepts that were to become universally followed in defining its bounds. In many places and in ordinary times the defendants would have been within their constitutional rights, Holmes said. But the character of every act depended on the circumstances in which it was done. When a nation was at war, many things that might be said in times of peace could not be endured. 'The most stringent protection of free speech would not protect a man in falsely shouting "fire!" in a crowded theatre and causing a panic,' he said, coining a still famous legal aphorism. 'The question in every case is whether the words used are used in such circumstances and are of such a nature to create a clear and present danger that they will bring about the substantive evils that Congress has a right to prevent. It is a question of proximity and degree.'

He would build on the phrase 'clear and present danger' in later judgements, until it became the main test – and for many years the only test – of when restrictions on free speech could be permitted. But he made it clear that the first amendment was not intended to give immunity to every possible use of language – 'we venture to believe that neither Hamilton nor Madison, nor any other competent persons, then or later, ever supposed that to make criminal the counselling of a murder would be an unconstitutional interference with free speech'.

The next case that came up involved the best known of all the defendants prosecuted under the Espionage Act, Eugene Debs, the leader of the American Socialist Party. Debs had run for president four times and in the election of 1912 had won 6 per cent of the vote in a race against Woodrow Wilson, William Howard Taft and Theodore Roosevelt. His party had gone on to oppose American intervention in the war and support the Bolshevik Revolution. Debs was arrested at a workers' rally in Canton, Ohio, after telling his listeners they were 'fit for something better than slavery or cannon fodder'. No soldiers were present at the rally. Not one word was said about the draft. Yet Debs was indicted by a federal grand jury for attempting to cause insubordination in the army. He was found guilty and sentenced to ten years in prison.

The Supreme Court were widely expected to overturn the conviction. Yet, for legal reasons, they felt unable to do so, Holmes once again concurring with the majority. It did not matter, he said, that Debs's opposition to American intervention in the war was just an incidental remark in a general plea for socialism. If its effect was to obstruct recruiting, it was not protected by the first amendment. As in other cases, it was a question of proximity and degree. In times of war, a little breath could be enough to kindle a flame.

Progressive opinion was shocked. 'So long as we apply the notoriously loose common law doctrines of conspiracy and incitement to offences of a political character, we are adrift in a sea of doubt and conjecture,' wrote Ernst Freund of the *New Republic*. 'To know what you may do and what you may not do, and how far you may go in criticism, is the first condition of political liberty. To be permitted to agitate at your own peril, subject to a jury's guessing at motive, tendency and possible effect makes the right of free speech a precarious gift.'

Holmes himself was much troubled by the judgement they had reached. Debs's talk had been almost innocent in its pattern of mild cant phrases, he thought, but was just enough to support conviction. 'Whether it was enough to justify putting into motion the complicated wheels of government machinery,' his secretary wrote, ' – ah! that was a different question, but a question which his New England conscience, his sense of human justice, could not shrug away.'

It was not the Espionage Acts which were unconstitutional, Holmes had concluded, it was the way they had been construed by the district judges. In Debs, that issue had again been unclear. He would therefore bide his time until a case came up so plainly wrong that he could give voice to his deepest thoughts about the right to free speech and the first amendment. Three months later, the case of Jacob Abrams gave him his opportunity. Then and thenceforth, he and Brandeis parted company with the majority of the court.

This time, the more repressive Sedition Act of 1918 was at issue, with its punitive sanctions against 'disloyal, profane, scurrilous, or abusive language about the form of government, the constitution, soldiers and sailors, flag or uniform of the armed forces'. The 29-year-old Abrams, a self-styled anarchist, was arrested under its provisions along with a group of young associates who had thrown hand-printed leaflets in English and Yiddish from the roof of a warehouse in New York City's Lower East Side. The leaflets protested in lurid language about the secret despatch of American troops to Russia in the summer of 1918 in an attempt to hinder the Bolshevik Revolution. Passers-by in Crosby Street were startled as the leaflets showered down on their heads, urging them to:

AWAKE! AWAKE, YOU
WORKERS OF THE WORLD!

The pamphlet told the people of America their president was too cowardly to come out openly and say the capitalist nations could not afford to have a proletarian republic in Russia. Instead, he lied to them, while secretly sending troops to crush the revolution. The puzzled passers-by were asked, 'Will you allow the Russian Revolution to be crushed? You: Yes, we mean you, the people of America!' The leaflet went on in this vein for several more paragraphs, and ended with a naive postscript: 'It is absurd to call us pro-German. We hate and despise German militarism more than do your hypocritical tyrants.'

Two army sergeants combed the building for the perpetrators of the outrage, eventually arresting six men and a woman, who all confessed. Four of them were indicted under the Sedition Act and tried in the New York Federal Court House, but under a judge from Alabama, a State, it was pointed out, where people were of one mind about the war, where Jewish immigrants were scarce, Bolshevism unknown and where the working class was more conspicuous for a submissive respect for law and order than for the criticism of high officials. Abrams, as the ringleader, was sent to prison for twenty years and fined $4,000, all he owned. The others also went to jail, one of them declaring, 'I did not expect anything better'. 'And may I add,' said the judge, 'that you do not deserve anything better.'

When they considered the case after the war, the Supreme Court again confirmed the savage sentences that had been handed down. Delivering the majority opinion, Mr Justice John Clarke of Ohio said the court had no power to revise the sentences. It could not lay aside the jury's verdict. It could merely correct any legal errors that had occurred. And these were not sufficiently serious to overturn the conviction. Clarke granted that the defendants' intent was to help Russia. This was not forbidden. But they had also called for a general strike. And this, if they had been successful, would have hindered the war effort. It would have persuaded people not to work in ammunition factories. The conviction must therefore stand.

Holmes, who had been profoundly troubled by the injustice of the long sentences, then delivered his first, and perhaps his greatest, dissent on the issue of free speech. Of course, he said, the anarchists' leaflet did urge the curtailment of production within the meaning of the statute. But the statute also required an intent to 'cripple or hinder the United States in the prosecution of the war', and he could not find that the intent had been proved. More important than this, though, was the principle of free speech protected by the first amendment.

He recalled his own test that speech could be punished when there was a 'clear and present danger', and more readily in time of war. But even in war, the principle was the same – there must be the present danger of immediate evil. In what he called 'the surreptitious publishing of a silly leaflet' he could find no such danger to the government. Even in wartime, Congress had no power to forbid all effort to change the mind of the country. He went on:

> In this case, sentences of twenty years imprisonment have been imposed for the publishing of two leaflets that I believe the defendants have as much right to publish as the government has to publish the Constitution of the United States now vainly invoked by them. Even if I am technically wrong and enough can be squeezed from these poor and puny anonymities to turn the colour of legal litmus paper, the most nominal punishment seems to me all that possibly could be inflicted, unless the defendants are to be made to suffer not for what the indictment alleges, but for the creed that they avow.

Writing these words, we are told by his secretary, Holmes felt his inadequacy to make them burn with the resentment and passionate conviction that he felt. The issue far transcended these three poor men,* so unimportant, and the girl, the victims of the hysteria of a war that had now been fought. It touched and tested the very experiment of life on which the American way, for which he had fought, and which he loved, was founded. He reached again for his pen and wrote of his deepest philosophical beliefs.

> Persecution for the expression of opinions seems to me perfectly logical. If you have no doubt of your premises or your power and want a certain result with all your heart you naturally express your wishes in law and sweep away all opposition. . . . But when men have realised that time has upset many fighting faiths, they may come to believe even more than they believe the very foundations of their own conduct that the ultimate good desired is better reached by free trade in ideas – that the best test of truth is the power of the thought to get itself accepted in the competition of the market, and that truth is the only ground upon which their wishes safely can be carried out. That at any rate is the theory of our constitution. It is an experiment, as all life is an experiment. Every year if not every day we have to wager our salvation upon some prophecy based upon imperfect knowledge. While that experiment is part of our system I think that we should be eternally vigilant against attempts to check the expression of opinions that we loathe and believe to be fraught with death, unless they so imminently threaten immediate interference with the lawful and pressing purposes of the war that an immediate check is required to save the country.

He ended by saying that he wholly disagreed with the argument that the first amendment left the common law as to seditious libel in force. 'History seems to

---

* One of the defendants had since died.

me against the notion. I had conceived that the United States through many years had shown its repentance for the Sedition Act of 1798, by repaying fines that it had imposed.' Only the emergency that made it immediately dangerous to leave the correction of evil counsels to time warranted making any exception to the sweeping command, 'Congress shall make no law abridging the freedom of speech.' 'Of course,' he concluded, 'I am speaking only of expressions of opinion and exhortations, which were all that were uttered here, but I regret that I cannot put into more impressive words my belief that in their conviction upon this indictment the defendants were deprived of their rights under the Constitution of the United States.'

Only Mr Justice Brandeis concurred with the great dissent, and by a vote of seven to two, the Abrams conviction was upheld. The four defendants stayed in jail until 1923, when President Harding used his powers of executive clemency to commute the sentences on condition that the defendants, who were all aliens, should embark at once for the Soviet Union, which they did. The Supreme Court had done nothing to overturn the injustice that had been done, and was still not ready to accept that the logic of Holmes's test of the need for 'clear and present danger' must *always* apply before free speech convictions could be upheld.

By now, Holmes had become known as the Great Dissenter, as in case after case the court upheld convictions under the Espionage Acts, Holmes and Brandeis always dissenting. Never had two so eminent judges had so little influence over the outcome of the cases they heard. But neither had dissenting voices ever had so profound an influence on shaping constitutional law for the future. Sometimes it was Holmes, and sometimes his younger colleague, who wrote their joint dissent, as they insisted again and again on the need for there to be a 'clear and present danger' before a conviction could be upheld.

The melancholy conclusion has to be that the first amendment's majestic command that 'Congress shall make no law abridging the freedom of speech', is reduced to a pious platitude if the courts decline to uphold it. As ever, the protection of free speech depends not merely on statements of law, but on the actions of men and women with the courage to defend it. The Supreme Court was shockingly careless of the right to free speech during the wave of wartime espionage cases it upheld, their reputation saved only by the long and lonely stand of Justices Holmes and Brandeis. They were the only ones who saw that free speech is more than an individual need; it is a social need, of importance to the entire community. As Professor Chafee so eloquently argued, free speech needs to be preserved in war even more than in peace, so that the fundamental issues of the struggle may be clearly and calmly defined by debate, the war aims kept under civilian control and not diverted to improper ends, or conducted with undue sacrifice of life and liberty, or prolonged after its just purposes are accomplished. That, at least, is the American belief, upheld by Justices Holmes and Brandeis and confirmed by experience from the Civil War through to Vietnam.

By the time the last espionage case had been cleared, Holmes was an old man. 'Cheer up, Wendell,' his wife told him on his eightieth birthday in 1921, 'it's going to get worse.' Neither can have foreseen he had another ten years to serve, and further battles for free speech still to fight. His faculties were unimpaired, and although he had stopped running to fires and had to take a nap in the afternoons, his capacity for work was undiminished, his sense of humour as dry as ever. He celebrated his birthday with a party for his staff, consuming some precious bottles of champagne sent to him as a gift before its prohibition under the eighteenth amendment. He told them, 'the eighteenth amendment forbids manufacture, transportation and importation. It does not forbid possession or use. If I send it back, I shall be guilty of transportation. On the whole, I think I shall apply the maxim of *de minimis*, and drink it.' And Fanny allowed him an extra cigar as he mused on his great age. 'I always thought when I got to fourscore, I could wrap up my life in a scroll, tie a pink ribbon around it, put it away in a drawer and go around doing the things I want to do. But I learned that when you have taken one trench, there is always a new firing line beyond.'

Life was painting a picture, not doing a sum, the greatest act of faith that of deciding you are not God. He read voraciously, with a taste for naughty French novels and the classics. He was so thrilled at discovering Dante that after reading the troubadour's line, '*jeu sui Arnaud, que plor e vau cantan,*' he declared, 'I had to rush out of doors to walk it off.'

He rose early, worked at home until half-past eleven, writing his opinions at a lectern, standing up. Then on conference days he set off to walk the 2 miles to Capitol Hill, where the court sat in the old Senate chamber, columned and draped in red velvet, but furnished more like a drawing room than a hall of justice. Here, with four pageboys sitting on a leather sofa to fetch water or cigars, the judges deliberated. And here, on Mondays, which was Decision Day, they solemnly read out their carefully crafted opinions.

The espionage cases were behind them, but after the war, a new bogey arose to haunt America: that of socialism, a creed that had already conquered Russia, was rampant throughout Europe and had even led to a brief period of Labour Party rule in Great Britain. Americans had an almost superstitious dread of the red menace, and Congress began to introduce repressive measures to stamp it out. Holmes, who had no more fear of sudden ruin than he had of immediate panaceas, was sceptical. Fear, he saw, was being translated into doctrines that had no proper place in the constitution, or in common law. Sure enough, it was not long before he was once again defending free speech against repressive legislation and disproportionate prosecutions.

The first case the court had to consider was that of a pamphlet advocating communism which was alleged to 'give you the creeps a little'. Benjamin Gitlow, the publication's business manager, was indicted under an archaic New York State law for advocating criminal anarchy. He was convicted in 1920 and sentenced to up to ten years hard labour.

When the appeal came to the Supreme Court in 1925, they could not consider it under the first amendment, which applies only to abridgements of free speech by Congress, and not by the individual States. But Holmes persuaded them that they were able to consider it under the fourteenth amendment, passed after the Civil War in order to speed up the emancipation of the former slaves, one clause of which prohibited the individual States from depriving any citizen of life or liberty without due process of law. One of those fundamental liberties was the freedom of speech, as defined in the Bill of Rights. It was a momentous decision, which cast the mantle of protection guaranteed by the first amendment over the acts of individual States. Its use by the Supreme Court led to intense legal controversy as lawyers argued the important questions of, first, whether the framers of the amendment had intended to incorporate the entire Bill of Rights in its 'due process of law' clause; and, secondly, whether the Supreme Court was entitled to apply the Bill of Rights to the States, *regardless* of the intention of the framers, in accordance with Mr Justice Holmes's celebrated 'felt necessities of the times'. The argument raged for over two generations, and has never wholly been resolved. But it did Benjamin Gitlow little good. Having decided they had jurisdiction over his case, the Supreme Court used it to uphold his conviction.

Holmes of course dissented. Brandeis again joined him. It was hard for anyone to tolerate the publication of such propaganda, they acknowledged, but unless they did so, they would not preserve the liberty to speak their own minds. Freedom was not about insignificances. To preserve it, there must be freedom to differ about things that are important. In voicing his dissent, Holmes's language was, as always, terse, lucid and to the point:

> It is said that this manifesto was more than a theory, it was an incitement. Every idea is an incitement. It offers itself for belief, and if believed it is acted on unless some other belief outweighs it or some failure of energy stifles the movement at its birth. The only difference between the expression of an opinion and an incitement in the narrower sense is the speaker's enthusiasm for the result. Eloquence may set fire to reason. But whatever may be thought of the redundant discourse before us it had no chance of starting a present conflagration. If in the long run the beliefs expressed in proletarian dictatorship are destined to be accepted by the dominant forces of the community, the only meaning of free speech is that they should be given their chance and have their say.

It has been said that the victories of free speech must be won in the mind before they can be won in the courts. In that battlefield of reason, the dissenting opinions of Holmes and Brandeis carved from a series of defeats a set of arguments worthy to stand beside those of Milton's *Areopagitica* or John Stuart Mill's *On Liberty*. Holmes's prescription of a 'clear and present danger' served the court for a further fifty years until it was superseded by an even clearer test. In striking down the conviction of a member of the Klu Klux Klan, the court laid down, in 1969, that speech can be suppressed only if it is intended and likely to produce 'imminent lawless action'. Otherwise, even speech that preaches violence is protected. This is the standard that prevails in America today.

AN HEROIC LIFE COMPLETE

Holmes's last years saw an inevitable and at the end a saddening diminution of his powers. But he faded away with immense dignity and spirit. Mrs Holmes died in 1929 at the age of eighty-eight, an event which he said not only took away half his life, but gave him notice. 'I bow my head,' he wrote to a friend. 'I think serenely, and I say as I told someone the other day, O Cosmos – now lettest thou thy ganglion dissolve in peace.' But he kept on working for a few more years, and delivered one last stinging dissent in favour of the liberty of conscience. The case involved a Hungarian-born pacifist, Rosika Schwimmer, who was refused American citizenship because she would not swear to bear arms to defend the constitution.

'So far as the adequacy of her oath is concerned,' Holmes remarked drily, 'I can hardly see how that is affected by the statement inasmuch as she is a woman of over fifty years of age, and would not be allowed to bear arms if she wanted to.' As to her opinions, she thoroughly believed in organised government and preferred that of the United States to any other in the world. Surely, it could not show any lack of attachment to the principles of the constitution that she thought it could be improved. 'I suppose the most intelligent people think it might be,' Holmes observed. 'Her particular improvement looking to the abolition of war seems to me not materially different in its bearing on this case from a wish to establish cabinet government as in England, or a single house, or one term of seven years for the President. To touch on a more burning question, only a judge mad with partisanship would exclude because the applicant thought that the eighteenth amendment should be repealed.'

It was an opinion, he confided to a friend that was designed to cause discomfort in certain quarters. He had not lost his sense of humour, but he was getting tired now and knew his colleagues were assigning him the easier cases. But he stayed on until he had become the longest serving justice in history. Harvard commissioned a full-length portrait, which hangs in a place of honour next to the one of Marshall.

And then he was ninety. On his birthday, a mountain in Alaska was named after him, and he was invited to speak on the radio, an invitation he accepted because he thought it might be fun. He heard the dour Chief Justice Charles Evans Hughes say to the nation, 'we honour him, but what is more, we love him. We give him tonight the homage of our hearts'. Deeply moved, the old man paused for a while, and then said slowly, 'In this symposium my part is only to sit in silence. To express one's feelings as the end draws near is too intimate a task.' Then he added a few words that showed how reluctant he was to go. 'The riders in a race do not stop short when they reach the goal,' he said. 'There is a little finishing canter before coming to a standstill. There is time to hear the kind voice of friends and to say to one's self "the work is done." But just as one says that, the answer comes, "The race is over, but the work is never done while the power to work remains . . . And so I end with a line from a Latin poet who uttered the message more than fifteen hundred years ago: Death plucks my ear and says, "Live – I am coming."'

He should have gone then, but went on working for almost another year, his hands beginning to shake now, his mind haunted by fatigue but hating to quit. At last, he accepted the inevitable and on 10 January 1932, he told his clerk 'I won't be coming in tomorrow.' That night he wrote to President Hoover and submitted his resignation.

He lived on until 1935, the shadows closing in. He dozed a lot, but could still listen to his secretary reading out loud from Spengler's *Decline of the West* and listen to Brahms or Beethoven on the radio. Once a week, he drove out to the cemetery at Arlington to touch Fanny's tomb, struggling on one occasion to recall some verses he had quoted at a Memorial Day speech more than forty years earlier about a soldier, buried on the battlefield, hearing lovers pass him by, and asking if he was still remembered:

> 'Not so, my hero,' the lovers say,
> 'We are those that remember not;
> For the spring has come and the earth has smiled,
> And the dead must be forgot.'
> Then the soldier spake from the deep dark grave:
> 'I am content.'

He lingered on until the eve of his ninety-fourth birthday and was buried next to Fanny in the soldiers' graveyard at Arlington. After his death, two army uniforms were found hanging in his home with a note pinned to them, which read, 'These uniforms were worn by me in the Civil War and the stains upon them are my blood'.

PART FIVE

A Citadel Defended

The ruling passion be it what it will
The ruling passion conquers reason still.

Alexander Pope, 1688–1744

CHAPTER FIFTEEN

'A Terrible Gift'

TOTALITARIAN CATASTROPHE

By the end of Holmes's life, his legacy seemed secure. Free speech had won its proper constitutional place, at least in the western democracies. Its legal and philosophical parameters had been defined. History seemed to be proving that it was possible for human beings to think, write and speak as they saw fit. The combination of economic liberalism, political democracy, religious emancipation and individualism in personal life fuelled the desire for freedom, and at the same time appeared to bring mankind nearer to its realisation. 'One tie after another was severed,' wrote the social psychologist, Erich Fromm. 'Man had overthrown the domination of nature and made himself her master; he had overthrown the dominance of the Church and the domination of the absolutist State. The *abolition of external domination* seemed to be not only a necessary but also a sufficient condition to attain the cherished goal: freedom of the individual.'

It was not to be. Communist and fascist dictatorships shattered the optimistic dream. Far from embracing freedom, whole nations – whole continents – seemed to be in flight from it. New systems emerged which denied everything that men believed they had won in centuries of struggle. Free speech was but one of dozens of human liberties that were ruthlessly cast aside in the twentieth century's descent into barbarism. A year after the Russian Revolution, Lenin declared, 'ideas are much more fatal things than guns. Why should any man be allowed to buy a printing press and disseminate pernicious opinions calculated to embarrass the government?'

And, of course, he quickly made sure that no man was so allowed. Those who seek absolute power in the name of an ideology always have a need to bring the press under State control. In Italy, after eliminating a third of all newspapers and compelling the rest to join the Fascist Party, Benito Mussolini boasted, 'I consider Fascist journalism as my orchestra'. And the moment he assumed power in Germany, Hitler enacted the infamous Editor's Law, which compelled all journalists to register with the State, all editors to accept appointments as servants of the State, and all publishers to follow Nazi discipline or face closure. The first priority of all tyrannical regimes is to stifle free speech.

For those who had the foresight to look for them, the portents of the totalitarian catastrophe had been apparent for generations. Although Mill's arguments had at first seemed to triumph, the freedom and individuality he so prized had already in his own lifetime begun to be undermined by feelings of isolation and insecurity. Just as the fifteenth and sixteenth centuries had seen men cast aside the old medieval certainties – and with them, their comforting sense of security – so the late nineteenth and early twentieth centuries saw individuality give way in turn to a new form of collectivism. It was the collectivism of the factory and the production line, of mechanised slaughter and mass unemployment, of dictatorship and revolution. Powerless and insecure in the face of impersonal forces over which they had no control, people surrendered their freedom for the sake of the illusory security offered by an authoritarian State. All principles became meaningless except the one they were ripe for: the leadership principle, or what was, in effect, a return to tribalism.

As far back as 1849, the Russian novelist, Fyodor Dostoyevsky, had foreseen its coming. While Harriet Taylor and John Stuart Mill were still mulling over their ideas on liberty, Dostoyevsky was penning his much quoted attack on the 'terrible gift' of freedom. This grew from his own experience in having been sentenced to be shot for writing a pamphlet critical of the Tsar. He and five fellow prisoners had been led out to a square in St Petersburg, where they found their coffins laid out in a row. They were stripped to their shirts, three of them were blindfolded and tied to posts in front of the firing squad. At that moment a horseman galloped up to announce that the Tsar had reprieved them. The execution had been staged as a lesson 'not to be forgotten'. They were to be sent instead to Siberia, even though one of them had lost his mind. Three days later, Dostoyevsky and two others were sent to the convict prison at Omsk, where he spent the next four years never out of fetters, never alone, his only book a copy of the Bible.

Out of this experience, so different to Mill's, or anyone else's in the west at that time, he emerged to become one of the world's great novelists – and by free choice, a supporter of the Tsar, the Orthodox Church and the reactionary Slavophil Party. Among his unforgettable creations was the Grand Inquisitor, who in *The Brothers Karamazov* says that so long as he remained free man has no more constant and agonising anxiety than to find as quickly as possible someone to relieve him of his terrible gift. There were three forces, and only three, which could lift this burden and bring him happiness. These forces were 'miracle, mystery and authority', forces which throughout his history had proved far more attractive to man than ever his freedom had done.

In rejecting the 'terrible gift', the Grand Inquisitor was, in effect, echoing the biblical myth of the expulsion from paradise. Before eating from the tree of knowledge, man and woman had lived peacefully in the Garden of Eden, without stress and without work, but also without choice and without freedom. Only by disobeying God did they acquire their freedom, that 'terrible gift'. Now, it seemed, the forbidden fruit was to be handed back. But it was not paradise to which twentieth-century mankind returned. It was a particularly nasty form of purgatory. Those nations which surrendered to totalitarian authority, or were conquered by it, also lost their freedom and their individuality. Millions died on the battlefield, millions more in the Gulags and concentration camps. As for the rest, the State took control over their entire social and personal life. Dissent was stifled or driven underground. The freedom of expression was brutally suppressed. By the time war broke out in 1939, liberal democracy, at least in Europe, appeared to be on the way to extinction, with authoritarian regimes outnumbering constitutional democracies by sixteen to twelve.

The effect was felt even in the nations who fought the war in the name of freedom. In the long run, they saved democracy, though in the process they were obliged to bring back censorship, impose secrecy and subordinate individual rights to the over-riding necessity of ensuring the survival of society as a whole. But at least the controls were well-defined and largely accepted, so that during the war itself there was only limited government interference with unorthodox or unpopular opinions, and, in America, no return to the sedition trials of the First World War. Indeed, the day after Pearl Harbor the US Justice Department issued the enlightened decree that no prosecutions were to be launched for allegedly seditious utterances without the direct permission of the attorney-general. When the war was over, Zechariah Chafee, the foremost legal expert on the problems of free speech in America, was able to report that there had been less suppression than he had anticipated. Then he added, perhaps more presciently than he knew, 'I expect some sort of outbreak of fear during the unsettled period before we get back to normal peace conditions.' In fact, another half century elapsed before anything approaching 'normal conditions' were restored. Instead, the Cold War froze relations between the former allies and America was swept by yet another wave of repression and intolerance.

THE DECLARATION OF HUMAN RIGHTS

Peacetime had begun optimistically enough. When he enunciated the principles for which the war would be fought, President Roosevelt idealistically declared that 'in the future days, which we seek to make secure, we look forward to a world founded upon four essential freedoms. The first is freedom of speech and expression everywhere in the world.' In 1946, the victorious allies resolved to achieve this ideal through the introduction of a universal declaration of human rights, similar to the Americans' own Bill of Rights. At that time, the only rights individuals had under international law were the treaties abolishing the slave trade, the Geneva and Hague Conventions on the conduct of warfare and certain clauses protecting national minorities contained in the Versailles Peace Treaty of 1919.

Now, for the first time, moral imperatives were to be articulated as rights for individuals throughout the world. The declaration was to recognise that free expression was literally the first freedom, underpinning all the other freedoms, the tool which everyone must have if they are to defend their other human rights.

The godmother of the Declaration was the formidable Eleanor Roosevelt, widow of the wartime president, who chaired a drafting committee of only eight people. What eventually emerged as Article 19 was as succinct and all-embracing as the American Bill of Rights itself. It reads, in full: 'Everyone has the right to freedom of opinion and expression; this right includes freedom to hold opinions without interference and to seek, receive and impart information and ideas through any media and regardless of frontiers.'

The hope was that, in time, the declaration would acquire the force of one of Madison's universal maxims and become the norm to which all nations would feel themselves ethically bound. Although acclaimed as the UN's most important achievement, its implementation never quite lived up to the expectations. While Article 19 expresses a noble ideal that should be universally honoured, it remains a statement of good intentions without legal force. No supreme court was created to rule on breaches. No government that signed it believed it to be binding in all circumstances. It was, and has remained, a piece of aspirational rhetoric, described as more poetry than reality and even dismissed (by an American ambassador to the United Nations, no less) as 'a letter to Santa Claus'.

PURGE AND PERSECUTION

When the declaration was sent off to be ratified in 1948, the most vehement opposition came, ironically enough, from the United States, its architect's homeland. Politicians on the reactionary right were determined to shut out what they termed 'socialism by treaty'. There was also widespread resentment across the segregated south that the declaration's pronouncements on race interfered with the rights of the individual States. Moreover the country was in the grip of a massive reaction against the dangers of domestic communism. There was a belief that, under the influence of treacherous fellow-travellers in the State Department, President Roosevelt had sold out to the Russians at Yalta and so facilitated the Soviet domination of Eastern Europe. The offence was compounded when, allegedly under the same influence, China, too, was 'lost' to communism. And when Alger Hiss, who had been one of Roosevelt's advisers at Yalta, was accused of being a Soviet spy, the scene was set for the most widespread and longest lasting political repression in US history.

The provisions of the first amendment were once again cast aside. The newly drafted Universal Declaration of Human Rights was ignored. Holmes's test of 'a clear and present danger' was discounted by the Supreme Court because of the supposed gravity of the evil they faced. Intolerance took over. At one extreme, Julius and Ethel Rosenberg were hanged for a crime it is now widely believed they did not commit. At another extreme, everyone who applied for a permit to fish in New York City reservoirs had to sign a loyalty oath. It was feared that if communists were allowed to go fishing, they might poison the city's drinking water.

In between the extremes, hundreds went to prison, thousands lost their jobs, dissent was stifled, careers blighted, and, just as seriously, the spectrum of accepted debate in America was drastically and perhaps permanently narrowed.

The persecutions, which lasted for at least a decade, are now indelibly known as McCarthyism, after the witch-hunting Senator from Wisconsin, Joe McCarthy. It is, however, strongly misleading to attach the blame for what happened to the activities of one man and his repellent committee. The repressions that poisoned American life in the late 1940s and 1950s were both longer lasting and far more widespread than is sometimes admitted. Indeed, recent research into the files of the Federal Bureau of Investigation suggest that the phenomenon would be more accurately termed 'Hooverism', after the FBI's director of forty-three years, J. Edgar Hoover. Thanks to the Freedom of Information Acts of the 1970s we now know that the FBI was at the heart of the anti-communist crusade. It organised the machinery of political repression, it drew up the loyalty programme, controlled the internal security apparatus, initiated the criminal prosecutions and conducted the undercover operations that pushed the communist issue to the centre of American politics. Hoover's position as head of the investigative arm of the justice department ensured that his own deeply reactionary vision of American communism would gain widespread acceptance, as did his pre-emptive way of dealing with it.

After the outbreak of the Korean War in 1950, his influence was further boosted by the passage of the so-called McCarran Act – legislation passed over President Truman's veto which authorised the FBI to draw up a national register of allegedly subversive influences. Not only did the act give the FBI *carte blanche* to decide what was subversive, it freed Hoover to embark on his self-imposed mission to purge the nation from the taint of communism. Supposedly dangerous suspects were put under surveillance, often illegally, and over 26,000 Americans had their names put on the Bureau's Security Index, the 'most potentially dangerous' of whom were scheduled to be arrested 'within one hour after the order is given' and detained in prison camps. It is now known that among those on the Index was the writer, actor and director, Orson Welles, who was considered so dangerous he was put under surveillance on a daily basis. The FBI had been keeping an eye on Welles ever since he produced *Citizen Kane*, a film based on the arch-conservative press baron, William Randolph Hearst, who had close links to Hoover. Although Welles was kept on the index until 1954, recently released FBI records show no evidence of any subversive activity, let alone communist affiliation. The actress Lucille Ball was put under surveillance after the FBI discovered she had registered to vote as a communist in the elections of 1936 'at the insistence of her grandfather'. Files were opened on Pablo Picasso because of his connections with 'various subversive groups that were of interest to the FBI', while the bureau compiled a 1,400 page dossier on Albert Einstein, another on Thomas Mann, the winner of the Nobel Prize for Literature, and even one on Eleanor Roosevelt, whose correspondence was monitored in an attempt to prevent her appointment to the US delegation at the United Nations.

The evidence against Einstein, such as it was, included the fact that he publicly advocated pacifism, civil rights, and racial equality; supported Hollywood's blacklisted film-makers; was a friend of Charlie Chaplin, Paul Robeson and Frank Lloyd Wright; advocated abolition of the House Un-American Activities Committee (HUAC); and published articles in *The Bulletin of Atomic Scientists* advocating world government and a less militaristic foreign policy. Other allegedly 'pertinent' data claimed that, before the war, Einstein had created a stir on a trans-Atlantic liner by refusing to stand for a rendition of the German national anthem, and in the 1950s was experimenting with a ray gun which could help destroy aircraft, tanks and armoured cars. 'He hopes that with it a dozen men could defeat five hundred,' the FBI's agent reported – and 'through it, five hundred could rule a nation'. Hoover's obsessive anti-communism ensured that even allegations as absurd as this were seriously entertained and investigated.

As well as administering the Security Index, the FBI also vetted people for employment under the various loyalty programmes, which operated in both the public and private sectors. By the beginning of 1952, they had checked some 2 million federal employees for evidence of subversive views, and by 1960 had assembled over 430,000 files on allegedly subversive groups and individuals. One particularly effective cull affected sailors and dock workers, all of whom had to be checked out before being allowed to go to sea in an American vessel or to load one with cargo – allegedly for security reasons, but in practice to destroy the power of militant unions. Nearly 3,000 seamen and longshore-men failed to pass the test, including workers on cruise liners, coastal freighters, fishing boats and ferries.

No sector of the economy, public or private, was exempt from political screening. Blacklisting was commonplace, the techniques used by the Loyalty Boards were uncannily similar to those of the Catholic Inquisition. When people were brought before the boards, the name of their accuser was invariably concealed, the accusations they had to face equally vague and in violation of natural justice. Sometimes the questions were entirely hypothetical: would the person before the board report fellow workers if they found they were communists? Would they fight for the United States if they got into a war with the Soviet Union? What did they think about the Marshall Plan, 'socialised medicine', public ownership of utilities, or race relations? Black people were asked if they had white friends, whites if they had black ones. People of all colours were asked if they owned Paul Robeson records. Some were quizzed about their tastes in art and literature and others about their religious beliefs, especially if they were Quakers or pacifists. All of them were asked the $64,000 question: 'Are you now, or have you ever been, a member of the Communist Party?' People whose replies were too radical, too evasive – or too honest – lost their jobs.

The manifest unfairness of the system led to many injustices. It was commonplace, for example, to condemn people by association. One young meteorologist was labelled a security risk because, as he put it, he had maintained a 'close and continuing relationship with my dad and sister' who had once subscribed to 'what are now called subversive newspapers'. A waiter on a passenger liner was told his presence on board was 'inimical to the security of the United States', though no reasons were given and he was therefore unable to defend himself. A music teacher at the University of Illinois lost his job after an anonymous typewritten document was dropped on the desk of his college president alleging unverified past associations with unidentified but 'undesirable' elements. Only later was the document shown to be a blind memorandum from the FBI. At least 800 such dismissals were engineered at schools and colleges across the country under the Bureau's Responsibilities Programme.

In all these cases, the victims rarely found out who had made the charges against them. The FBI always insisted on withholding the identity of its informers, even from the Loyalty Boards who held the hearings. Usually, all they knew was that the information had come from what the FBI called a 'reliable' source, which was just as likely to be an illegally conducted wiretap or break-in as it was one of the bureau's undercover informers. Such was the FBI's prestige at the time that board members seldom questioned the source of the bureau's allegations.

The nation's judiciary was equally reluctant to intervene. Despite the obvious injustices that the loyalty programme's procedures entailed, judges invariably upheld the over-riding need to protect national security. In a test case involving a union leader, Dorothy Bailey, whose job was to draw up training manuals for the government's Labour Department, the FBI's use of secret informers was upheld by the federal courts. Bailey had no involvement with the Communist Party, though she was described as 'a hell of a good union person'. After intensive interrogation, she came out of her hearing 'pure as the driven snow'. Nevertheless, in the summer of 1948, she was suspended from her job. The Regional Loyalty Board had been given derogatory – and, of course, anonymous – information about her. She was never told what specific charges she faced, nor who had made them. In any other circumstances, her case would have been upheld as a cut and dried infringement of her civil liberties. So blatantly unfair did it seem that her lawyer, the future Supreme Court Justice Abe Fortas, took her case to a federal appeals court, where he assumed she would win. But she did not. A judge in Washington ruled that the issue was not whether she should have had a fair trial but rather the woeful state of the 'world situation'. Even if Bailey was granted the right to trial, he said, the 'inexorable necessities of the government' would require the protection of FBI informers. Three years later, his ruling was upheld on appeal by the US Supreme Court. The highest court in the land had legitimised the secrecy, the intolerance and the unfairness that characterised the FBI's crusade, even though their processes were in clear violation of several rather basic personal and political rights, including the UN's recently ratified declaration that everyone has the right to hold opinions 'without interference'.

Throughout the unsavoury episode, the FBI successfully strove to protect its image as a stalwart upholder of American virtues, and even as a champion of civil liberties. They were masters of what has later become known as 'spin', leaking information to favoured supporters in Congress or the press and bullying its critics. To cover its tracks, leaks were made either orally, or in the form of blind memoranda accompanied by explicit warnings not to let on where the information had come from. Bullying took the form of opening files on writers and journalists who criticised the bureau, or looked too deeply into its methods. Those critics Hoover termed 'coyotes of the press' found themselves systematically disparaged and their careers disrupted. When necessary, the director resorted to downright blackmail. For example, when the bureau learnt that a US Senator had been involved in a hit-and-run accident with a pretty girl by his side, 'by noon of next day the good Senator was aware that we had the information and we never had any trouble with him on appropriations since'. In most cases, Hoover did not have to blackmail his victims directly – it was sufficient for them to know he was capable of doing so. It is now known that the bureau compiled dossiers on every member of Congress and every congressional candidate, though at the time the bureau consistently denied it.

Hoover himself was virtually untouchable. The sexually-repressed bachelor director was a consummate bureaucrat and brilliant propagandist, projecting himself as guardian of the nation's security, incorruptible, superprofessional, the boss whose sycophantic staff formed an honour guard along the corridors when he came to address them and showered him with gifts on his birthday and at Christmas. Sometimes they were ordered to write flattering letters when he returned from giving evidence to a congressional committee, telling him 'what a marvellous job he had done up there on the Hill'. Hoover's ghost-written speeches reinforced the aura of almost salvationist zeal that pervaded the bureau's work. 'Here and abroad,' Hoover would say, 'mortal enemies of freedom and deniers of God Himself conspire to undermine the fundamental forces which are the lifeline of our country's vitality and greatness.' With the supporters of the New Deal in full retreat, no national politician could afford to challenge Hoover's leadership of the FBI without facing an attack on his own patriotism or his alleged subversive tendencies. Opponents were routinely wiretapped or subjected to what the FBI termed 'a black bag job' – an illegal break-in to a suspect's home or office. One long-time critic of the FBI's tactics, the National Lawyers' Guild, was subjected to a prolonged vendetta of this nature. Long before Watergate, the FBI routinely conducted illegal burglaries of the NLG's offices and planted wiretaps on its phones and those of its leading officers – the difference being that, unlike the Watergate burglars, they were not found out. The counter-measures they took to cover their tracks were equally ruthless. On the day before the NLG was to hold a press conference demanding an investigation into the FBI's clandestine activities, Hoover leaked damaging information about them to a friendly politician, Congressman Richard Nixon. He at once called for an investigation 'to determine the truth or falsity of charges that it is being used as a Communist front organisation'. There was no evidence to back up the charge, but the smear was effective. Next day's headlines were dominated by Nixon's allegations, not the NLG's report, which was largely ignored. Thereafter, Hoover peppered the attorney-general's office, the White House, his allies in Congress and the press with so much derogatory material about the NLG that its activities lost their impact, even when it produced evidence to support its charge that 'the FBI may commit more federal crimes than it ever detects'.

Nowhere was the crusade against the influence of the red peril conducted more zealously than in Hollywood, the American dream factory. A radical left-leaning community of screenwriters and producers had flourished there since the 1930s, attracted to the communist movement in its Popular Front period because of its commitment to social justice and its strong stand against Hitler. By the late 1940s, all but the most tenacious of them had shed their illusions and 'jumped off the Moscow Express' to use the contemporary if pejorative phrase. But the taint remained. The Loyalty Board's question was to be, 'Are you now, *or have you ever been*, a member of the Communist Party?' In Hollywood, it became just as potent a taint to have been a member of the Screen Writers Guild, a left-leaning union formed just before the war and open to communists and non-communists alike. In those idealistic days, it was hard to tell where the liberals left off and the fellow travellers began. To many of them, communists were seen simply as enthusiastic archetypes of their own New Deal. The guild was opposed by the ultra-conservative Motion Picture Alliance, which had been formed to combat 'the growing impression that this industry is made up of, and dominated by, communists, radicals and crackpots' and to oppose all efforts 'to divert the loyalty of the screen from the free America that gave it birth'.

The two sides came face to face early in 1947 at hearings before the HUAC, which played a major role in consolidating the machinery of the anti-communist crusade. Contempt proceedings taken by HUAC made it impossible for witnesses to rely on their constitutional right to free speech. It also led to the practice of blacklisting, which was central to the success of the crusade. The role of the FBI, though clandestine, was crucial. For some time, the bureau had been running informers within the film community. It now began bugging the phones of Los Angeles leftists and burglarising the headquarters of the Screen Writers Guild. The bureau's local agents regularly supplied HUAC with blind memoranda that detailed the supposedly subversive connections of people it wanted to investigate and even prepared questions for the committee to use in interrogating witnesses.

When the committee began its hearings early in 1947, its motives were openly ideological: movies, it held, should treat businessmen as heroes, not villains, and trade union activists as communist-inspired troublemakers. When it wanted to know how Hollywood's communists got their propaganda onto the screen, a friendly witness told them it was a sure sign of communist influence if a film left the impression that 'American industrialists were greedy monsters'. Having established that it was as keen to eliminate left-wing ideas from Hollywood movies as it was in purging trade unionists, HUAC was now ready to strike at individuals. In September of that year it issued forty-three subpoenas, many of them to friendly witnesses such as Ronald Reagan, who could be relied on to deplore the influence of the left and congratulate the committee on its work. Nineteen of the other subpoenas went to potentially hostile witnesses, some of them known communists, but some barely active in the party. At least three went to people who had never been communists at all and one to the German poet and playwright Bertholt Brecht, who promptly left the country.

From the start, the potentially hostile witnesses determined to present a united front, but quickly realised that they were sailing in uncharted waters. Until that time, no one had gone to jail for defying the HUAC, no one in Hollywood had yet been blacklisted, but it was not known to what extent the courts would protect their right to hold unorthodox opinions or whether HUAC could question them about their political affiliations. After much debate, they chose to present themselves as civil libertarians fighting for their right to free speech. As one of them said later, 'we had not come to Washington to defend ourselves. We had come to defend the First Amendment.'* The film colony's liberal majority rallied to their support; they feared that the HUAC hearings were an attempt to censor the movies and violate their freedom of speech. Three hundred of them formed an *ad hoc* group to defend the first amendment, including such glittering stars as Humphrey Bogart, Judy Garland, Danny Kaye, Gene Kelly and Burt Lancaster. The studios stood rather nervously on the sidelines, though their spokesman promised that they would never be party to anything 'as un-American as a blacklist'. 'Tell the boys not to worry,' he added. 'We're not going totalitarian to please this committee.'

His words turned to ashes in his mouth. The hearings were a disaster. When called to the stand, each of the unfriendly witnesses tried to read out a formal statement explaining his position and why he was refusing to cooperate. The committee chairman, Parnell Thomas, refused to let them read their statements, insisting instead that they answer the committee's questions. As a result, the hearings degenerated into a shouting match. The witnesses accused the committee of muzzling them, calling its members 'fascist' and 'reactionary', but they were gavelled down by Thomas, who summoned US marshals to escort the disorderly ones from the room. After ten such confrontations, the committee suspended the hearings, but not before recording the witnesses' communist affiliations and, where relevant, producing a photocopy of his Communist Party membership card.

While the committee may have come across as authoritarian and unfair, the image of the now notorious 'Hollywood Ten' was damaged beyond repair. Instead of appearing as dignified defenders of their right to free speech, they were perceived as rowdy ideologues, evasive about their ties to the Communist Party and in contempt of the accepted procedures of the elected Congress. Within days, their liberal support had evaporated. The stars who had so recently rallied in support of their right to free speech now hastened to recant. 'I detest Communism just as any other decent American does,' said Humphrey Bogart in a statement that admitted his trip to Washington to support the Ten had been 'ill-advised, even foolish'. However sincere their belief in their own right to free speech, American liberals and moderates could never bring themselves to defend the civil rights of communists, whose views they now regarded as beyond the pale.

It was not long before Hollywood itself caved in. All of the Ten lost their jobs and the studios who had employed them pledged never again to knowingly take on a communist or a member of any other group which used illegal or unconstitutional methods. The Ten had not only become unemployable, they now faced a jail sentence for contempt of Congress. As their appeals wound their way upwards towards the Supreme Court, they remained confident that their right to free speech under the first amendment would be upheld. Only slowly did it dawn

---

* Rather than rely on the fifth amendment which would protect them from incriminating themselves, but which would give the impression that they had something to hide. Hence McCarthy's later sneer at 'Fifth Amendment Communists'.

on them that they were going to lose. At a hearing before a federal appeals court in 1949, Judge Bennett C. Clark based his judgement on the 'current ideological struggle between the communist-thinking and democratic-thinking parts of the world' on which, he said, 'the destiny of all nations hangs'. Because the movies were such a potent means of disseminating propaganda, he held that the Ten's refusal to say whether or not they were members of the Communist Party actually endangered the nation.

In November that year, the Supreme Court refused to consider the case at all and the Ten served out their one-year jail sentences. By the time they were released, the blacklist had claimed almost everyone in films who had ever been connected with the Communist Party, though no one else from Hollywood would go to jail: unfriendly witnesses had learned to take the fifth amendment, which protected their right not to incriminate themselves, rather than the first, which had proved to be a nullity in hearings before Congress. But the process did not stop there. Although the blacklist was at first confined to communists, it was extended before long to cover anyone whose activities had antagonised such bodies as the American Legion or the fiercely right-wing (and corrupt) technicians' union, the International Alliance of Theatrical Stage Employees. Those they named included many of the Hollywood liberals who had joined the Committee for the First Amendment and anyone else who held unorthodox or radical views. If they wanted to save their careers, they were obliged to recant. In 1952, Marlon Brando was forced three times to revise his statement explaining why he had signed the Stockholm Peace Petition before he was allowed to go back to work. Naturally enough, dissent dried up, the studios took no risks and Hollywood would never again take on issues that were regarded as too contentious or controversial. Even films made by independent producers were denied a showing if their message was held to be subversive.

In Hollywood, more than anywhere, the anti-communist crusade succeeded in demonising the views of the far left and purging the movies of any taint of un-American ideology. Gone for ever was the class consciousness and emphasis on collective struggle that had pervaded a good deal of Hollywood's output during the 1930s and 1940s. Gone too was its stream of movies about the heroic struggles of exploited miners and poor farmers that had culminated in the classic film version of John Steinbeck's bestseller about Dust Bowl refugees, *The Grapes of Wrath*, the only American film ever allowed to be shown in countries behind the Iron Curtain.

MCCARTHY'S NEMESIS

The anti-communist crusade was already well under way when, in February 1950, Senator McCarthy joined in with his now infamous speech at Wheeling, West Virginia. Barely three weeks after Alger Hiss had been convicted of perjury, McCarthy waved a piece of paper at a Lincoln's Birthday dinner, saying that he held 'here in my hand' a list of 205 communists working in the state department – clear evidence that the Truman administration was 'crawling with traitors'. The charges were wild and unsupported. And although he was later forced to change his tune – maybe they were not all 'card-carrying' communists, he said, though they were certainly 'loyalty risks' or 'people with communist connections' – McCarthy was on his notorious way, riding a tide of anti-communist fervour that he whipped up into an outbreak of national hysteria. A communist conspiracy, he claimed, threatened the very existence of the United States. Hearings were held in which he accused the State Department, the Army, the Voice of America and the US Information Agency of being infested with spies. A political brawler and a reckless, hard-drinking demagogue, McCarthy seemed to relish every minute of his notoriety, though he was to declare, 'I don't enjoy this task. It is a dirty, disagreeable job, but a job which must be done.' He likened it to his boyhood job of killing the skunks that attacked his mother's chickens, a 'dirty, foul, unpleasant, smelly job. And sometimes after it was done, people did not like to have us sit next to them in Church'.

People were named as communists or fellow-travellers with scant regard for the truth and without the least personal research. (McCarthy commonly got his hit lists ready-made from the professional anti-communist network, which now flocked to his side. He gave their movement his name and in return they gave him his agenda and his information.) Though he was reckless with his facts, he was a genius at propaganda and an expert at gaining publicity. The more outrageous his claims, the more eagerly the press lapped them up, for in that pre-television age newspapers were still the main source of hard news. Deadlines were more important to them than detailed investigation, and McCarthy's allegations were given more prominence than careful analysis. The Wisconsin senator was especially skilled at releasing his information just in time to make the headlines but without any time for further checks. Besides, as one editorial writer ruefully admitted, it seemed unbelievable that such a respected figure as a US Senator would make up such charges if he did not have the evidence to support them.

Perhaps McCarthy's best known victim was Owen Lattimore, a teacher at Johns Hopkins University and one of the nation's leading commentators on East Asian affairs. An outspoken liberal with no illusions about the corrupt regime of Chiang Kai-shek, Lattimore had long been under surveillance by the FBI, though they had never found anything in the least incriminating. Always on the lookout for treason in high places, the more reckless McCarthy announced that he was about to name 'the top espionage agent in the United States, the boss of Alger Hiss'. When Lattimore's name was revealed by a friendly journalist, McCarthy further embroidered his story. The distinguished sinologist was no longer merely a spy. He was no less than 'the main architect of America's China policy'. The allegation was quickly denounced as a 'fraud and a hoax', but again the damage was done. Lattimore was summoned before a Senate Judiciary Committee and eventually arrested and put on trial for perjury for denying that he had been 'a promoter of communism or communist interests', and even more vaguely that he was 'a follower of the communist line'.

The charges were eventually thrown out by the federal judge, Luther W. Youngdahl, who declared that such allegations were impossible to prove. Many of the policies cited in the indictment were identical to those of the American government. Though McCarthy had failed to show that Lattimore was a communist, he had made him controversial. And in the atmosphere of the times, that was enough to end his academic career. His students were blacklisted, his speaking engagements dried up and his reputation was permanently damaged. He eventually left America to teach at the University of Leeds in England, his case an eloquent reminder of how attacks on the far left could so easily expand into an attack on the liberal mainstream. The effect on the spectrum of what views were permissible in America has lasted to this day.

McCarthy continued his anti-government crusade even after Dwight Eisenhower came to the White House in 1953. But in attacking his own party, McCarthy had launched himself on a self-destructive path that would end his career. His well-known nemesis came first in a courageous television documentary presented by the respected CBS commentator, Edward R. Murrow, who revealed the emptiness of McCarthy's charges and the unfairness of his methods, and then in the so-called Army-McCarthy hearings, in which the new medium of television again showed up the repellent and bullying nature of his methods. The hearings lasted for two months, and became one of the first – and arguably one of the most important – examples of how live broadcasts of public events can influence opinion. The issues were complex, and the hearings constantly interrupted by McCarthy's crude and insulting remarks, bullying of witnesses and lectures on the 'whining, whimpering appeasement of the Truman-Acheson regime'. The denouement came when the Senator launched a vindictive personal assault on an assistant to the Army's principal counsel, Joseph Welch. While Welch was cross-examining another witness about subversion in the Army, McCarthy interrupted with a characteristic smear: 'I think we should tell him he has in his law firm a young man named Fisher . . . who has been for a number of years a member of an organisation which was named, oh years and years ago, as the legal bulwark of the Communist Party.' Fred Fisher, a member of Welch's Washington law firm, had once been active in the National Lawyers' Guild. Welch, who had been prepared for McCarthy's intervention, launched into a dramatic riposte:

> Until this moment, Senator, I think I never really gauged your cruelty or your recklessness. Little did I dream that you could be so reckless and so cruel as to do an injury to that lad. It is true he is still with Hale and Dorr [Welch's law firm]. It is true that he will continue to be with Hale and Dorr. It is, I regret to say, equally true that I fear he will always bear a scar needlessly inflicted by you. If it were in my power to forgive you for your reckless cruelty I would do so. I like to think I am a gentle man, but your forgiveness will have to come from someone other than me.

Oblivious to what he had done, McCarthy blundered on with a further assault on Fisher. Welch had to beg him to stop. 'Let us not assassinate this lad further, Senator. You have done enough. Have you no sense of decency, sir, at long last? Have you left no sense of decency?' The electrifying exchange, broadcast live on television and carried that evening on every network news programme, effectively ended McCarthy's career. The following year he was censured by his colleagues in the Senate, and two years later, discredited and pathetic, he died of drink.

THE LEGACY OF PARANOIA

'We have condemned the individual,' remarked Senator Herbert Lehman after the 1954 vote to censure McCarthy. 'But we have not yet repudiated the "ism".' It was all too true. The country may have repudiated the crude and repulsive methods of the Wisconsin Senator, but the wave of anti-communist fervour lasted for the rest of the 1950s and into the 1960s. It was a phenomenon that affected mainstream liberals as well as radicals and has had a lasting impact on institutions ranging from the State Department to the local high schools who had purged their staff rooms of dissidents. From Hollywood to Harvard thousands of lives were blighted, careers damaged, reputations destroyed and marriages wrecked. And for what? There was never any realistic need for the loyalty oaths, the blacklists or the FBI's index of subversives.

True, there *were* Communists in America, albeit not many; and a few had found their way into the labour unions and public services. But domestic communism was never likely to enter the American mainstream, nor was it the threat to the freedoms that Hoover, McCarthy and HUAC represented it to be. By first demonising and then eliminating the views of a tiny, though admittedly extreme minority they caused unnecessary damage to almost every facet of American life. Of course it should never be forgotten that all this – and much, much worse – was going on in the communist world. What made the (relatively mild) repression in America so shocking was that it was conducted in the name of freedom and in the country that regarded itself, quite sincerely, as 'the last best hope' of mankind and the guardian of its liberties, free speech prominent among them.

Beyond the effect it had on individuals, the anti-communist crusade had other consequences, no less profound though more difficult to assess. It has been convincingly argued that it intensified the Cold War and contributed to the US disaster in Vietnam. Robert McNamara, one of the architects of the Vietnam War, has admitted that if experienced and knowledgeable China hands had not been driven out of government, the United States might well have avoided the conflict. In a 1970 interview President Johnson declared that he could not have risked a communist takeover in Vietnam because it would have led to 'an endless national debate – a mean and destructive debate – that would shatter my presidency, kill my administration and damage our democracy'. Johnson believed that the Truman administration lost its effectiveness from the day the communists took over in China, adding, 'I believe [it] had played a large role in the rise of Joe McCarthy'. It clearly also influenced Johnson's own decision to escalate the American involvement in Vietnam, with such disastrous consequences.

By drastically narrowing the debate, the anti-communist crusade limited the options available to American foreign policy makers for almost four decades. From 1948 to the end of the 1980s, US foreign policy was dominated by the priorities of the Cold War, sometimes with a catastrophic effect on human rights. In country after country – from Chile to Guatemala, Haiti to Iran, Paraguay to Zaire – the United States supported repressive military or oligarchic regimes that were anti-communist, regardless of their often appalling record in other areas, and, what is worse, they did so in the name of freedom and democracy.

At home, intellectual doors closed in the cultural world as well. In the words of Ellen Schrecker, who spent twenty years studying the phenomenon, 'It is clear that the anti-communist crusade transformed the mental contours of American life, changing the way that millions of ordinary people thought about themselves and their society.' Self-censorship became common in thousands of subtle ways as opinion formers, such as teachers, writers, artists and film makers, modulated their views and removed the sharp edges from their opinions and their commissions. University professors curtailed their off-campus political activities – not surprising when HUAC had demanded a list of the books they kept in their libraries. Organisations in the liberal mainstream, such as the NAACP and the American Civil Liberties Union, hung back from controversy for fear of being tarred with the communist brush. Anything too radical – such as a call for free health care or an end to racial segregation – would invariably be labelled 'communistic'. All too often, the liberals chose to keep silent, worried that they would be ostracised as 'fellow travellers' or, even worse, as communists themselves.

In the climate of the times, the infant television industry became even more timid than Hollywood. Here the main pressure came from private sponsors, who censored the content of programmes and were so terrified of controversy they forced the networks to drop hundreds, perhaps thousands, of actors, writers and technicians from their payrolls. As one critic noted in the early 1950s, television had become so timid that 'virtually everything from pregnancy to freedom of religion is considered a controversial subject, leaving almost nothing except homicide as a fit topic to enter our houses'. There were honourable exceptions, notably in the networks' own newsrooms, but elsewhere blandness ruled. As one senior CBS producer complained, 'The trouble with people who've never joined anything and therefore are "safe" for us to use is that they usually aren't very good writers or actors or producers or, hell, human beings.'

His words might well serve as an epitaph for the entire era. It frightened ordinary decent people into sheepish conformity, and it ostracised those who chose not to conform. It also showed that in an open society, the right to free speech really is indivisible. To deny that right to unpopular and even extreme minorities diminishes the quality of the right available to the rest of us; and that can lead on to evils greater than those they set out to eliminate, as the McCarthy era so graphically demonstrated.

CHAPTER SIXTEEN

Challenging the Censors

THE KING'S CHIMNEY

Whatever rescued America from the scourge of McCarthyism it was not an awakened sense of public liberty. Speaking as an alien who had come from a libertarian country, the English journalist Alastair Cooke was surprised to find when he first arrived in the United States that 'liberty is not in our time a markedly American passion'. Equality was the watchword: equality of privilege in prosperity, and equality of care in hard times. In his day, that was almost exactly the reverse of the situation in Great Britain, a country of inequalities, but one where radical and unorthodox views were widely held and generally tolerated, up to and including a belief in socialism, communism and the ultimate victory of the proletariat. At least since Mill, the freedom to hold unorthodox opinions had been widely and, on the whole, placidly accepted. British concerns about free speech tended to focus more on the questions of official secrecy, draconian laws of libel, and to an almost prurient extent on the problems raised by obscenity, profanity and pornography.

In a society that prided itself on its reputation for tolerance, it was regarded as perfectly legitimate to hold advanced political views – indeed, the Communist Party regularly put up candidates to stand for election to Parliament and one or two of them even served as MPs. The British concept of tolerance did not, however, extend to views that were thought likely to corrupt the minds of society's weaker members, particularly its womenfolk and children. It seems extraordinary, looking back, that as late as 1954, a total of 167,000 books were confiscated by Scotland Yard and incinerated in what they called the 'King's Chimney' because magistrates had adjudged them to be obscene. A confidential Home Office 'blue book' circulated to each of the country's police forces that year listed over 4,000 titles that were subject to confiscation. Most of them were otherwise worthless pulp novels with titles like *Amorous Nymph* and *Arabian Passion*, but some were simply popular thrillers by Mickey Spillane and James Hadley Chase, and a few were works of fiction by important writers like Jean Paul Sartre, Upton Sinclair and Daniel Defoe, whose *Moll Flanders* had been listed in the blue book for years.

All these decisions were taken under the terms of the 1857 Obscene Publications Act, drawn up in the heyday of Victorian prudery, which was used to uphold convictions against Charles Bradlaugh and Annie Besant for publishing a pamphlet about their pioneering research into birth control. Both were jailed for six months. A decade later, publishers were imprisoned for issuing translations of Gustave Flaubert's *Madame Bovary* and Emile Zola's *La Terre*.

American prudery was just as grotesque. Mark Twain's *Huckleberry Finn* was termed unfit reading for 'pure minded lads and lasses' (as it still is, though for different reasons). Walt Whitman was discharged from his post with the Interior Department after his *Leaves of Grass* was condemned as obscene and Nathaniel Hawthorne's *Scarlet Letter* was banned because of its 'brokerage of lust'. About the same time, a standard work on etiquette recommended that books by male and female authors should be placed on separate library shelves. Under a federal statute known as 'the Comstock Law', after the post-office agent who sponsored it, some 397,000 books were confiscated and over 5,000 people arrested on obscenity charges.

Change came only slowly, but in the earlier part of the twentieth century, two infamous test cases at last brought this sort of prurient censorship into disrepute – the banning in both Britain and America of one of the century's greatest novels, James Joyce's *Ulysses*, and the prosecution in Britain of a novel which had dared to explore the life of two lesbians, Radclyffe Hall's *The Well of Loneliness*.

The first edition of *Ulysses* was published in Paris in 1922. When attempts were made to import copies into the United States and Great Britain, the authorities immediately confiscated them. In Britain, customs officials sent a note to the Director of Public Prosecutions declaring that 'the importer describes it as a noteworthy work of art by an author of considerable repute which is being seriously discussed in the highest literary circles'. This mitigating note cut little ice with the DPP, Sir Archibald Bodkin, who somewhat pompously replied: 'I have not had the time, nor may I add, the inclination to read through this book.' He had, however, read the salacious passages drawn to his attention on pages 690 to 732, in which Molly Bloom describes her orgasms, and on that basis issued his considered legal opinion that the book was full of 'glaring obscenity and filth . . . and filthy books are not allowed to be imported into this country'. For good measure, he threw in his opinion that 'it is not only deplorable but at the same time astonishing that publications such as the *Quarterly Review* and the *Nation* should have devoted any space to a critique upon *Ulysses*'. On the basis of this opinion, and without any reference to a court of law, a literary masterpiece was banned from entering England for the next fourteen years. When some 500 copies of the second edition arrived at Folkestone, they were seized by customs officers and committed to the 'King's Chimney'.*

Joyce's novel retained its notoriety throughout the 1930s. There was much embarrassment at the Home Office when a copy was found among the books offered for sale from the estate of the late Lord Birkenhead, a former lord chancellor. On the advice of the DPP, it was discreetly withdrawn from the auction. In 1931, the distinguished critic Harold Nicolson was dismissed by the BBC after being personally forbidden by Lord Reith to refer to *Ulysses* in a series of talks on English literature. It was not until the end of the decade that, under pressure from academic and literary figures led by T.S. Eliot, the ban on *Ulysses*

---

* A device that was itself outlawed under the Clean Air Act of 1959, which forbade the emission of black smoke, including that caused by burning books (though it did not mark the end of censorship – they shredded the books instead).

was finally lifted. The first unlimited edition appeared in 1937, and with the publication of the paperback edition in 1968 the book became one of the biggest best-sellers of the twentieth century, without causing any discernible harm to the ½ million people who bought it.

Radclyffe Hall's *Well of Loneliness* was subject to even more shameful treatment by the Home Office authorities. The first British novel to deal seriously with lesbianism was first published in 1928 to sympathetic reviews. The *Daily Herald* described it as 'a profound and moving study of a profound and moving problem'. Certainly there was nothing pornographic about it: its most physically explicit line simply said, 'Then Stephen took Angela into her arms and kissed her full on the lips as a lover'. It was not the treatment, but the subject matter itself that outraged the political establishment, led by the ever-censorious home secretary, Sir William Joynson-Hicks. In a speech as the book was about to be published he complained:

I am attacked on the one hand by all those people who put freedom of speech and thought and writing before everything else in the world, as if there were freedom in God's world to pollute the generation growing up. There must be some limit to the freedom on what a man may write or speak in this great country of ours. That freedom, in my view, must be determined by the question as to whether what is written or spoken makes one of the least of these little ones offended.

Critics quickly poked fun at his idea that obscenity consisted of material that would offend the least of the little ones, or 'bring a blush to the cheeks of Little Nell', as one of them put it. But equally quickly, copies of *The Well of Loneliness* were seized in a police raid on the publisher, Jonathan Cape, which was summoned to 'show cause' why they should not be destroyed. When the case came to court, the defence called on the cream of literary England to pronounce on the book's merits: Arnold Bennett, John Buchan, T.S. Eliot, George Bernard Shaw, Lytton Strachey and Virginia Woolf among others. But the magistrate sent them all home. The book might well be a fine piece of literature, he pronounced, but that was not the point: it was obscene. It must, moreover, 'appear to anyone of intelligence that the better an obscene book is written, the greater is the public to whom it is likely to appeal. The more palatable the poison, the more insidious it is.'

Perverse though his reasoning was, it did at least motivate a renewed call for the reform of an outdated and discredited act. But it was not until 1949 that the *Well of Loneliness* was finally published, taking its place as one of the milestones in the development of feminist literature in Britain. And it took until the 1960s before the views of literary experts were heard in any obscenity case held in a British court. In the meantime, absurd cases of censorship continued until well after the war, culminating in what amounted to a wholescale purge in 1954, a year which also saw the start of a witch-hunt against homosexuals and 'vice' generally, including a solemn attempt by the authorities to destroy copies of *The Kinsey Report*, a scientific investigation into human sexual behaviour. Alan Travis, who has conducted an exhaustive study of the Home Office files of the period, concluded that the total of 167,000 publications destroyed by Scotland Yard that year was more than the total for the previous four years put together. One hundred and eleven people went to prison and their sentences were getting longer.

Saucy seaside postcards were one favourite target for the censors and the town of Swindon even ordered the destruction of Boccaccio's *Decameron*. Other towns seized translations of works by Aristophanes, Ovid, Juvenal and Rabelais. Publication of Norman Mailer's war novel, *The Naked and the Dead*, was allowed to be published only on condition that the soldiers' obscenities should be replaced with dashes and capital F's – though Mailer was permitted to use the word 'fu' a few times, leading to Tallulah Bankhead's classic riposte on meeting him: 'Are you the young man who can't spell fuck?'

As the almost century-old test of obscenity fell into further disrepute, a long and ultimately successful campaign for reform was conducted by A.P. Herbert and Roy Jenkins, a later home secretary. Although forced to make many compromises before they got it through Parliament, a new Obscene Publications Act finally reached the statute book in 1959. It allowed the effect of the publication to be considered as a whole and 'the public good' to be taken into account. If it could be shown that a publication was in the interests of science, literature, art or learning a case against it would fail. And, at last, the views of literary experts could be heard in a book's defence.

The new act came of age during the landmark trial of *Lady Chatterley's Lover*, the novel by D.H. Lawrence which had been listed in Scotland Yard's blue book for thirty years and subjected to countless confiscations and prosecutions. It came before a jury in 1961 after Penguin announced they were to publish a cheap unexpurgated paperback edition and handed over pre-publication copies to the police in order to test the waters. A copy found its way to the DPP, who decided to charge Penguin with publishing an obscene work. The defence called thirty-five distinguished witnesses to vouch for the book's literary merits, though the trial is now largely remembered for one of the choicest gaffes in British legal history, when the prosecution counsel, Mervyn Griffith-Jones, asked a jury made up of radio dealers, teachers, dock labourers and cabinet makers to ask themselves the question: 'Would you approve of your young sons, young daughters – for girls can read as well as boys – reading this book? Is it a book that you would have lying around the house? Is it a book you would wish your wife or servants to read?'

When the guffaws had subsided, the jury listened to the evidence and returned a verdict of 'not guilty'. Within a year, *Lady Chatterley* was outselling the Bible, proving once again that attempts at this sort of censorship can defeat their own ends and more often than not bring the law itself into disrepute. At any rate, the permissive age had now begun. From then on it became increasingly difficult to uphold a case of obscenity against the written word. But in other areas, what Mill would have called the 'rags and remnants' of censorship continued to bring ridicule on the whole antiquated system. Bizarre though it now seems, every play produced on a British stage had to be approved by the Lord Chamberlain, a functionary attached to the royal household with offices in St James's Palace.

Far from being a 'vast sounding board' for the social and political concerns of the day, as it had been in ancient Athens, the presence of the lord chamberlain ensured that the output of the theatre in nineteenth- and twentieth-century Britain was largely restricted to stilted escapist entertainment. Serious questioning of orthodox values was taboo, the stage completely detached from the concerns of modern life and subject to more censorship that it had been during the reign of Queen Elizabeth. Stultified and repressed, it became, in the words of the theatre historian, Nicholas de Jongh, 'a reactionary, unintellectual outpost of Europe', a 'petrified island' scarcely involved with the modern theatre movement. Plays ruled unsuitable for public performance included some of the most outstanding works of the age: Ibsen's *Ghosts*, Tolstoy's *Power of Darkness*, Shaw's *Mrs Warren's Profession*, and Pirandello's *Six Characters in Search of an Author*.

Even theatre managers argued for the retention of censorship. They had no wish to see their profitable places of amusement turned into political arenas for socialists, suffragettes or other assorted radicals. They wanted their audiences to wake after a night at the theatre with glamorous recall: 'What a nice play, what clever people, how smart the house, what pleasant hours.' They of course got their way and the English stage sank further into its complacent state of somnolence, impervious to the bracing new wave of *avant garde* art and literature that was sweeping France or the great works of literature coming out of Russia.

Their timidity prevailed for a further sixty years, and until the very end, the lord chamberlain wielded his blue pencil with authoritarian relish: no living member of the royal family could be impersonated on stage, nor could any other friendly head of state; homosexuality could not be referred to, while words such as 'pouf' 'rogered' and 'get stuffed' were cut from John Osborne's play *The Entertainer*; Harold Pinter was prevented from putting on his play *Landscape* altogether, and a play based on *Private Eye's Mrs Wilson's Diary* was heavily censored, even though all the jokes had already appeared in print. That, and the absurdity of banning live performances seen by a few hundred when the same play could be safely shown to millions on television finally led to the Lord Chamberlain's unlamented demise in 1968.

Although the Lord Chamberlain had gone, Scotland Yard's Obscene Publications Squad plodded on. Two years after the *Chatterley* trial they launched raids on two of London's world renowned art galleries – the Tate and the Victoria and Albert – to enquire about the 'obscene prints' they had displayed of Aubrey Beardsley's black and white line drawings of Aristophanes' *Lysistrata*. Although the permissive sixties were now in full swing, these sorts of raids only came to an end after corruption was uncovered in the Obscene Publication Squad's own ranks. It transpired that Soho pornographers were being given a 'licence to trade' in exchange for large bribes, which were then shared out among the squad's officers. Other pornographers simply bought back their own wares – at inflated prices – from the police officers who had seized them. What shocked the liberal community was the fact that while all this was going on, the police regularly raided underground magazine and book publishers connected with the radical, anti-establishment youth movement for what seemed more like political than puritanical motives. Like prohibition in America, the law was fostering a far worse crime than the one it was supposed to prevent. If pornography did not corrupt its readers, it certainly corrupted the police.

By that time, large parts of the 1959 act were seen to be unworkable. Juries were regularly throwing out the cases that were brought and in a more permissive age terms like 'obscene', 'indecent' and 'deprave' had lost much of their original meaning. It became almost impossible to uphold an obscenity conviction against the written word. And in any case, the area of concern about pornography had moved away from the printed word to the moving image – cinema, television and video, all of which were already heavily regulated in Britain. The debate on what controls can be imposed without impinging on civil liberties is yet to be resolved. For those who believe in maximising the freedom of the individual to control his or her own life, the test is no longer to ask whether the material causes shock, outrage or offence, but whether it causes actual harm – and whether more harm would be done if it was banned.

LAST CHANCE SALOON

In the post-permissive years of the 1970s and 1980s, it was not novels or plays or even lurid videos that caused the most outrage in the ranks of the British establishment. It was the antics of the tabloid newspapers. Such was the disgrace into which mass popular journalism had sunk that by 1989 a senior government minister felt impelled to warn them that they were drinking 'in the last chance saloon'. Over the next five years, Britain's newspapers – good and bad alike – lived under the threat of statutory controls not seen since the seventeenth century. Proposals were aired that would have imposed fines for inaccuracy, a compulsory right of reply and a press tribunal presided over by a High Court judge with powers, if necessary, to suspend publication. There would also be new laws on privacy to guard against intrusion. After a series of spectacular rows – often centred on the turbulent life of Diana, Princess of Wales – the crisis eventually passed. But at times it was a close-run thing, with the right to free speech once again open to question.

For all that it endured as a bulwark of British liberties for 300 years, the freedom of the press had never been specifically asserted or offered legal protection, as it had been in the United States and most other societies in the western tradition. This led to a paradoxical tendency for the British popular press to regard its freedom as something coming without strings, whereas a freedom guaranteed by the constitution has corresponding obligations, albeit unspoken ones. Where most American journalists acknowledge and take pride in their constitutional role in upholding free speech, British journalists feel themselves beholden to no such obligation: their press is as free to be disreputable as it is to be reputable.

This tendency is reinforced by the fact that journalism in Britain has never been recognised as a profession requiring special training or education. Since newspapers are simply exercising the right of free speech open to everyone, its practice cannot be restricted only to those who have obtained formal qualifications of the sort that apply to doctors, lawyers, clergymen, accountants or engineers. Journalism, in both principle and in practice, is open to all. It has no organised structure, no professional body to speak for it and no required certificates of competence. Highly skilled though they are, most journalists have been trained in the workplace. Perhaps for these reasons, theirs has never been a particularly reflective occupation. Its practitioners tend to be reluctant to conduct research into their work and have shown a marked distaste for analysing or justifying what they do. There was, until very recently, a notable absence of effective quality control, even into such basic matters as factual accuracy and intrusions into privacy.

In its Victorian heyday, this did not seem to matter too much. Newspapers like *The Times* cherished their independence, but under such editors as Barnes and Delane they also tended to serve *bourgeois* readers who were as high-minded and well-educated as they were. The change began in 1896 when Alfred Harmsworth launched his sprightly new *Daily Mail*, which he sold at ½*d* to a middle- and working-class readership in the suburbs. Though dismissed by Lord Salisbury as 'a newspaper for office boys written by office boys', the *Mail* proved to be a phenomenal success and made the fortune that enabled Harmsworth, by now ennobled as Lord Northcliffe, to buy up the bankrupt *Times*. By the end of the First World War, Northcliffe and his imitators had established the popular press as a major industry with daily circulations running into many millions, though ominously becoming 'more and more the monopoly of a few rich men'.

As the press barons who succeeded Northcliffe grew in power and self-importance, they themselves came to be perceived as a threat to the diversity of opinion and the freedom of speech – such pretensions punctured by Stanley Baldwin, who in 1931 denounced them for aiming at 'power without responsibility – the prerogative of the harlot throughout the ages', a withering put-down penned by the prime minister's cousin, Rudyard Kipling.

The Second World War took these concerns off the agenda. Newsprint was strictly rationed, with most national newspapers limited to around four pages, which left little space to carry much more than reports from the various theatres of war.

With the end of wartime paper rationing, competition once again intensified. Lord Beaverbrook's *Daily Express* had already overtaken the *Daily Mail* and was in turn shouldered aside by the brash new tabloid *Daily Mirror*, which had made its name during the war as the voice of the common soldier. Events gathered pace towards the end of the 1960s, when Rupert Murdoch launched the tabloid *Sun*, which achieved an even vaster circulation by offering its readers a relentless diet of gossip, scandal, trivia and, on its infamous page three, bare breasts.

The establishment was scandalised. The *Sun* was excoriated in the House of Lords as 'one of the most irresponsible newspapers in any western democracy' and 'a disgrace to decent standards of journalism'. The paper's Australian proprietor, who relished his nickname 'the Dirty Digger', dismissed his critics as stuffy and class-bound. The *Sun* continued on its lurid way to success, with a circulation in excess of 4 million a day. And, inevitably, other tabloids joined in, all offering the same frivolous mixture of sex, scandal and gossip. In the 1980s there was a showdown with the printing unions as one by one, the old Fleet Street newspapers converted to modern technology and moved out to premises in London's dockland, led by the Murdoch papers, including *The Times*, which he had bought in 1982.

After a series of lurid exposures, the press woke up to the fact that they now faced the real possibility of statutory regulation. Although the measures that were being proposed were primarily aimed at those drinking in 'the last chance saloon', they also represented a real threat to the future of serious investigative journalism, as well as the probability of endless entanglements with the courts, and even the return of prior restraint. Some of the more responsible broadsheets threatened to break ranks with the tabloids in order to protect their own position, but after much backroom manouevering, the industry as a whole made a belated attempt to set up an effective complaints body, backed by a nationally accepted code of practice to be drawn up and administered by the industry itself. The result was the creation in 1990 of a Press Complaints Commission headed by a distinguished and independent academic, Lord McGregor of Durris. He was given eighteen months to prove its worth.

He had barely settled in before an even greater storm broke around the activities of the popular press. It began with reports that the marriage of the Prince and Princess of Wales was in serious trouble. 'Charles and Diana: Cause for Concern', was the headline in the *Daily Mail*. While the stories later turned out to be substantially true, they caused outrage in Parliament. MPs called for a halt to the 'unhealthy and damaging' inquest into the royal marriage and demanded action from the Complaints Commission.* It was only the realisation that the Prince and Princess had themselves been responsible for much of the malicious tittle tattle that changed the climate of hostility towards the press. Before then, they came dangerously close to being put under Statutory Control. In 1993, a government-appointed committee headed by Sir David Calcutt QC proposed a regime of censorship and control more draconian than anything seen since the reign of the Stuarts. In place of the PCC, Calcutt proposed a press tribunal presided over by a high court judge appointed by the government. Among its many duties would be that of compiling its own code of practice and restraining publication of material deemed to be in breach of the code. It would have the power to award compensation, impose fines and award costs. Three new criminal offences of press intrusion were to be created, with an additional civil tort for invasions of privacy. As if these draconian proposals were not enough in themselves, Sir David couched his report in tones so sneeringly disdainful that even the ministers who had commissioned it were shocked and the proposals allowed to lapse.

In any case, a new weapon to control the press had now come to hand and cynical lawyers and politicians were not slow to exploit it. This followed a decision by the new Labour government to incorporate the European Convention on Human Rights into English law. The proposed legislation was originally put forward as a measure intended to protect the individual from actions by the State. It was not envisaged that it would allow private individuals or bodies to take legal action against other private individuals or bodies. On that basis, many newspapers were in favour of adopting the convention; indeed some

---

* A full account of these manoeuvrings can be found in Richard Shannon's *A Press Free and Responsible* cited in the bibliography.

of them had been campaigning for such an outcome for several years. But when it was published in 1997, they discovered that the Human Rights Bill applied not only to the various branches of government, but also to private bodies, including the media. In the case of both the press and broadcasting, the bill would empower the courts to issue injunctions to block publication when invasions of privacy were alleged. Here was their old enemy 'prior restraint' back with a vengeance.

Since the clause in the bill protecting privacy was incompatible with that protecting the freedom of expression, conflicts were to be resolved by the courts. This meant that complainants could sue for compensation, obtain prior restraint of publication, and ask for fines to be imposed on errant newspapers. Serious investigative journalism would be hamstrung. Remedies for invasions of privacy would be available only to those who could afford to take legal action. In the view of the new chairman of the PCC, Lord Wakeham, the proposals amounted to a privacy law 'by the back door'. While this might protect those in the public eye with nothing to hide, 'it would be used mercilessly by those with everything to hide. It would be a villains' charter'.

A simple amendment to exclude disputes between private persons from the provisions of the bill would have avoided these problems, but appeals to this effect fell on deaf ears. The lord chancellor, Lord Irvine, simply confirmed his attachment to the bill as drafted and actually welcomed the prospect of people being able to censor stories they claimed would breach their privacy. His attitude made it clear that the Labour Party's election promise that adoption of the European Convention was a limited, technical measure that would apply only to various branches of government no longer obtained.

After an intense lobbying campaign, the government reluctantly introduced an amendment to the bill that in considering cases under the new legislation the courts must pay 'particular regard' to the principle of free expression. Admittedly, thresholds were set before judges could award a pre-publication injunction and the burden of proof was put on the applicant to show why publication should be stopped. But the judiciary had got its foot in the door and the bill as amended passed untroubled through its remaining Parliamentary stages and came into legal force in 2000.

The question now was how the judges would interpret their new powers. As cases began to come before the courts, the answer was depressingly clear: judge-made privacy laws had become a reality and would almost certainly erode the freedom of speech. In several cases, judges were granting injunctions to prevent the publication of news stories where an invasion of privacy had been alleged, and in one case even issuing an anonymity order to prevent disclosure of the identity of either the applicant or the defendant. Having heard the evidence in secret, the judge concluded that 'he was satisfied on the facts that the claimant was likely to succeed at trial ensuring that his right to privacy should prevail over the newspaper's right to the freedom of expression'. So much for the obligation to give 'particular regard' to free speech. When it came to hard cases, judges showed themselves as dismissive of the freedom of the press as they had always been. Privacy laws were being introduced into England not through statutes passed after due consideration by Parliament, but by secretive judicial fiat.

This may not be thought to matter too much where privacy laws are used to suppress personal – often sexual – scandals. As the PCC's own code of practice lays down, everyone is entitled to respect for his or her private and family life, home, health and correspondence. In the case of complaints, 'a publication will be expected to justify intrusions into any individual's private life without consent'. Justification usually takes the form of an exposure of crime or wrong-doing, or, in the case of public figures, the exposure of gross hypocrisy or double standards.

The problem with admitting the law into this process is threefold: it usually involves censorship, with no opportunity for newspapers to demonstrate the need for public exposure; it restricts the ability to make complaints to those able to meet the considerable legal costs involved; and it can all too easily be used by powerful litigants to suppress information that in a free society *ought* to be in the public domain. In Europe, where the convention has been in force for many years, the record in balancing the right to privacy with that of free expression has not been a happy one. Protected by draconian privacy laws, politicians in several European countries have grown deeply corrupt, the absence of an inquisitive press allowing them to conceal the most serious malpractices from the public. The most obvious example is France, where the press has been prevented by privacy laws from exposing the corruption of at least two of their recent presidents, who in Britain would almost certainly have been exposed by the press, and could never have been elected. They got away with it only because they were able to sweep their sleaze under a carpet of legal protection.

In Britain, the introduction of press laws for the first time in 300 years has not enhanced the freedom of the press; it has diminished it. However tentatively, it has allowed for the judicial invasion of free speech without any kind of democratic control. Judges now make the rules which decide the balance between the conflicting rights of privacy and free expression. On the evidence so far, their record in defending a free press has been as poor as any of their predecessors.

PENTAGON PAPERS

At about the time the British press began to confront the threat of prior restraint over its exposure of the royal family's marital problems, the American press was just emerging from its own encounter with prior restraint over a more substantive matter. Newspapers there had been fighting for the right to disclose the secrets of how they were governed. After an intense struggle, they eventually emerged victorious, though the price they had to pay was the lost support of large segments of the general public. Far from upholding the rights of a free and inquisitive press, public opinion polls conducted at the height of the crisis revealed that the constitutional guarantees of the first amendment no longer commanded majority backing. Fifty-five per cent of the people polled said that even in peacetime they would deny the press the freedom to report any news story 'if the government feels it's harmful to our national interest'.

Like so many of the ills that afflicted America in that generation, it had begun with the war in Vietnam. As early as 1962, President Kennedy had been infuriated by a small group of young newsmen in Saigon who were reporting that developments there were far graver than public statements indicated. The president failed to persuade the *New York Times* to withdraw its reporter, David Halberstam, who, with several others, found himself systematically belittled by officials in Saigon and Washington. One of them described the young correspondents as 'two-bit, half-baked Cassandras who are doing a disservice of almost treasonable proportions to the great American public'.

The bitterness against them had to be seen to be believed. 'Here come the men from the *Hanoi Times*,' exclaimed a senior White House press officer as two reporters from the *New York Times* walked into his briefing. For five long years, honest correspondents ploughed a lonely and unpopular furrow, until the Tet offensive of 1968 finally awoke the American public to the gravity of the situation they faced. Even the reporters' own head offices did not always accept their on-the spot assessments, while others in the press sometimes turned on their own, as when Harrison Salisbury of the *New York Times* became the first American newsman to visit Hanoi. When he filed eye-witness reports that, contrary to US communiqués, American bombing had inflicted heavy civilian casualties, he was either not believed or dismissed as a tool of enemy propaganda. Reporting the war constantly placed such blood-and-bone issues before working journalists. To whom did they owe their primary allegiance: to the government, to the people, to their papers or to the truth? The answer was not always easy, especially when telling the truth (as they saw it) was regarded by many people as unpatriotic or even treasonable.

That journalists were unpopular and out of tune with large segments of public opinion was forcibly brought home during the Democratic National Convention of 1968, when Chicago's police officers went on the rampage against them. 'Man, the pigs have gone wild,' one fleeing demonstrator called to the newsmen covering the riot. 'They're not after us; they're after you!' According to the official Walker Report on the riots, forty-nine newsmen were clubbed, gassed or arrested without reason as they went about their job of reporting the news. When it was over, Mayor Daley blandly put the blame for the riot on 'biased coverage' by both press and television. For journalists who were there, it came as a shock to find that the vast majority of people believed the mayor rather than what they had seen with their own eyes on television or read in the morning newspapers.

During the Nixon regime of the 1970s, attitudes towards the media were to grow more hostile than ever. Early in the administration, a concerted campaign to intimidate both press and television was launched by the vice president, Spiro Agnew. 'The day when the network commentators and even the gentlemen from the *New York Times* enjoyed a form of diplomatic immunity from comment and criticism of what they said is over,' he warned. 'Yes, gentlemen, the day is past.' He went on in similar vein in other speeches, referring in his alliterative style to 'the nattering nabobs of negativism,' 'the apocalyptic analysis' and the 'querulous questioning' of the reporters, backing up his criticisms with open threats of legal and economic reprisals.

Again, what most worried newsmen about Agnew's onslaught on their freedom of speech was the fact that it seemed to have won the support of a majority of the American people. When all three networks carried the vice president's first speech live, it triggered an avalanche of letters, telegrams and phone calls. They favoured Agnew by a majority of two to one. Here was shocking evidence that the blame for the so-called credibility gap had shifted away from the politicians in the White House on to the shoulders of the journalists who reported them. The conclusion, disturbing but irrefutable, was that the American people no longer trusted their sources of news.

The road back to credibility would be long and arduous. But over the course of the next decade, the press's tenacious reporting redressed the balance, often in the face of the most intense hostility. Their coverage of the Watergate affair, the massacre at My Lai, the racist background of one of Nixon's nominees to the Supreme Court, the corruption of Spiro Agnew and the real effect of the bombing of North Vietnam provided living proof of the need in a free society for a press active and courageous enough to exploit to the limit its rights of disclosure under the first amendment.

The greatest of all their tests came in June 1971 when the *New York Times* was prohibited by court injunction from continuing its publication of the Pentagon Papers, a secret history of the American involvement in Vietnam commissioned by the Department of Defence. For the first time in American history, a newspaper was faced with a prior restraint on publication. It was to lead to the biggest clash in a lifetime between the press on the one hand and the government on the other.

The story had dropped into the *Times*'s lap three months earlier when Daniel Ellsberg, one of the authors of the study, had handed over an enormous bundle of documents to Neil Sheehan of the *Times*'s Washington bureau, who ten years earlier had been one of the young reporters in Saigon whose despatches had so infuriated President Kennedy. Ellsberg, as a former government employee, had been an early hawk in the war and gone on ground combat missions there, but had grown more and more disillusioned as the war went on. Believing the American people had been deliberately misled, he secretly copied thousands of pages of the Pentagon's own study of the origins of the war, which he himself had helped to compile. After attempting to show them to 'authorised' politicians – who backed away – Ellsberg went to the press.

Senior editors at the *Times* soon established the authenticity of the papers and, after prolonged and often agonising debate, decided to publish. Their decision was not taken lightly. There were many practical and moral issues to consider: should the *Times* publish the full text of the documents they had obtained, which might compromise military security? How could they justify publishing 'stolen' documents? What god-given right did a newspaper have to declassify government secrets? How would they respond if taken to court? They concluded that their constitutional right to free speech meant more than the freedom to publish only what the government would allow them to publish. In their view, the only way to establish the right to publish was to publish. As to the charge that the documents were stolen, the editor of the *Times*, Abe Rosenthal, replied, 'How can you steal a decision that has caused consequences the country now pays for? How can you steal the mental processes of elected politicians or appointed officials?'.

Once the decision had been taken, the *Times* embarked on the colossal, months-long task of sifting through the papers, checking each document against the facts that had been reported at the time, analysing the historical background and putting each episode into its correct perspective. It was an impressive intellectual exercise, involving seventy-five employees working in complete secrecy in a suite of rooms the *Times* had hired in the Hilton Hotel. When it was finally published on Sunday 13 June, the story appeared under an unsensational three-column headline and, at first, seemed to have passed unnoticed. The networks ignored it, the expected 'quick government response' never came, and the Associated Press which serves thousands of newspapers and broadcasting outlets carried not a word.

Next day, the *Times* ran the second instalment of the massive archive. Awake now from its weekend slumbers, official Washington stirred itself into action. After urgent conferences at the Justice Department and the Pentagon, a stiff note was telephoned through to the *Times*, advising them that the documents were classified as 'Top Secret' and, as such, their publication was illegal. Further publication, it said, would cause 'irreparable injury' to the country's defence interests. The *Times* was asked to desist from further publication and return the documents to the department of defence.

After a frenzied argument on the editorial floor of the *Times*, the matter was referred for a decision to the publisher, Ochs 'Punch' Sulzberger, who was in Europe. He agreed with the editor, Rosenthal, and gave orders for the series to go ahead. A few hours later the presses began to roll with the third story in its series, showing how President Johnson had secretly opened the way to ground combat in Vietnam. Sensational though these revelations were, they were overshadowed by an even larger headline stating that John Mitchell, the attorney-general, had sought to halt the series, but the *Times* had refused. The emphasis had shifted from the content of the Vietnam documents on to the right of the newspapers to publish them. Rosenthal said, 'Think what it would have meant . . . if the headline had been: "Justice Department Asks End to Vietnam Series and *Times* Concedes." I think it would have changed the history of the newspaper business.'

A year later, when the dust had begun to settle, he wrote his own assessment of how the *Times* had been forced to face, in one big bundle, issues that people spent lifetimes evading: 'In the bundle were the meaning of true patriotism and national interest; the meaning and purpose of a profession, a lifetime; the meaning, duties, obligations of a free press; fear for self, for career, for the future of a newspaper; the need to see clearly what was judgement, what was ego, what was morality. As somebody said, except for sex, there it all was.'

For three days, readers of the *Times* with the stamina to persevere were treated to rare insights into the methods, the manner, the planning processes, and the intellectual assumptions that had led their country into the most divisive war in its history. Here, for all the world to see, were the liars, the villains, the honestly misguided men, the baffled leaders, their mistakes and miscalculations exposed by the most massive leak of government documents in American history.

But on the fourth day, it abruptly ended. A district judge who was serving his first day on the bench granted the government's request for a restraining order until a full hearing could be heard later in the week. It was, said the *Times*, 'an unprecedented example of censorship'. But, as it had promised all along, it dutifully agreed to abide by the court's decision. Thinking that they had been cowardly in refusing to defy the courts, Ellsberg leaked further copies of the archive to the *Washington Post*, but by the end of the week they, too, were proscribed from publishing further extracts. It was now up to the courts to resolve the issue.

The first test came in the same federal court in New York that had issued the initial injunction. The *Times* argued strenuously that unravelling government secrets was at the very heart of a free press. Everything the American government did, planned, thought, heard and contemplated in the realms of foreign policy was stamped and treated as secret – and then revealed by that same government in its daily round of contacts with reporters and politicians. Max Frankel, the *Times*'s Washington Bureau chief, told the court of the countless occasions he had been made privy to government secrets: when President Kennedy, at the height of the Cuban missile crisis, had provided him with a transcript of his conversations with Andrei Gromyko, the Soviet foreign minister; when President Johnson, waist-deep in his Texas swimming pool, had recounted his confidential conversation with Prime Minister Kosygin; when Dean Rusk told him that Laos was not worth the life of a single Kansas farm boy; and many other examples. The purpose of such dealings was not to amuse or flatter a reporter, but to put diplomatically useful information into the public domain without official responsibility and, occasionally, to explain and illustrate a policy that could publicly be described in only the vaguest terms. 'This,' Frankel concluded, 'is the coin of our business and of the officials with whom we regularly deal.' To urge that the press publish 'no further information of this character', as the attorney-general had done, was in effect to tell reporters to stop doing their job.

A day later, Judge Murray Gurfein delivered a verdict favourable to the *Times*: the government had shown no cogent reason why the documents should be suppressed. 'The security of the nation is not at the ramparts alone,' he said. 'Security also lies in the value of our free institutions. A cantankerous press, an obstinate press, a ubiquitous press must be suffered by those in authority in order to preserve the even greater values of freedom of expression and the right of the people to know.' His brave judgement was immediately overturned on appeal. The prohibition continued. The great constitutional issues that had been presented would now be settled by the US Supreme Court.

They, too, upheld the right to free expression, but only after the chief justice, Warren Burger, had accused the press of setting up a double standard of conduct – one set of principles for themselves, another for the government. He protested against the 'unseemly haste' in which the case had been conducted. Would it have been unreasonable, he asked, for the *Times* to have given the government the opportunity to review the entire collection of documents and determine whether agreement could be reached on publication?

That seemed to suggest the *Times* should go cap in hand to the White House each time it uncovered a fact which might be displeasing to the government. Such a course would be tantamount to giving politicians powers of censorship that ran counter to the very principle of an independent press. But the chief justice had more to say:

To me it is hardly believable that a newspaper long regarded as a great institution in American life would fail to perform one of the basic and simple duties of every citizen with respect to the discovery or possession of stolen property or secret government documents. That duty, I had thought – perhaps naively – was to report forthwith to responsible public officers. Thus duty rests on taxi drivers, Justices and the *New York Times.*

Luckily for the newspapers, the authoritarian chief justice possessed only one vote out of nine, and the court as a whole returned a decision in favour of the press by a majority of six votes to three. So exercised were they about the importance of the issues that had been raised that, uniquely, the nine justices produced nine separate opinions. The liberal Justice Hugo Black declared that 'far from deserving condemnation for their courageous reporting, the *New York Times* and the *Washington Post* . . . should be commended for serving the purpose that the Founding Fathers saw so clearly. In revealing the workings of government that led to the Vietnam war, the newspapers nobly did precisely that which the Founders hoped and trusted they would do.'

The press had won a famous victory. After the most testing fifteen days of its history, the presses of the *New York Times* resumed publication of the Pentagon Papers, to the illumination of the general public and the embarrassment of the Department of Justice. No discernible harm was done to national security. When the euphoria wore off, however, the newspapers were to make a more sober assessment of their victory. Prior restraint – death to a free press – now had a precedent. The Department of Justice may have lost the overall argument, but it had proved it *could* obtain a prohibition on publication while a case was being reviewed in the courts. The hostility shown towards the press by some members of the Supreme Court carried its own ominous portents. The Pentagon Papers case turned out to be the very last to be heard by a court that still retained a bare liberal majority. Before its next term began, the liberal Justices Black and Harlan had been replaced by two out-and-out conservatives nominated by President Nixon.

In 1971, the press had won; but would it have won in 1972 or 1982? Would it win today, in 2002? There are many who doubt it. The freedom of the press depends, as always, on the willingness of society to uphold it and on the courage of its practioners to defend it. Are those qualities as prevalent today as they were a generation ago? Will the editors and journalists of the twenty-first century show the same clear-headed resilience as their predecessors? Will their profit-driven corporate shareholders grant them the editorial freedom they will need to do so? And, perhaps above all, will the law be as supportive of a free press as it was then? It is hard to be sure. Americans can take comfort in the promise of their Bill of Rights that governments may make no law restraining the freedom of speech or of the press, but when the winds of intolerance begin to howl, it takes more than a comforting legal rubric to supply the courage to withstand them. Yet it is precisely when public support is least that a free press is needed most, as the turbulent events of the 1970s clearly showed.

CENSORING CYBERSPACE

The debate about the future of a free press has been infinitely complicated by the arrival of a new means of communication which, in theory at least, seemed to open up the prospect of unfettered freedom of speech for everyone in the world. By the beginning of the twenty-first century an estimated 200 million people were hooked up to 'cyberspace', a unique and wholly new medium of communication based in no particular geographic location, but available to anyone, in any country, with access to the internet. In addition to that, the prospective merger of television and the internet brought about by digital technology promised to make the current systems of broadcasting and film regulation redundant, with thousands of channels available to every home from around the world.

When that day comes, it was originally thought that it would bring with it a global information environment in which freedom of speech had no limits. In 1997, the US Supreme Court ruled that, as the most participatory form of mass speech yet developed, the internet deserved the highest protection from government intrusion. In a case brought by the American Civil Liberties Union against a law that would have made it illegal to transmit material that was 'indecent' or 'patently offensive', the court declared that the law contravened the free speech provisions of the first amendment. Just as the strength of the internet was chaos, so 'the strength of our liberty depends on the chaos and cacophony of the unfettered free speech the First Amendment protects'. The internet was not an 'intrusive' medium and so should not be subjected to the same sort of controls as those applied to network television. Offensive material was not accessed by chance, but required the user to take 'affirmative steps'. The odds were therefore slim that a user would enter a sexually explicit site by accident. Children were protected by the fact that access to sexually explicit sites could usually be obtained only by the production of a credit card to verify the user's age.

In Britain and elsewhere, the debate about controlling the internet has taken a more censorious turn. That there should be *some* sort of control over pornography is accepted by even the most liberal advocate of free speech. Films or videos showing real acts of torture, 'snuff movies' or the sexual abuse of children are always unacceptable, whatever the audience. There is also widespread agreement that children themselves need to be protected from hardcore pornography and even that adults should be protected from having it thrust upon them if they find it offensive. There is genuine anxiety also about sites that entice children away from home, or tell them how to commit suicide or make bombs. In Germany, there is concern about neo-Nazi sites and sites that incite racial hatred, or even, in one case, murder. In Britain, the government's stated position is that what is illegal offline is illegal online – in other words, the Obscene Publications Act applies equally to the net as to any other medium. The problem, however, is policing it, especially where the material comes from jurisdictions outside the reach of the English courts.

Though it is still in the future, the government's preferred answer seems to lie in the introduction of voluntary blocking and rating schemes operated by the internet service providers themselves. A European-funded organisation called

Incore was set up in 2000 to create a system whereby illegal sites would be screened out by ISPs across the continent. All legal sites would be electronically tagged so that individual users of the net could build up their own filters, based on an internationally agreed set of labels which rated material according to the degree of sex, nudity, violence and bad language it contained – or even create the ability to screen out unwanted advertisements, or sites that promoted undesirable activities such as drug taking, smoking cigarettes, advocating revolution or drinking alcohol. This would be coupled with the creation of hotlines to report illegal content and a code of practice for the ISPs.

Civil libertarians are wary of this solution, which in their view contains a very real threat to free speech. The ACLU, which has led the worldwide fight against the cyber censors, says they amount to a prior restraint on publication. It adds: 'In the physical world people censor the printed word by burning books. But in the virtual world you can just as easily censor controversial speech by banishing it into the furthest corners of cyberspace with blocking and rating schemes.' By their nature, government-coerced schemes for the ISPs to police themselves hark back to the seventeenth-century practice of giving the Stationers' Company control over its own members' output. Such systems play safe. Controversy is avoided. Controls tend to be over-inclusive. In the few years since it was first introduced, the internet's 'censorware' has already displayed many of the classic faults of self-regulation. Most ISPs take their decisions in secret. There is usually no appeal against their bans. Far from empowering individual end-users to control the content they wish to receive, censorware in fact relies on a centralised system of classification which imposes an undesirable cultural hegemony on the net. As happened with commercial television, there will be a tendency for the ISPs to tone down their material to conform to the lowest common denominator in order to maximise their profits and keep out of trouble.

The use of the net by paedophiles, however, is a real area of concern. It is regarded practically everywhere as an arrestable criminal offence, as is the distribution of such material and, in many countries, its possession. Rather than impose heavy-handed and probably unworkable prior restraints on the internet, it is generally recognised that the most effective approach to such crimes is to target the perpetrators – helped in Britain by the creation of hotlines run by the Internet Watch Foundation, a voluntary organisation funded by the ISPs. Once they locate illegal content, the IWF informs the police and the ISPs, who then have no excuse in law that they are unaware of the offending material, and so could be prosecuted if they fail to remove it. The ISPs consistently comply with such advice as they would otherwise end up in court on obscenity or other public order charges.

So long as it stopped there, issues of free speech would not arise. Paedophiles are committing a revolting crime. The harm they do needs strong measures to prevent it, including some sort of control over their use of the internet. There is also strong support across many nations for a system of rating websites to protect children from accessing pornography. However, there is also huge disagreement about how extensive the controls should be. Civil liberty campaigners fear that self-regulation of the sort operated by the IWF simply invites government intervention. Once such systems are established, they argue, it becomes very tempting for governments to impose mandatory filter use and the whole paraphernalia of government-backed regulation – or even, in Europe, supranational regulation. Beyond all that looms the worst-case scenario in which ISPs are made criminally liable for the content of every one of the millions of sites that their subscribers can access from anywhere in the world.

And the process will not stop with pornography. Already, German ISPs are under pressure to install filters to shut out vulgar language, 'hate speech', intolerance and sites that encourage gambling and even the sale of alcohol. From there, it will be just a short step to censoring undesirable political content and even some religious sites. Those campaigning to keep the net free from such controls stress the immense difficulties that would be involved in trying to impose a common standard across widely different cultures. They point out that anyway much of the material on the net originates in the United States, where the courts have so far refused to sanction any form of outside control. Furthermore, the vast majority of internet users in Britain and in Europe are already denied access to illegal content because all the big ISPs screen it out on the advice of the IWF. Short of what is illegal, they argue, the net should be free to any user in possession of his or her civil liberties.

This includes those who make use of the internet to spread what is sometimes known as 'hate speech' – material in support of the Ku Klux Klan, for instance, or fundamental religious groups, or even neo-Nazis. The ACLU, among others, argue that if the free speech rights of the most unpopular groups in society are lost, then no one's liberty is secure. In that sense, freedom of speech is indivisible. In the ACLUs' view, censoring so-called hate speech also runs counter to the long-term interests of the racial, ethnic, religious and sexual minorities who are the most frequent victims of hate. If government is given the power to decide which opinions are hateful, history teaches that it is more apt to use this power to prosecute minorities than to protect them. Tolerating hateful speech, they argue, is 'the best protection we have against any Nazi-type regime in this country'. At the same time, freedom of speech does not prevent punishing conduct that intimidates, harasses, or threatens another person, even if words are used. Threatening phone calls, for example, are not constitutionally protected. The court has also held that so-called 'fighting words . . . which by their very utterance inflict injury or tend to incite an immediate breach of the peace', are similarly unprotected.

Ever since Gutenberg assembled his first printing press in the 1450s, new forms of communication have aroused alarm about the evil effects they may have. Printed books were put under the control of heavy-handed licensers because of the harm they might do. So in their turn were newspapers, the cinema, radio, television, satellites and video, the regulatory vestiges of which have persisted into the twenty-first century. Now it is the internet's turn, where the battle over imposing controls has barely begun. What is already clear is that the old anarchic days of unfettered free speech enjoyed by its pioneers are over. What takes its place is still a matter for conjecture. But what is clear beyond doubt is that the principles of free speech as it applies to the internet will have to be fought out and thought out just as vigorously by the coming generation as they have for every other new form of communication.

CHAPTER SEVENTEEN

Taking Stock

FREE SPEECH DEFINED

Progress towards establishing a universal principle of free speech has been neither as even nor inevitable as once supposed. Indeed, it is worth remembering that for much of human history the very concept of 'free speech' would have been quite meaningless. Even in democratic Athens, the liberty of speech so extolled by Pericles was put forward more as a civic duty than as a 'right' in the modern sense of the word. Two thousand years later, when the conditions for civil liberty were again beginning to take shape, the precursors of that liberty had other, quite different, objectives in mind. Neither Luther nor Galileo ever thought of 'free speech', even as he accidentally advanced it. Later still, when free speech did begin to emerge as a principle to be defined and defended, the arguments put forward in Milton's *Areopagitica*, Locke's *Letter on Toleration*, Madison's Bill of Rights and Mill's *On Liberty* were, in spite of superficial similarities, arguments for different things, in pursuit of different aims in entirely different circumstances. In the middle of a civil war, Milton sought the liberty of unlicensed printing for Protestant intellectuals like himself; Locke was concerned to distinguish between political and religious rights; Madison strove to limit the power of the new federal government; Mill set out to establish a sweeping general principle that may, or may not, be as relevant today as it was when he wrote it. While there are important lessons to be learned from them all care must be taken not to project their ideas too literally into the present. As the great nineteenth century historian, Leopold von Ranke, taught, every historical age is 'immediate to God'. So it is with individuals. Their contributions to the modern concept of free speech must be judged by their own lights, used by us when they are relevant, while recognising that the ruling passions of one age are not necessarily those of another. If it is to endure, free speech must never become mere 'dead dogma', an inheritance from the past that needs no further examination. It is, after all, part of the principle itself that the best-warranted beliefs must be constantly tested in the crucible of criticism. Reliance on past authority is never enough. The freedoms of the mind, including that of free speech, need to be continually examined, expanded and revitalised in order to determine their current validity.

What is clear from an examination of the past is that not one but several notions of what is loosely called 'free speech' exist, related to one another and in many ways interdependent, but each with its own distinct character and pedigree. The struggle to establish the liberty of conscience, for instance, was conducted independently from the struggle for a free press and based on quite different arguments. Then again, the nature of the free enquiry needed to establish a scientific truth is different in kind from the freedom needed by a politician to get his ideas accepted in the democratic marketplace. Does the right to free speech extend to the visual arts? Some have said not, and continue to censor various forms of visual expression in the name of sexual morality. Is television covered by the same principle that guarantees the freedom of the press? Judging by the regulatory framework surrounding most television systems, the answer, at least for the moment, is no.

Another question that then arises is that of the *quality* of the speech to be protected. Are the tabloid newspapers as worthy of protection as a learned dissertation in *The Economist*? Is an impartial source of news more valuable than commercial advertising? Is a book worth fighting for and a comic not? When it comes to art, Picasso's banned *Guernica* and Shostakovich's outlawed symphonies are clearly easier to defend than *The Chain Saw Massacre*, though perhaps not so much because they are a higher form of art, but because banning them was designed to prevent people being politically influenced by them. The question is further complicated when an act of communication is coupled with another sort of conduct – aggressive picketing of non-union workers during a strike, for instance. Clearly, what is at stake here is more the 'freedom of expression' than 'free speech', though the two concepts are often conjoined. In short, the generic term 'free speech' is colloquially used to cover a diverse range of freedoms, each subject to its own definition and its own type of defence or justification.

THE ARGUMENT FROM TRUTH

The classic defence of free speech, going back to Milton, is that it is important first and foremost because it leads to the discovery of truth. 'Let her and falsehood grapple,' Milton wrote in his *Areopagitica*, 'for whoever knew truth put to the worse in a free and equal encounter?' Mill picked up the same argument: open discussion, freedom of enquiry and the interplay of competing beliefs will inexorably lead truth to reveal herself. More recently, the search for truth has been likened to the process of cross-examination in a court of law. When all opinions have been freely heard, the jury of public opinion will deliver its verdict and pick the version of truth it prefers. Oliver Wendell Holmes believed the best test of the truth of an idea was to get itself accepted in the competition of the market. His colleague, Felix Frankfurter, made a similar point when he said, 'the history of civilisation is in considerable measure the displacement of error which once held sway as official truth by beliefs which have in turn yielded to other truths'. Man's liberty to search for truth should, therefore, remain unfettered 'no matter what orthodoxies he may challenge'. In all these formulations, the right to free speech is not put forward as an end in itself but as a means towards something else: the discovery of truth, which is held to be the dominant good. The process is seamless; truth is simply what for the moment survives until a greater truth comes along to replace it. There are no absolutes.

Modern philosophers find the formulation unconvincing. It fails to give a clear answer to the critical question – does truth *always* emerge triumphant when sent out to grapple with falsehood? Where is the empirical evidence that in every argument reason will prevail? They point to the example of pre-war Germany, where the Nazis put forward views about the racial inferiority of the Jews that were widely accepted. Does this then make their theories true? One hopes not. What survives as a truth in the marketplace is just as likely to lead to error, ignorance, folly or even to unspeakable crimes. There is therefore no link in logic between the right to free speech and an increase in human knowledge and understanding. At best, truth may emerge from a seminar of intellectuals trained to think rationally. That is by no means the same as saying it will prevail when subject to the scrutiny of the public at large. People are not nearly so rational as the leaders of the eighteenth-century Enlightenment assumed who first articulated the idea of rationality. Their optimistic naiveté has long since been discredited by history and bitter experience. Without this assumption, the empirical support for the argument from truth evaporates. As Pope said:

> The ruling passion be it what it will,
> The ruling passion conquers reason still.

Clearly then, there are major flaws in basing a theory of free speech on the assumption that reason will always prevail. But while the freedom to express contrary views may not always lead to truth, it does have another, perhaps more important virtue. By focussing on human fallibility, it posits the admission in every argument that 'I may be wrong and you may be right'. Indeed, in most arguments, I am very likely to be wrong. I therefore need my free speech in order to test my opinion against yours. Even when I reject it, your thought has then helped to shape my thought. This process is especially valuable when applied to matters of ethics, morals and politics, where there is little consensus and, consequently, a large risk of suppressing an opinion which may later turn out to be the right one. That is why the classic defence of free speech based on the collision of competing ideas has been held so strongly and for so many years. What is true and what is false, what is right and what is wrong, what is sound and what is foolish are, in these fields at least, essentially subjective judgements. And if individuals can be fallible in these matters, then so too can those who rule over them. Just as we are properly sceptical about our own ability to distinguish truth from error, so should we be even more sceptical about the motives and abilities of those to whom we grant political power. The treatment meted out to Socrates, Galileo, Lilburne, Wilkes and Cobbett, the prosecutions for seditious libel of those now regarded as heroes, the banning of *Ulysses* and *Guernica*, Hoover's persecution of dissidents and countless acts of petty censorship are proof enough that authority is a spectacularly bad arbiter in matters of free speech. While not infallible, the free exchange of competing ideas is likely to get nearer to the truth than is any governmental agency. Even when he is wrong, Galileo's enquiring mind is preferable to the dogma of the Inquisition.

It must, however, be conceded that a defence of free speech based on the collision of competing ideas is unlikely to achieve all that Voltaire, Jefferson and Mill hoped it would. It demonstrably does not always lead to the truth. And even though it retains its validity as a negative justification of free speech – in the sense that it assumes the fallibility of human judgement – it does not provide a justification for the right to free speech in all circumstances. In particular, it does not begin to address the question of the liberty of conscience or the freedom of the press. In order to defend those categories of free speech, other arguments are needed.

THE ARGUMENT FROM DEMOCRACY

One of the strongest of these arguments is that free speech is necessary to the proper working of democracy. In a sense this goes back to the *isêgoria* of ancient Athens, the right whereby 'free born men, having to advise the public, may speak free'. However, it must always be remembered that for the vast bulk of intervening history, democracy was not a highly regarded form of government. Until two centuries ago, it was associated with mob rule and dark, almost fathomless threats from the lower orders. The ruling classes of Europe and the leaders of the Church looked on it with oligarchic disdain, as did the American Federalists. Not until the days of Jefferson and Madison did it achieve anything like political respectability, and even by the 1930s less than half the countries of Europe could claim to be self-ruling liberal democracies. In most of the non-western world the concept was quite unknown.

It is only where democracy has taken root that a coherent principle of free speech can be based upon it – and then only in genuinely democratic societies that choose their rulers from opposing political parties through elections open to all, by agreement and without violence. This is an argument for free speech that was simply unavailable in the era of Milton, Locke and Voltaire. Even in the early days of the American republic, it took several decades of controversy before they felt able to discard the notion of seditious libel, the belief that governments should be protected from criticism, even during a hotly fought election campaign. Before then, the law in both Britain and America held that governments could be criminally assaulted by mere words and opinions. Any comment about the established order that tended to lower it in the public's esteem was seditious libel, subjecting its author to criminal prosecution. Freedom of speech protected debates in Parliament from encroachments by the crown. It did not give the individual citizen the right to speak his mind. Freedom of the press simply meant the absence of prior restraint, the liberty to print without a licence and answer for the consequences.

Free speech became a necessary civil liberty only after the people themselves became the source of sovereignty, the masters rather than the servants of government. But once that had occurred, the political argument in its favour became irresistible. For a sovereign electorate to choose between rival political parties, it must have an unimpeded supply of information on which to base that choice. Because people cannot intelligently cast their votes without access to the relevant arguments, to deny them access to those arguments is as serious an infringement of their democratic rights as denying them the vote. Furthermore, because a democracy's leaders are answerable to the people, free speech is needed to keep them under constant critical scrutiny. The freedom to criticise government policy and officials, which used to be regarded as seditious libel, is actually a necessary check on the power of elected politicians. Without it, democracy itself would become corrupted. In a modern society, it is, as Walter Lippmann once observed, not so much a privilege as an organic necessity.

There is, however, a paradox at the heart of this argument. Democracy is, in essence, rule by the majority. But the right to free speech entails allowing an individual to put forward an unpopular or even a hated idea which the majority might wish to suppress. As we have seen, decisions taken by majorities can be as wrong and tyrannical as those taken by an individual despot. In classical times, a democracy voted to put Socrates to death for expressing his dissent and Horace spoke of '*civium ardor prava jubentium*', which can be translated as 'the frenzy of the citizens in urging what is wrong'. De Tocqueville coined the phrase 'tyranny of the majority' and Mill used it to expound his own views on free speech. To take it for granted that free speech comes as part and parcel of democracy is clearly mistaken. What then can be done?

If it is accepted that free speech is vital to the working of democracy, the only way to resolve the paradox is by granting it special protection, to shield it from encroachment even by the sovereign will of an otherwise all-powerful people. This can be justified on the grounds that to deny a minority point of view the right to be heard removes the moral basis for accepting the decisions of the majority. The law of the land then loses its authority and people will not feel bound by decisions from which they have been excluded. Democracy can function effectively only if the majority grant minorities the right to dissent. They need their freedom of speech in order to persuade others to share their point of view. It therefore merits a privileged status. In this case, at least, liberty takes precedence over democracy.

Modern representative democracy is, of course, far removed from the idealised open democracy of the Athenian *polis*, where the ordinary citizen could – and usually did – take an active part in the decision-taking process. Today, that is neither possible nor even desirable. Other means have to be found to enable individual citizens to join in the political debate and, if they feel the need, to express their own dissenting views. And while ordinary members of the public may appear to have little power compared to that exercised by the Athenian citizen, public opinion as a whole can have a great deal of power, not only in choosing its representatives at election time, but constantly, through the processes of modern communications. The press, radio and especially television can bring politicians into citizens' homes to be scrutinised and cross-examined on a daily and even hourly basis. Such coverage has become an essential adjunct to the public's right to participate in the decision-making process and an integral part of the system of checks and balances that enables representative democracy to function. Freedom of speech not only means the freedom to say what you want, but also the freedom to read what you want, or to hear it, or see it on television. The freedom of the recipient therefore implies freedom for their chosen means of communication.

It should be recognised, though, that by basing the argument for the freedom of speech and the press on its value to democracy, its application is confined almost exclusively to public affairs, government and politics. In spite of its almost unassailable strength in its own field, it once again fails to provide an over-arching principle to cover the right to free speech in all its forms any more than did the argument from truth.

THE ARGUMENT AGAINST CENSORSHIP

The nearest we are likely to come to an over-arching principle covering all forms of free speech is the negative one that censorship and suppression are themselves intrinsically evil, and will always tend to do more harm than good. Mill certainly thought so when he argued that governments have no authority to suppress an opinion for all mankind and exclude every other person from the means of judging its merits. Milton, too, contended that censorship was not only wrong, it was usually pointless. The crown's efforts to control the flow of ideas through the licensing laws had been as futile as 'trying to pound up the crows by shutting the park gates'. 'Believe it Lords and Commons, they who counsel you to such a suppressing, do as good bid ye suppress yourselves.'

While Milton spoke rhetorically, there is ample empirical evidence to support him. As it has just been seen, the process of regulating speech has historically been prone to fairly spectacular errors. The attempt by the American Federalists to suppress criticism from their political opponents by means of the Alien and Sedition Acts is a typical, though not unique, example of how even a democratically elected government can mistake legitimate criticism for criminal sedition. In our own age, democratically elected politicians have sometimes felt the need to cast aside their attachment to free speech and resort to censorship, which they then tend to justify with varying degrees of sophistry. In 1971, the Nixon administration went to court to prevent the *New York Times* from publishing the Pentagon Papers, described by the administration as 'a deliberate betrayal of government secrets'. In Britain, a similar attempt was made by the Thatcher administration to prevent the broadcast of *Death on the Rock*, a television programme which examined the fatal shooting of three unarmed Irish nationalists by British forces in Gibraltar. The Foreign Secretary, Sir Geoffrey Howe, made an attempt at suppression in person, but he was rebuffed by the television regulator, who stood firm against this attempt to ban a programme the government had not even seen.

These and several similar examples provide eloquent reason why governments should not themselves be allowed to act as censors. They are generally acting as judges in their own cause. Their attempts to regulate critical speech is a clear conflict of interest. This renders them ineligible to make the necessary distinctions between opinions that are false and harmful and those that are true and useful. No group of fallible human beings is able to make such distinctions, least of all one with an interest in the outcome. We should always mistrust the motives and abilities of those who seek to prescribe opinions to us and determine what doctrines, what facts or what arguments should be allowed to be heard. The power of government to regulate speech and the press should always be more limited than are its other powers.

Although this argument may be valid when applied to serious matters of public policy, it is harder to justify its application to more trivial matters. The content of Britain's tabloid newspapers is a case in point. It is nowadays made up almost entirely of trivia – gossip about the lives of royalty, television personalities and footballers, and, only slightly more seriously, revelations about the sexual peccadilloes of politicians, judges and prominent businessmen. If they are to avoid the laws of libel, most such stories need to be true and many of them are harmless. But should they be protected by such concepts as 'freedom of speech' and 'liberty of the press'? In his treatise on *Free Speech*, Alan Haworth thinks not, and uses the example to attack the argument that free speech is necessary in order to reveal the truth, which Mill and his followers hold to be the pre-eminent good. Material in the tabloid press is utterly trivial and meretricious, Haworth says, therefore its suppression would not be a matter of any great significance. Who cares if 'all mankind is robbed' of the opportunity to know what soap-opera stars get up to with their nineteen-year-old boyfriends?

While this point of view is superficially persuasive, it does not stand up to closer scrutiny. People may not care if 'all mankind is robbed' of trivial tittle-tattle, but they ought to care about the machinery of censorship that would be required to ensure that such tittle-tattle was suppressed. To ban it would call either for a repressive system of fines and punishments in case it were published, or an even more repressive system of pre-publication scrutiny to prevent it from being published in the first place. And imagine the cumbersome list of bureaucratic rules and regulations that would be drawn up to decide just which items of tittle-tattle were allowable and which were forbidden. Nor is it likely that the process would stop with trivia. Once the machinery of censorship was in place, the temptation to extend its use to other areas would be all but overwhelming. Each would be justified in the name of public decency or protecting privacy or ensuring fair reporting or any number of other desirable ends. They would, however, never justify the means. The machinery of censorship is by its very nature oppressive.

Freedom of expression exists only where there is no prior restraint on publication and where everything may be published, subject to the sanction of laws applying to all citizens. Part of the price of such freedom is an abundance of shallow tittle-tattle, some irresponsible journalism and the occasional embarrassment of private and public figures. We may not like it, but it is not possible to impose sanctions on meretricious journalism without restricting the responsible and necessary exercise of the freedom of speech.

None of this should be taken to imply that the freedom of speech has no bounds and cannot cause harm. Printing something scurrilous about people can damage their reputation, invade their privacy or cause emotional distress. Pornography can corrupt them. Inciting an angry crowd can cause a riot. Revealing military secrets can compromise national security. Intemperate speeches on immigration can stir up racial hatred. What is dangerous is to try and control these harmful effects through laws that apply only to the press, which are pernicious in themselves. The harm can best be dealt with, quite legitimately and without encroaching on the freedom of speech, by recourse to the ordinary laws of the land and to nothing else.

More than 100 years ago, the constitutional historian A.V. Dicey noted that the abolition of censorship was final in England because the exercise of discretionary power by the crown was inconsistent with the ideas of English law. In France, by contrast, censorship though constantly abolished had been just as constantly revived, because the exertion of discretionary powers by the government had been and still was in harmony with the French concept of *droit administratif.* The contrast was made all the more striking by the paradox that the statesmen who tried, with little success, to establish the liberty of the press in France really intended to proclaim the freedom of opinion, while the statesmen who would not pass the Licensing Act, and thereby founded the liberty of the press in England, held theories of toleration which fell far short of favouring unrestricted freedom of discussion. The contrast was not only striking in itself, but also afforded the strongest illustration that could be found of English conceptions of the rule of law.

The point is well worth pondering as Britain adopts more and more European-style legislation in the name of 'harmonisation', including the so-called human rights bills. In spite of what they say on their face, such laws have a historical tendency to restrict rather than extend the freedom of speech. An important reason for the long survival of a free press in England is that for 300 years after the lapse of the licensing laws in 1695 there was no such thing as a press law and the terms 'press offences', 'censorship of the press' and even 'liberty of the press' were all but unknown in the law courts, simply because any offence that could be committed by the press was governed by the ordinary law of the land. That is also the case in America, where press laws are forbidden by the constitution. That does not mean that the press is exempt from all control. It means it is subject to the same laws as everyone else. Equal liberty under law is the one sure foundation of a principle of free speech that comes closest to covering all aspects of that elusive concept.

Voltaire thought that 'liberty consists of dependence on nothing but law'. He spoke after a visit to England, where he had enjoyed 'in a free country the greatest benefit I know, and humanity's most glorious right, which is to depend only on men's laws and not upon their whims'. Throughout his life, he constantly repeated the phrase, 'laws, not whims'. As a passionate advocate of the power of reason, he saw that reason could become useful to society only when its findings were communicated; hence freedom of expression was an indispensable corollary of the freedom of thought, and with it a long series of other liberties. Freedom of expression depends on law; therefore the best government is that which guarantees to all, without distinction, the utmost liberty of speech they can enjoy without harm to their fellows. It follows from this that the concept of free speech under law cannot be an absolute freedom. But as John Locke recognised, man was never really free even when he lived in a state of nature. Far from surrendering his liberty when he created political societies, Locke believed he in fact increased it. Law provided the security in which he was more able to express himself than he was in the hazardous conditions of primitive anarchy. Though there is more *theoretical* liberty in a state of nature, there is less *actual* liberty. Free speech, too, flourishes best under the rule of law.

AN UNCERTAIN FUTURE

Equal liberty under the law underpins a concept of free speech which implies a profound respect for the individual and the acceptance of diversity. These are qualities commonly considered to be the primary components of the western liberal credo. At the same time, conventional wisdom holds that the liberal emphasis on individuality undermines social cohesion, shows a selfish disregard for others and emphasises rights at the expense of duties. The words 'liberal' and 'liberalism' have themselves become pejoratives, associated with permissiveness and personal greed. This interpretation in fact turns liberalism on its head – the rights liberals proclaim necessarily impose obligations towards others – but there is no doubt that it is an interpretation that has taken hold. It is also likely that the pressures it imposes on free speech will grow, both as a result of the felt need to restore a sense of stability and social conformity and a desire to eliminate views regarded as divisive, dangerous, politically incorrect, or simply too provocative to tolerate.

Society's loss of faith in its liberal credentials leads not so much to the tyranny of the majority as the ability of intolerant minorities to tyrannise *over* the majority. Add to this the rival moral traditions that now live side by side in most western societies and a further threat to free speech becomes manifest. We live in a world where loosely held traditions of tolerance are constantly under challenge from a number of other contending, often incompatible ideologies, many of them hostile to the very concept of free speech.

A disturbing example of these conflicts was the Islamic *fatwah*, or death sentence, passed in 1988 on Salman Rushdie for the crime of blasphemy in publishing his novel *Satanic Verses*. For more than a decade, Rushdie was forced to live as a prisoner in his own country, with each side staring uncomprehendingly at the other over a seemingly unbridgeable cultural divide. Islamic fundamentalists saw the book as a deliberate assault on their most deeply held beliefs; western liberals saw the issue as a clear breach of the right to free speech. It could, of course, be both of those things. If that is the case, then which of them should take priority over the other? And who, ultimately, should decide these things? With both sides claiming the protection of a universal and abstract moral authority, such questions would seem to be logically insoluble. The liberal case was not helped by unsympathetic western commentators claiming Rushdie 'knew just what he was doing' or that he had 'brought it upon himself'. The author's motives in writing the book are in fact irrelevant. Either he had the right to free speech or he did not. For anyone who holds to the principles of tolerance and free expression there is a citadel to defend. In a liberal democracy, as Britain is, the basic civil rights on which that society is built should be inviolable. They are, after all, what protect the rights and the diversity of views held by minorities.

For many, the most worrying aspect of the Rushdie affair was not the *fatwah* imposed by a distant Ayatollah, but the fact that the author received such grudging support from a supposedly open liberal society that counts the right to free speech as one of its bulwarks. It revealed to an alarming extent how confused that society had become about its moral identity and how feeble it was in defending its basic civil rights. The episode gave an ironic twist to the concept of Mill's tyranny of the majority, the social pressures which impose conformity, stifle individuality and enslave the soul itself. In the Rushdie case, the harm was caused by an intolerant minority in the face of a tolerant but passive majority. A generation previously the same trait had enabled fanatical minorities to impose totalitarian rule in much of Europe, and even today it remains one of the greatest challenges faced by modern society. It is a trait which has even led some people to abandon any sort of defence of western liberal values. Everything is relative, they argue: we have no more right to defend and propagate the values of our own culture than any other culture. Those who do defend it are dismissed as imperialist, racist or shockingly out of touch with the need to embrace values we do not share. Rather than defending the citadel, they seem to say, they would be better employed on pulling it down.

The shallowness of such views was cruelly exposed by the terrorist attacks on New York and Washington in September 2001. In one autumn morning, the fragility of our modern civilisation and how easily its values can be subverted by barbarism became suddenly and brutally apparent. The postwar generation's complacent illusion that a free and affluent lifestyle came as their birthright rather than something that needed nurturing and defending lay among the ruins of the assaulted city. No longer could they take for granted the humane complexities of the civilisation in which they lived. Like the Rushdie *fatwah*, but on an infinitely greater scale, the fundamentalist assault on America threw down a challenge for them – and for all of us – to redefine the values of the tolerant and, yes liberal, civilisation in which we live. For all its evil effects, the assault did at least reveal how precious are the values of freedom and tolerance, as well as how fragile. If it created an awareness of what they have to lose, one hopes it might also bring a realisation that modern civilisation rests on more than just material well-being and the right to be left alone. It rests just as much on a delicate network of moral and cultural values that have taken centuries to create, but which can take only seconds to destroy.

Among those cultural values is the right to free speech as defined, struggled for and defended over at least the past three centuries. Yet within days of the outrages in America, authorities in countries around the world were calling for more controls, more restrictions and even the suspension of laboriously won human rights. Restrictions were called for, as they always are, in the name of combating evil. In America, the provisions of the first amendment were put aside yet again and critics of the government's response to the atrocities bludgeoned into silence. The US media went along with the view that its role was to support the government's response without qualification. Debate was seen to equate with dissent and dissent with a lack of patriotism. In Britain, new laws were proposed forbidding the incitement to religious hatred – a concept almost impossible to define in any meaningful legal sense and precisely the sort of law that Tom Paine fought against in publishing *The Age of Reason*. He established then – and one hoped, for all time – that religious beliefs are as open to criticism, ridicule and abuse as any other form of belief. The only legitimate boundary to such criticism is to prevent a direct incitement to violence, which would be covered anyway, under existing laws. When Paine's arguments were eventually accepted, they also established that what makes our civilisation worth defending is not the fact that it is specifically western or Christian, but that it is secular, tolerant and democratic, and shows a proper respect for individual liberties. As previous chapters have tried to show, free and rational thinking came about only when individuals had been released from the chains of religious and political dogma. However well meant, renewed attempts to protect such dogmas from criticical scrutiny represent a dangerous regression, negating the very thing which western governments were trying to defend: their people's liberty and their inalienable civil rights. Far from suppressing deeds that threaten life and liberty, blasphemy laws criminalise thought itself.

Whether the religion they seek to protect is Christian or Islamic, such laws have no place in the modern, secular, multi-cultural world. The battle of ideas must always be fought in conditions of free speech. Indeed, it is worth reflecting that Christianity itself would probably never have taken hold if the Jewish elders had been given their way and persuaded the Romans to silence St Paul because his preaching was stirring up religious hatred. Any set of beliefs, whether secular or religious, works best through the power of persuasion. There should be no room in a pluralist society for totalitarian ideologies, which, through indoctrination and coercion, seek to exclude all dissent. However much the opinions of others are deplored, debate must never be curtailed by laws which undermine the liberty to disagree peaceably about the eternal verities.

If liberal values are to be properly defended it is essential to know what free speech entails. It entails the freedom to be provocative – to say things that cause offence, to insult the opinions of others, to impart information others may wish to suppress, to voice views others may hate. It also entails the duty to be tolerant of those who voice such views, however much one personally disagrees with them. Those charged with conducting the debate on such burning issues as the threat of terrorism, the future of Europe, or maintaining the standards of a free and responsible press must learn to apply to their task the principles that have been won by the efforts of their predecessors, including that of free speech. If this book has helped to illuminate those efforts, it has been well worth the writing.

Bibliography

Published in London unless stated otherwise.

CHAPTER ONE

Acton, Lord, *Essays on Liberty*, London, 1907.
Aristophanes, *The Clouds*, trans. A.H. Sommerstein, Harmondsworth, Penguin, 1973.
——, trans. K.J. Dover, Oxford, Oxford University Press, 1968.
——, trans. J. Henderson, Loeb, 1998.
——, *The Wasps*, trans. D.M. McDowell, Oxford, Oxford University Press, 1971.
——, trans. B.B. Rogers, Loeb, 1924 and reprints.
Berlin, I., *Four Essays on Liberty*, Oxford, Oxford University Press, 1969.
Brickhouse, T.C. and Smith, D. *Socrates on Trial*, Oxford, Oxford University Press, 1989.
Bury, J.D. ed., *Cambridge Ancient History*, vol. v, Cambridge, Cambridge University Press, 1923–54.
Critias (attrib. by some), *The Old Oligarch*, Loeb translation, 1998.
Euripides, *The Suppliant Women*, trans. Philip Vellacot, Harmondsworth, Penguin, 1972.
Guthrie, W.K.C., *A History of Greek Philosophy*, vol. 5, Cambridge, Cambridge University Press, 1962–81.
Hammond, N.G.L., *The Classical Age of Greece*, Weidenfeld & Nicolson, 1979.
Hayek, F.A., *John Stuart Mill and Harriet Taylor*, Routledge & Kegan Paul, 1951.
Herodotus, *The Histories*, trans. Aubrey de Selincourt, Harmondsworth, Penguin, 1954.
Howatson, M.C., ed, *Oxford Companion to Ancient Literature*, Oxford, Oxford University Press, 1989.
MacDowell, D.M., *The Law in Classical Athens*, Thames & Hudson, 1978.
Milton, J., *Areopagitica*, 1644: World Classics, Oxford, Oxford University Press, 1929.
Mulgan, R., *Freedom in Ancient Greece*, Athlone Press, 1984.
Muller, H.J., *Freedom in the Ancient World*, Secker & Warburg, 1962.
Plato, *Apology*, trans. H. Tredennick, Harmondsworth, Penguin, 1954.
——, *The Socratic Dialogues*, various trans., Harmondsworth, Penguin, 1987.
——, *Symposium*, trans. M. Joyce, Loeb, 1924.
——, *Gorgias*, trans. W. Hamilton, Harmondsworth, Penguin, 1960.
Pohlenz, M., *Freedom in Greek Life and Thought*, Dordrecht, Holland, D. Reidel & Co, 1966.
Russo, C.F., *Aristophanes: An Author for the Stage*, London and New York, Routledge, 1962, Florence: English edn, 1997.
Stone, I.F., *The Trial of Socrates*, Jonathan Cape, 1988.
Taplin, O. ed., *Literature in the Greek and Roman Worlds*, Oxford, Oxford University Press, 2000.
Thucydides, *History of the Peloponnesian War*, trans. Rex Warner, Harmondsworth, Penguin, 1954.
Xenophon, *Memorabilia*, trans. B.B. Rogers, London and New York, Loeb, 1924 and reprints.
——, *Hellenica*, trans. Rex Warner, Harmondsworth, Penguin, 1966.

CHAPTER TWO

Aurelius, M., trans. A.S.L. Farquarson, *Meditations*, Everyman, 1961.
Barnes, T.D., *Tertullian*, Oxford, Oxford University Press, 1971.
Baus, K., *Handbook of Church History I*, Oxford, Oxford University Press, 1965.
Benko, S., *Pagan Rome and the Early Christians*, Batsford, 1985.
Bible, authorised version (AV).
Catholic Encyclopaedia, The, New York, Robert Appleton Co., online edn, 1999.
Eusebius, *Ecclesiastical History*, vol. vii, London Library copy.
Fox, R.L., *Pagans and Christians*, Viking, 1986.
Gibbon, E., *The Decline and Fall of the Roman Empire*, abridged edn, Chatto & Windus, New York, Harcourt Brace, 1960.
New English Bible (NEB).
Patterson-Smyth, J. *The Story of St Paul's Life and Letters*, London, 1935.
Pliny, *Letters*, trans. B. Radice, Harmondsworth, Penguin, 1963.
Studies in Ancient Society, Routledge & Kegan Paul, 1974.
St Croix, G.E.M., 'Why Were the Early Christians Persecuted?', *Past & Present*, 26 (1963).
Taplin, O., *Literature in the Greek and Roman Worlds: A New Perspective*, Oxford, Oxford University Press, 2000.
Tertullian, *Apologeticum* (trans. C. Becker) London Library copy.
de Urbel, P., trans. P. Barrett, *St Paul, the Apostle of the Gentiles*, Elek, 1958.
Wilson, A.N., *Paul: the Mind of an Apostle*, Random House, 1997.

CHAPTER THREE

Acton, Lord, *History of Freedom*, London, 1907.
Berlin, I., *Two Concepts of Liberty*, Oxford, Oxford University Press, 1969.
Burckhardt, J., trans. S.G.C. Middlemore, 1990, *The Civilisation of Renaissance Italy*, Harmondsworth, Penguin, 1990.
Daniell, D., *William Tyndale: A Biography*, New Haven, Yale University Press, 2001.
Dawson, C., *The Making of Europe*, London, 1934.
Dickens, A.G., *Martin Luther and The Reformation*, London, English Universities Press, 1967.
Eisenstein, E., *The Printing Press as an Agent of Change*, 2 vols, Cambridge, Cambridge University Press, 1979.
Erasmus, D., *Collected Works*, various trans., Toronto University Press, 1974.
——, *Praise of Folly* (trans. B. Radice), Harmondsworth, Penguin, 1984.
Febvre, L. and M., H.-J., trans. David Gerard, *The Coming of the Book*, New Left Books, 1990.
Foxe, J., ed. J. Pratt, *The Acts and Monuments of John Foxe* (known as his *Book of Martyrs*), 8 vols, London, 1877.
Halkin, L.E., trans. John Tonkin, *Life of Erasmus*, Oxford, Blackwell, 1987.
Jardine, L., *Worldly Goods*, Macmillan, 1996.
Mackinnon, J., *Luther and the Reformation*, 4 vols, Longman Green, 1923–8.
McGrath, A., *In the Beginning: the Story of the King James Bible*, Hodder & Stoughton, 2001.
Mozley, J.F., *William Tyndale*, London Library, 1937.
Muller, H.J., *Freedom in the Western World*, New York, Harper & Row, 1963.
Oberman, H., *Luther: Between God and Devil*, New Haven, Yale University Press, 1989.
Rakil, A., Jr., *Renaissance Humanism*, Philadelphia, University of Pennsylvania Press, 1988.
Rupp, G., *The Righteousness of God*, Hodder & Stoughton, 1953.
Todd, J.M., *Luther: A Biographical Study*, Crossroad, 1969, 1982.

CHAPTER FOUR

Baiguent, M. and L.R., *The Inquisition*, Viking, 1999.
Burman, J., *The Hammer of Heresy*, Wellingborough, Antiquarian Press, 1984.
Brodrick, J., *Galileo: The Man, His Work, His Misfortunes*, New York, Harper & Row, 1964.
Dickens, A.G., *The Counter Reformation*, New York, W.W. Norton & Co, 1968.
Donne, J., *Collected Works*, London Library.
Galilei, G., trans, S. Drake, *Selected Works*, Oxford, Oxford University Press, 1980.
Koestler, A., *The Sleepwalkers*, New York, Macmillan (Danube edn), 1966.
Redoni, P., trans. R. Rosenthal, *Galileo Eritico*, Allen Lane, Penguin Press, 1988.
Sobel, D., *Galileo's Daughter*, Fourth Estate, 1999.
de Santillana, G., *The Crime of Galileo*, Heinemann, 1956.

CHAPTER FIVE

Frank, J., *The Beginnings of the English Newspaper*, Cambridge, Mass., Harvard University Press, 1961.
Gardiner, S.R., *History of the Great Civil War* (reproduction edn, The Windrush Press, 1987).
Gregg, P., *Freeborn John*, Harrap, 1961.
Hill, C., *Puritanism and Revolution*, Secker & Warburg, 1958.
——, *Century of Revolution*, Sphere Books, 1969.
——, *England in the Seventeenth Century*, Sphere Books, 1970.
Howell's State Trials, vols iv, vi.
Lilburne, J., *Work of the Beast*, London, 1638.
——, reprinted in Haller, W., *Tracts on Liberty in the Puritan Revolution*, vols, i, ii, iii, New York, Columbia University Press, 1934.
——, *Revolt of the Pamphleteers*, New York, Columbia University Press, 1934.
Milton, J., *Areopagitica*, 1644, Oxford Classics, 1924.
Paterson, A., *Censorship and Interpretations*, Madison, University of Wisconsin Press, 1984.
Siebert, F., *Freedom of the Press in England 1476–1776*, Urbana, University of Illinois Press, 1965.
Sharpe, K., *The Personal Rule of Charles I*, New Haven, Yale University Press, 1992.
Wedgwood, C.V., *The King's Peace*, Penguin, 1964.
Wilson, A.N., *The Life of John Milton*, Oxford, Oxford University Press, 1983.

CHAPTER SIX

Aytoun, E., *The Penny Universities*, Secker & Warburg, 1956.
Black, J., *The English Press in the Eighteenth Century*, London and Sydney, 1987.
——, *The English Press*, Stroud, Sutton.
Blagden, C., *The Stationers' Company*, George Allen & Unwin, 1960.
Collett, D., *History of the Taxes on Knowledge*, Watson & Co., 1906, Thinkers Library edn, 1933.
Cranston, M., *John Locke*, Longman Green, 1957.
Dunn, J., *The Political Thought of John Locke*, Cambridge, Cambridge University Press, 1969.
——, *Locke*, Past Masters, Oxford, Oxford University Press, 1984.

Hamburger, P., 'Development of the Law of Seditious Libel', *Stanford Law Review*, 1985.
Locke, J., *A Letter Concerning Toleration*, London, 1689, reprinted by Hackett, Indianapolis, Indiana, 1983.
——, *An Essay Concerning Human Understanding*, London, 1690, Oxford, Clarendon Press, 1975.
Macaulay, Lord, *History of England*, Longman Green, 1871.
Pollock, F. and Maitland, F., *History of English Law*, vol. ii, Cambridge, Cambridge University Press, 1898.
Schwoerker, L.G., 'Liberty of the Press and Public Opinion' (published in *Liberty Secured?*, ed. Jones, J.R.), Stanford, Stanford University Press, 1992.
Steele, R., *Tudor and Stuart Proclamations*, Oxford, 1910.
Trevelyan, G.M., *England Under the Stuarts*, Methuen, 1965.

CHAPTER SEVEN

Almon, J., *Wilkes's Life and Correspondence*, London, 1805.
Bleackley, H., *Wilkes: The Life*, John Lane, 1917.
Chevenix Trench, C., *Portrait of a Patriot*, William Blackwood & Son, 1962.
Nobbe, G., *The North Briton, A Study in Political Propaganda*, New York, Columbia University Press, 1939.
Postgate, R., *That Devil Wilkes*, Constable & Co., 1930.
Sherrard, O.A., *John Wilkes, A Life*, George Allen & Unwin, 1930.
Thomas, P.D.G., *John Wilkes, A Friend to Liberty*, Oxford, Clarendon Press, 1996.
Walpole, H., *Selected Letters*, London Library Copy presented by Earl Spencer.
Wilkes, J., *The North Briton* (collected single-vol. edn), 1763.
——, *Essay on Woman* (reconstructed text by A.H. Cash, AMS Press Inc. New York, 2000).

CHAPTERS EIGHT AND NINE

Ayer, A.J., *Voltaire*, London, Weidenfeld & Nicolson, 1986.
Ayer, A.J., *Thomas Paine*, Secker & Warburg, 1988.
Besterman, T., *Voltaire*, Oxford, Blackwell, 1969.
Boorstin, D., *History of the American People: The Colonial Experience*, New York, Vintage, 1958.
Brogan, H., *History of the United States of America*, Longman Green, 1985.
Conway, M., *The Life of Thomas Paine*, New York, 1892.
Foner, E., *Tom Paine and Revolutionary America*, New York, Oxford University Press, 1976.
John, K., *Tom Paine: A Political Life*, Bloomsbury, 1995.
Levy, L,W., *Legacy of Suppression*, Cambridge, Mass., Belknap Press, 1960.
Paine, T., *Selected Writings* (ed. M. Foot and I. Kramnick), Harmondsworth, Penguin.
Schlesinger, A.M. Sr., *Prelude to Independence*, New York, Northeastern University Press, 1958.
Trevelyan, Sir O.T., *The American Revolution*, London, 1905.
Voltaire, *Treatise on Tolerance*, trans. B. Masters, Cambridge University Press, 2000.
Williamson, A., *Thomas Paine*, London, George Allen & Unwin, 1892.

CHAPTER TEN

Brodie, F.M., *Thomas Jefferson: An Intimate History*, Methuen, 1974.
Brogan, H., *History of the United States*, Guild Publishing, 1985.

Ellis, J.J., *The Passionate Sage, The Character and Legacy of John Adams*, New York, Random House.
Federalist Papers, The, ed. I. Kramnick, Harmondsworth, Penguin, 1987.
Levy, L., *Legacy of Suppression*, Cambridge, Mass., Belknap Press, 1960.
——, *Jefferson and Civil Liberties*, Cambridge, Mass., Belknap Press, 1963.
Madison, J., ed. D.B. Mattern, *Writings*, vol. 17, University Press of Virginia, 1991.
Malone, D., *Thomas Jefferson and the Ordeal of Liberty*, Boston, Little, Brown & Co., 1962.
Miller, J.C., *The Federalist Era*, Hamish Hamilton, 1960.
Mitchell, B., *Alexander Hamilton, The National Adventure*, New York, Macmillan, 1962.
McCullough, D., *John Adams*, New York, Simon and Schuster, 2002.
Peterson, M.D., *Thomas Jefferson and the New Nation*, Oxford, Oxford University Press, 1970.
Rutland, R.A., *Birth of the Bill of Rights*, Raleigh, University of North Carolina Press, 1955.
Schachner, N., *Alexander Hamilton*, New York, Thomas Yosseloff, 1946.
Smith, J.M., *Freedom's Fetters*, Ithaca, New York, Cornell University Press, 1956.

CHAPTER ELEVEN

Aspinall, A., *Politics and the Press, 1780–1850*, Home & Van Thal, 1949.
Chesterton, G.K., *Essays*, Hodder & Stoughton.
——, *William Cobbett:* © Royal Literary Fund, House of Stratus, 2000.
Cobbett, W., Political Register, various edns.
——, *Collected Writings*, London Library.
——, *The Life and Adventures of Peter Porcupine*, 1796.
——, *Advice to Young Men*, 1830.
——, *Last Hundred Days of English Freedom*, ed. J.L. Hammond, 1921.
——, *Selected Writings*, Folio Society edn, 1968.
Cole, G.D.H., *William Cobbett*, Collins, 1924.
Cole, G.D.H. and Postgate, R., *The Common People*, Collins, 1921.
Collet, D., *History of the Taxes on Knowledge*, Thinker's Library, 1933.
Halevy, E., *History of the English People*, Ernest Benn, 1961.

CHAPTER TWELVE

Berlin, I., *Two Concepts of Liberty*, Oxford, Oxford University Press, 1969.
Hayek, F.A., *John Stuart Mill and Harriet Taylor*, Routledge & Kegan Paul, 1951.
Mill, J.S., *On Liberty*, London, 1859, Penguin, 1974, ed., Gertrude Himmelfarb.
——, *Autobiography*, New York, Columbia University Press, 1924.
Stephens, Sir J.F., *Liberty, Equality, Fraternity*, Smith, Elder, 1874.

CHAPTER THIRTEEN

Ayerst, D., *Guardian: Biography of a Newspaper*, Collins, 1971.
Brandon, P., *Life and Death of the Press Barons*, Secker & Warburg, 1988.
Cook, Sir E., *Delane of The Times*, Constable, 1915.
Dasent, A.I., *John Thadeus Delane: Editor of The Times*, Murray, 1908.
Van Deusen, G.G., *Horace Greeley: Nineteenth-Century Crusader*, Philadelphia, University of Pennsylvania Press, 1953.

Elton, O., *C.E. Montague*, London, 1929.
Hammond, J.L., *C.P. Scott of the Manchester Guardian*, G. Bell & Sons, 1934.
Herd, H., *The March of Journalism*, George Allen & Unwin, 1952.
Lippmann, W., *Public Opinion*, George Allen & Unwin, 1922.
Official History of the Times, The, vol. iii, Times Publishing.
De Tocqueville, A., trans G. Lawrence, *Democracy in America*, New York, Doubleday, 1966.
Williams, F., *The Right to Know*, Longman, 1969.
——, *Dangerous Estate*, Longman, Green & Co., 1957.

CHAPTER FOURTEEN

Abraham, H.J., *Freedom and the Court*, 4th edn, Oxford University Press, New York, 1982, Ch. V.
Bent, S., *OWH*, Vanguard Press, New York, 1932.
Biddle, F., *Memorials of Oliver Wendell Holmes*, New York, 1936.
Chafee, Prof. Z., *Free Speech in the United States*, Harvard University Press, Cambridge, Mass., 1941.
Donelly, J., *International Human Rights*, Westview Press, Boulder, Colorado, 1998.
Frankfurter, Mr Justice F., *Holmes and the Supreme Court*, Cambridge, Mass., Harvard University Press, 1938.
Holmes, O.W., Sr, *Collected Works*, Cambridge, Mass.
Holmes, O.W., Jr, *Collected Legal Papers*, New York, 1920.
——, *Common Law*, Boston, 1881.
Howe, M. de Wolfe, *Oliver Wendell Holmes*, 4 vols, Belknap Press, Cambridge, Mass., 1957.
Menand, L., *The Metaphysical Club*, Flamingo Press, 2002.
McCloskey, G., *The American Supreme Court*, Chicago, University of Chicago Press, 1960.
Williams, J.S., *The Supreme Court Speaks*, Austin, Texas, University of Texas Press, 1956.

CHAPTER FIFTEEN

Ceplair, L. and Englund, S., *The Inquisition in Hollywood*, Garden City, New York, Anchor Press/Doubleday, 1980.
Cooke, A., *A Generation on Trial, USA v Alger Hiss*, Penguin, Baltimore, Md, 1968.
Emerson, T. and others, *Political and Civil Rights in the United States*, Boston, Little, Brown & Co., 1967.
Friendly, F.W., *Due to Circumstances Beyond Our Control*, New York, Random House, 1967.
Fromm, E., *The Escape from Freedom*, New York, Henry Holt & Co., 1994.
Ignatieff, M., *'Out of Danger'*, *Fifty Years of Free Expression, Index on Censorship*, London, 1998.
Index on Censorship, London, various edns, esp. *Fifty Years of Free Expression, Index on Censorship*, London, 1998.
McCloskey, R.G., *The Modern Supreme Court*, Cambridge, Mass., Harvard University Press, 1972.
Newman, R.P., *Owen Lattimore and the 'Loss' of China*, Los Angeles, University of California Press, 1992.
Orme, B., 'Rhetoric and Reality', *Fifty Years of Free Expression, Index on Censorship*, London, 1998.
Oshinsky, D.M., *A Conspiracy So Immense: The World of Joe McCarthy*, New York, Free Press, 1983.

Schrecker, E., *Many Are the Crimes (McCarthyism in America)*, Princeton, New Jersey, Princeton University Press, 1998.

Smith, D.L., *Zechariah Chafee Jr, Defender of Liberty and the Law*, Cambridge, Mass., Harvard University Press, 1986.

Theoharis, A.G. and Cox, J.S. *The Boss: J. Edgar Hoover and the Great American Inquisition*, Philadelphia, Temple University Press, 1988.

Thurman, A., *Fair Fights and Foul: A Dissenting Lawyer's Life*, New York, Harcourt Brace, 1965.

CHAPTER SIXTEEN

Akdeniz, Y., *Sex on the Net: The Dilemma of Policing Cyberspace*, Garnet, Reading, 1999.

Arnold, B., *The Scandal of Ulysses*, St Martin's Press, New York, 1992.

Hargreaves, R., *Superpower*, St Martin's Press, New York, 1974.

Herd, H., *The March of Journalism*, George Allen & Unwin, 1954.

Internet Watch Foundation, website www.inf.org.uk (and others), 2002.

de Jongh, N., *Politics, Prudery and Perversions: The Censorship of the English Stage*, Methuen, 2001.

Robertson, G. and Nicol, Andrew G.L., *Media Law* (2nd edn), Ch. 3, Longman, 1990.

Rolph, C.H., *The Trial of Lady Chatterley*, Penguin, 1966.

Shannon, R., *A Press Free and Responsible*, John Murray, 2001.

Sheehan, N. and others, *The Pentagon Papers, New York Times*, 1971.

Souhami, D., *The Trials of Radclyffe Hall*, Virago Press, 1999.

CHAPTER SEVENTEEN

Dicey, A.V., *The Law of the Constitution*, Macmillan, 1885, repub. Liberty Fund Indianapolis, 1982.

Haworth, A., *Free Speech*, The Problems of Philosophy Series, Routledge, 1988.

Levy, L.W., 'Freedom of Speech in Seventeenth-century Thought', *Antioch Review*, Spring 1999.

Schauer, F., *Free Speech: A Philosophical Enquiry*, New York, Cambridge University Press, 1982.

Small, W., *Political Power and the Press*, New York, W.W. Norton, 1971.

Notes

CHAPTER ONE

2   Alcibiades's description from Plato's *Symposium*, 220bl–cl.
3–4   Aristophanes *Clouds*, trans. Alan H. Sommerstein.
5   Herodotus, bks VII–VIII. Quotes from Euripides *The Suppliant Women*, trans. Philip Vellacot.
6–7   Myteline debates in *Thucydides*, III, pp. 36–5
7–8   For free speech in the theatre see *Powers of Horror and Laughter*, Peter Wilson. Aristophanes's *Wasps* (adapted from literal trans. in Loeb), ll. 1,286–91.
9 ff   For background on Alcibiades and Critias see Xenophon *Hellenica*, II.2.1.
11   Mill quote from letter to his wife, 22 March 1855 (quoted in Hayek).
11–12   The speech by Critias is carried in full in Xenophon, *Memorabilia*, bk II.3.22. The response and death of Theramenes follows in bk II. 3.34ff.15. For the overthrow of the Thirty see Xenophon's *Hellenica*, bk II.4.16–20, 41.
13   Trial of the admirals related in Xenophon's *Hellenica* bk I.7.1–35. See also Plato's *Apology* 32B. For background to Anytus see *Oxford Companion*, Stone pp. 173–8. Quote is from Xenophon's *Memorabilia*, bk II.2. 23.
14 ff   For analysis of the events which brought Socrates to trial see Brickhouse, Smith and Guthrie, vol. 5 The two accounts of Socrates's speeches at the trial by Plato and Xenophon are here interwoven.
21   Acts of the Apostles, 17:20–1.

CHAPTER TWO

22   Polybius 'History' quoted in the *Oxford Companion to Ancient Literature*. For background see Pohlenz, pp. 107–8; Muller, pp. 249–50, 274–9, 282.
23 ff   For freedom of speech in the later Republic see esp. *The Beginnings of Latin Literature*, Matthew Leigh. *Literature in the Greek and Roman Worlds*, pp. 319–20. For Livy's account of Cicero's death see Seneca the Elder, *Suasasoria*, 6.17 (trans. M. Winterbottom). For a discussion of the subsequent servility and Tacitus quotes see *Prose Literature from Augustus to Hadrian*, Christina S. Krause essay in *Literature in the Greek and Roman Worlds*, pp. 439–42.
24 ff   The commentaries on Paul's works are by Perez de Urbel: trans. from the Spanish by Paul Barrett, and the splendidly straightforward account by J. Patterson Smyth: Paul's quotes are from I Thess. 2: 9–12, II Tim. 4. 7–13 and II Corinthians 11: 24–28.
26   Paul's quotes are from Acts 22: 3 and Romans 3: 6. The story of Paul's conversion on the road to Damascus is told three times, almost word for word. The first account is related in Acts 9:1–43. His presence at the stoning of Stephen is confirmed in Acts 7: 58.

27–8   For Paul's freedom to preach under Roman protection see esp. Romans 13: 1–7; Acts 23: 23 ff; 26: 1–13 and 28–32. Paul's appearance before Gallio from Acts 18: 12–17.

28   The dispute about circumcision, Acts 15. Paul loses his temper at Corinth, Acts 18: 6.

29   Paul's salutations, see e.g. Coloss. 4: 18; the verses on charity are in Cor. 13: 1–13.

29 ff   There is a full account of Paul's arrest and dispatch to Rome in Acts 21–7. An account of Nelson reading the 'Sailor's Chapter' is given in Patterson-Smyth, p. 199; Paul's stay in Rome comes from the last few pararaphs of Acts, 28: 30–1.

30   Brethren emboldened: Phil. 1: 14; Paul's thoughts on death: Phil. 1: 3–4. For Paul's legacy see esp. Muller, pp. 289–95.

31   Paul speaks of a planned journey to Spain in Romans 15: 24. Quotes from his last letter: II Tim. 4: 2–8, 13–19. Paul's presence at the first book burnings is related in Acts 19: 19.

32   *Letters of the Younger Pliny*, Bk 10: 96–7, trans. Betty Radice.

33   Tertullian quote from his *Apologeticum* trans. C. Becker

34 ff   The definitive analysis of the persecutions is by G.E.M. St Croix, 'Why Were the Early Christians Persecuted?' published in *Studies in Ancient Society*. Other helpful accounts include Robert Lane Fox *Pagans and Christians*, Stephen Benko *Pagan Rome and the Early Christians* and the Gibbon, esp. xv and xvi. Comparison with Islam, Fox, p. 220. For the number of martyrs see Gibbon, ch. xvi, p. 219; for modern views see esp. Fox, ch. 9. The death of Polcycarp and the Christians' use of literature discussed in *Pagans and Christians*, Jane L. Lightfoot, *Literature in the Greek and Roman Worlds*, pp. 278–84.

35 ff   *The Seed of the Church* from Tertullian's *Apologeticum* quoted in T.D. Barnes, *Tertullian: The Passion of Perpetua*, see K. Baus, *Handbook of Church History I*, pp. 447 ff, Fox, pp. 438–40. For Tertullian quote, see Barnes, pp. 60–2; for Alexander Severus, see ref in *Oxford Companion*. For the effect of the Decian persecution see Fox, p. 450, Gibbon, ch. xvi; Dionysius's account quoted in Eusebius's *Ecclesiastical History*, ch. vii, 11.7.

36   Diocletian's persecution is described by the Church historian Eusebius, often at first hand. The collapse of the pagan cults is described by Frend, pp. 276–80. Constantine's conversion, see esp. Fox, pp. 609 ff and the *Oxford Companion*.

37–8   Symmachus's letter, quoted in Benko, p. 59. Closure of the schools, Gibbon, ch. 40. For decisions at the Council of Nicea see *Catholic Encyclopedia: Censura Librorum*.

CHAPTER THREE

39   Boots are sometimes superior to books, quoted without further identification, in Isiah Berlin, p. 124. The quote about monasteries is from Dawson, pp. 36–8.

40   Burckhardt quote, p. 136.

41   'Liberalism began then': John Rawls, *Political Liberalism*, pp. xxiii–xxiv.

41 ff   Erasmus, *Praise of Folly*, trans. Betty Radice. See also *The Collected Works of Erasmus*, Toronto University Press. For the *Life of Erasmus* see Leon E. Halkin.

42   *No Erasmus, no Shakespeare*, E. Jones, *The Origins of Shakespeare*, Oxford 1977 (cited in Daniell's biography of William Tyndale, p. 42).

46 ff   For Luther's life and translated quotes I have used the standard English biography by James Mackinnon. There is a good modern account by Heiko

Oberman, and intepretations from a Catholic point of view by John M. Todd,
For the theological arguments see esp. Gordon Rupp, *The Righteousness of God*
and A.G. Dickens, *Martin Luther and the Reformation.*

48   *The Righteousness of God*: from Romans 1: 17. The supposition that inspiration
            came while he was on the lavatory is based on his own account in his *Table Talk*
            of how the idea came to him while sitting in 'the tower room'.

50 ff   For the spread of print see Lisa Jardine, *Worldly Goods*, Lucien Febvre and
            Henri-Jean Martin, *The Coming of the Book*, and Eisenstein, *The Printing Press as
            an Agent of Change.* For an estimate of the number of books printed in Europe
            see Eisenstein, p. 13, and the spread of Luther's ideas by print see pp. 148, 153.

56   Catholic Praise of Luther's German Bible, Todd, p. 186.

57–8   For the dispute between Luther and Erasmus see Mackinnon, vol. IV,
            pp. 245–66, and Halkin, *Life of Erasmus.* See John Stuart Mill, *On Liberty*, World
            Classics edn, p. 37. Melanchthon took his text from II Kings 2: 12.

59 ff   For general background to the Bible in English see esp. Dickens, McGrath and
            Daniell, from which the statistics have been drawn. For the church's
            opposition see McGrath, p. 19. For the edict of 1408, see McGrath, p. 33.
            Colet's suspension – though sometimes disputed – was reported by Erasmus,
            Tyndale and Foxe IV, pp. 618–19.

61   Bible read 'till all in pieces,' see Daniell, p. 196. 'Ignorant and illiterate monks
            . . .' see Daniell, p. 295.

62–3   For Thomas More's role see esp. Daniell, pp. 258–9, 274–80. For importance
            of Antwerp see Eisenstein, p. 162, McGrath, pp. 80–1. For the burnings see
            Foxe, various vols. Also Daniell, pp. 174–82. Quote on More from Daniell,
            p. 280.

64   For accounts of Tyndale's arrest and execution see Foxe, V, pp. 124–9, Mozley,
            pp. 325–8 and Daniell, pp. 375 ff.

CHAPTER FOUR

66 ff   Much of the voluminous literature on Galileo is highly partisan and often
            contradictory. For the general reader the indispensable guides in English are
            Giorgio de Santillana's *The Crime of Galileo*, Heinemann, 1956, and Arthur
            Koestler's challenging survey of man's changing vision of the universe, *The
            Sleepwalkers.* Stillman Drake's *Galileo*, is an invaluable source of translations of
            Galileo's own writings. For many years the standard work was Karl von Gebler's
            Galileo Galilei and the Roman Curia, translated from the German in 1879 and
            still invaluable for background and documentation. *Galileo: the Man, his Work,
            his Misfortunes* by James Brodrick gives an interesting brief survey from a
            Catholic point of view; Redoni's *Galileo Eretico* provides many insights into the
            complex politics of the Roman curia, mostly based on new research. Even now,
            there is no consensus about why Galileo was brought to trial and many of the
            detailed manoueverings that went on are still hotly debated by scholars. Where
            dispute exists, I have tried to indicate this in the text.

72–4   For a further background see *The Hammer of Heresy*, John Burman. For the
            effect of Trent see Dickens, *Counter-reformation*, also Eisenstein, pp. 160 ff.
            Milton's quote is from his *Areopagitica.*

75   The Koestler quote is from *The Sleepwalkers*, p. 421: Galileo's Italian biographer
            from whom the quotes are taken is A. Banfi, *Vita di Galileo Galilei*, p. 148.
            Quoted in Brodrick, p. 98.

79   Barberini's remarks on the death of Richelieu are quoted in Koestler, p. 471.
82   For a Jesuit view of Galileo's 'underhand' methods see Brodrick, p. 127. For
          Barberini's tangles with Spain see esp. Redondi, pp. 229–30.
88   Milton's quotes are from the *Areopagitica.*   .

CHAPTER FIVE

89–92   The account of Lilburne's trials and punishment is from his *Work of the Beast,*
          1638, published in William Haller's *Tracts on Liberty in the Puritan Revolution,*
          vol. II. See also his *Revolt of the Pamphleteers* in vol. I, pp. 9–14. Quote on the
          government's attempt to silence its critics is from S.R. Gardiner's standard
          history on the Puritan Revolution.
93–6   For background see Haller, vol. I, and Pauline Gregg's *Freeborn John.* Press
          grown cheap and prolific and historian's concept of the doctrine of liberty is
          from Haller, vol. I, introduction, pp. 2–3. For general background on the
          licensing laws, see esp. Siebert's *Freedom of the Press in England 1476–1776,* For
          the effect of the licensing laws in the 1630s see Kevin Sharpe's *The Personal
          Rule of Charles I,* ch. xi, pp. 644–713. 'Thou shalt commit adultery' anecdote
          quoted in Siebert, p. 138. Effect of Star Chamber decree, see Siebert, p. 131.
          For rise of the corantos see Siebert, pp. 148 ff and Sharpe, pp. 646–50. Lupton
          quote is from Joseph Frank's *The Beginnings of the English Newspaper.* Sir Henry
          Herbert quoted in Sharpe, 646–7. For analysis of the 1637 decree see Siebert,
          pp. 134 ff. Sir Henry Wotton's quote is from Paterson's *Censorship and Inter-
          pretations,* p. 209. The historian of the seventeenth-century press is Frederick
          Siebert, see esp. pp. 173–4.
96–101   I have used the OUP World Classics edition of Milton's *Areopagitica,* Oxford
          1929. For background see Haller's *Puritan Tracts,* vol. I, pp. 64 ff and App. B,
          and A.N. Wilson's *Life of John Milton.*

CHAPTER SIX

102–3   For an account of the regulation of printing after the Restoration see Siebert,
          ch. 12, pp. 237 ff and *Liberty of the Press and Public Opinion, 1660–95,* Lois G.
          Schwoerker, published in *Liberty Secured?,* pp. 199–231. For an account of
          Twyn's trial and sentence see Howell's *State Trials,* vol. 6, pp. 513–39.
103 ff   For the importance of the London coffee houses see Aytoun, *The Penny
          Universities.* For Locke's life and association with Shaftesbury see esp. *Locke* by
          John Dunn, pp. 1–21. For general background to the era see esp. G.M.
          Trevelyan, *England Under the Stuarts,* chs 11 and 12.
106   For lapse of the licensing laws see Trevelyan, pp. 239–40. Bossuet cited in
          Trevelyan, p. 423.
107 ff   Locke's letter to his friend William Molyneux, January 1698, in JL's
          correspondence, Clarendon. John Locke, *Epistolia de Tolerantia* (1688) and
          Letter Concerning Toleration (London 1689). Full text reprinted by Hackett
          Publishing Co., Indianapolis.
111 ff   For the end of the Licensing Act, see Siebert, pp. 261 ff. For Macaulay
          quotes see his *History of England,* vol. iv. Other accounts appear in Schwoerker,
          p. 199.

114–15   For Queen Anne's proclamation see Robert Steele, *Tudor and Stuart Proclamations*, Oxford, 1910, No. 4315. For the introduction of the Stamp Acts see Dobson Collett's *History of the Taxes on Knowledge*, 1st pub. 1906. Swift and Addison from the *Spectator* and *Journals to Stella*, 1712, quoted in Siebert, p. 313.

115–16   For the development of seditious libel see esp. Frederick Pollock and F. Maitland's *History of English Law*, vol. 2, p. 503, also Philip Hamburger, 'Development of the Law of Seditious Libel', *Stanford Law Review*, 37 (1985), pp. 661–75. For the prosecution of Daniel Defoe see *Daniel Defoe: His Life*, by Paula R. Backscheider. For accounts of the effects of the Stamp Acts, the laws of Seditious Libel and the restrictions on parliamentary reporting in this period see G.C. Gibbs, *The Press and Public Opinion*, published in *Liberty Secured?*, pp. 231–65, and Jeremy Black, *The English Press in the Eighteenth Century*. The Holt judgements are detailed in Gibbs, pp. 246, 253. 'Legal terrorism' is also from Gibbs, p. 248.

116–17   Macaulay's *History of England*, vol. iv. For a discussion of parliamentary privilege see Gibbs, p. 253 and Siebert ch. 17, pp. 346 ff.

CHAPTER SEVEN

118 ff   I have drawn heavily on the account by Wilkes's contemporary, John Almon, *Wilkes's Life and Correspondence*, London, 1805, as have all the standard biographies. The most authoritative modern study is *John Wilkes: a Friend to Liberty* by Peter D.G. Thomas. *That Devil Wilkes*, Raymond Postgate and O.A. Sherrard's *Life* are good on the contemporary background and *Portrait of a Patriot*, Charles Chevenix Trench, provides a sympathetic and up-to-date account of Wilkes's extraordinary life. The date of Wilkes's birth is a matter of dispute. Wilkes himself thought he was born in 1727, but most modern authorities settle on 1725. Copies of *The Essay on Woman* are hard to come by. The most authoritative edition is probably the reconstruction by an American scholar, Professor Arthur H. Cash, published in 2000 in New York.

119   The description of Bute is Frederick's, the Prince of Wales, who appointed Bute to tutor his son, later George III. The quotes from Horace Walpole are all from his *Letters*, published in several volumes (various publishers). I have used the edition presented to the London Library by Earl Spencer.

120 ff   There is a copy of Wilkes's single-volume edition of *The North Briton* in the London Library, 1763. There are extensive quotes and an analysis in *The North Briton: a Study in Political Propaganda*, George Nobbe, New York, Columbia University Press, 1939.

121   Almost all Wilkes's aphorisms were first given currency by Almon and subsequently quoted in the standard biographies, though occasionally attributed to different occasions. Some are doubtless apocryphal.

127   The question of forgery has excited historians for generations. The work of H.S. Ashbee in the nineteenth century is as near to the truth as one is now likely to get. Postgate was the first biographer to give it credence, and it is now generally accepted that parts at least of the *Essay* were forged by the government, though it is not now known whether this was done in order to attribute the verses solely to Wilkes or to add even more salacious words to the manuscript. The former seems more probable.

128   Pitt's remark on lawyers is from Sherrard, p. 109, as is the description of his behaviour during the debate.

130   The satire is quoted without attribution in Sherrard, p. 130.
135   'This curious error', noted Horace Walpole, 'was that the proceedings were
             stated as at the County Court for the County of Middlesex' instead of, as
             Mansfield said they should have been, 'at the County Court of Middlesex for
             the County of Middlesex'. The difference was so trifling, the only conclusion
             can be that the courts were so desperate to find a way out of their dilemma
             almost any excuse would do.
140   The verses on Burke are quoted by Trench, p. 284 (unattrib.).
142   Wilkes was buried in the Grosvenor chapel in South Audley Street, now the
             heart of London's Mayfair.

CHAPTER EIGHT

143   Quote from Sir O.T. Trevelyan's *The American Revolution*, London, 1905. Cited
             in Michael Foot's introduction to the Penguin Classics edition and Williamson,
             Thomas Paine, p. 75.
143 ff   The key biography of Paine, on which all other authors have drawn, is the two-
             volume work by Moncure Conway, published in New York in 1892. I have also
             drawn on the modern biographies by John Keane and Audrey Williamson,
             which, although sometimes maddeningly discursive, contains valuable new
             research. *Tom Paine and Revolutionary America* by Eric Foner is excellent on
             Paine's early American years. A.J. Ayer's *Thomas Paine* combines a sketch of his
             life with a rigorous critical examination of his philosophical and political
             writings. For Paine's own writings, I have relied on the Penguin Classics
             edition edited by Michael Foot and Isaac Kramnick. For minor works and
             letters I have relied on Moncure Conway.
148 ff   Three invaluable but very different works give the background to the history of
             the colonial American press: Daniel Boorstin's volume in his history of the
             American people, *The Colonial Experience, Prelude to Independence*, by Arthur M.
             Schlesinger, Sr, which deals exhaustively with the newspaper war on Britain in
             the period 1764–76; and *Legacy of Suppression*, Leonard W. Levy's challenging
             survey of free speech and the press in early American history.
149–52 ff   The Zenger case is dealt with by both Schlesinger, pp. 64–8, and Levy, pp. 132
             ff. The full case is examined in Howell's *State Trials*, vol. 17. Blackstone's quote
             dates from 1765 and is dealt with elsewhere. Francis Hopkinson is cited in
             Schlesinger, p. 298. Adams and Hutchinson quotes cited in Levy, p. 87.
153   Vigilante quotes cited in Levy, p. 178. Quotes from Schlesinger, p. 189.

CHAPTER NINE

154 ff   For the state of free speech in pre-revolutionary France, see Simon Schama's
             Citizens, pp. 174–83. For the history of ideas during the Enlightenment see
             Muller, *History of Freedom in the Western World*, pp. 314–49.
156 ff   Voltaire's life is well sketched in the biography by A.J. Ayer. See also Theodore
             Besterman, *Voltaire*. See also Voltaire's own *Treatise on Tolerance*, trans. Brian
             Masters.
161 ff   Paine's writings are again drawn from the Penguin Classics edition. For Pitt's
             response to *The Rights of Man* see esp. Williamson, p. 160. Chelmsford's
             response cited in Foner, pp. 234 ff.

164–7   For Paine's trial and Erskine's defence I have used the 1810 edition of Thomas Erskine's speeches while at the bar. See also account in Howell's *State Trials*. Rickman's letter is drawn from Conway, vol. II, pp. 67–8.

173   Paine's letter cited in Conway's biography, II, pp. 354–5.

174   Madame Bonneville's account of the funeral cited in Williamson, p, 275. The return of Paine's bones in recounted by all the modern biographers. The account of his missing skull is related in Williamson, pp. 282–4.

CHAPTER TEN

175–6   The role of Madison and Hamilton in the constitutional convention of 1789 and the subsequent Bill of Rights comes from John C. Miller, *The Federalist Era*. The 'whip-syllabub' quote was made during the ratification debate by Aedemus Burke of South Carolina. A full account of the debate and the federalist/anti-federalist split is given in Rutland, p. 208. For ratification by the states see Rutland, pp. 217–18, Franklin cited in Levy, p. 200. It was Virginia's vote that, appropriately, secured the necessary majority for the Bill of Rights, while Massachusetts, Connecticut and Georgia assented only in 1939 on the sesquicentennial anniversary of the constitution.

176 ff   For American attitudes towards the Bill of Rights and free speech in this era see L. Levy, *Legacy of Suppression*, ch. 5, pp. 179 ff and 280–1.

177   Adams's 'damn 'em' quote in Jefferson's diary is cited in Jefferson's biography by Merrill D. Peterson, p. 594. For the character of the Federalist administration see Miller, pp. 118 ff, Adams's correspondence with Jefferson, 9 July 1813, cited in Ellis, p. 296.

179–80   A full account of the effects of the Alien and Sedition Acts is given in J.M. Smith, *Freedom's Fetters*. The account of the ratification debate in the Senate is drawn from Malone, p. 388. Madison quote from his letter to Jefferson, 5 May 1798, University of Virginia edition 1991, p. 126. Judge Addison is cited in Malone, p. 387.

180 ff   An excellent account of the debate about the meaning of free speech in this era is given in L. Levy, *Legacy of Suppression*, pp. 249–60.

183 ff   There are many biographies of Thomas Jefferson, of varying quality. I have used two of the standard works, the single volume account by Merrill D. Peterson, and the magisterial study by Dumas Malone, vol. 3, *Jefferson and the Ordeal of Liberty*. Jefferson's letter to his young friend is cited in Malone, p. 418.

184   James Parton's description cited in Peterson, p. 30. Jefferson's suspicions that his post was spied on is cited in Malone, p. 410. A detailed account of Jefferson's role in the Virginia and Kentucky Resolutions is given in Malone, pp. 402–6 and 419–20, Peterson, pp. 609–11.

185–7   A full account of the wave of prosecutions under the Sedition Act is given in Smith, *Freedom's Fetters*.

188   Peterson gives a colourful account of the election outcome, from which I have drawn the newspaper quotes. See pp. 642–3. The epitaph on the Federalist era is Miller's, pp. 275–7.

190 ff   For Jefferson's complicated relationship with Callender, see esp. Fawn M. Brodie, *Thomas Jefferson: An Intimate History*, ch. 23, pp. 315–24 and Peterson, pp. 569–72 and 635–8.

191 ff   An account of Jefferson's role in subsequent prosecutions for seditious libel is given in Levy, *Jefferson and Civil Liberties*, ch. 3, 'A Few Wholesome

Prosecutions', pp. 42–69. For accounts of Hamilton's defence of Harry Crosswell see Broadus Mitchell, *Alexander Hamilton, The National Adventure*, Macmillan, New York, 1962, pp. 503 ff.

193   Jefferson's role in the Dennie prosecution is cited in all the authorities. The details about the Port Folio is from Fawn Brodie, *Intimate Life*, p. 544.

CHAPTER ELEVEN

195 ff   The best of all sources for the life of William Cobbett is Cobbett himself. Only his *Rural Rides* remains commonly in print, but there are extensive collections of his works in The London Library, and elsewhere. Of particular value are his *American Letters of Peter Porcupine*, his *Advice to Young Men*, and the annual editions of *Cobbett's Political Register*. The Folio Society has published a helpful sample of Cobbett's writings, which includes one or two articles not found elsewhere. The definitive biography is that by G.D.H. Cole, Collins, 1924. His *Common People* (jointly with Raymond Postgate) is good on the social background.

196   Cobbett's quote from *The Last Hundred Days of English Freedom, Political Register* (*PR*), July 1817. G.K. Chesterton's essay on Cobbett, p. 51. Cobbett's early adventures are related in *The Political Register* of 19 February 1820; reprinted in Folio Society selection, pp. 25–6. Cobbett is thought by later historians to have been fourteen at the time of his visit to Kew. His Canadian army experiences are related in *Life and Adventures of Peter Porcupine*, 1796, and *Advice to Young Men*, 1829; reprinted in Folio selection, pp. 30 ff.

198 ff   For his life as Peter Porcupine see *Advice to Young Men*, how he became a writer on politics, *PR*, 6 September 1804. His farewell to America from *Porcupine's Works*, cited in Cole, p. 68.

199   For the birth of the Register see Cole, pp. 79–90. See also Arthur Aspinall, *Politics and the Press, 1780–1850*, Home & Van Thal, 1949.

200–1   Article on flogging, *PR*, 1 July 1809. His comments of earlier floggings cited in Cole, p. 150.

201   For an analysis of Cobbett's manoeuvres prior to sentence see Cole, pp. 156–9. Chesterton's quote from his Cobbett essay, pp. 88–9.

202   The story of his wife's miscarriage is told in *Advice to Young Men*; Folio selection, pp. 51–2. For the Luddite riots see Cole and Postgate, *Common People*, ch. xv.

203   'Open Your Mouth and Shut Your Eyes', *PR*, 7 September 1816.

204 ff   For the success of the twopenny *Register* see Aspinall, pp. 29–31. For the effect of the Stamp Acts see Dobson Collet's *History of the Taxes on Knowledge*, pp. 9–12. Bamford quote from *Passages in the Life of a Radical*, cited in Cole, p. 211.

205 ff   For an account of Sidmouth's gagging laws see Aspinall, pp. 44–7. Cobbett's reaction is reprinted from his autobiography in Folio selection, p. 58.

206 ff   For his life in exile see Cole, ch. xv. For the effect of the Six Acts on the press see Aspinall, pp. 56–60. Collet, scattered references indexed under 60, George II, cap. 9. For its general effects see Cole and Postgate, pp. 219–28.

208   Hetherington's career is described in Aspinall, p. 28, and Collet, pp. 18, 22, 43, 46.

209   Cobbett's article on rick burnings, *PR*, 11 December 1830. Goodman's various confessions quoted in *PR*, January 1831. Cobbett's account of the trial is taken

from *PR*, 16 July 1831. See also *A Full Account of Mr Cobbett's Trial*, W. Strange, 1831.

211   An account of Cobbett's death was published in the *Register* by his two sons, J.P. and J.M. Cobbett, reprinted in Folio selection, pp. 78–9.

212   There is an interesting analysis of the role of the English press in this period in Elie Halevy, *History of the English People*, vol. I, *England in 1815*, Ernest Benn edn, 1961, 159–72, from which the quote from Sheridan is taken.

CHAPTER TWELVE

214 ff   The definitive account of Mill's life is his own *Autobiography*, one of the most candid accounts of a person's spiritual and mental development ever written. I have used the 1924 edition, Columbia University Press, to which all citations refer. The other indispensable account of Mill's life is *John Stuart Mill and Harriet Taylor*, a compilation of their correspondence through their friendship and subsequent marriage, with a commentary by F.A. Hayek. For Mill's early education see *Autobiography*, pp. 3–9. It was an 'appalling success', Isaiah Berlin, *Two Concepts of Liberty*, p. 175.

217–19   Mill's relationship with Harriet Taylor is examined in Hayek, from which Mill and Harriet's quotes are taken. Carlyle's description of the pair is cited by Hayek, pp. 29, 35. The description of Harriet's beauty is cited on p. 24 and the break with Roebuck on p. 29. Harriet's writing on liberty is from *An Early Essay*, cited in full as App. II, in Hayek, pp. 275–9. Mill's letters on Harriet's death, Hayek, p. 263.

220 ff   Penguin Classics edition of *On Liberty*, London, 1974. The sections relevant to his arguments on free speech are mainly the introductory section, pp. 59–75 and pt II, *On the Liberty of Thought and Discussion*, pp. 75–119.

225 ff   The response to the initial publication of *On Liberty* is fully recounted in Gertrude Himmelfarb's introduction to the 1974 Penguin Classics edition. The tutor from Cambridge was Leslie Stephen, brother of Sir James Fitzjames Stephen, who later wrote the book-length refutation of *On Liberty*. Macaulay and Morley are cited by Himmelfarb on pp. 36–40, Kingsley on p. 46. Mill's own response comes from *Autobiography*, pp. 177–80.

226–7   The quotes from Sir James Fitzjames Stephen are from *Liberty, Equality, Fraternity*.

227–9   Mill's relevance today was tellingly defended by Sir Isaiah Berlin in two lectures he gave in the 1950s, subsequently published as *Two Essays in Liberty*. I have used the OUP paperback edition of 1969. See esp. *John Stuart Mill and their Ends of Life*, pp. 175–206.

229   Mill's parliamentary career related in his *Autobiography*, pp. 198 ff.

CHAPTER THIRTEEN

230   For de Tocqueville on American newspapers see *Democracy in America*, New York, Doubleday, 1966 (trans. George Lawrence), pp. 180–6 and 317. Rebecca West cited in Francis Williams, *The Right to Know*, Longman, 1969, p. 1.

231–7   The definitive life of Delane is A.I. Dasent, *John Thaddeus Delane, Editor of The Times: his Life and Correspondence*, Murray, 1908, 2 vols, from which most of the personal quotations have been drawn. There is also a good single-volume life by Sir Edward Cook, *Delane of the Times*, Constable, 1915. A brief modern sketch will be found in Piers Brandon, *The Life and Death of the Press Barons*, 1988.

232 ff   See the official *History of the Times*, vol. iii, for the period from which most of the quotes from the paper are drawn.

236 ff   There is a good brief analysis of the effects of the abolition of Stamp Duties in Harold Herd, *The March of Journalism*, pp. 147–60, from which the quotes have been drawn. See also Dobson Collet's splendid monograph, *Taxes on Knowledge*. Hazlitt cited in Brandon, p. 37.

238–44   There are many biographies of Horace Greeley. The most useful for his life as a journalist is Glyndon G. Van Deusen, *Horace Greeley: Nineteenth-Century Crusader*, American Historical Association, University of Pennsylvania Press, Philadelphia, 1953. There is also a good sketch in Brandon's *Press Barons*, pp. 50–63.

239   Greeley's advice to Friend Fletcher, see Walter Lippmann, *Public Opinion*, George Allen & Unwin, London, 1922, p. 331. Lippmann's quote on the fountains of truth is from the same work, p. 321.

244–51   Scott's political life is in J.L. Hammond's biography, *C.P. Scott of the Manchester Guardian*, G. Bell & Sons, 1934. Good on his political career and correspondence, less so on his role as a journalist and editor. There is a separate chapter by W.P. Crozier giving a charming though sketchy account of Scott's life in the office. For Scott as a newspaperman see bk II of David Ayerst's *Guardian: Biography of a Newspaper*.

245   Scott's denigration of reporters is from Francis Williams, *Dangerous Estate*, pp. 164–5.

247   The chronicler of the *Guardian* is Ayerst, pp. 247, 448, 438.

250–1   Oliver Elton's biography of C.E. Montague (1929) gives the best analysis of Scott's moral influence. Scott's own quotes on the duties of a newspaper come from his celebrated leader in the centenary edition of the *Manchester Guardian* published in 1922 – the only article he ever wrote under his own by-line. W.P. Crozier quote from his chapter in Hammond's biography 'Scott in the Office'.

CHAPTER FOURTEEN

252 ff   The most comprehensive biography of OWH is the 4-vol. work by Mark de Wolfe Howe, Belknap Press, Harvard, Cambridge, Mass., 1957. The contemporary biography by Silas Bent, Vanguard Press, New York, 1932, is good on the life, but less so on the benchmark court cases. All have drawn on Holmes's own writings, the most important of which are the *Collected Legal Papers*, New York, 1920, and his *Common Law*, Boston, 1881. Dr Holmes's letter of introduction to John Stuart Mill is quoted in Bent, p. 134. Walter Lippmann cited in Bent, p. 21.

253–4   Holmes's exploits in the war are recounted with little variations in all the biographies and drawn from Holmes's own account, *Touched with Fire*, and his father's memoirs, published in his *Collected Works*. See also Howe, pp. 80 ff, Bent, pp. 74–104. The shaping of his philosophy is dealt with at length in *The Metaphysical Club* by Louis Menard, ch. 3.

255   'To think . . .' Biddle, p. 30.

256   De Tocqueville on the Supreme Court in *Democracy in America*, pp. 149 ff. See also the *American Supreme Court*, Robert G. McCloskey.

256 ff   The indispensable guide to the free speech cases brought under the Espionage
            Acts of 1917–18 is Professor Zechariah Chafee, *Free Speech in the United States*,
            first pub. 1920, and revised when America entered the Second World War in
            1941. For the quote on the court's nineteenth-century legacy, see p. 14; his
            account of the passage of the Espionage Acts see pp. 38–40; the wartime
            prosecutions, pp. 55 ff; The Montana case, p. 286.

259 ff   There is a good account of Holmes's later career by one of his many
            secretaries, Francis Biddle, from whom these and later personal anecdotes are
            taken. The clear and present danger test is articulated by Holmes in *Schenk v.
            United States*, 249 US 47 (1919). Analysis of Holmes's approach to free speech
            cases is set out in the work of a later justice, Felix Frankfurter, *Mr Justice Holmes
            and the Supreme Court*, Harvard University Press, 1938, ch. 3, 'Civil Liberties and
            the Individual', pp. 49 ff. The text of Justice Holmes's opinions on free speech
            are widely available in law libraries. I have used Jesse S. Williams, *The Supreme
            Court Speaks*, Austin, Texas, University of Texas Press, 1956. The full
            background to the Abrams case is given in Chafee, ch. 3, pp. 108–40. The
            technical reference is *Abrams v. US*, 1919, US 616. For Holmes's feelings when
            he wrote the Abrams opinion see Biddle, pp. 157–9.

263 ff   Holmes in old age, see esp. Biddle, pp. 168 ff. Also Bent, p. 321. *Gitlow v. New
            York*, Supreme Court of the US 1925, 268 US 652. The quotation is from
            Dante's poem '*Mime Petrose*', written in 1296 for a lady Pietra who had harshly
            rejected his love. 'O Cosmos', Biddle, pp. 186–7. 'Cheer up, Wendell', p. 195.
            US v. Schwimmer, 1929, US 644.

266   Radio tribute, Biddle, pp. 191–2.

267   Memorial Day speech and poem cited in Biddle, p. 204. The full poem is in
            Bent, p. 117.

CHAPTER FIFTEEN

268–70   Fromm quote in *Escape from Freedom*, p. 2. Dostoevsky quote from *The Brothers
            Karamazov*. For Chafee report on wartime extent of free speech see Smith
            biography. Article 19, UN Declaration of Human Rights, texts reproduced in
            Donnelly, App. 1, pp. 161–8. American Ambassador to UN, Jeanne Kirkpatrick,
            quoted in *Fifty Years of Free Expression*, IOC, 1998.

271   For an account of the Hiss trials and their effects see Cooke, *A Generation on
            Trial*. New York City edict on fishing quoted in Emerson, p. 269.

272   Hoover's role discussed at length in Schrecker, pp. 203 ff. McCarran Act
            enacted 1950. Discussed in McCloskey, pp. 71–3. Examples are from the FBI's
            website, recently made available under the 1975 Freedom of Information Act
            (www.foia/FBI.gov).

273 ff   Loyalty Board questions, Schrecker, pp. 277–9. Bailey case in Arnold, pp. 297
            ff. Campaign against NLG: Theoharis and Cox, pp. 189–91, 202, 256, Nixon's
            role, p. 258. See also Schrecker, pp. 224–5.

275–8   HUAC and the Screen Writers' Guild, see Ceplair and Englund, pp. 257 ff.
            Trials of Hollywood Ten, Ceplair and Englund, pp. 257–77. See also Schrecker,
            pp. 316–30. Studios' spokesman was Eric Johnson, former head of the National
            Chamber of Commerce. Quoted in Ceplair and Englund, p. 260. The
            inglorious career of the Committee to Defend the First Amendment, including
            Bogart etc, quotes in Ceplair and Englund, 285–92.

278   For a discussion of the Supreme Court attitude in this era see McCloskey, ch. 2. Brando recants, Ceplair and Englund, pp. 387 ff.

278 ff   For McCarthy's career and downfall see Oshinsky–Skunk quotes, Oshinsky, p. 233. Editor quote, Schrecker, p. 243. Lattimore case dealt with exhaustively in Newman, see also FBI website. Youngdahl judgment, Schrecker, p. 252. McCarthy-Army hearings, Oshinsky, pp. 458–9.

281   Senator Lehman quote, Oshinsky, p. 492. LBJ interviewed by Doris Kearns, Schrecker, p. 373. For general discussion on McCarthyism's effects on US foreign policy see Donnelly, p. 87.

282   Schrecker's analysis from *Many Are the Crimes*, ch. 10, pp. 359 ff. CBS producer David Susskind in Schrecker, p. 400.

CHAPTER SIXTEEN

283   Alastair Cooke quote from a *Generation on Trial*, p. 17. 1954 statistics in Travis, p. 94.

285–6   The *Ulysses* discussion draws heavily on Public Record Office files, HO144/20071. Much new material in Travis pp. 18 ff. See also Bruce Arnold, *The Scandal of Ulysses*, New York, St Martin's Press, 1992. *Well of Loneliness* material drawn from documents released in 1998, HO144/2 2547, see Travis, pp. 45 ff.

287   de Jongh quote from introduction to *Politics, Prudery and Perversions*, p. xiv. For Edwardian complacency see pp. 41–2. Hall quote, p. 96. Lord Chamberlain's demise from Travis, pp. 216 ff.

288–90   For development of popular press see Herd, ch. xii, pp. 252–84.

290   For the history of the PCC during these years see Shannon. Calcutt Report *Review of Press Regulation*, CM 2135 HMSO, 1993.

290–2   Concerns about the effect of human rights legislation reported in UK *Press Gazette*, October and November 1997 and Newspaper Society's 'Privacy Laws which spell the end of Press Freedom', 27 November 1997. Quotes on effect of human rights legislation, see *The Times Law Report*, 2 November 2001.

292–7   Material drawn from author's own files as ITN Washington correspondent during these years. For more detail see Ungar. The definitive edition of the papers was published by the *New York Times* in 1971.

298–300   The debate about sex on the net is well covered by Yaman Akdeniz (lecturer at Leeds University's Centre for Criminal Justice Studies), *Sex on the Net*, Garnet, Reading, 1999. For ACLU quotes see www.aclu.org (under issues/cyber).

300   Examples drawn from various websites, see especially www.censorware.org and www.cyber-rights. Analysis of filtering systems provided by The Electronic Privacy Information Centre, Washington, DC (www.epic.org). For information of the Internet Watch Foundation see their website, www.iwf.org.uk.

CHAPTER SEVENTEEN

302   For a full discussion of the Argument from Truth, see Schauer, ch. 2, pp. 15–34. For Frankfurter quote see *Dennis v. United States*, 341 US 494 (1951). *Ranke: Immediate to God*, cited by Trevor Roper.

303   Pope quote from Epistles iii, p. 153.

304   For a full discussion of the argument from democracy, see Schauer ch. 3, pp. 35–46.

305   Horace lines from *Odes*, bk III, ode iii. Quoted by Jefferson in a letter to Madison, 20 December 1787.

307   Haworth on tabloid press, p. 92.

308   For a comparison of French and English law on this point see Dicey, ch. vi, pp. 146–69. Voltaire cited in Besterman, pp. 311 ff. Bagehot quote from *The Metaphysical Basis of Toleration.*

309   Criticism of Rushdie made to author by a publisher and a literary agent while reporting on the 1988 *fatwa*. For the power of public opinion see Schauer's discussion of Meiklejohn's theories of liberty, pp. 43–4.

310   For free speech issues raised by the terrorist attacks on America, see esp. Mary Kenny, *Observer*, 14 October 2001 and Bryan Appleyard, 'In Defence of Civilisation,' *Literary Review*, October 2001.

Index